North America

Latin America
and the Caribbean

Antarctica

OCEAN

Beaufort
Sea

Great Bear
Lake

Great Slave
Lake

Lake
Athabasca

Hudson
Bay

Labrador
Sea

ATLANTIC
OCEAN

Canada

Lake
Winnipeg

Gulf of
Alaska

Great Salt
Lake

United States

PACIFIC   OCEAN

Gulf of
Mexico

The Bahamas

Cuba

Mexico

Jamaica   Haiti   Dom. Rep.   St. Kitts & Nevis
Belize   Caribbean   Antigua & Barbuda
Guatemala Honduras   Sea   St. Lucia   Dominica
El Salvador Nicaragua   St. Vincent &   Barbados
Costa Rica   Grenadines   Grenada
Panama   Venezuela   Trinidad & Tobago
                  Colombia   Guyana
                              Suriname
                          French Guiana (Fr.)

Cabo
Verde

The Ga
G

Samoa

Tonga

Ecuador

Peru

Amazon R.

Brazil

Bolivia

Paraguay

Chile

Uruguay

Argentina

Bellingshausen
Sea

Amundsen Sea

Weddell
Sea

Source: Orvis, *Introducing Comparative Politics,* 5e, pp. ii, SAGE Publications.

Latin American Politics

Sara Miller McCune founded SAGE Publishing in 1965 to support the dissemination of usable knowledge and educate a global community. SAGE publishes more than 1000 journals and over 800 new books each year, spanning a wide range of subject areas. Our growing selection of library products includes archives, data, case studies and video. SAGE remains majority owned by our founder and after her lifetime will become owned by a charitable trust that secures the company's continued independence.

Los Angeles | London | New Delhi | Singapore | Washington DC | Melbourne

Latin American Politics

Eduardo Alemán

University of Houston

FOR INFORMATION:

CQ Press
An Imprint of SAGE Publications, Inc.
2455 Teller Road
Thousand Oaks, California 91320
E-mail: order@sagepub.com

SAGE Publications Ltd.
1 Oliver's Yard
55 City Road
London, EC1Y 1SP
United Kingdom

SAGE Publications India Pvt. Ltd.
B 1/I 1 Mohan Cooperative Industrial Area
Mathura Road, New Delhi 110 044
India

SAGE Publications Asia-Pacific Pte. Ltd.
18 Cross Street #10-10/11/12
China Square Central
Singapore 048423

Printed in Canada

Library of Congress Cataloging-in-Publication Data

Names: Alemán, Eduardo, 1969- author.

Title: Latin American politics / Eduardo Alemán.

Description: Thousand Oaks, California : CQ Press, 2021. | Includes bibliographical references.

Identifiers: LCCN 2020012045 | ISBN 9781506326610 (paperback) | ISBN 9781071816295 (epub) | ISBN 9781071816264 (epub) | ISBN 9781071816240 (ebook)

Subjects: LCSH: Latin America—Politics and government—21st century. | Political culture—Latin America. | Political stability—Latin America. | Democracy—Latin America.

Classification: LCC JL960 .A428 2021 | DDC 320.98—dc23

LC record available at https://lccn.loc.gov/2020012045

This book is printed on acid-free paper.

MIX
Paper from responsible sources
FSC
www.fsc.org   FSC® C103567

Acquisitions Editor: Anna Villarruel
Editorial Assistant: Lauren Younker
Production Editor: Megha Negi
Copy Editor: Erin Livingston
Typesetter: Hurix Digital
Proofreader: Rae-Ann Goodwin
Indexer: Integra
Cover Designer: Candice Harman
Marketing Manager: Jennifer Jones

20 21 22 23 24 10 9 8 7 6 5 4 3 2 1

• Brief Contents •

List of Figures	**xi**
List of Tables	**xiii**
Preface	**xv**
Acknowledgments	**xix**
About the Author	**xxi**

PART I •	**BACKGROUND**	**1**
Chapter 1 •	Colonial Legacy and the Post-Independence Period	3
Chapter 2 •	Political Regimes and Democratic Stability	35
Chapter 3 •	Guerrillas and Revolutions	65
Chapter 4 •	U.S.–Latin American Relations	97

PART II •	**INSTITUTIONS**	**125**
Chapter 5 •	Latin American Presidentialism	127
Chapter 6 •	Legislatures in Latin America	151
Chapter 7 •	Elections and Electoral Rules	175
Chapter 8 •	The Judiciary	203

PART III •	**POLITICAL ATTITUDES, POLICIES, AND OUTCOMES**	**229**
Chapter 9 •	Political Culture	231
Chapter 10 •	Corruption	255
Chapter 11 •	Civil Liberties and Press Freedom	285
Chapter 12 •	Income Inequality, Poverty, and the Gender Gap	311

Glossary	**339**
Notes	**351**
Index	**397**

• Detailed Contents •

List of Figures	xi
List of Tables	xiii
Preface	xv
Acknowledgments	xix
About the Author	xxi

PART I • BACKGROUND   **1**

Chapter 1 • Colonial Legacy and the Post-Independence Period   **3**

Colonial Latin America	3
Colonial Institutions	4
Colonial Policies	8
Colonial Societies	12
Independence and the Struggle for Political Order	16
Independence	17
Turmoil after Independence	22
The Sources of Post-Independence Instability	27
The Emergence of Political Order and Economic Growth	28
Conclusions	32
Key Terms	34
Bibliographic Recommendations	34

Chapter 2 • Political Regimes and Democratic Stability   **35**

What Is Democracy?	36
Minimalist Definitions	37
More Complex Procedural Definitions	39
Maximalist Definitions	43
Non-Democratic Regimes	45
Disagreements on Difficult Cases	49
Regime Transitions and Democratic Survival	53
The Economy	53
Political Institutions	55

Cultural Factors · 56
Agency: Political Elites · 59
The International Context · 61
Conclusions · 63
Key Terms · 64
Bibliographic Recommendations · 64
Web Resources · 64

Chapter 3 • Guerrillas and Revolutions · **65**
Guerrilla Movements in Latin America · 66
The Cuban Revolution · 70
The Nicaraguan Revolution · 76
Failed Revolutions in El Salvador and Guatemala · 82
El Salvador · 83
Guatemala · 85
Guerrillas and the Peace Process in Colombia · 88
Peace Agreements · 90
Conclusions · 93
Key Terms · 94
Bibliographic Recommendations · 94
Web Resources · 95

Chapter 4 • U.S.–Latin American Relations · **97**
The Cold War · 99
The Aftermath of the Cold War · 106
The Early 21st Century · 111
How Latin Americans View the United States · 119
Conclusions · 121
Key Terms · 122
Bibliographic Recommendations · 123
Web Resources · 123

PART II • INSTITUTIONS · **125**

Chapter 5 • Latin American Presidentialism · **127**
Presidentialism and Its Critique · 128
Constitutional Variations in Latin American Presidentialism · 133
Differences between U.S. and Latin American Presidentialism · 136
The Right to Initiate Legislation · 136

Veto Power 138

Legislative Agenda Setting 139

Decree Power 140

Presidential Instability 141

Causes and Implications of Presidential Interruptions 146

Conclusions 148

Key Terms 149

Bibliographic Recommendations 149

Web Resources 149

Chapter 6 • Legislatures in Latin America 151

The Legislative Branch 152

Representation 152

Lawmaking 158

Oversight 160

Organization 163

Bicameralism 163

Committees and Procedural Rules 165

Legislative Voting Behavior 168

Conclusions 171

Key Terms 172

Bibliographic Recommendations 172

Chapter 7 • Elections and Electoral Rules 175

Suffrage Extensions 176

Compulsory Voting 181

Rules for Electing Presidents 183

Presidential Reelection Rules 186

Rules for Electing Members of Congress 188

Proportional Representation 188

Majoritarian Rules: Incomplete List and Plurality 192

Mixed-Member Electoral Systems 192

The Consequences of Congressional Electoral Rules 194

The Relationship between Share of Votes and
Share of Seats 195

The Personal Vote versus the Partisan Vote 197

Conclusions 200

Key Terms 201

Bibliographic Recommendations 201

Web Resources 202

Chapter 8 • The Judiciary   **203**

  Judicial Independence   204
    Appointment Rules   205
    Length of Tenure   208
    Removal Proceedings   210
    Size of Higher Courts   212
    The Political Context   213
  Judicial Authority   215
    Instruments of Judicial Authority   216
    Judicial Authority in Six Latin American Countries   218
  Perceptions of the Judiciary   220
    Experts' Assessments   222
  Conclusions   226
  Key Terms   227
  Bibliographic Recommendations   227

PART III • POLITICAL ATTITUDES, POLICIES, AND OUTCOMES   229

Chapter 9 • Political Culture   **231**

  Support for Democracy   232
  Confidence in Institutions and Interpersonal Trust   239
  Ideological Positions   246
  Conclusions   252
  Key Terms   254
  Bibliographic Recommendations   254
  Web Resources   254

Chapter 10 • Corruption   **255**

  Corruption   256
    The Causes of Corruption   258
    The Consequences of Corruption   261
  Efforts to Combat Corruption   263
  Measuring Corruption   268
  Corruption Scandals   277
    Odebrecht   277
    The CICIG and The Anti-Corruption Fight in Guatemala   279
    Other Major Scandals   280
  Conclusions   281
  Key Terms   282

Bibliographic Recommendations   283
Web Resources   283

Chapter 11 • Civil Liberties and Press Freedom   **285**

What Are Civil Liberties?   286
The Right to Life and Liberty   290
Free Expression, Peaceful Assembly, and
Religious Freedom   295
Press Freedom   299
Property Rights   303
Conclusions   307
Key Terms   308
Bibliographic Recommendations   309
Web Resources   309

Chapter 12 • Income Inequality, Poverty, and the Gender Gap   **311**

Income Inequality   312
    Why Is Income Inequality Considered a Problem?   314
    Trends in Income Inequality   314
    Poverty Rates   319
    Reducing Poverty and Inequality   322
The Gender Gap   326
    Women in Public Office   328
    Economic Participation and the Income Gap   332
Conclusions   336
Key Terms   337
Bibliographic Recommendations   337
Web Resources   338

Glossary   **339**

Notes   **351**

Index   **397**

• List of Figures •

Figure 1.1   Annual Growth of Exports Per Capita, 1850–1912   29
Figure 2.1   Democracy in Latin America, 1901–1950   38
Figure 2.2   Democracy in Latin America, 1951–2000   39
Figure 2.3   Political Regimes in Latin America, 1900–2011   41
Figure 2.4   EIU's Democracy Index, 2019   44
Figure 2.5   Average Number of Years in Power by Authoritarian
             Regime Type, Latin America 1946–2010   49
Figure 2.6   Executive Constraints and Authoritarianism   55
Figure 2.7   Illiteracy and Authoritarianism   59
Figure 6.1   Ideal Points Derived from Roll-Call Votes from
             Chile's Chamber of Deputies   170
Figure 7.1   Disproportionality and District
             Magnitude in Five Chambers   196
Figure 8.1   Combinations of Judicial Instruments   217
Figure 8.2   Public Trust in the Judiciary, 1995–2018   222
Figure 8.3   Judicial Independence, 1985–2018   223
Figure 8.4   The Judiciary's Ability to Check
             Government Powers, 2019   225
Figure 9.1   Democracy Is Better Than Any Other Form of
             Government, 2016–2017   233
Figure 9.2   Tolerance for Citizens Who Speak Poorly of the
             Regime, 2016–2017   238
Figure 9.3   Tolerance for Gay Persons Running for
             Office, 2016–2017   239
Figure 10.1 Corruption Perception Index, 2012–2019   268
Figure 10.2 Corruption and Open Government, 2019   270
Figure 10.3 Corruption and Rule of Law, 2018   271
Figure 11.1 Security and Safety, 2010–2017   291
Figure 11.2 Freedom from Torture, 2000–2018   293
Figure 11.3 Support for Free Speech, Freedom of the
             Press, and Internet Freedom   297
Figure 11.4 Freedom of Expression and Assembly, 2019   298

Figure 11.5 Press Freedom, 2013–2019   302

Figure 11.6 Expropriation Risk and Property Rights Protection   307

Figure 12.1 Income Inequality, 2000–2017   317

Figure 12.2 Income Decile Dispersion Ratio, Circa 2017   318

Figure 12.3 Percentage of the Population Living on
              Less than $5.50 a Day, 2000–2017   321

Figure 12.4 Salary of Women as a Percentage of the
              Salary of Men   333

Figure 12.5 Salary of Women as a Percentage of the Salary of
              Men, Latin American Average by Education   334

Figure 12.6 Factor-Weighted Gender Pay Gap   335

• List of Tables •

Table 1.1	Indigenous Population in the Americas, 1492	13
Table 1.2	Composition of the Population in the Americas, 1570–1825	14
Table 1.3	Deaths in War and Civil Conflict, 1810–1879	22
Table 1.4	Gross Domestic Product per Capita, 1800–1900	26
Table 2.1	Freedom Status and Democracy in Latin America, 2018	42
Table 2.2	Types of Authoritarian Regimes	46
Table 3.1	Examples of Guerrilla Organizations	67
Table 4.1	Latin American's Opinions about the United States	120
Table 5.1	Distinct Attributes of Some Presidential Constitutions	134
Table 5.2	Presidential Interruptions	142
Table 6.1	Latin American Legislatures	156
Table 7.1	Restrictions to Universal Suffrage	177
Table 7.2	Suffrage Extensions	180
Table 7.3	Presidential Election Rules	184
Table 7.4	Rules for Electing Members of Congress	189
Table 8.1	Rules for Appointing High Court Judges and Length of Tenure	209
Table 8.2	Rules for Removing High Court Judges and Whether the Size of the Court Is in the Constitution	212
Table 9.1	Justifying Authoritarian Takeovers, 2016–2017	236
Table 9.2	Confidence in the President, Congress, and Political Parties, 2016–2017	242
Table 9.3	Interpersonal Trust	244
Table 9.4	Left–Right Self-Placement, 2016–2017	248
Table 9.5	Policy Preferences and Left–Right Self-Placement, 2016–2017	250
Table 10.1	Survey of Business Leaders, 2017–2018	272
Table 10.2	Public Services Corruption, 2016	274
Table 10.3	Private Firms' Experience with Corruption	275
Table 12.1	Poverty and Extreme Poverty	319

Table 12.2   Percentage Who Agree That a Wife
            Must Obey Her Husband   327
Table 12.3   Percentage of Women in Congress, 2019   330
Table 12.4   Women in Cabinets and High Courts   331

• Preface •

Latin America looks very different today than in the mid-20th century, when social scientists began to rigorously compare the politics of the region. Back then, most Latin Americans were poor, lived in rural areas, and were governed by dictatorial regimes. Civil liberties were frequently violated, mortality rates were high, and few women participated in the labor market. Nowadays, most Latin Americans live in urban areas, are not poor, and elect governments in competitive elections. Access to education and health care has also increased markedly. Women's participation in the labor force has grown significantly, and the gender gap in education has shrunk dramatically. While it is certainly true that poverty, political instability, sexism, and economic underperformance continue to be major problems, the region has made substantial progress in raising standards of living, strengthening political institutions, and overcoming authoritarianism.

Relations between the United States and Latin America have also changed substantially over the last decades. While in the 1950s, some academics could argue that it was a "slight exaggeration to say that the most important thing the two groups have in common is the hemisphere in which, by geographic accident, they live," it is nowadays evident that people on both areas of the Americas share a lot in common.[1] Economically, the United States (U.S.) is much more connected to Latin America. Mexico has become the country's second most important trading partner (after Canada), and since the mid-1990s, the U.S. has signed free trade agreements with 11 Latin American countries. Other policy issues, such as immigration, crime, human rights, and the environment, have also entered into the U.S.–Latin America agenda during the last few decades. Moreover, people of Latin American descent, who accounted for 1 percent of the U.S. population in 1950, are today the largest minority group, with around 18 percent of the U.S. population. More than half of the foreign-born population of the U.S. comes from Latin America.

The transformation of Latin American politics has been reflected in the main topics examined by academics and discussed by political pundits. While contemporary studies of Latin American politics continue to underline the importance of social conflict and economic performance, most have moved away from historical explanations centered on deterministic views of the legacy of Iberian culture and religion. Comparative studies of political institutions, elections, and public opinion are much more common these days. We also have access to a lot more data, which has stimulated empirical analyses of new and old theories. In short, the comparative analysis of Latin American politics has changed significantly over the last couple of decades, and this book seeks to reflect this transformation.

Approach of the Book

This book is about Latin America and how political scientists and other academics have explained political trends in the region. It is organized into research topics. Some of the big questions that have drawn substantial interest over time—What are the causes of political instability? What explains the gap in economic and political development between the U.S. and Latin America? Why have some revolutionaries triumphed when most have failed?—will be examined in light of recent research. Other topics central to the comparative politics literature but rarely examined in textbooks on Latin America—such as the effects of electoral rules, the organization of legislatures, judicial independence, and political culture—will also be addressed. New subjects that have become important to comparative studies, ranging from corruption, civil liberties, and press freedom to income inequality and the gender gap, are also incorporated into the book.

Professors and students should find the book well suited for a Latin American politics class. It should also work well as a complimentary book in comparative politics, third world politics, and Latin American studies courses. The book combines theoretical insights with descriptive material and historical background and explains the main arguments of each chapter with the help of data and illustrative figures. The chapters familiarize students with the main areas of research in Latin American politics and how social scientists think about the questions that dominate the field.

Each chapter concludes with suggested readings, a list of key terms, and (where appropriate) web resources that students can access to expand their knowledge and use in their own research. References throughout the book offer a useful bibliography of scholarly work on the main topics addressed in each chapter.

Organization

The first part of the book introduces students to some of the big questions of the discipline and examines political events over long periods of time. This includes analyses of the colonial period, its legacy, and the conflict that followed independence; political regimes and regime transitions since the early 20th century; and civil wars and revolutions. It also examines U.S.–Latin American relations, with a focus on the period following the end of World War II.

The second part concentrates on contemporary political institutions and highlights their differences across the region and their implications for political outcomes. It examines the presidency, the legislative branch, elections and electoral rules, and the judiciary. Among other topics, this section addresses the sources of presidential instability (also known as *presidential interruptions*), the extension of voting rights, the debate over compulsory voting, and the rules that promote judicial independence.

The last part of the book focuses on political attitudes, policies, and outcomes. It evaluates Latin Americans' support for democracy, confidence in institutions, interpersonal trust, and perceptions of corruption. It also examines the region's civil liberties record, factors influencing poverty and income disparities, and the progress and challenges on the road to gender equality.

• Acknowledgments •

The idea for this book originated while teaching Latin American politics to an enthusiastic group of students at the University of Houston, many of whom were children of Latin American immigrants or were themselves born in this region. I am grateful for their interest and encouragement and for their reading and discussion of drafts of various chapters. I am also indebted to the University of Houston, which has provided me with a supportive intellectual environment.

I would also like to thank the scholars who offered suggestions, shared sources, provided feedback, or commented on different aspects of the book: Gregg B. Johnson, Valparaiso University; Lydia Tiede, University of Houston; Julio Ríos Figueroa, CIDE; Patricio Navia, New York University; Pablo Pinto, University of Houston; Daniel M. Brinks, University of Texas at Austin; Francisco Cantú, University of Houston; Marisa Kellam, Waseda University; Aníbal Pérez-Liñán, University of Notre Dame; Eugenia Artabe, University of Houston; Mark P. Jones, Rice University; and Jamie Michelle Wright, University of Houston. Their suggestions greatly benefitted this book. Of course, responsibility for any remaining errors and omissions remains my own. I would also like to thank the CQ Press and SAGE staff and editors for their help, particularly Scott Greenan and Anna Villarruel, who stewarded this project during the last stages. Nancy J. Deyo, who helped with proofing and editing early drafts, also deserves my gratitude.

SAGE wishes to thank the following reviewers for their assistance:

Tiffany D. Barnes, University of Kentucky

T. Adam Golob, University of South Florida

Miguel Carreras, University of California, Riverside

• About the Author •

Eduardo Alemán is an associate professor of political science at the University of Houston. Professor Alemán teaches courses in comparative politics, political institutions, and Latin American politics. He specializes in the comparative analysis of political institutions and the politics of Latin America. Professor Alemán has published numerous articles in such journals as *World Politics*, *Comparative Politics*, *Legislative Studies Quarterly*, *Latin American Politics and Society*, and *Latin American Research Review*. He is also the co-editor of the book, *Legislative Institutions and Lawmaking in Latin America* (2016), with George Tsebelis.

Background

PART I

Background

Colonial Legacy and the Post-Independence Period

Most Latin American countries became independent in the first decades of the 19th century, after three hundred years of colonialism. Politics in the newly independent nations were significantly influenced by their colonial past. Likewise, the types of societies that characterized these nations in their early years were shaped by the colonial societies that had developed over the prior centuries. Political conflict and institutional development during the decades following independence had a lasting effect on Latin America. This chapter reviews the main traits of the colonial period, the political turmoil that followed independence, and the arrival of political order and economic growth in the second part of the 19th century. More specifically, it discusses the institutions and policies that shaped colonial Latin America, the independence movement, the causes of the widespread conflict that followed independence, and the characteristics surrounding the emergence of political stability and **export-led growth**. This chapter should enhance your understanding of the early politics, institutions, and economy of Latin America and provide you with a background that will lead to a better understanding of the politics of the region in subsequent eras.

Colonial Latin America

European countries began the colonization of the New World soon after the arrival of Christopher Columbus at the Caribbean islands of Bahama, Cuba, and Hispaniola in 1492. The kingdom of Spain, which had funded Columbus's voyage, colonized the largest area, including most of Latin America. Portugal, another leading European power, colonized much of the eastern part of South America. These two kingdoms signed the **Treaty of Tordesillas** in 1494, resolving controversies over land in the Americas by establishing a line of demarcation along a meridian 370 leagues west of the Cape Verde islands, a Portuguese possession on the west coast of Africa. Territories to the west of the line would be ruled by Spain and those to the east by Portugal. This treaty gave Spain control over most of the New World and Portugal control over the eastern area of what would become Brazil. Although other European countries ignored it, the treaty was mostly respected by Spain and Portugal. England, France, and the Netherlands established permanent colonies in the New World during the 17th century.

Spain and Portugal used soldiers and explorers, called **conquistadores**, to take control of new territories. Most of the early conquests were organized and financed by these individuals and their backers. Conquistadores were motivated primarily by personal wealth as well as, to some extent, by their contribution to the spread of the Catholic faith. They were also driven by the prestige and potential noble rank associated with military distinction and service to the crown. Conquistadores led the fight against the most numerous and advanced indigenous civilizations of the New World: the Aztecs and the Incas.

Hernán Cortés commanded the campaign against the Aztecs, who inhabited central Mexico. The Aztecs had brought several other indigenous tribes under their control and had developed a complex civilization. Ruled by Emperor Montezuma II, they had their capital and political center in Tenochtitlan, where about 300,000 people lived. Cortés began his campaign against the Aztecs in 1519 with around 600 men. He eventually allied with the Tlaxcalans, an indigenous tribe that had resisted Aztec domination and provided Cortés with thousands of warriors. Following a series of bloody confrontations and a 75-day siege of Tenochtitlan, the Spaniards finally defeated the Aztecs in August of 1521.

Francisco Pizarro led the campaign against the Incas, who ruled the largest empire in the pre-Columbian era. The Incas' territory extended across what is now Peru, Ecuador, and Chile. Its political and military capital was Cusco, located in the Andes mountains. In 1532, Pizarro arrived at what is today Peru. Atahualpa, the last Inca emperor, was captured and later killed by the Spaniards in August of 1533. After the arrival of reinforcements, Pizarro proceeded to take over Cusco, which fell in November of 1533. Following the defeat of the Incas, a violent dispute among the conquistadores ensued, which led to the assassination of Pizarro in 1541.

Spain ruled most of the region until the wars of independence in the 1810s and 1820s and remained in control of Cuba until 1898. Portugal ruled Brazil until 1822, when the independent empire of Brazil was founded. Colonial powers established institutions, implemented policies, and shaped societies in ways that would have a lasting impact on the countries of Latin America.

Colonial Institutions

The Spanish colonies were ruled by an elaborate bureaucracy. At the top of the administration was the **Council of the Indies**, which was created in 1524. The council, residing in Spain, acted as the king's advisory committee on colonial policy, drafting and issuing laws as well as appointing and supervising colonial authorities.

In Spanish America, the most senior officials were the **viceroys**. For most of the colonization period, there were two viceroyalties: New Spain (which extended from New Mexico to Panama) and Peru (which covered most of the Spanish territories in South America). The boundaries are shown in Map 1.1.

MAP 1.1 ● Colonial Latin America in the 16th and 17th Centuries with Boundaries of Viceroyalties and Audiencias

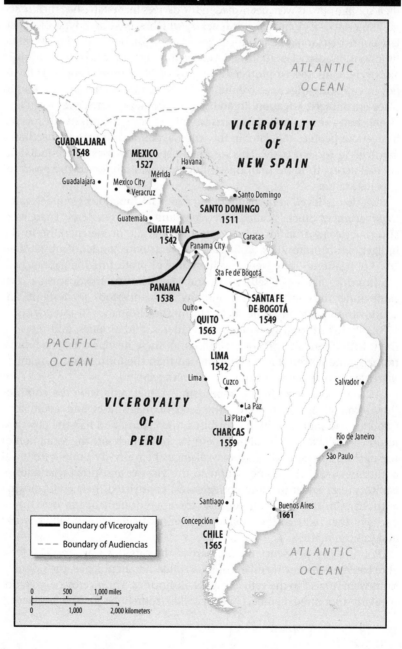

In the 18th century, two additional viceroyalties were created: New Granada (which encompassed the areas that are now Colombia, Ecuador, Panama, and Venezuela) and Río de la Plata (which encompassed the areas that are now Argentina, Bolivia, Paraguay, and Uruguay, as well as a portion of the north of Chile). Governors and captain generals were appointed by the Spanish crown to rule over frontier territories and those at a considerable distance from the capital of the viceroyalty. They typically had special military functions, and their specific powers were delineated in the decrees that established their posts.

The crown also created **audiencias**, which served as a type of appellate court that, in some instances, also had legislative and administrative functions. Audiencias addressed complaints against colonial authorities and were supposed to protect the rights of indigenous people. Difficulties in enforcing the excessive number of laws, regulations, and decrees in place encouraged litigation. In addition to ordinary courts, the crown also established a series of special courts for military officers, priests, aristocrats, indigenous people, and, later in the colonial period, miners and merchants involved in foreign trade. This fostered disputes in cases where individuals had access to more than one tribunal, which reinforced the power of appellate courts.

At a lower level, administrative and judicial functions were delegated to government officials called *corregidores* and *alcaldes mayores*. There were also *corregidores de indios*, who controlled the sale of merchandise in the indigenous communities, collected native tribute, and organized their labor obligations. They were also in charge of protecting indigenous people from the abuses of settlers. In the 18th century, the Spanish crown came under the control of the Bourbons, who undertook some significant administrative reforms. One such reform, the Ordinance of Intendants of 1782, abolished local governors, corregidores, and alcaldes, and replaced them with intendants. The appointment of these new provincial administrators, more powerful and better trained than the former ones, sought to increase the revenue sent from the colonies to Spain.

At the lowest level in the administrative hierarchy were the **cabildos** (town councils), which were composed of magistrates and councilors. Cabildos had judicial duties, controlled town lands, and had the power to impose local taxes, issue building permits, and coordinate the formation of self-defense forces. Low budgets weakened their already limited financial authority, and their subordination to the viceroy and provincial administrators (e.g., governors and corregidores) constricted their policymaking authority.[1] In the late 18th century, the appointment of the new intendants further reduced the cabildos' power, particularly over public works and judicial matters.

Political independence on the part of the cabildos was rare. The local elite could elect some members of the cabildo but, in practice, the nominations were subject to the veto of higher authorities. The viceroy or governor regularly appointed members of the cabildo (sometimes for life), frequently left elective offices unfilled, and, on occasion, would punish cabildo members for their behavior (e.g., with fines).[2]

In short, the institutions of Spanish America centralized power in an appointed bureaucracy. Most of the top positions in the bureaucracy were staffed with individuals born in Spain. Local elites were restricted in terms of their ability to exercise power within the colonial bureaucracy. Some of them took advantage of the crown's decision to sell appointments in the audiencias beginning in 1687, but this practice began to be curtailed in mid-18th century and their participation in the colonial bureaucracy was subsequently reduced.

Portugal had a less structured bureaucracy in Brazil than Spain in its colonies. It relied on appointed governors and only in the 18th century sent a viceroy to the region. The royal government was established in San Salvador da Bahia, where it remained until 1763, when it was moved to Rio de Janeiro. First the governor general and later the viceroy held significant powers, including executive, judicial, economic, and military authority. In practice, however, the Portuguese colony was rather decentralized because of its large territory and difficulties in transportation.[3] The provincial-level bureaucracy was less developed than the one in Spanish America. At the municipal level, governmental authority was in the hands of a town council called *senado da câmara*. The town councils were composed of members appointed by the royal authorities, with some elected from the local elites. During the first part of the colonial period, the town councils in Brazil enjoyed significant administrative, judicial, and fiscal powers, but during the 18th century, administrative reforms began to erode their authority.

In the New World colonies, there was a close association between civil and religious authorities. The affiliation between the Catholic Church and the Spanish crown during the colonial period came to be known as the **royal patronage (*patronato real*)**. Under this arrangement, the Pope gave the Spanish monarchs control over the church in the colonial territories. The monarch was responsible for organizing and financing the evangelization of the new colonial territories. In return, the clergy became responsible to the crown, which had the power to appoint bishops, archbishops, and parish priests, subject to papal approval. The monarch also had the right to establish dioceses, modify their boundaries, and collect the ecclesiastical tax (tithe). Members of the clergy were exempted from most taxes, and the special court system spared them from prosecution in common criminal courts. Communication between the Pope and the clergy in the colonies was under the control of the monarch (*regium exequatur*), who had to approve the publication of papal resolutions and who could screen bishops' petitions.[4] These powers isolated the Holy See from the clergy in the colonies, weakened the authority of bishops, and subjected the church to the power of the Spanish crown.

The Pope also ceded to the Portuguese crown a royal patronage (patronato real) for their colonial territories.[5] The Portuguese king was responsible for safeguarding the clergy, promoting evangelization, and collecting the ecclesiastical tax (tithe). Appointments to all ecclesiastical offices were made by the Board of Conscience and Orders (*Mesa de Consciência e Ordens*). As in Spanish America, the Portuguese colony had special ecclesiastical courts for the clergy, which, in comparison to the common criminal courts, were considered to be rather lenient.

In colonial Latin America, the Catholic Church was typically responsible for birth, death, and marriage certificates and running hospitals and schools. Catholic missions spread throughout the region, particularly in frontier areas, where they concentrated on the religious conversion of natives.[6] Catholic orders—Franciscans, Dominicans, Augustinians, and Jesuits—undertook most of the missionary work.

The Spanish and Portuguese crowns banned the immigration of non-Catholics to the colonies. Religious persecution was carried out by the Holy Office of the Inquisition, which dealt with matters of faith and morals. Church edicts informed colonists about the practices of Jews, Moors, and Protestants so they could identify and expose them to the Inquisition. Those suspected of homosexuality or advancing scientific ideas opposed by the Catholic Church were also persecuted. While persecution of the indigenous peoples was not actively pursued, many other groups were tortured, sentenced to be lashed, and killed as a result of the Inquisition's recommendations. In colonial Brazil, the influence of the Inquisition was much more limited than in the Spanish colonies.

Colonial Policies

The economic policies of Spain and Portugal were heavily influenced by the economic theory of **mercantilism**, which linked affluence with the accumulation of capital.[7] Both countries sought prosperity by accumulating gold and silver through external trade. This demanded a favorable trade balance, meaning a situation in which the value of exports exceeded the value of imports. To this end, both colonial powers required their colonies to buy all commodity imports from them and to sell all commodity exports to them. The resulting trade deficit was financed by the transfer of mineral resources to the colonial powers.[8] A trade monopoly assured both Spain and Portugal that their colonies could not reduce this deficit by trading with other countries. In addition, taxes on mining and other local taxes flowing to the colonial powers further increased that deficit. As a result of this economic strategy, colonial powers paid particular attention to mineral-rich areas.

The Spanish crown established the *Casa de Contratación de Indias* to control commerce with the New World. This institution, based in Seville, was in charge of inspecting and regulating the flow of trade. The city's merchant guild was authorized to manage trade transactions and royal monopolies for the crown. Only members of the guild could purchase commodities for distribution and sale across Europe. During the 17th century, the port of Cadiz was occasionally authorized to be used for trade with the Spanish colonies. In the early 18th century, Seville permanently lost its monopoly to Cadiz. In the New World, the ports of Veracruz (Mexico), Cartagena (New Granada), and Portobello (Panama) were those authorized to receive the commodities arriving from Spain and where exports were loaded to be sent back.

The Spanish colonial economy focused on the extraction of mineral resources, particularly gold and silver from the viceroyalties of Peru and New Spain. At first, there was the gold that had been previously accumulated by the indigenous civilizations, which was plundered by the conquistadores. Gold deposits decreased rapidly in Peru and New Spain but became important in regions such as New Granada and Chile.[9] Instead, silver production increased in importance and, by the 1540s, surpassed gold in terms of value. The most important silver mines were in Potosí (Bolivia), Zacatecas (Mexico), and Guanajuato (Mexico). Silver mining increased significantly during the 16th century, experienced a decline during the 17th century, and then recovered after the early 18th century.[10] Mercury, which was used for processing silver, also became economically significant. Most of the mercury used in the colonies came from deposits in Huancavelica (Peru) and the south of Spain. Mineral wealth did not become relevant in Brazil until the 1690s, when gold was discovered.

Labor from indigenous people was crucial for the mining industry. Originally, labor came from **encomienda**, which involved the granting of labor or tribute from indigenous people to the conquistadores, and from enslaved natives. Most of the latter had been captured in the wars of conquests or bought from indigenous chiefs and Spaniards.[11] The enforcement of laws limiting indigenous slavery and the wane of conflict after the conquest sharply decreased the number of enslaved indigenous workers by the mid-16th century.

Widespread abuses under the encomienda system led to its gradual replacement by crown-managed draft labor starting in the 1550s. In New Spain, draft labor was called *repartimiento*; in Peru, it was called *mita*. It required indigenous communities to supply a portion of their population to work for a prescribed time. For example, indigenous communities were forced to send one-seventh of their adult male population to work for one year in the silver mines of Potosí.[12]

From the late 16th century onward, wage labor also became significant and, by the 18th century, it was the predominant form of labor in the mines. Labor from blacks brought from Africa and their descendants (slaves and free men) represented a small portion of the labor in silver mines but served as a predominant portion of the labor in tropical lowland gold mining.

Revenue from mining represented a substantial source of income for the Spanish crown. Not only did the crown receive a royalty on mining production but it also set the price of mercury and monopolized its distribution. In addition, mining stimulated trade, which provided revenues in the form of sales taxes and customs duties. In short, the Spanish had a vital interest in colonial mining and greatly influenced it through its control of draft labor, the supply of mercury, and the imposition of royalties.

Mining promoted roadbuilding, commerce, and intra-colonial trade. However, not much capital obtained from mining was reinvested locally to help colonial economies become self-sustaining.[13] Nonetheless, the economy diversified during the 17th century, and local agriculture became more important. During this period, elites extended their control over land through purchases and usurpation.

Agriculture in the colonies can be divided into two types. The first was oriented toward internal demand, including the supply of provisions to the mining centers and subsistence farming. The second focused on the demands of the international market and centered on plantation agriculture.

Extensive land grants from the crown were allocated early on as rewards for military endeavors during the conquest. The first large estates were close to the emerging markets created around mining areas and colonial administrative centers. There were many small farms, called *ranchos*; the large ones, called *haciendas*, grew in importance during the 18th century. Ecclesiastical land holdings also increased significantly over time, often as a result of donations from devout Catholics. Jesuits, for example, owned a great deal of land, including plantations and vineyards, which were ultimately confiscated by the Spanish crown when it expelled them from its colonies in 1767.

Towns first relied on provisions from indigenous farming. Indigenous communal lands, which included a sizeable share of the land in the highlands and even some of the best arable land, lasted throughout the colonial period.[14] Indigenous people and **mestizos** (people of mixed native and European blood) provided most of the labor in the Andean and Mexican regions, whereas African slave labor was crucial in the tropical lowlands. The encomienda, mita, and repartimiento were also used to supply agricultural workers. For the most part, the working conditions of indigenous people in the haciendas were less abusive than those of mine workers and, over time, the share of free labor in agriculture increased markedly.

In the colonial centers and around mining towns, legal private holdings were common, but in general, there was widespread insecurity over legal titles in cultivated lands. Some areas with dubious titles included occupied public lands and abandoned indigenous lands. The insecurity of most land titles prevented individuals from securing loans, led to competing ownership claims, and had a negative impact on land productivity in the colonies.[15]

Plantation agriculture took place in tropical climates, focusing on crops such as sugar, cotton, coffee, and tobacco that offered particular economic advantages when produced on large-scale plantations. The preeminent plantation colony was Brazil. After land was first granted by the Portuguese crown to a set of twelve proprietary captains, most sought to establish sugar plantations, but the majority failed when confronted with the difficulties of attracting settlers, raising capital, and dealing with the natives. However, sugar plantations took hold in the northeast. During the second part of the 16th century, the captaincy of Pernambuco established dozens of sugar plantations and mills and became the economic engine of the colony. By the early 17th century, a successful sugar industry had developed in northeast Brazil, providing the Portuguese crown with substantial export taxes.

Initially, Portuguese settlers used enslaved natives for plantation labor, but the indigenous population declined due to disease, and many of the survivors fled inland. The availability of indigenous people for plantation work was further limited after the Portuguese king issued decrees in 1570 and 1573 restricting their enslavement. Settlers then turned to the importation of slaves. African slaves represented a small share of plantation labor in the 16th century, but soon after, they became the main source of labor. From the beginning of the colonization period until 1820, the number of African slaves brought to Brazil has been calculated to be close to 3.6 million; an additional 1,269,400 would arrive between 1821 and 1867.[16]

Sugar plantations spread from Brazil to the Caribbean and lowland regions of tropical Spanish America. This fostered an increase in the slave trade during the second half of the 18th century. Most of those brought to the Spanish colonies after the mid-18th century ended up in Cuba and Puerto Rico. The northern coast of South America also had a significant proportion of African slaves, many of them working at cacao plantations on the coast of Venezuela.

Policies in the Spanish colonies began to change after the House of Bourbons replaced the Hapsburgs in the Spanish throne. Most of the policy changes, known as the **Bourbon Reforms**, took place during the second half of the 18th century. They included institutional changes, such as the creation of the viceroyalties of New Granada and Río de la Plata and the autonomous captaincies of Venezuela and Chile, and the recentralization of administrative power under the intendancy system. The establishment of special courts for miners and export–import merchants was part of these reforms. Also, the sale of offices to creoles (persons born in the Americas of European ancestry), which had become common in the first part of the 18th century and had allowed many of them to join the colonial bureaucracy, was ended.

The Bourbon reforms extended the reach of royal monopolies to cover tobacco, gunpowder, salt, and some alcoholic beverages, among other goods.[17] The crown assumed direct administration of tax collection, increased sales taxes, and improved their enforcement. Some mining costs were reduced, and mining infrastructure improved. In addition, a royal decree issued in 1778 lessened restrictions on intra-colonial trade and opened additional Spanish ports to transatlantic trade. Military defenses were also strengthened, partly to prevent further losses, such as those that took place in the Caribbean to the British, French, Dutch, and Danes during the 17th century. In Brazil, a set of similar reforms, known as *the Pombaline Reforms*, was implemented during the second half of the 18th century.

The reforms reasserted the crown's authority over the colonies, which creoles resented. Overall, the economy became more diversified and grew, but at the end of the colonial period, Latin American colonies lagged behind the United States. Latin American colonies were comparatively far from the principal world markets, and the region's geography posed many obstacles to accessing and transporting goods. More importantly, the Spanish and Portuguese crowns failed to establish institutions that would clearly define, protect, and enforce property rights, which discouraged investment, entrepreneurship, and inventive activity.[18] Furthermore, colonial powers invested little in education and physical infrastructure and prevented settlers from developing advantageous trade links with other world markets.[19]

Colonial Societies

Latin America experienced tremendous demographic changes during the colonial period. Indigenous populations were devastated; millions of Africans were brought in as slaves; and the proportion of mestizos grew significantly. In addition, creoles and Spaniards had an uneasy coexistence in a social system that privileged both of them over other groups

One of the most terrible legacies of the colonization period in Latin America is the collapse of indigenous populations after 1492. The estimates of the number of indigenous people in the eve of the conquest vary extensively, and there is an ongoing debate among scholars regarding the correct numbers. Estimates provided by geographer William M. Denevan put the number of indigenous people in 1492 at 53.9 million. The population breakdown per region appears in Table 1.1.

After the conquest, the number of indigenous people experienced an enormous decline, the most abrupt of which occurred in the Caribbean and the Brazilian coast, where natives came close to extinction. Researchers have estimated that the population of Central Mexico declined from 16.9 million in 1532 to 1.1 million in 1608.[20] In the Andes and Central America, there was also a very significant reduction in the indigenous population. In general, the indigenous people living in the highlands had a greater rate of survival than those living in the lowlands. The decline of the indigenous population in New Spain and New Granada continued until the middle of the 17th century, when it reached its lowest point. In Central America, the lowest point was in the late 16th century, while in the Andes, it was in the early 18th century. Afterward, the numbers began to grow again, albeit rather moderately.

Several factors explain the drastic decline in the number of indigenous people after 1492. The violence inflicted by the conquerors, including killings in military confrontations, enslavement, and overworking, was one factor. Malnutrition resulting from changes in diet, confiscation of food, and alterations in food production also had an effect. Another cause was a sharp decline in fertility rates. This has been associated with pervasive hopelessness among indigenous communities, which negatively impacted the tendency to have children.[21] However, the most significant cause of population decline was disease. The Europeans brought with them diseases for which indigenous people had no immunity. Epidemics of smallpox, malaria, measles, typhus, and influenza had a devastating effect. The arrival of yellow fever with the slave ships coming from Africa also led to a high number of deaths.

While the proportion of indigenous people experienced a profound decline from the days before the conquest, the number of Africans brought involuntarily to the colonies increased markedly. First, they went to the Caribbean and Mexico, and later to Peru and Brazil. The estimated numbers for the period prior to 1641 are 265,500 arriving in Brazil and 529,800 arriving in Spanish America.[22] The numbers increased drastically between 1641 and 1820, with the propagation of the plantation economy. During this period, around 3.3 million African slaves arrived in Brazil, 417,400 in Spanish America, and 3.5 million went to the British and French Caribbean and the Dutch West Indies.[23] For the most part, the birth rate of the black population living in these colonies was low, and their growth in terms of the share of the population was the result of forced migration.

TABLE 1.1 ● Indigenous Population in the Americas, 1492	
Region	Estimated Population
North America	3,790,000
Mexico	17,174,000
Central America	5,625,000
Caribbean	3,000,000
Andes[1]	15,696,000
Amazonia[2]	5,664,000
Chile and Argentina	1,900,000
Paraguay, Uruguay, and southern Brazil	1,055,000
Total	53,904,000

[1.] It includes the highlands and coast of Peru, Bolivia, Ecuador, Venezuela, and Colombia.
[2.] It includes the eastern lowlands beside the eastern and southern flank of the Andes.

Source: William M. Denevan (ed.) 1992. *The Native Population of the Americas in 1492.* 2nd ed. Madison: University of Wisconsin Press.

The pattern of migration from Europe to the Americas changed over time. Between 1500 and 1760, the number of Europeans immigrating to the colonies in the New World was approximately 2 million.[24] Of these, 33 percent went to Spanish America, 26 percent to Portuguese America, and 37 percent to British America. After the mid-1600s, the British colonies became the main destination of European immigration to the New World.

The composition of the population in Spanish America, Brazil, and the United States and Canada during the period 1570–1825 appears in Table 1.2. It shows how the indigenous portion dropped drastically in the three types of colonies. In 1825, it only remained a majority in the Spanish colonial territories. The proportion of black population grew in all three regions but only became a majority in Brazil. In contrast, white population grew to become the largest group only in the United States and Canada, where they amounted to four out of five inhabitants in 1825.

The social structure of colonial society was greatly influenced by race and birthplace. A specific legal structure, the **castas**, developed to detail the relations between indigenous people and the Spaniards and creoles. This caste system, which entailed a set of rights and responsibilities based on ethnicity, was put in place after the abolishment of indigenous slavery in the Spanish colonies. Geographic mobility and occupational opportunities were regulated. Indigenous people (and, in most cases, mestizos as well) were excluded from holding public office and could not undertake several activities, such as law, medicine, and wholesale business. They could not bear arms or own horses and needed special permission to reside outside

TABLE 1.2 ● Composition of the Population in the Americas, 1570–1825				
Region	Year	Indigenous (%)	Black (%)	White (%)
Spanish America	1570	96.3	2.5	1.3
	1650	84.4	9.3	6.3
	1825	59.5	22.5	18.0
Brazil	1570	94.1	3.5	2.4
	1650	78.9	13.7	7.4
	1825	21.0	55.6	23.4
United States and Canada	1570	99.6	0.2	0.2
	1650	85.8	2.2	12.0
	1825	3.7	16.7	79.6

Source: Stanley L. Engerman and Kenneth L. Sokoloff. 2012. *Economic Development in the Americas since 1500: Endowments and Institutions.* New York: Cambridge University Press.

indigenous villages. As previously noted, indigenous people were also subject to draft labor, although during the 17th century, free private labor became the norm in most places.

Starting in the late 16th century, mestizos of legitimate descent could buy from the crown a certificate classifying them as Spaniards, which gave their descendants greater opportunities, including the chance of higher education.[25] In 1783, King Charles III of Spain put in place a process called *cédulas de gracias al sacar* by which free blacks and **mulattos** (individuals of mixed white and black ancestry) could receive a royal certificate to alter their racial status. In 1795, a new law established that these individuals could purchase such a license, which gave them the right to apply for permission to be educated, marry a white person, have a government job, or become a priest. These legal processes establishing racial and ethnic flexibility were primarily the result of the crown's perpetual shortage of funds.[26] They met with strong opposition from the white population in the colonies, which sought to defend their privileges.

The Portuguese also established a caste system in Brazil, although less elaborate than in Spanish America. Indigenous slavery was in place for a longer period of time than in Spanish America despite legal limits, and the enslavement of black people continued until after Brazil's independence. Blacks were not allowed to hold public office, become priests, bear arms, own horses, or wear certain clothes.[27] Black slaves could buy their freedom or become free as a result of a decision from their master (considered a gift or charity). In the latter case, a slave's freedom could be revoked for acts of ingratitude toward their former master.[28]

Following the fall of Spanish rule, slavery collapsed in places such as Mexico, Central America, Chile, Bolivia, and Argentina. In Venezuela, Peru, Ecuador, and Colombia, where there was greater resistance, this took place in the 1850s. In Cuba and Puerto Rico (where Spain retained control) as well as in Brazil, slavery was abolished in the 1880s.

In the Spanish and Portuguese colonies, the white population had significant legal advantages and much greater educational and commercial opportunities than others. But even among themselves, there were important inequalities in terms of political power. Only individuals born in Spain (called ***peninsulares***) and creoles could hold public office and positions in the Church, but the former group occupied the most prominent positions. The renowned Prussian scholar Alexander von Humboldt, who traveled throughout the colonies, remarked on how the government, suspicious of creoles, reserved the best offices for native Spaniards. He noted the mutual dislike between peninsulares and creoles and wrote that "the most miserable European, without education, and without intellectual cultivation, thinks himself superior to whites born in the continent."[29]

Although traditionally depicted as dominant, there were significant constraints placed on the settlers by the colonial system. Settlers did not control policymaking; the crown limited their economic opportunities with the imposition of high taxes, royal monopolies, trade restrictions, and forced monetary donations. Moreover, the property rights of settlers were less than secure, and in some instances, they had to endure economic losses resulting from Spain's debt defaults, wealth expropriation, and compulsory loans.[30] This limited settlers' political influence and investment incentives.

Settlers also depended on the crown for security. Concerns about indigenous and slave rebellions were common, and they frequently occurred during the 18th century, even if most were small in scale. While local militias consisting of settlers (and often mulattos and mestizos) dealt with most rebellions and riots in the colonies, they ultimately depended on the forces of the crown to suppress the most serious uprisings. External threats were also relevant, as shown by the occupation of many Spanish settlements in the Caribbean, frequent attacks on trading routes, and the temporary control of parts of northeastern Brazil by the Dutch. The complicated relationship between the settlers and the Spaniards regarding security and social privileges, as well as the frequent conflicts over economic matters and political influence, would eventually play important roles in the events leading to independence.

Independence and the Struggle for Political Order

The events leading to the independence of Latin American countries originated with the **Peninsular War** in Europe, a conflict involving France versus Portugal, Spain, and Great Britain. It started after Portugal, a long-time ally of England, refused to join Napoleon Bonaparte's continental system, which sought to blockade British products from continental Europe. Then, France occupied Portugal at the end of 1807. Before the French troops arrived in Lisbon, the Portuguese royal family, the administration, and the court sailed to Brazil protected by warships and accompanied by several merchant ships. Spain originally allied with France, but in early 1808, Napoleon Bonaparte turned against Spain and seized much of its territory.

The political turmoil generated by the invasion of Spain together with growing animosity toward King Charles IV led to his abdication in favor of his son Ferdinand VII. Napoleon Bonaparte did not recognize Ferdinand VII as the King of Spain, kept him captive in France, and instead named his brother Joseph Bonaparte as ruler. Although Spanish administrative bodies acquiesced, rebellions against Napoleonic rule spread across the country.

The Peninsular War would last until 1814. During that period, the governing structure of the Spanish kingdom was in disarray. The Cádiz Cortes (an elected assembly composed of nobles, clergymen, and the common people) emerged as a governing body in 1810 but was severely constrained and had to operate surrounded by French troops. Some representatives from the Spanish colonies also participated in the Cádiz Cortes.

Regulations passed by the Cádiz Cortes had a profound impact on the kingdom and the colonies. For example, the Cádiz Cortes abolished the viceroyalties and the Inquisition and declared equality for subjects in the colonies. It also abolished indigenous tribute and draft labor and ordered the breakup of indigenous communal land and its distribution among adult indigenous individuals. A liberal constitution was then passed in 1812, ending the absolute monarchy and establishing a constitutional one, which allowed the national parliament to pass legislation despite the king's opposition.

The Spanish constitution was nullified by King Ferdinand upon his return to the throne in 1814. An absolute monarchy was restored and the Cádiz Cortes dissolved, and supporters of the liberal constitution began to be persecuted and sometimes killed. An era of instability followed, exacerbated by Ferdinand's change of the rules of royal succession in favor of his daughter Isabella II. It was during this time of occupation, resistance, restoration, and internal conflict that the Latin American colonies began the self-rule that would eventually lead them to independence.

Independence

The immediate cause of the emergence of the first autonomous local governments in the colonies, called **juntas**, was the political vacuum left by the French occupation of Spain. But the underlying tensions that facilitated the move toward self-government and independence can be traced back to earlier events. These included conflicts stemming from the economic grievances of settlers, the centralization of political power in Spanish administrators, a long-standing animosity between creoles and peninsulares, and the concerns of settlers about the ability of the crown to provide security.

Tax pressures, which increased with the Bourbon reforms, generated substantial opposition in the colonies. Rebellions against fiscal policies took place in New Granada in 1765 (Quito) and 1781 (Socorro). Forced donations and loans to pay for Spain's military expenses and debts became common. One particularly controversial measure was the consolidation decree of 1804, which led to the confiscation of charitable church funds in the colonies. In New Spain, where the church had put its capital to work becoming one of the most crucial lending institutions, this decree had a tremendous effect, leading to property seizures and farmers having to sell their proprieties on unfavorable terms to pay their debts.[31] This royal decree, which angered the propertied classes, was finally suspended when France invaded Spain.

Opportunities for trade remained limited by colonial policies, which was particularly upsetting to agricultural producers. During the British blockade of Spanish ports that took place during the Anglo–Spanish War (1796–1802), many colonists experienced the advantages of freer trade and resented the reimposition of colonial controls that followed. Demands for free trade, for example, were common among the representatives from the colonies in the Cádiz Cortes during the French occupation of Spain.[32] Also upsetting to colonists was legislation issued at the beginning of the 19th century that sought to restrict the establishment of manufacturing to protect competing industries in Spain.

Another grievance had to do with governmental actions that weakened the political power of settler elites. The recentralization of power that shifted administrative authority to the intendants weakened the influence of settler elites. After the mid-18th century, the participation of creoles in public office was reduced significantly. Historian John Lynch observed that the proportion of creoles among audiencia appointees dropped from 44 percent during the period 1687–1750 to 23 percent in the period 1751–1808.[33] There were also fewer creoles in top Church and military positions.

Security concerns also played a role in the events leading to self-government. As noted before, local militias dealt with most internal security matters and settlers relied on royal military power for suppressing major rebellions and external threats, but this arrangement was shaken in the early 19th century. For example, when the British invaded the viceroyalty of the Río de la Plata in 1806 and 1807, it was the locals that drove them out, with little help from Spain.

Settlers also feared a potential conflict with the indigenous masses and slaves. In the words of historian J. H. Elliott, "Spaniards and the upper ranks of the creoles lived in fear of an explosion among the ethnically mixed populations that crowded the streets of New Spain and Peru."[34] A violent indigenous uprising began in Peru in late 1780 and led to a major confrontation pitting creoles and Spaniards against the forces led by Tupac Amaru. After thousands of deaths, the rebellion was suppressed in early 1782 and the indigenous leaders were killed. Also influential was the violent slave revolt that took place in the French colony of Saint-Domingue in 1791, which eventually led to the newly independent state of Haiti in 1804. This event was particularly worrisome for plantation owners in the Spanish Caribbean, Venezuela, and Brazil. After France occupied Spain in 1808, many settlers doubted whether the royal forces defeated in Europe could fulfill their commitment to protecting their lives and property.

The last decades of colonial rule also saw the beginnings of nationalist ideas that underlined an identity different than that of the colonial power. The ideas of the Enlightenment also reached intellectual circles and generated concern among an ecclesiastical hierarchy troubled by the principles of equality and liberty and challenges to tradition and authority. In addition, the independence of the United States proved that a revolt against a powerful European country could actually succeed.

After France invaded Spain, locally run juntas began to emerge across the colonies. The first were established in Mexico and Uruguay in 1808. The one in Mexico was short-lived; loyalist groups regained control and devolved power to a new viceroy. The one in Uruguay was a loyalist junta formed in opposition to the provisional viceroy of the Río de la Plata, whom some perceived as having an ambivalent position regarding the conflict in Spain.

However, the juntas formed in 1809 in La Paz (upper Peru) and Quito (New Granada) sought greater autonomy and were not fully committed to the Spanish central junta that had emerged to fill the vacuum after Ferdinand's captivity. The Quito junta collapsed that same year as royalist troops were closing on the city. The next year, forces sent by the viceroy of Peru captured and punished the leaders of the La Paz junta who had sought to establish new self-government institutions.

In 1810, a creole-led rebellion in Caracas deposed the captain general of Venezuela and established a junta to govern autonomously from Spanish institutions. Soon after, juntas emerged in Bogota, Buenos Aires, Santiago, and again in Quito. After appointing the viceroy as its president, the Bogota junta deposed him. In Buenos Aires, the viceroy was removed by rebel creoles after a failed attempt by loyalists to place him as the head of the newly established junta. A few months later, a new governing junta formed in Santiago. In all these cases, the autonomous juntas claimed to govern in the name of Ferdinand, who remained captive in France.

Venezuela saw the most intense conflict during the wars of independence, mainly as a result of its proximity to the Spanish Caribbean and Europe. The junta in Caracas called for an election to a congress, which declared independence in 1811. The following year, the city was captured by royalist forces helped by reinforcements sent from Puerto Rico but was lost again to independent forces in 1813. Royalist forces retook Caracas in 1814 and remained in the city until it was finally liberated in 1821 by independence hero, Simón Bolivar.

In neighboring New Granada, the junta of Cartagena declared independence in 1811. Forces coming from Venezuela restored New Granada to royalists' hands in 1816 but were defeated three years later by Bolivar. Royalists were then expelled from Guayaquil in 1820 and Quito in 1822.

The Buenos Aires junta had refused to recognize the authority set in Spain in the absence of Ferdinand and moved to take areas of the viceroyalty of the Río de la Plata in upper Peru (Bolivia) that remained in control of royalists. The forces sent north temporarily experienced success but were ultimately defeated. The Buenos Aires junta also sent forces to Paraguay, which were also unsuccessful. Paraguay established its own junta in 1811 and became de facto independent in 1813 when an elected congress established the Republic of Paraguay without any mention of Ferdinand.

The junta that had been set up in 1808 in Montevideo (Uruguay) maintained its allegiance to the provisional government in Spain and did not join the autonomous-minded junta in Buenos Aires. Political and military turmoil followed. Portuguese forces occupied the Uruguayan territory in 1811 at the request of Spanish loyalists. Subsequent confrontations between royalists, local independent forces led by José Gervasio Artigas, and forces loyal to the Buenos Aires junta continued until Artigas took the city of Montevideo in early 1815. The next year, Portuguese forces invaded Uruguay and remained there until 1825, when the country declared independence.

The United Provinces of the Río de la Plata, as Argentina was then called, formally declared independence in 1816. The following year, military leader and then–governor of Cuyo, José de San Martín, crossed the Andes with a sizeable army to liberate Chile from royalist control. After recurrent conflict, Chile's junta had collapsed and loyalist forces sent from Peru in 1813 had regained control. Following the defeat of the royalist by San Martín's forces, Chile declared independence in 1818.

San Martín arrived at the outskirts of Lima, still controlled by royalist forces, in 1820. Northern coastal cities had already switched sides, but Lima remained loyal to Spain. At that time, Spain was undergoing significant political developments, which had brought **liberals** back to power and the reestablishment of the 1812 Constitution. This made **conservatives** in Lima uneasy about restoring ties with the motherland. Meanwhile, the new Spanish government seemed ready to reach some type of settlement with the revolutionaries. In 1821, faced with uncertainty and eroding support, the Spanish authorities and the bulk of the royalist army left Lima for the highlands. A few days later, San Martín proceeded to enter Lima and declare the independence of Peru.

After meeting Bolivar in Guayaquil in 1822, San Martín withdrew from the region. Bolivar's army then took the offensive against the remaining royalist forces. Bolivar's lieutenant, General Antonio José de Sucre, led the independent forces in the Battle of Ayacucho, which took place in December of 1824 and resulted in the defeat of the remaining royalist forces in Peru. Not long after, General Sucre marched into upper Peru. Royalist forces surrendered in April of 1825, and a newly formed congress proceeded to declare the independence of upper Peru, which took the name of Bolivia in honor of the liberator.

In New Spain, loyalists had taken control of the government after the 1808 junta in Mexico City had been quickly dissolved. But in 1810, they faced a massive uprising led by Manuel Hidalgo, a charismatic priest who appealed for profound social reforms and racial equality. Hidalgo's sizeable forces, which were primarily composed of mestizos and indigenous people, marched into the city of Guanajuato, where they killed hundreds of Spaniards and creoles. They then moved toward Mexico City. Despite having the upper hand and winning some confrontations in the outskirts of the city, Hidalgo decided to retreat. The royalist forces then pursued the rebels, eventually defeating them and killing Hidalgo and other leaders of the insurgency. José Maria Morelos, another priest, took over the leadership of the movement and scored some victories, but in 1815, he was finally captured and sentenced to death.

The independence movement in Mexico lost its impetus after 1815. Smaller forces, such as those led by Vicente Guerrero in Oaxaca, continued to fight but were not close to achieving a military victory. When the Spanish revolution of 1820 brought the liberal movement back to power, royalist forces led by creole Agustín de Iturbide were poised to defeat Guerrero's uprising. The political change in Spain led conservatives in Mexico to reassess their options, with Iturbide then changing positions and negotiating with Guerrero. In early 1821, he proposed a path to independence that would recognize the equality of all citizens, solidify the primacy of Catholicism, and establish a monarchical system. Ferdinand would be invited to assume the throne, and if that could not be worked out, his brothers would be offered the position. Property was to be protected, clergy privileges upheld, and administrative and military positions would be preserved for those who accepted the independence plan. On August, Iturbide met with an envoy of the Cádiz Cortes, who recognized the independence of Mexico and agreed to persuade the remaining royal troops to surrender.

In Central America, there was no major uprising as in Mexico, but there were smaller rebellions. Two of these took place in San Salvador, with Manuel José de Arce as a key player. He would later become the first president of the Federal Republic of Central America. As in Mexico and Peru, the move toward independence accelerated after the 1820 liberal takeover of government in Spain. Central American elites did not look favorably on the changes Spain was undergoing. Many became particularly displeased after the Spanish Cádiz Cortes suppressed the Bethlehemite Brothers' religious order, which had been founded in Guatemala in 1653. After Iturbide's independence plan became known, Chiapas joined Mexico's path. Soon after, Guatemala and the other provinces of Central America declared independence.

To summarize, the events that triggered the move toward autonomous governments across the colonies originated in Europe. However, many of the underlying tensions between settlers and Spaniards that facilitated the move toward independence had originated with the Bourbon Reforms in the second part of the 18th century, before France occupied Spain. The capture of Ferdinand in France, hostility toward the Cádiz Cortes, and the experience of autonomy gained after 1808 accelerated the cause of independence. The more peripheral areas of Latin America made the transition prior to the conservative centers of colonial rule, such as Peru and Mexico. The latter regions were finally swayed to support independence after liberals in Spain retook control of the government.

In Brazil, the move toward independence came after the 1820 Liberal Revolution in Portugal. The Portuguese Cortes summoned King João VI who, together with the Portuguese royal court, had been living in Rio de Janeiro since 1808. Before departing, the king named his son, Dom Pedro, as regent in charge of governing Brazil in his place. The Portuguese Cortes then revoked the status of Brazil, which, in 1815, had been elevated to a kingdom equal to Portugal. This move generated strong opposition throughout Brazil. Afterward, the Portuguese Cortes demanded the return of Dom Pedro, but he refused to comply. In the midst of the impasse, Dom

Pedro supported the election of a Brazilian constituent assembly and, soon after, openly called for independence. The separation from Portugal was formalized in September of 1822, and by November of the following year, the last Portuguese troops in Brazil surrendered.

Turmoil after Independence

The wars for independence caused significant hardships in Latin America. Between 1810 and 1829, war and civil conflict led to approximately 780,000 deaths.[35] Political power fragmented, and weak states without clearly delineated borders emerged. After a decrease in the 1830s, the number of deaths increased markedly. The region faced recurring civil conflict, economic instability, and intense disagreements over how to organize the new countries. Wars between bordering countries also added to the political instability of the region. It was only after 1870 that the intensity of these conflicts declined. Table 1.3 presents data on the number of deaths in war and civil conflict between 1810 and 1879.

Disputes emerged over the type of government that should be established. Some advocated for a monarchical structure; early on, it was promoted in Argentina and Chile, but soon dismissed. In Mexico, after failing to convince Ferdinand and his brothers to assume the throne, Iturbide was crowned Emperor Agustin I in July 1822. Less than a year later, he was forced to abdicate, and Mexico became a republic. After a few decades, Mexican conservatives again attempted to establish a monarchy, conspiring with Napoleon III to enthrone a foreign noble, Archduke Maximilian of Austria, as emperor of Mexico. Backed by the French army, he was crowned Emperor Maximilian I in June 1864. His supporters would eventually be

TABLE 1.3 ● Deaths in War and Civil Conflict, 1810–1879		
Decade	Number of Deaths	Deaths per 1,000 People
1810–1819	474,360	32.0
1820–1829	307,439	18.3
1830–1839	8,565	0.4
1840–1849	147,680	6.8
1850–1859	220,688	9.0
1860–1869	357,141	12.8
1870–1879	18,500	0.6

Source: Robert H. Bates, John H. Coatsworth, and Jeffrey G. Williamson. 2007. "Lost Decades: Post Independence Performance in Latin American and Africa." *Journal of Economic History*, 67(4): 917–943.

militarily defeated in 1867. Maximilian I was captured and executed three years after assuming power. The monarchy proved more stable in Brazil. Emperor Pedro I reigned from 1822 to 1831, when he was replaced by his son, Pedro II, who reigned from 1831 until 1889. The latter's rule was ended by a military coup that abolished the monarchical system of government.

Most countries sought to establish republican governments, with separation of powers and some embracement of individual liberties. Inspiration came from the Spanish constitution of 1812, the constitution of the United States and the British system, as well as the strong Napoleonic state. Early constitutions reflected these various influences. The first constitutions were more likely to establish powerful presidents than constrained executives, but most were short-lived and, most importantly, not embraced as legitimate by the people they were supposed to restrain. Those in power did not respect the rights of outgroups and used the resources of the state to perpetuate themselves in government. Those out of power did not believe the in-groups would agree to give up power as constitutionally prescribed.

Conflicts between advocates of a federal structure and those seeking a centralized form of government were common. There were major differences between the two political groups formed after independence: liberals and conservatives. Those coalescing around the conservative pole tended to support a strong central government and a powerful executive. They also sought to preserve a central role for the Catholic Church and a stratified social system. The emerging liberals tended to support a more decentralized federal structure and sought to curtail the influence of the Catholic Church and eliminate its privileges. Liberals, unlike conservatives, advocated for free trade.

Violent disputes between liberals and conservatives became commonplace. In New Granada, which became Gran Colombia after independence, advocates of a strong central government fought those seeking decentralized federal arrangements. Gran Colombia was originally composed of Venezuela, Ecuador, Colombia, and Panama, but internal struggle led to its formal break-up in 1831. Colombia continued to face recurrent civil war throughout the 19th century. A particularly bloody conflict between liberals and conservatives was the Thousand Days War (1899–1902), after which Panama seceded from Colombia.

Central America was also engulfed in severe conflict between liberals and conservatives. The United Provinces of Central America was formed in 1823, after about one and a half years as part of the empire of Mexico. The new political entity included Guatemala, Nicaragua, Honduras, El Salvador, and Costa Rica, but the union faced internal conflicts from the start. Liberals controlled the federation's government and passed a series of anticlerical and trade policies, which were vehemently opposed by conservatives and the clergy. A civil war began in 1838, when former military officer Rafael Carrera, supported by the Catholic Church, rose up and captured Guatemala City. The war would last until 1840, when the federation dissolved.

Similar conflicts erupted in other countries as well. In post-independent Chile, liberals and conservatives quarreled over whether a unitary or federal arrangement should organize the nation. The promulgation of a liberal constitution in 1828, the anti-clerical tendency of the liberal government, and a dispute over the appointment of a vice president prompted a conservative uprising. The ensuing civil war of 1829–1830 would end with the establishment of a centralized conservative government, which was able to maintain relative stability for a much longer period than most others in the region. In Venezuela, a major civil war between liberals and conservatives took place between 1859 and 1863, following conflicts over the federal character of the constitution and the forced exile of several politicians associated with the federal cause. In Bolivia, which had established a centralized unitary government after independence, uprisings in favor of federal arrangements ensued in Santa Cruz on several occasions. Finally, a civil war took place in 1898–1899, ending with the triumph of the federal forces.

Conflict between the center and the periphery of the country was recurrent in post-independence Argentina. A series of civil wars were fought between defenders of a strong central government with Buenos Aires at its head and those seeking confederal arrangements with extensive provincial autonomy. Unlike what was common in most of the other Latin American countries, the unitary faction tended to embrace liberal values in matters of the economy and the role of the Catholic Church, while the federalists were more conservative. A short-lived unitary constitution was passed in 1826, but the country was soon again subsumed in a civil war. A federal constitution was finally enacted in 1853, when Buenos Aires had temporarily split from the Argentine confederacy. In 1861, following the defeat of a federalist force, Buenos Aires joined the rest of the country as part of the Argentine Republic. Subsequent conflict over the status of the city continued until 1880, but Argentina maintained its federal structure and embraced several of the liberal policies advocated by the unitary faction.

International conflicts were also common throughout the 19th century. The Mexican–American War of 1846–1848 was one of the first major international conflicts following independence. Tension between both countries had been exacerbated by the annexation of Texas by the United States in 1845 as well as the unresolved dispute over Texas's western border. President James Polk decided to send a special envoy to Mexico to resolve the dispute and to purchase additional land, but this strategy failed. Subsequently, a scuffle between Mexican and American troops at the disputed border provided Polk with the excuse to declare war on Mexico. The conflict ended with Mexico's occupation and defeat in 1848. As a result of the war, Mexico lost a vast territory in the north of the country, including California and New Mexico.

One of the first major international conflicts in South America was the War of the Triple Alliance, which involved Paraguay against Argentina,

Brazil, and Uruguay. It began in 1864 after Paraguayan President Francisco Solano Lopez attacked Brazilian troops because of his objection to Brazil's involvement in the civil war in Uruguay. Next, he declared war on Argentina for refusing to allow Paraguayan troops to cross its territory. Paraguay, which suffered tremendous losses, was finally defeated in 1870. Brazil and Argentina then proceeded to annex significant portions of Paraguayan territory.

Another major conflict was the War of the Pacific, which confronted Chile with Bolivia and Peru. It originated with a dispute over policies affecting Bolivia's mineral-rich Atacama Desert, where Chilean companies and settlers had become very influential. In 1878, Bolivia imposed a new tax on nitrates exported by Chilean firms in violation of a prior international treaty, which led to the companies' refusal to pay and the government confiscating their holdings. After protests from the Chilean government, Bolivia declared war on Chile in 1879. Peru, which had signed an alliance treaty with Bolivia, was drawn into the war. Chile ultimately defeated both countries, signing a truce with Peru in 1883 and one with Bolivia in 1884. The war led to the annexation of a sizeable territory by Chile, including a slice of southern Peru and the western part of Bolivia, which thereafter was left landlocked.

War and political instability had negative economic consequences for Latin America. Military expenses grew as well as law enforcement costs. Recurrent conflicts damaged property and productive assets, and there were numerous challenges to the normal development of commerce.[36] Fiscal deficits became common after independence, which further weakened the new governments.

Other economic costs were associated with the breakup of the colonial union into several smaller states, such as the burdens of establishing new administrations, fiscal and monetary institutions, and financial markets. New barriers to intra-regional trade were put in place, and transaction costs increased. Moreover, political turmoil made it more difficult for governments to stabilize their economies and build effective institutions. In Mexico and Peru, mining declined; there was a deterioration in the physical capital of the mines, a rise in the price of mercury, and a decrease in silver production. This exacerbated budget deficits.

Independence also brought some economic benefits, particularly free trade and access to capital. Soon after independence, trade imbalances were common, but over time, this unfavorable context began to change. Latin American exports grew modestly during the first half of the 19th century and strongly during the second half. Most exports came from the primary sector of the economy—agriculture, livestock, and mining.

The opening of the economies to trade benefited coastal regions more than others. In Chile, new silver deposits were found, and international demand for copper expanded rapidly. In Argentina and Uruguay, exports of livestock products significantly increased. In Cuba, still under the control of Spain, sugar exports thrived. Exports also grew in Costa Rica—first gold and then coffee. These five countries had the highest per capita exports in 1850 and 1870.[37]

Table 1.4 presents data on income per capita for ten countries for the 19th century.[38] This sample is limited because exact figures are not available for all countries. Nonetheless, it shows salient differences across countries and over time. Income per capita surged during the last decades of the century in several countries, such as Argentina, Chile, and Cuba. These countries benefited greatly from export-led growth. Mexico underperformed for most of the 19th century, but its economy grew strongly by the end of it. In contrast, per capita income in Peru shrunk considerably at the end of the century. Brazil's dismal economic performance is made evident by these figures: The country's per capita income in 1900 was almost identical to the one it had 100 years earlier.

The richest countries at the start and the end of the 19th century were Argentina and Uruguay. Chile, which experienced an impressive period of economic growth in the second part of the century, ended up as the third richest country in Latin America, with a per capita income slightly higher than that of Cuba. Peru and Mexico, the centers of colonial rule in Spanish America, lagged behind considerably.

TABLE 1.4 ● Gross Domestic Product per Capita, 1800–1900								
Country	1800	1820	1850	1860	1870	1880	1890	1900
Argentina	1,594	1,710	2,144	2,321	2,514	2,748	4,139	4,925
Brazil	600	600	600	687	751	734	751	606
Chile			616	1,011	1,187	1,397	1,808	2,174	2,533
Colombia	819	739	681	794	937	985	995	946
Cuba[1]	844		1,294			1,846	2,531	2,448
Ecuador					624	624	734	903
Mexico	985	760	795	695	789		1,184	1,374
Peru					731	933	479	471	604
Uruguay	1,643	1,773	2,205	2,681	3,286	3,070	3,243	3,027
Venezuela	514	464	903	949	848	1,032	1,281	885

[1.]Data for Cuba are for 1792, 1850, 1881, 1892, and 1902.

Source: Maddison Project Database, version 2018.

To sum up, the post-independence era was characterized by high levels of political instability. Civil wars broke out in most countries, and many of them were engulfed in international wars. The lack of agreement over the type of government to be established in the new nations fueled recurrent conflict. In many nations, such as Peru, Venezuela, and Guatemala, military rulers established dictatorial regimes. Others, such as Argentina and Uruguay, experienced prolonged periods of internal disunity. These conflicts generated a high number of casualties and were economically costly. The burdens of independence slowed economic growth during the first decades after independence, but as the intensity of conflict declined, the economy picked up steam and export-led growth became the norm. By the 1870s, political order began to take hold and, in many countries, elites established agreed-upon political institutions to resolve disputes. This signaled the transition between turmoil and political order.

The Sources of Post-Independence Instability

The chaos that followed independence was costly. Most of the region lacked sufficiently strong institutions to prevent recurrent aggression by one group against others. It took decades until governments could exercise effective and stable authority. Why was Latin America unable to find stability after independence?

One important reason was the lack of self-governing institutions during the colonial period. Under Spanish rule, political power was vested in a centralized absolute monarchy that prevented violent conflicts among groups. When independence came about and ended the authoritarian colonial order, the inhabitants of the new nations could not resort to some preexisting political institutions. They had no experience with autonomous government, aside from the limited role played by cabildos, nor were they familiar with the workings of republican institutions. This exacerbated the difficulties of state building and contributed to political disorder. According to economist and Nobel Prize winner Douglass C. North and his coauthors, "In the absence of any institutions from the colonial era that would either dampen that uncertainty about the intentions of competing groups or constrain the attempts of groups that might aggress against others, open warfare became the norm."[39]

Many of the leaders that emerged after independence, often from the military, sought to reconstruct political order along the lines of the personalist Spanish tradition. However, they lacked the legitimacy and strength of the colonial power. Important social groups did not coalesce around these emerging leaders, who could not muster enough power to impose political order. Liberalism kept winning new followers, who challenged the hierarchical societal structure and economic order sought by traditional conservatives.

In addition, economic problems eroded the authority of those governments that emerged after independence. Fiscal problems made it difficult to coopt elites and to sustain the loyalty of militias, which further complicated government stability. Budgetary problems also made it difficult to pay members of the public administration. Under such conditions, governments were hard-pressed to defend themselves from insurgent groups.

The lack of consensus among elites was not only the result of the lack of a common belief system but also of the apparent absence of shared economic interests. For instance, historian Frank Safford notes that in many countries, the regions most likely to initiate rebellions against the central government were those located where it was difficult or impossible to play a part in the export trade.[40] He argued that the lack of economic opportunities encouraged elites to engage in politico-military enterprises.

During the chaotic first decades following independence, only Chile and Brazil managed to maintain some degree of political stability. In Chile, early prosperity strengthened the state. During the conservative hegemony that emerged after 1830, governments had the resources and determination to suppress dissent. In Brazil, most of the elite considered the monarchy a useful institution to foster national unity and maintain social stability.[41] Political stability was also facilitated by growth in the production and export of coffee.

The Emergence of Political Order and Economic Growth

The end of violence and political turmoil came to Latin America around the 1870s. Internal war and recurrent rebellions gave way to the centralization of government power, which facilitated the resolution of intra-elite disputes through nonviolent mechanisms.[42] Secular modernizing governments began to emerge across the region. Some of the institutional reforms implemented during the second part of the 19th century included the establishment of new civil and commercial codes and new financial institutions, such as public and private banks and insurance firms. Governments also lessened the political and economic role of the Catholic Church.

Peace and the consolidation of political power strengthened the security of property. Countries began to improve their tax revenues and consolidated their burdensome public debts. Several countries saw a significant improvement in infrastructure, such as the modernization of ports and the development of railways. Given the high costs of transportation inside the region, the expansion of railway infrastructure was heralded as a major advancement. Some of these projects were partly financed with foreign capital. British capital spending in the region grew markedly after 1865.

In the second part of the 19th century, there was an emerging agreement across Latin American countries that the best path to development rested on further integration with world markets. Increasing exports was seen to be the engine of economic growth. The development of railways facilitated access to natural resources, and more modern ports and reductions in

FIGURE 1.1 ● Annual Growth of Exports per Capita, 1850–1912

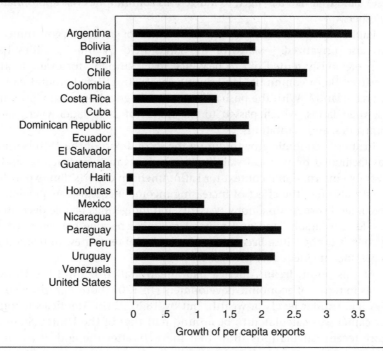

Growth of per capita exports

Source: Victor Bulmer-Thomas. 2014. *The Economic History of Latin America since Independence.* New York: Cambridge University Press.

international transport costs benefited international trade. Industrialization in Western Europe and the United States increased demands for primary products. Some of the major exports from Latin America were maize, wheat, wool, and meat from temperate climates; coffee, sugar, cacao, and bananas from tropical climates; and silver, tin, copper, and nitrates from mineral-producing regions.

The growth of exports strengthened the links between Latin American countries and the world economy. Their main trading partners were the United States, United Kingdom, Germany, and France.[43] The success of the export-growth model was most evident in the Southern Cone: Argentina, Chile, and Uruguay. Figure 1.1 presents data on the annual growth of per capita exports for nineteen Latin American countries and the United States.

Across Latin America, governments promoted agrarian development. As commercial agriculture progressed, significant reforms in land tenure were put in place. In countries where communal land systems had remained, those systems were eliminated in favor of individual private property. This led to the abolishment of indigenous communal property. While indigenous people had the option of registering their land as private property, comparatively few were able to undertake the process of doing so. In many cases, land that had belonged to indigenous communities was appropriated by others.

Public land controlled by municipalities or national governments was also privatized.[44] Many of the lands held by municipalities had been previously rented out to peasants. In El Salvador, for example, the privatization of communal land during the 1880s affected around half of all arable land.[45] With the push of commercial agriculture, many peasants lost their lands, which passed to the hands of large landowners, land companies, and plantations.

In short, economic growth during the second part of the 19th century was facilitated by political stability, investments in infrastructure, and a favorable international context for Latin American exports. But export-led growth also had the effect of increasing income inequality. As previously noted, land ownership among peasants and indigenous people decreased. In addition, arable land and mineral resources became concentrated in the hands of the elites. Because land and mineral rents grew in relation to wages, income inequality increased.[46]

At this point, Latin America had already fallen behind the United States in terms of economic development. In 1700, both European colonies had similar levels of wealth, but by 1820, Latin America's income per capita was calculated to be around half that of the United States.[47] More recent calculations show that in 1870, after the end of colonial rule and 50 years of political turmoil, the per capita income of Latin American countries represented 25 percent of the per capita income of the United States.[48] The substantial gap in development between both regions was already there. During the following decades, however, this gap remained relatively unchanged: The ratio of per capita income went from 25 percent in 1870 to 23 percent in 1930. After the arrival of political order in 1870, Latin America's annual rate of growth of per capita income was not too different from that experienced by the United States.

The modernizing governments that brought order to the region came to power as a result of a series of military and political victories by liberal-minded forces. These governments put in place reforms that fortified the power of the central government, limited the power of the Catholic Church, secured the property of elites, and strengthened law and order. They differed, however, in their level of political competition and the constraints they placed on executives.

In Mexico, many liberal reforms, such as the prohibition of corporate (i.e., church and civil institutions) ownership of real estate and the abolition of special courts for clergy and the military, were passed in the 1850s, before the emergence of political order. It was after Porfirio Díaz seized the presidency in 1876 that Mexico achieved a sustained period of political stability. During the last decades of the 19th century, Mexico saw a significant modernization of infrastructure, the establishment of financial institutions, a significant increase in mining exports, and economic growth. The country also experienced an erosion of republican principles and the rise of authoritarianism. After one term in office, Díaz was succeeded in the presidency by Manuel González, his handpicked candidate. Díaz then returned to power in 1884, when he established a personalist dictatorship that would last until 1911.

In Central America, liberal reforms and some modicum of political stability came in the 1870s. The wave of modernizing liberal presidents included Tomás Guardia (1870–1882) in Costa Rica, Justo Rufino Barrios (1873–1885) in Guatemala, Rafael Zaldívar (1876–1883) in El Salvador, and Marco Aurelio Soto (1876–1883) in Honduras.[49] Liberalism arrived later in Nicaragua with the presidency of José Santos Zelaya (1893–1909). These modernizing presidents promoted agricultural development, particularly the expansion of coffee and banana production for export. The privatization of communal lands was most extensive in El Salvador and Nicaragua. In these countries and Guatemala, government policies favored the creation of large commercial estates and the implementation of coercive labor regulations in rural areas.[50] Unlike its neighboring countries, Costa Rica developed an oligarchic republic by the late 19th century, with elites competing in electoral contests, alternation of the presidency, and limits on executive power.

South American countries also found order under various types of liberal regimes. For instance, in Argentina, an oligarchic republic emerged in the 1860s and became stabilized by 1880. Liberal factions competed against each other in elite-dominated elections, and presidents governed under strict term limits that prevented them from running for reelection. During this period of time, Argentina's economy grew and the country became one of the richest in the world. In addition, literacy rates increased markedly, new European immigrants arrived, and a comparatively large middle class began to play a more prominent social role.

Peru initiated an era of modernization and economic growth under relative political stability after José Nicolás de Piérola, a former president, seized power in 1895. This change signaled a transfer of influence from military leaders to the oligarchy. Presidential turnover after the end of the stipulated term would become the norm. Under this oligarchic republic, Peru embarked on a period of reconstruction following the defeat in the War of the Pacific, strengthening the links of the country with international markets, promoting commercial agriculture, and delivering economic growth.

Political order and an oligarchic republic had emerged in Chile before any other country in Latin America. The period known as the "Liberal Republic" began in 1861 and brought about reforms that limited the power of the executive, prohibited the immediate reelection of the president, strengthened the role of congress, and reduced the influence of the Catholic

Church. A brief and violent conflict between the president and congress in 1891 was resolved in favor of the latter and gave way to a new era of congressional predominance known as the "Parliamentary Republic."

Political order and liberal reforms arrived in Venezuela after Antonio Guzmán Blanco, a liberal politician and former vice president, seized the government in 1870. During his personalist dictatorship, the government promoted international trade, expanded railway and road construction, and improved the country's ports. He also lessened the influence of the Catholic Church and established religious freedom. Guzmán Blanco would govern directly or indirectly until 1887, when he left for Europe after hand-picking his successor.

Political order and economic growth became the norm in most countries after 1870. However, Latin America continued to be characterized by regimes that limited the political participation of most of its citizens. Even in those republics in which elections took place regularly, the franchise tended to be limited to a small minority of men. Formal restrictions such as wealth and literacy requirements were in place in many countries, and the lack of secret ballot was the norm. These governments would lead the region into the dawn of the 20th century.

Conclusions

This chapter focused on the colonial period and its aftermath. It described the institutional structure put in place by the colonial powers, including its hierarchical and centralized organization as well as its administrative and judicial functions. It highlighted the limited independence of local town councils and the dominant role given to Spanish bureaucrats. The close association between civil and religious authorities and the control of the monarchy over the clergy were also explained.

Policies established during this period influenced the region's development. As noted in the chapter, the practice of mercantilism and a strict trade monopoly were characteristic of this era. The obsession of the colonial powers with the extraction of mineral resources, mainly gold and silver, impacted the colonial economy and its administrative development. Agriculture eventually grew in importance, particularly the plantation economy geared toward the export market. Plantation agriculture became central to the economies of Brazil, the Caribbean, and other coastal regions of tropical Latin America. The economic strategies of the colonial powers influenced labor and immigration policies. The chapter reviewed the coercive labor mechanisms used to draft indigenous labor for mining and agriculture as well as highlighted how labor shortages spurred a massive slave trade.

Colonial societies evolved in ways that would have a profound impact on the region. Indigenous populations were devastated, and millions of Africans were brought forcefully to the region as slaves. The chapter described the composition of the population over time and the characteristics of the caste system put in place by the colonizers. The inequalities in terms of political power that divided Spanish-born peninsulares from the local creoles were also reviewed.

The immediate events leading to independence had their origin in Europe, but long-standing political and economic grievances in the colonies also played an important part. Some of these were the result of the Bourbon reforms, which Spain undertook to modernize its colonial policies. Political instability in Europe and local reaction to the impact of liberalism in Spain and Portugal also influenced the movement toward independence. The chapter examined these factors and described the emergence of autonomous governments in Latin America.

Independence was followed by widespread turmoil. Civil wars, political violence, and international conflict characterized the region in the decades after independence. The chapter described these events, including the confrontation between liberals and conservatives, and examined the possible sources of such conflict and instability. It then moved on to address the arrival of political order and economic growth in the latter part of the 19th century. It highlighted the impact of export-led growth and noted the income gap that had already developed between Latin America and the United States. The chapter concluded by reviewing the various types of governments that emerged in Latin America by the late 19th century and how they differed with regards to political competition and the constraints placed on executives.

Knowledge of the political, economic, and social institutions that characterized the colonial period; the process leading to independence; the chaotic aftermath; and the emergence of political order and growth at the end of the 19th century not only illuminates a crucial aspect of the region's history but also helps us understand the political and institutional developments of the subsequent eras. The next chapter continues our examination of Latin American politics with a look at the emergence and stability of different regime types throughout the 20th century.

Key Terms

Bourbon Reforms 11

Cabildos 6

Conservatives 20

Council of the Indies 4

Export-led growth 3

Junta 17

Liberals 20

Mercantilism 8

Peninsular War 16

Royal patronage
   (patronato real) 7

Viceroy 5

Bibliographic Recommendations

Leslie Bethell (ed.). 1984/1985. *The Cambridge History of Latin America*, Volumes I–III. London: Cambridge University Press.

Victor Bulmer-Thomas. 2014. *The Economic History of Latin America since Independence*. New York: Cambridge University Press.

Victor Bulmer-Thomas, John H. Coatsworth, and Roberto Cortés Conde (eds.). 2006. *The Cambridge Economic History of Latin America*, Volume I. New York: Cambridge University Press.

John H. Elliott. 2006. *Empires of the Atlantic World: Britain and Spain in America 1492–1830*. New Haven: Yale University Press.

Stanley Engerman and Kenneth L. Sokoloff. 2012. *Economic Development in the Americas since 1500: Endowments and Institutions*. New York: Cambridge University Press.

Francis Fukuyama (ed.). 2008. *Falling Behind: Explaining the Development Gap between Latin America and the United States*. New York: Oxford University Press.

2

Political Regimes and Democratic Stability

Currently, most Latin American countries are considered to be democratic. The situation was strikingly different over most of the 20th century, when authoritarian governments prevailed. During the mid-1970s, for example, most Latin Americans lived under dictatorial regimes that severely curtailed civil rights and freedom of the press. In some cases, these dictatorships embarked on violent campaigns to eliminate opponents. While dictatorial regimes sometimes allowed elections to take place, the results were often questionable. Most of the democratic regimes that emerged before the 1970s were relatively short-lived and politically weak. It was only after the wave of regime change that began at the end of the 1970s that **democracy** became the norm across the region.

There are good reasons to consider democracy as the best form of government. According to the philosopher Karl Popper, democracy is the best type of political system because it provides a nonviolent, institutionalized path to get rid of bad rulers.[1] Democracies are more likely to produce accountable government than non-democracies and to make governments more responsive to a wider range of citizens.[2] The extent to which democracies work to make governments responsive and accountable varies across countries and often has to do with their institutional arrangements, as will be discussed further in this book.

In a democracy, citizens choose governments in free elections. If one assumes that an adult is the best judge of his or her own interests, then a free vote makes equal consideration of everyone's interests more likely. Democracy offers an arena favorable to peaceful compromise. According to political theorist Robert A. Dahl, democracy provides a more extensive domain of personal freedom than any other political regime, increases the likelihood that people live under laws of their own choosing, and provides an orderly and peaceful process that a majority of citizens can utilize to induce the government to do what they most want it to do.[3]

Scholars have long debated the proper way to define different political regimes. The first part of this chapter reviews various definitions of democracy and describes patterns of democracy and **authoritarianism** across Latin American countries. It reveals which countries have been democratic underachievers and which have had a more consistent record of competitive elections, with long-term patterns illustrating the instability of democracy over most of the 20th century. The second part of the chapter examines the emergence and fall of democracy. It discusses the impact of economic, institutional, cultural, and international factors as well as the role of the military.

What Is Democracy?

The word *democracy* originated in ancient Greece, combining two concepts: *demos*, which meant the citizens of a city-state, and *kratos*, which meant rule. While various cities in ancient Greece had governments characterized by "rule by the people," Athens was the first city to have a long-lasting regime called *democracy*. For Aristotle, the basis of a democratic regime was liberty. Greek philosophers advanced a classification of political regimes that remained influential until the 19th century. These early approaches tended to divide political regimes into three categories: monarchies, oligarchies, and democracies. According to the definition advanced by the Greek historian Herodotus, *monarchies* concentrate power in a single individual; *oligarchies* concentrate power among a few members of the elite; and *democracies* are based on equality with accountable office holders selected by lot.

Modern analyses of political regimes abandoned these early classifications and advanced alternative definitions of democratic and non-democratic regime types. For most scholars, democracy did not originate until the 19th century and was not embraced by most countries until the late 20th century. In Latin America, the only countries that are consistently identified as having had democratic governments before 1945 are Argentina, Chile, Costa Rica, and Uruguay.

Contemporary definitions of democracy can be placed along a continuum from minimalist to maximalist, depending on the number of features considered to be necessary to qualify as a democratic regime. Minimalist approaches focus on competitive elections, and their related indicators tend to produce rather reliable cross-national indices. Middle-range definitions expand on the procedures considered to be democratic to include some core political freedoms and limited military interference. Maximalist definitions of democracies incorporate a variety of characteristics that go beyond a handful of procedures to include various governance indicators and aspects of **political culture**.

Minimalist Definitions

Procedural definitions underline processes and rules to define democracy. According to the minimalist perspective, a democracy is a system in which rulers are selected in competitive elections. The classic definition comes from Joseph Schumpeter, who stated that a democracy is "that institutional arrangement for arriving at political decisions in which individuals acquire the power to decide by means of a competitive struggle for the people's vote."[4] In his view, democracy was a method for arriving at political decisions based on free competition for a free vote.

Several scholars have adopted Schumpeter's minimalist definition of democracy. The best-known contemporary advocate of this definition is the political scientist, Adam Przeworski. He argued that democracy, as defined by the minimalist perspective, is highly consequential: **Contested elections** mean that a government may change, and this possibility opens the door to the peaceful regulation of conflicts.[5] The long-term benefits of alternation in office overcome both the short-term incentives of rebellion for the electoral losers and the short-term benefits of refusing to give up power for the electoral winners. The simple fact that political contenders expect to take turns helps to avoid bloodshed and allows for conflicts to be processed according to rules.

Supporters of the minimalist conceptualization of democracy disagree with the idea of attaching normatively desirable political, social, or economic characteristics to the definitional features of democracy. By defining democracy in minimalist terms, they provide a simple and analytically clear definition that is well-suited to empirical analyses. In short, it avoids conceptualizing democracy based on outcomes we would like to see democratic governments deliver. This is particularly helpful because it facilitates a nonarbitrary way of classifying countries and allows us to examine whether democracies are, in fact, more likely to deliver desirable political, social, and economic outcomes.

Consider the operationalization of democracy in the following two data sets built by scholars who embrace the minimalist perspective. The first one has three specific requirements for a country to be classified as democratic: an elected chief executive and legislature, more than one party competing in the elections, and an alternation in power under the same rules as the ones that brought the executive to office.[6] Countries not meeting these three requirements are classified as authoritarian. The second one defines a country as democratic if it has competitive elections and has enfranchised a majority of the male population.[7] This approach retains the dichotomous classification, which means countries are either democratic or authoritarian, but also adds a minimum level of participation as a defining feature.

Figure 2.1 shows the number of democratic years for the period 1901–1950 from the second data set, which was built by Carles Boix, Michael Miller, and Sebastian Rosato. It shows that authoritarianism prevailed during the first half of the 20th century, with half of the countries not having

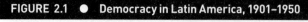

FIGURE 2.1 ● Democracy in Latin America, 1901–1950

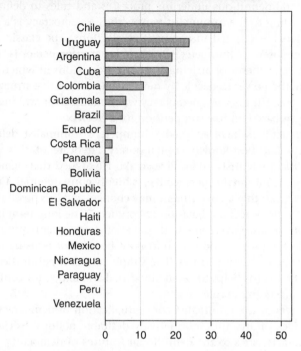

Source: Carles Boix, Michael Miller, and Sebastian Rosato. 2013. "A Complete Data Set of Political Regimes, 1800-2007." *Comparative Political Studies*, 46(12):1523–1554.

a single year of democratic rule before 1951. Among those that experienced some degree of democracy, only Chile had more years of democracy than authoritarianism. Uruguay is a close second in terms of years of democracy, followed by Argentina, Cuba, and Colombia, respectively.

Figure 2.2 shows the number of democratic years for the period 1951–2000, according to the two mentioned sources that follow the minimalist perspective. The first bar is based on the data set constructed by Boix and his colleagues. The second bar is based on the data set constructed by José Antonio Cheibub, Jennifer Gandhi, and James Raymond Vreeland, who adopt the narrower minimalist operationalization of democracy that does not consider enfranchisement levels.

Democracy was much more common during the second half of the 20th century than during the first half, with twelve of the twenty countries having more years of democracy than authoritarianism. Both sources agree in terms of the best democratic performers in the second half of the century. Costa Rica ranks on top and is the only country that was consistently democratic throughout this period. Colombia and Venezuela follow it. At the bottom of the list are Haiti, Paraguay, Mexico, and Cuba.

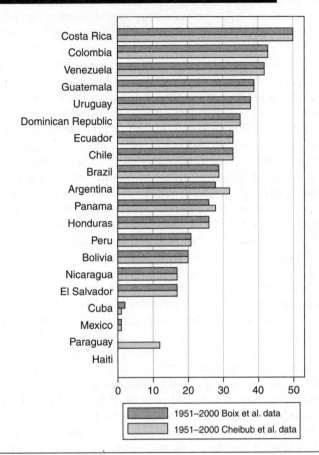

FIGURE 2.2 ● Democracy in Latin America, 1951–2000

Source: Carles Boix, Michael Miller, and Sebastian Rosato. 2013. "A Complete Data Set of Political Regimes, 1800-2007." *Comparative Political Studies*, 46(12):1523-1554. José Antonio Cheibub, Jennifer Gandhi, and James Raymond Vreeland. 2010. "Democracy and Dictatorship Revisited." *Public Choice*, 143(1): 67-101.

When looking at the entire 20th century, four countries had more years of democracy than years of authoritarianism: Chile, Uruguay, Colombia, and Costa Rica. The two sources discussed are very consistent in their classification of democracy in Latin American countries. In sixteen of the twenty countries, they provide the same classification, and in two cases (Cuba and Panama), the difference is minimal. Differences are more significant in the cases of Paraguay and Argentina, which will be discussed later in greater detail.

More Complex Procedural Definitions

Not everyone agrees with the minimalist conceptualization of democracy; a common critique is that such definitions do not consider civil liberties. While holding free and fair elections and alternation in power are essential components of democracy, many have argued that some basic freedoms are essential as well. For example, political scientist Larry Diamond argues that without civil liberty, electoral competition and political participation cannot be truly meaningful.[8] Among these civil liberties, freedom of speech and freedom of the press are considered to be paramount. From this perspective, governments elected in competitive elections that impinge on these civil liberties cannot be considered to be fully democratic.

Another criticism is that minimalist definitions do not consider whether elected individuals actually govern. This challenge highlights situations, present in several instances in Latin American countries, where de facto power was retained by the military despite the holding of elections. Military influence may be manifested by holding veto power over policy in areas not related to the armed forces or by dominating outright major policy areas. Examples of this state of affairs are Guatemala between the presidential election of 1985 and the signing of the 1992 peace accords, which ended that country's civil war; and El Salvador between the presidential election of 1984 and the signing of the 1996 peace accord, which brought that country's civil war to a close.

With these criticisms in mind, some scholars have advanced alternative conceptualizations of democracy, retaining the focus on procedural characteristics but extending necessary conditions beyond those of the minimalist perspective. One influential classification that follows this alternative view was offered by political scientists Scott Mainwaring and Aníbal Pérez-Liñán.[9] For a country to be democratic, they argued, four characteristics must be present: free and fair competitive elections, inclusive adult citizenship, protection of civil and political rights, and a military that is under civilian control. They observed that dichotomous classifications are insufficiently sensitive to regime variations and instead proposed a trichotomous classification that builds on all four dimensions of their definition of democracy. If a country suffers a partial (but not flagrant) violation of any of the four principles, it is classified as semi-democratic. When one or more flagrant violations of these principles take place, a country is considered authoritarian. Figure 2.3 shows the total number of countries in each category from 1900 to 2011.

This figure illustrates the incidence of political regimes over the long term. The first country to be classified as democratic under this scheme is Argentina in 1916, the second is Uruguay in 1919, the third is Costa Rica in 1928, and the fourth is Chile in 1932. The proportion of democratic countries begins to increase slowly during the 1940s and has a first peak in the late 1950s and early 1960s. Afterward, it decreases until reaching a low point in the mid-1970s. From the late 1970s onward, the number of democracies increases markedly. A turning point comes about in 1990, when democracy becomes the most common regime type in the region.

When evaluating the entire 20th century under this classification, three countries had more years of democracy than years of authoritarianism and

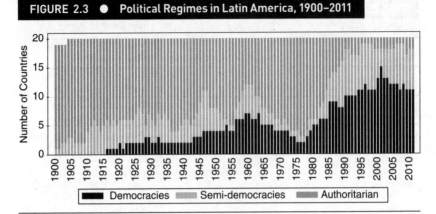

FIGURE 2.3 ● Political Regimes in Latin America, 1900–2011

Source: Scott Mainwaring and Aníbal Pérez-Liñán. 2013. *Democracies and Dictatorships in Latin America: Emergence, Survival, and Fall.* New York: Cambridge University Press.

semi-democracy combined: Costa Rica, Uruguay, and Chile. These three countries are also among the top democratic performers, according to the minimalist classifications discussed in the prior section. Among the worst democratic performers are Haiti, Cuba, and Paraguay, which were also poorly ranked under the minimalist classification.

One relevant difference between this ranking and the ones discussed before is the classification of Colombia. Mainwaring and Pérez-Liñán classified Colombia as a semi-democracy for most of the 20th century but never as a full democracy. However, under the minimalist classifications discussed in the prior section, it is one of the countries with the best democratic record. This discrepancy will be addressed further in this chapter.

Another well-known source that provides a trichotomous classification of democracy is Freedom House. It utilizes information on political rights and civil liberties to construct a rating that determines whether a country is *free, partly free,* or *not free.* As does the prior source, it includes information on the electoral process, political pluralism and participation, and civil liberties but also considers information on corruption and government transparency. Table 2.1 shows the status of each Latin American country during the year 2018. The last column shows whether Freedom House considers the country an *electoral democracy,* which is a less restrictive category that considers whether countries have met certain minimum standards for political rights and civil liberties. This measure gives greater weight to the electoral process category, and as a result, partly free countries may or may not pass this threshold.[10]

According to Freedom House, the vast majority of Latin American countries are classified as electoral democracies, with only five failing to meet this standard in 2018: Cuba, Haiti, Honduras, Nicaragua, and Venezuela. Among this group, Cuba, Nicaragua, and Venezuela are also classified as not free. Freedom House characterized the 2018 presidential elections in Venezuela as

TABLE 2.1 ● Freedom Status and Democracy in Latin America, 2018

Country	Freedom Status	Electoral Democracy
Argentina	Free	Yes
Bolivia	Partly Free	Yes
Brazil	Free	Yes
Chile	Free	Yes
Colombia	Partly Free	Yes
Costa Rica	Free	Yes
Cuba	Not Free	No
Dominican Republic	Partly Free	Yes
Ecuador	Partly Free	Yes
El Salvador	Free	Yes
Guatemala	Partly Free	Yes
Haiti	Partly Free	No
Honduras	Partly Free	No
Mexico	Partly Free	Yes
Nicaragua	Not Free	No
Panama	Free	Yes
Paraguay	Partly Free	Yes
Peru	Free	Yes
Uruguay	Free	Yes
Venezuela	Not Free	No

Source: Freedom House. 2020. Freedom in the World 2019. https://freedomhouse.org

"profoundly flawed" and noted bans on prominent opposition candidates and voter intimidation.[11] That same year, the Nicaraguan government pursued a brutal crackdown on political opponents, which included the imprisonment of opposition figures and "violence by state forces and allied armed groups resulting in hundreds of deaths."[12] Freedom House labeled nine Latin American countries as partly free and eight as free. This highlights how, even if most countries meet the basic standards of an electoral democracy, several fall short in some aspects of civil liberties and political rights.

Maximalist Definitions

Not everyone agrees with the idea that democracy should be measured solely by a few essential procedural features. Some see the focus on voting and elections as too narrow. They propose instead a maximalist definition that goes beyond procedures to include practices and beliefs considered to be beneficial to a thriving democracy. From this perspective, democracy is seen as a principle to be aimed at rather than a method. As a result, this "thick" approach to conceptualizing democracy may more accurately reflect the ideals of democracy than do minimalist conceptualizations.

Maximalist definitions, however, are controversial among political scientists. On the one hand, it is difficult to agree about which of the many possible desirable features of an ideal democracy should be counted. On the other hand, assessing the actual scores of countries along many of these features can be highly subjective and difficult to replicate. By incorporating desirable characteristics and political outcomes into the definition, a maximalist definition precludes studying whether democracy (in a narrow sense) is actually more likely to produce such outcomes.

Maximalist definitions work well to differentiate among countries, as they favor more detailed classifications than two or three categories. One good example of this approach is the Democracy Index produced by the Economist Intelligence Unit (EIU). This index is based on a total of sixty indicators grouped into five categories: electoral process and pluralism, civil liberties, the functioning of government, political participation, and political culture. The resulting Democracy Index is a continuous measure that ranges from 0 to 10.

Several aspects of politics not included in the indices previously discussed are incorporated into the sixty indicators that make up this index. For example, the category "electoral process and pluralism" goes beyond questions regarding the free and fair contest for the executive and the legislature to include an assessment of whether laws provide for broadly equal campaigning opportunities, whether the process of financing political parties is transparent and generally accepted, and whether municipal elections are also free and fair. In the category "the functioning of government," the Democracy Index moves past evaluating whether the elected government is free of undue influence by the military to examine, for example, public confidence in government and political parties, levels of corruption, and the willingness and capability of the civil service sector to implement policies.

As in middle-range conceptualizations, the Democracy Index also includes categories for "political participation" and "civil liberties" but evaluates a variety of other features. For example, in the former category, it considers the proportion of women in parliament; adult literacy; authorities' efforts to promote political participation; the extent to which adults follow politics in the news; and whether ethnic, religious, and other minorities have a reasonable degree of autonomy and voice in the political process. In the latter category, it considers political restrictions on access to the Internet, freedom to form trade unions, the use of torture by the state, judicial independence, religious tolerance, and the protection of property and human rights.

Lastly, the Democracy Index is unique in including a "political culture" category within which it assesses such things as popular support for democracy, separation of Church and State, proportion of the population that would prefer military rule, whether there is a degree of societal consensus and cohesion sufficient to underpinning a stable functioning democracy, and the proportion of the population that desires a strong leader who bypasses parliament and elections.

The Democracy Index has been calculated by the EIU since 2006, which precludes its usage for evaluating long patterns of democracy. However, it presents a revealing picture of contemporary politics in the region. Figure 2.4 shows the score for each Latin American country in 2019: the higher the number, the closer to the democratic ideal.

Among the top performers, we find three countries that were among the best ranked under the most restrictive classifications: Uruguay, Costa Rica, and Chile. Remarkably, the best-placed country in Latin America, Uruguay, ranks among the top fifteen countries in the world. Uruguay,

FIGURE 2.4 ● EIU's Democracy Index, 2019

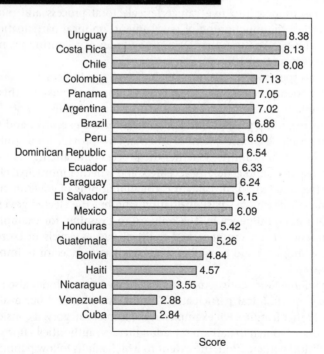

Score

Source: The Economist Intelligence Unit. 2020. *Democracy Index 2019: A Year of Democratic Setbacks and Popular Protest.* Available at http://www.eiu.com

Costa Rica, and Chile have scores greater than eight and are, according to the Democracy Index, *full democracies*, which means that they enjoy not only basic political freedoms and civil liberties but also a political culture conducive to the flourishing of democracy.[13]

Ten Latin American countries have a score greater than six and lower than eight which, according to the Democracy Index, means that they are democracies, even if they are flawed. Countries in this category are characterized as having free and fair elections and respecting basic civil liberties, although there are some weaknesses in the other essential features (e.g., governance, political culture, or political participation).

Four countries (Honduras, Guatemala, Bolivia, and Haiti) have scores between four and six, which, according to the Democracy Index, makes them *hybrid regimes*. It means that there are substantial irregularities regarding electoral competition and severe weaknesses in other fundamental aspects of its characterization of democracy. The worst-ranked countries in the Democracy Index are Nicaragua, Venezuela, and Cuba, which have scores below four and are labeled as *authoritarian*. As noted in the previous section, these three countries are also considered not free by Freedom House.

Just as the EIU's Democracy Index underscores that all democracies are not the same, several scholars have argued that there are substantial differences among authoritarian countries. The next section examines these claims.

Non-Democratic Regimes

Authoritarianism is an important research topic in political science. One of the main findings from this field of research is that authoritarian governments differ in significant ways, which affects how they govern as well as their survival in office. A well-known classification of authoritarian regimes was developed by political scientists Barbara Geddes, Joseph Wright, and Erica Frantz.[14] They considered whether control over policy, leadership selection, and the security apparatus are in the hands of a governing party, a royal family, the armed forces, or a small group centered around an individual dictator. While they classified a variety of authoritarian regimes all over the world from 1946 to 2010, the Latin American cases they examined can be grouped into five distinct types. Definitions for each of these appear in Table 2.2.

Military regimes were the most common type of authoritarian regime in Latin America during the 20th century. Such regimes are characterized by the prominent role of the armed forces in controlling policymaking, the selection of leaders, and the security forces. In these regimes, the formal leader is typically a military officer, but the military institution constrains the behavior of whoever happens to hold such a leadership position.

Examples of military governments abound. For instance, Brazil was governed by a military dictatorship between 1964 and 1985. This authoritarian

TABLE 2.2 ● Types of Authoritarian Regimes

Regime Type	Definition	Examples
Military	Control over policy, leadership selection, and the security apparatus is in the hands of the military institution.	Argentina 1976–1983 Brazil 1964–1985
Indirect military	Formal political leaders are chosen through competitive elections, but the military either prevents parties that would attract large numbers of voters from participating or controls key policy choices.	Guatemala 1985–1995 El Salvador 1984–1992
Personalist	Control over policy, leadership selection, and the security apparatus is in the hands of a narrower group centered around an individual dictator.	Dominican Republic 1930–1962 Nicaragua 1936–1979
Dominate party	Control over policy, leadership selection, and the security apparatus is in the hands of a ruling party.	Colombia 1949–1953 Mexico 1915–2000
Oligarchy	Regimes in which leaders are chosen through competitive elections but most of the population is disenfranchised.	Bolivia 1946–1951

Source: Barbara Geddes, Joseph Wright, and Erica Frantz. 2014. "Autocratic Breakdown and Regime Transitions: A New Data Set." *Perspectives on Politics* 12(2): 313–331.

regime came to power after the armed forces overthrew the government of João Goulart. He had been elected vice president in 1960 and became the head of government after the elected president, Jânio Quadros, resigned in 1961. During this authoritarian period, five different military men held the presidency, while the armed forces controlled government policy.

Military dictatorships ruled Argentina on several occasions. The last time was between 1976 and 1983, after overthrowing Isabel Perón, who had become president after the death of her husband, Juan Perón, in 1974. The government was organized as a **military junta** (administrative council) made up of the leaders of the different branches of the armed forces, with one officer assuming the formal role of president. During its eight-year rule, four different officers held the position of president. The dictatorship finally fell from power after being defeated militarily by Great Britain in the 1982 Falklands War.

Another type of authoritarian government is the **indirect military regime**. In this type of regime, elections lead to the selection of a president, but the military plays a preponderant role by either controlling key aspects of policymaking or preventing the participation of parties that would attract a large number of voters.

The governments of Guatemala (1985–1995) and El Salvador (1984–1992) in the years before the end of their respective civil wars are examples of the indirect military regime category. In El Salvador, the military withdrawal began with the elections of 1982, which led to a constituent assembly and an indirectly elected civilian president. Subsequent elections took place in 1984 and 1989, but the armed forces continued to play a prominent role in policymaking, and the guerrilla forces continued to boycott the electoral contests. This changed in 1992, when a peace agreement ended the civil war and the Farabundo Martí National Liberation Front (FMLN) guerrillas became a legal political party. In Guatemala, the military withdrawal began after the election of 1985 but, despite subsequent elections in 1990 and 1993, the armed forces remained highly influential and significantly constrained the authority of elected presidents. The peace process between the guerrillas and the government culminated in 1996, when the Guatemalan National Revolutionary Unity (URNG) guerrillas laid down their arms.

Personalist regimes are the third category of authoritarian governments identified by Barbara Geddes and her colleagues. This type of regime is characterized by an individual dictator who is unconstrained by the armed forces or a strong party. Policy and the security apparatus are typically in the hands of a narrow group centered around the ruler. These regimes often begin with a **military coup**—the abrupt overthrow of a government by the armed forces or a military faction—but soon after, power shifts to an individual officer who becomes the country's ruler.

A classic example of a personalist dictatorship is the regime led by Brigadier General Rafael Trujillo in the Dominican Republic. He came to power in 1930 after the military overthrew Horacio Vásquez, who had been elected president after the end of the country's occupation by United States (U.S.) military forces. Trujillo maintained a tight grip on power for three decades and vigorously persecuted political opponents. During his reign of power, he appointed others (including his brother) to the presidency but remained the country's undisputed political leader. In May of 1961, he was assassinated by other military officers.[15]

Another well-known example of a personalist dictatorship is the regime led by the Somoza family in Nicaragua between 1936 and 1979. Anastasio Somoza García, the head of the army, led a military coup that ousted a civilian president in 1936. He then became president in an election boy-cotted by the opposition. Until his assassination in September of 1956, he ruled the country either as the formal president or as the real power behind handpicked figureheads. His eldest son, Luis Somoza Debayle, became president after Anastasio's murder and controlled the government until 1967, when he died from a heart attack. After this, power shifted to Luis's younger brother, Anastasio Somoza Debayle, who had been the head of the army. He ruled directly and indirectly until being ousted from power by the Sandinista Revolution in 1979.

Another authoritarian category is the **dominant-party regime**. It is characterized by a single party that controls policymaking and access to political office although, on occasion, small parties are allowed to exist and sometimes compete for office. In this type of authoritarian regime, leaders are constrained by the party organization, which exercises control over the career paths of officials and the legislature. In dominant-party regimes, elections frequently take place, but opposition parties are either illegal, subject to persecution, or must confront severe institutional disadvantages.

The best-known dominant-party regime in Latin America is the one that was in place in Mexico between 1915 and 2000. The regime, which originated after the end of the Mexican Revolution, created the National Revolutionary Party in the 1920s, which was renamed the Mexican Revolutionary Party in 1938 and the Institutional Revolutionary Party (PRI) in 1946. The ruling party monopolized Mexican politics for most of the 20th century. The first time the PRI lost a gubernatorial election was in 1989, and the first time it lost its majority in the lower chamber of congress was in the 1997 election. Mexico's dominant-party regime came to an end in the year 2000, when the PRI lost the presidency for the first time in its history.

Another example of a dominant-party regime is the one that was in place in Colombia between 1949 and 1953. Laureano Gómez Castro of the Colombian Conservative Party came to power in 1949 amid widespread political violence and the killing and intimidation of political opponents, who boycotted the presidential election and the subsequent congressional elections. The Conservative-dominated regime came to an end as a result of a military coup that took place in 1953.

The last authoritarian category identified by Barbara Geddes and her colleagues is the **oligarchic regime**, which is characterized by leaders chosen in competitive elections but with most of the population disen-franchised. In Latin America, such a regime was common at the beginning of the 20th century but later disappeared. The only oligarchic regime in the post–1945 era was in Bolivia between 1946 and 1951. During that time, less than 5 percent of the Bolivian population voted. Most individuals were excluded from voting as a result of restrictions based on literacy and wealth requirements. This regime was overthrown by the Bolivian Revolution of 1952, which ended the prior restrictions on voting rights.

Authoritarian regimes differ with regards to their relative stability, how they come to an end, and whether they are likely to be followed by democracy. The second part of this chapter addresses outcomes related to the transitions away from authoritarianism, but one relevant finding from the literature on authoritarian regimes worth noting here is the difference in their survival rates. Typically, dominant-party regimes stay in power much longer than others, with military regimes remaining in power for the shortest time.[16]

From 1946 to 2010, there were 11 dominant party regimes, 20 personalist regimes, 28 military regimes, four indirect military regimes, and one oligarchic regime in Latin America. Figure 2.5 shows the average number of years in power for the first four categories. Consistent with prior cross-national findings, dominant-party regimes tend to stay in power the longest: On average, they rule for 25.1 years. Personalist regimes last an average of 9.5 years, indirect military regimes 8.5 years, and military regimes 7.2 years.

Disagreements on Difficult Cases

So far, this chapter has explained alternative definitions of democracy and has described how experts classify democracies and dictatorships. As noted previously, despite differences in how democracy is conceptualized, there is agreement on how to classify many governments in Latin America. Most measures underline the long democratic history of countries such as Uruguay, Costa Rica, and Chile; the prevailing authoritarianism in Haiti and Cuba; and the lasting dominant-party regime in Mexico.

However, there are some significant disagreements on the classification of particular cases that reflect more than merely subjective assessments by those constructing those classifications. They underline noteworthy

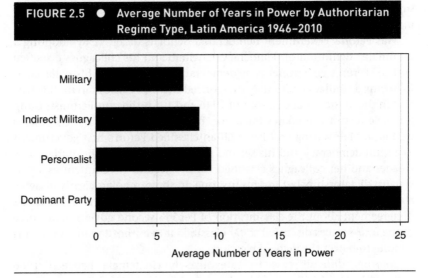

FIGURE 2.5 ● Average Number of Years in Power by Authoritarian Regime Type, Latin America 1946–2010

Source: Barbara Geddes, Joseph Wright, and Erica Frantz. 2014. "Autocratic Breakdown and Regime Transitions: A New Data Set." *Perspectives on Politics,* 12(2): 313-331.

differences regarding what constitutes a democracy. Discussing some of these cases can exemplify substantive differences in how we define political regimes. The rest of this section reviews some disagreements in the classifications of governments in five Latin American countries: Argentina, Colombia, Guatemala, Paraguay, and Venezuela.

One significant disagreement revolves around the classification of Juan Perón's first two governments in Argentina. Perón was one of the classic populist leaders of the mid-20th century. He was a military officer who rose to prominence during the military dictatorship that ruled the country in the period 1943–1946, when he occupied the positions of secretary of labor, minister of war, and vice president. He was then elected president in 1946 and again in 1951. During this time, he founded the most prominent political party of Argentina, which remains the largest one in the contemporary era.

Perón was accused of using the state resources at his disposal and his prominent role in the military dictatorship, when political parties were banned, to promote his candidacy for the 1946 elections. Once in power, he modified electoral rules to benefit his political movement, packed the Supreme Court, purged the state administration of non-Peronists, and changed the constitution to eliminate presidential term limits. Perón also restricted freedom of the press and his supporters harassed the opposition, often violently. Violations of civil liberties intensified around the 1951 presidential election, when the government suspended constitutional guarantees, restricted opposition access to the media, and imprisoned several opposition politicians. Political conflict between the government and the opposition increased dramatically during Perón's second term in office. As political polarization grew, Perón publicly encouraged his supporters to respond violently to those attacking the government. Finally, in 1955, the military rose up and overthrew him from power.

Was Perón's government democratic? Scholars disagree. By adopting a minimalist definition of democracy, Cheibub and his colleagues classified both of Perón's governments as democratic, but Boix and his colleagues, following a similar perspective, categorized them as authoritarian. It is true that in the presidential elections of 1946 and 1951, the non-Peronists camp was able to run candidates for office, but the fairness of such contests is in doubt. Mainwaring and Pérez-Liñán classified Perón's first government as a semi-democracy and his second government as an authoritarian one. Geddes and her colleagues classified Perón's second government as a personalist dictatorship, but not his first one. In short, scholars clearly disagree about the democratic credentials of Perón's first government. There is less disagreement about the classification of Perón's second government: three of the four sources discussed so far classified it as authoritarian, despite his coming to power through an election.

Another difficult case to categorize is Guatemala between 1966 and 1981. In 1966, Julio Méndez Montenegro was elected president in an election from which several political parties were banned from participation. Despite being a civilian who had advocated democratic reforms, he was not allowed to act independently from the military, which remained in control of important areas of policy beyond security. During his government, the armed forces began a major anti-guerrilla campaign and committed widespread violations of human rights. In 1970, he was succeeded in the presidency by Colonel Carlos Arana Osorio, who ran as a candidate of the military-dominated Institutional Democratic Party in an election where, once again, several political parties were not allowed to participate. During this government, top administrative positions were in the hands of the military, and the killing of members of the opposition at the hands of death squads linked to the government was common. Subsequent presidential elections in 1974 and 1978 were also won by officers belonging to the military-backed Institutional Democratic Party. They took place in contexts of violent political conflict and widespread violation of human rights, with several parties excluded from electoral participation and amid accusations of fraud. In early 1982, a faction of the military led by General Efraín Rios Montt overthrew the president and took control of the government.

Was Guatemala democratic during the 1966–1981 period? According to the two sources advocating a minimalist definition of democracy, the answer is yes. Elections took place and several parties competed for office. However, Mainwaring and his colleagues classified these four governments as authoritarian. For Geddes and her colleagues, the civilian government of Méndez Montenegro represents an example of indirect military rule, while the three governments of the military-run Institutional Democratic Party are examples of a military dictatorship.

The case of Paraguay has also generated different assessments among experts. All agree that Paraguay was a dictatorship under the rule of General Alfredo Stroessner, who governed with the support of the Colorado Party and the military from 1954 to 1989. However, there is disagreement regarding the time at which the country actually democratized.

According to Cheibub and his colleagues, Paraguay democratized after the multiparty elections of 1989, which followed the overthrow of Stroessner by a faction of the military. Geddes and her colleagues disagreed because the winner of the 1989 election, Lieutenant General Andrés Rodríguez, was Stroessner's former right-hand man, his son-in-law, and the leader of the military insurrection that overthrew him. Rodríguez ran as a candidate of the Colorado Party in a context not unlike those of previous elections; however, the new government proceeded to undertake various democratizing reforms. So, for Geddes and her colleagues, Paraguay democratized with the subsequent presidential election, which took place in 1993.

Mainwaring and Pérez-Liñán argued that Paraguay transitioned from dictatorship to semi-democracy in the 1989 election and to a full democracy in 2008 when, after 61 years, the long-ruling Colorado Party was defeated in a presidential election by a candidate from an opposition party. For Boix and his colleagues, the transition to democracy took place in 2003, when Nicánor Duarte Frutos was elected president. He came to power following a period of turmoil associated with the resignation of the prior president, Raúl Cubas, amid accusations of complicity in the assassination of his vice president. Duarte Frutos belonged to the Colorado Party but was its first candidate from outside the military and Stroessner's inner circle.

Disagreement regarding the classification of Colombia was noted earlier in this chapter. Most sources classify the country as democratic since the election of 1958, which took place after a bloody civil war and the signing of a power-sharing agreement, called the National Front, between the two main political parties of the country, Liberal and Conservative. However, Mainwaring and Pérez-Liñán disagreed and classified it as semi-democratic over the same period of time.

There are two main issues that raise concerns about Colombia's democratic credential, the first having to do with restrictions to political competition during the period 1958–1974. As a result of the power-sharing agreement that helped to end the civil war, the two major parties agreed to alternate in the presidency and share bureaucratic appointments. Furthermore, the constitution stipulated that only candidates from the Liberal and Conservative parties could run for election. The second issue has to do with the state's ability to guarantee civil rights. For most of the period following the end of the National Front, the Colombian state failed to exercise a monopoly on the use of force: The country suffered political violence perpetrated by guerrillas, paramilitaries, drug cartels, and death squads. Among the victims of political violence were numerous political activists from leftist political parties, including several members of congress, dozens of mayors and local councilors, trade unionists, and four presidential candidates, who were assassinated in 1987, 1989, and 1990. Electoral campaigns often stimulated violence, particularly at the municipal level. These events have raised questions about Colombia's democratic credentials.

A more recent example of a controversial regime classification is the case of Venezuela during the government of Hugo Chávez. He was a former military officer who went to jail for attempting to overthrow a democratic government and was subsequently elected as president in competitive multiparty elections. Most sources classify Chávez's short first government (1999–2000) as democratic and disagree about how to classify his second (2001–2006) and third governments (2007–2013). But none of the previously discussed sources cover the entire period of Chávez's government. The disagreement centers on assessments of the fairness of political competition—the extent to which the government manipulated electoral procedures and used state resources and institutions to severely curtail the electoral chances and rights of the opposition—as well as on the erosion of civil rights—the often-violent intimidation of members of the opposition and the weakening of press freedoms. These actions have led many observers to characterize Chávez's last two governments as non-democratic.[17]

To conclude, the first part of this chapter reviewed definitions of democracy and authoritarianism and provided examples from various Latin American countries. This section presented some examples of cases that are not easily categorized and showed why it is not a simple task to codify political regimes. Part of the reason for the different categorization of governments stems from the different conceptualizations of democracy, but also relevant is how authors judge such aspects as the conditions that surround political competition and the respect of basic civil rights. The next section shifts attention to the analysis of **regime transitions**.

Regime Transitions and Democratic Survival

For many decades, the study of the emergence and breakdown of democratic regimes has been an important research topic among social scientists. The topic is not only relevant to academics but also to politicians, activists, and others interested in the survival of democracy. Since most Latin American countries transitioned to democracy not long ago and democracy does not appear fully consolidated across the region, it seems particularly appropriate to investigate what could facilitate regime stability and prevent a slide back into dictatorship.

The political science literature has underlined the importance of several factors to explain regime change. In this section, we review the most significant ones: the economy, **political institutions**, cultural factors, agency, and the international context. While debates about the relative importance of each factor continue, it is important to understand what is meant to be the underlying mechanism linking each of them to regime transition. Reviewing these arguments and describing some relevant long-term patterns should contribute to enhancing our knowledge of the region's politics.

The Economy

The idea that economic development affects the emergence and stability of democracy has a long history in political science. It was a key argument advanced in the 1950s by the well-known scholar Seymour M. Lipset in his seminal work on the social prerequisites for democracy. According to Lipset, economic development was supposed to bring about a series of social changes that would favor the emergence of democracy.[18]

Among the most consequential changes associated with economic development is the growth of the middle class. The idea that a middle class is favorable to democracy goes back to Aristotle. Lipset thought that the middle class would help to mitigate social conflict, rewarding moderate and democratic parties over extremist ones. He also thought that economic development would make the rich less likely to fight off democratization and the poor less likely to support radical antidemocratic movements. As incomes rose, the rich would be less fearful of democratization because the threat that a popularly elected government would pursue drastic wealth redistribution would be lessened. Higher levels of economic development would also bring about greater economic security among those with relatively low incomes, which was supposed to promote moderation, longer time perspectives, and the legitimization of democratic institutions.

Evidence shows that democracy is more common among economically developed countries than among poor countries. However, proving a causal relation is statistically complicated. Several recent cross-national studies have concluded that levels of per capita income increase the likelihood of democratization.[19] They recognize that regime transitions may be facilitated by multiple factors but argue that higher levels of economic development increase the chances that a country will become democratic (even if this effect varies in different periods and even if some authoritarian rulers are better at insulating themselves from this effect). Additionally, democracy tends to be more stable (i.e., less likely to break down) at high levels of economic development.[20]

Some scholars have looked separately at a set of Latin American countries to evaluate the effect of economic development on democracy. Peter Smith, for instance, underlined that the most prosperous nations in Latin America (i.e., Argentina, Chile, and Uruguay) were the first ones to shift toward democracy in the period before the 1940s, but he believed that economic development was less crucial in those transitions occurring later in the 20th century.[21] Focusing on this latter period, Mainwaring and Pérez-Liñán found no direct association between economic development and transitions from dictatorship to democracy in Latin America.[22] However, they discovered that economic development increased the normative preferences for democracy among the region's key political actors, and this, in turn, had a significant effect in promoting the emergence and stability of democratic regimes.

Not all academics embrace the hypothesis that economic development causes democracy. Some have disputed the causal relationship and argued that both economic development and democracy are caused by historical factors that have made both outcomes more likely to occur simultaneously.[23] For instance, Guillermo O'Donnell, writing in the early 1970s, was skeptical of the democratizing effect of economic development in countries that industrialized late and noted that, at that time, both the richest and poorest Latin American countries had dictatorial regimes.[24] He went on to coin the term *bureaucratic authoritarianism* to characterize the military dictatorship of the more modernized countries, such as Argentina and Brazil, and to distinguish them from the oligarchic and personalist forms of authoritarianism prevalent in poorer Latin American countries.

Aside from the effect of overall levels of economic development, scholars have argued that short-term economic growth also affects the stability of political regimes.[25] Poor economic performance weakens support for governments and can erode their legitimacy. For example, Stephan Haggard and Robert R. Kaufman argued that transitions to democracy in Argentina, Bolivia, Brazil, Peru, and Uruguay took place in a context of economic crises that favored the opposition to the authoritarian regime.[26]

Political Institutions

Political institutions affect policymaking as well as the relationships between the different branches of government. Political scientists have long argued that institutional design impacts the stability of democracy. Since institutions establish the "rules of the game," they affect the incentives of the different political actors to obey by democratic norms.

An important debate within the institutional literature focuses on the power of the executive. Several scholars have argued that constraints on the executive have favorable implications for both democracy and development. In a series of articles, economists Daron Acemoglu, Simon Johnson, and James Robinson argued that executive constraints at the time of independence have a significant impact on the likelihood of democracy and the emergence of institutions conducive to economic development.[27] Executives with weaker constraints are expected to have fewer incentives to bargain with other political actors and to respect the rights of the opposition and more incentives to bypass congress and ignore existing rules. Constraints on the executive are also associated with institutions that protect property rights, which has been found to have a favorable effect on economic development.

The association between executive constraints and regime type in Latin America is illustrated in Figure 2.6. The horizontal axis shows the countries' executive constraints score in the last two decades of the 19th century,

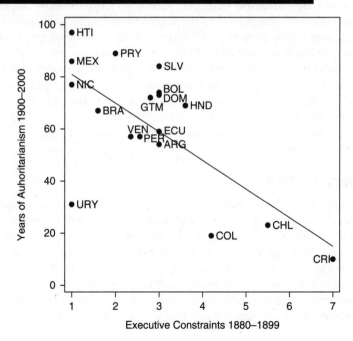

FIGURE 2.6 ● Executive Constraints and Authoritarianism

when political stability came to the region and political institutions began to take hold. The data comes from the Polity IV Project, which provides a score for executive constraints that goes from 1 (representing no limitations on the executive's actions) to 7 (representing situations in which legislatures and other accountability groups have effective authority equal to or greater than the executive on most areas).[28] On the vertical axis, the figure shows the number of years of authoritarianism between 1900 and 2000 from the political regime data set of Mainwaring and Pérez-Liñán. The black line inside the figure represents the linear prediction of executive constraints on authoritarianism. Each country is indicated by a dark point with its associated label.

The figure reveals a significant association between executive constraints at the end of the 19th century and regime type in the 20th century. The direction of this association can be seen in the black line that goes down from the upper left corner of the figure toward the lower right corner. Countries where executives had few limits tended to have more years of authoritarianism. This suggests that early institutions in Latin America explain a substantial amount of variation in the presence of dictatorial regimes in the subsequent century.

In addition to the effect of early institutions on the future incidence of democracy, scholars have also debated the influence of current institutions on democratic stability. Along the lines of the earlier argument, it has been observed that institutional rules that give strong legislative powers to the president in comparison to the legislature are problematic for the stability of democracy. For example, political scientists Matthew Shugart and John Carey made the argument that presidential systems allocating weaker constitutional powers to the executive are more stable than those that allocate strong powers to it.[29] Using the measure developed by these authors, Mainwaring and Pérez-Liñán found some evidence that democratic stability after the middle of the 20th century has been negatively affected by strong executive powers. A more recent study that examines Latin American countries from the early 20th century until the early 21st century found evidence that presidential hegemony over the other branches of government (congress and the judiciary) represents a major threat to democratic stability.[30]

Cultural Factors

Democracy has also been linked to political culture, which consists of the beliefs, values, and norms of a society. For some, political culture also includes an emotional and expressive element. The origins of a society's political culture are typically found in historical events, the individual experiences of its members, and the process of schooling. While it has been central to the work of many political theorists for centuries, modern research on political culture flourished after the end of World War II. Insights from this literature have had a significant influence on studies regarding the emergence and stability of democracy. Because democracy is associated with tolerance of the opposition, acceptance of different opinions, the rule of law, and the legitimacy of political institutions, many scholars have argued that democracy is fostered by a particular set of views and ideals.[31]

Political culture affects how individuals evaluate political institutions and political outcomes. For example, it influences whether the government is considered a legitimate authoritative body as well as the desirability of particular government activities. As a result, it can strengthen a society's commitment to democracy and help governments survive difficult crises. Many important aspects of political culture have been the focus of extensive research. Chapter 9 of this book will examine the attitudes and beliefs of Latin Americans in more detail. Here, we address how religion and education—two key aspects of political culture—affect democracy.

For a long time, scholars thought that religion played an important role in influencing the likelihood of democracy. The first countries to democratize were in Protestant Europe and in Britain's former overseas colonies. In contrast, at least until the second half of the 20th century, Catholic, Islamic, and Confucian countries seemed to offer an unwelcoming environment for democratic development.

Protestantism, particularly the Calvinist strand, has been described as highly receptive to democracy, given its emphasis on individualism, acceptance of pluralism of ideas and secular life, and promotion of civic associationalism. However, Catholicism, the prevalent religion in Latin America since colonial times, was for a long time characterized as being unreceptive to democratic values. For example, the late sociologist Kingsley Davis wrote in 1942 in an article about Latin America that

> Catholicism attempts to control so many aspects of life, to encourage so much fixity of status and submission to authority, and to remain so independent of secular authority that it invariably clashes with the liberalism, individualism, freedom, mobility, and sovereignty of the democratic nation.[32]

One influential view of the cultural challenges to democracy in Latin America was advanced by political scientist Howard Wiarda, who argued that the region's Catholic history and corporatist sociopolitical structures were fundamentally different from the Anglo-Protestant tradition.[33] According to this perspective, a corporatist, Catholic, and authoritarian tradition was brought over from Spain and Portugal during the colonial period. Wiarda contrasted the individualism and liberalism of the United States with the hierarchical conservative Catholic tradition of Latin America which, according to him, has been historically hostile to democracy. He and Margaret MacLeish Mott argued that Latin America has had a "political culture that values order over participation and natural law over a mere constitution."[34]

But the apparent incompatibility of Catholicism and democracy has been challenged by more recent events. For instance, during the third wave of democratization (1974–1990), Catholic countries were more likely to democratize than others.[35] This fact may be explained if one considers that cultures often have heterogeneous values and that religion is able to change over time.[36] Catholicism has undergone profound changes since at least the 1960s that have helped to make liberalism acceptable. Liberal Catholics have been vocal in politics for many years, but scholars often underline the lasting impact of the Second Vatican Council (1962–1965), which was an assembly of Roman Catholic religious leaders seeking to address doctrinal matters. It was at that time that the Catholic Church redefined its position on various issues and embraced a favorable view of religious freedom, the secular state, and civil liberties. Many of the ideas that helped to promote this shift in the Catholic Church had been brewing for some time before being adopted by the church's hierarchy. In addition to doctrinal changes, authoritarian regimes, which had attracted many European Catholics before World War II, were profoundly discredited by the 1960s.[37]

Aside from religion, another component of political culture is education. The view that education promotes attitudes and values that favor democracy has been common in the social sciences for over a century. There are several mechanisms through which education works to shape a society's receptivity to democracy. One view argues that education helps to promote tolerance and that more tolerant individuals are more likely to embrace democratic principles. Another view maintains that education instills civic skills and political interests that make individuals more likely to participate in politics and demand voting rights. Various empirical works have found a positive correlation between levels of schooling and democracy at the national level and between years of education and democratic attitudes at the individual level.[38]

In an illuminating analysis of political legitimacy and democratic values across Latin American countries, a group of political scientists found that education had the largest positive effect on political tolerance.[39] This finding is consistent with other studies of public opinion in the region, which found that increases in schooling enhance an individual's democratic values. At an aggregate level, there is also some indication that education positively affects democratic values. For example, Figure 2.7 shows the association between levels of illiteracy in 18 Latin American countries in 1900 (horizontal axis), and years of authoritarianism between 1900 and 2000 in the vertical axis.[40] It reveals a positive association between illiteracy at the turn of the century and years of authoritarianism in the subsequent century. While the association is less robust than that between executive constraints and democracy, it is still significant.

FIGURE 2.7 ● Illiteracy and Authoritarianism

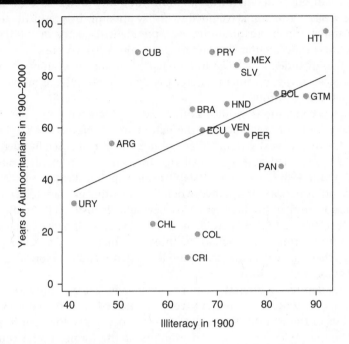

Agency: Political Elites

Explanations about the emergence and stability of democracy not only focus on cultural or structural features, such as institutions and the economy, but also on the actions of individuals at a particular juncture in time. Whether key political actors work to strengthen or undermine democracy can significantly impact political outcomes. Such key political actors include individuals such as presidents and influential party, religious, business, and labor leaders as well as organizations, including the military, social movements, trade unions, and guerrillas.

The frequency with which the military overthrew elected (and non-elected) governments in Latin America led to a rich literature focused on the armed forces. Military coups varied across countries and over time. Bolivia, Ecuador, Honduras, and Paraguay all experienced more than a dozen coups in the 20th century. Others, such as Costa Rica and Uruguay, only had two each during the same period of time. On some occasions, the military would overthrow a government and quickly withdraw to the sidelines, allowing civilians to form a government; at other times, the military would expel a sitting president and take direct control of the government. While military coups are no longer common, they used to be the most frequent cause of democratic breakdown in Latin America.

The reasons that the military in Latin America overthrew governments varied. Officers typically highly valued the survival of the military institution and their autonomy from politicians and would resent attempts by civilian governments to act in ways they interpreted as contrary to these ideals.[41] The military tended to dislike attempts by presidents to create parallel armed organizations (e.g., presidential guards or militias) or to politicize and interfere in military promotions. They were also keen on maintaining order, which was interpreted in various ways but often meant that officers saw governments unable to fulfill this objective as problematic for their own institution.

After a coup, military officers often excused their actions by highlighting the need to restore order to the nation and to protect the fatherland from the threat of extreme or violent groups. The threat posed by guerrillas, which represented a serious challenge to many governments from the 1960s to the 1980s, worked to destabilize many political regimes in Central and South America. For instance, when the Argentine military took control of the government in March of 1976, they publicly justified their intervention by claiming that they would end the prevailing climate of ungovernability and corruption as well as the threat of violent subversive groups. In reality, they ushered a new era of state-led violence and widespread human rights violations.

Dominant-class interests cannot adequately explain military interventions. In some cases, military coups coincided with the conservative interests of the wealthy classes but, on other occasions, they put in place left-leaning policy programs. An example of the former is the coup of 1954 in Guatemala, which deposed the progressive government of Jacobo Arbenz and led to a military government that proceeded to reverse various recently enacted social policies. An example of the latter type of coup is the intervention led by General Juan Velasco in Peru in 1968, which deposed the centrist government of Fernando Belaúnde Terry and instituted a leftist military dictatorship.

Military coups have deposed not only democratic governments but often authoritarian governments as well. Civilian elites have frequently conspired with military officers to depose sitting governments. This was the case, for example, with the military coup of 1958 in Venezuela, when a civilian–military movement overthrew the dictatorship of General Marcos Pérez Jiménez and later called for democratic elections.

On some occasions, **political elites** helped to usher in transitions to democracy; on others, they knocked on the barrack's door, seeking to depose elected governments. Political elites who saw democratization as contrary to their interests often worked to prevent it. In a study about democratic breakdown in Latin America during the 1970s, political scientist Nancy Bermeo emphasized the choices of political elites in bringing about the fall of democracy.[42] She underlined how errors of perception made conservative and leftist elites overestimate the threat and strength of their respective enemies and misinterpret citizens' preferences, which remained (for the most part) supportive of democracy.

The influence of the preferences of political elites was also emphasized in the work of Mainwaring and Pérez-Liñán.[43] The authors argued that policy preferences and beliefs about the desirability of democracy or dictatorship determine the actions of political elites. To study their effect on the stability of political regimes, they built a measure to capture the preferences of key political actors. Then, they used statistics to examine its effect on democratic stability in Latin America. Results showed that when key political actors had normative preferences favorable to democracy, the likelihood of competitive politics increased and the likelihood of reverting to authoritarianism decreased.

The International Context

Domestic politics are not immune to the international context. Regime change has been linked to significant international events as well as to the actions of major powers. The fact that regime transitions have come in waves and that democracies and dictatorships are usually regionally clustered hint at the importance of non-domestic factors.

Great powers can have a significant influence over other countries in their sphere of influence. During the Cold War era, the two major world powers were the United States and the Soviet Union. Many countries in Eastern Europe were under the constant threat of Soviet intervention, and attempts to move away from communism and toward democracy were met with military interventions (e.g., in Hungary and Czechoslovakia), violent repression, and the imprisonment of significant numbers of people.

The major power influencing politics in Latin America during this period was the United States. Driven by a Cold War mentality, governments in the United States tended to perceive left-leaning governments in Latin America as a potential security problem. Military governments, in contrast, were often (but not always) perceived to be more reliable allies. Political instability and the threat of leftist guerrillas worried policymakers in the United States. The Cuban missile crisis of 1962, which revealed the intention of the Cuban government to deploy Soviet ballistic missiles in Cuba, fueled the idea that the United States should actively intervene in the region to prevent further threats to its national security. However, policymakers often overreacted to the threat of communism, which led them to undermine democratic governments and support dictatorial regimes that committed widespread human rights abuses.

One well-known intervention was the Central Intelligence Agency (CIA)–orchestrated coup that took place in Guatemala in 1954, which deposed the left-leaning government of Jacobo Arbenz and installed a military dictatorship led by Carlos Castillo Armas. The operation to depose Arbenz was carried out during the presidency of Dwight D. Eisenhower, who thought the Guatemalan government to be influenced by communists. The military operation, which also received the support of the right-wing dictators of Nicaragua, the Dominican Republic, and Venezuela, led to the establishment of a violent dictatorship and triggered a civil war that would last until the 1990s.

In a cross-national study using data covering two centuries, Carles Boix examined how the structure of the international system affected the strategies of pro-authoritarian and pro-democratic domestic factions.[44] He found that the international system was detrimental to democracy during the Cold War era (1948–1990): Being in an alliance with the Soviet Union lessened the chances of a democratic transition, and being in an alliance with the United States made democratic breakdowns more likely. However, being allied with the United States at a time other than the Cold War appears to have had a favorable effect on democracy.

International organizations can also have a significant effect on the promotion of democracy. The Organization of American States (OAS) has played an active role in the promotion of democracy in Latin America since the last wave of democratization. For example, in the 1990s, it worked to prevent the breakdown of democracy (or semi-democracy) in Guatemala and Paraguay.

In September of 2001, the general assembly of the OAS adopted the Inter-American Democratic Charter. This binding charter states that governments have an obligation to promote and defend democracy. It was invoked for the first time in April of 2002 after an attempted coup against Venezuelan President Hugo Chávez. However, Chávez was returned to power soon after and before the OAS' general assembly was convened. The second time the charter was invoked was in June of 2009, when a coup deposed Honduran President Manuel Zelaya. The OAS suspended Honduras from the organization and many Latin American and European countries withdrew their ambassadors from the country.

The stability of democracy may also be affected by the regional context. A common view holds that democracy is contagious. Academics tend to refer to this phenomenon as the "diffusion" of democracy. This perspective stems from the idea that there are connections among countries that facilitate the flow of information that affects democratic (and authoritarian) trends. Academics disagree about whether the effects of democratic diffusion operate primarily through political elites or public opinion, but the evidence suggests that there are clear temporal and spatial effects associated with the spread of democracy. For instance, political scientist Samuel P. Huntington identified three waves of democracy around the world: The first began in the early 19th century with the expansion of the right to vote to a large portion of the male population in the United States; the second began after the end of World War II; and the third wave began in the mid-1970s in Southern Europe.[45] In Figure 2.2, shown in the first part of this chapter, we can observe how the number of democracies in Latin America increased during the second and third waves identified by Huntington.

Conclusions

When the 20th century began, Latin America lacked democratic regimes. While authoritarianism prevailed for most of the prior century, today, most countries in the region enjoy democratic governments. The move toward democracy was difficult, and many countries experienced significant reversals that delayed the establishment of competitive elections. But overall, the region has made a significant shift away from authoritarianism, which has brought not only free and fair elections but also a much greater respect for human rights.

This chapter focused our attention on the type of political regimes that have been prevalent in Latin America for over a century. It began with a review of the alternative definitions of democracy, including the advantages and disadvantages of each approach. Examples from various classifications helped to illuminate long-term trends across the region and the rationale behind coding schemes that assign countries to one category or another. The chapter also discussed the classification of some controversial cases and reviewed some significant differences between authoritarian regimes.

Transitions from authoritarianism to democracy and the breakdown of democratic regimes have attracted significant attention among academics and policymakers. The second part of the chapter looked at five different factors that are commonly associated with regime transition. First, it examined arguments linking higher levels of economic development to democracy and economic crises with regime instability. Second, it reviewed the connection between political institutions, particularly executive powers, and democratic breakdown. Third, the chapter went over the connection between two aspects of political culture, religion and education, and democracy. Next, it examined the impact of political elites on democratic stability. This included a discussion of the role of the military, which was a significant source of democratic instability throughout the 20th century. The chapter concluded with a discussion of the effect of the international context. Some of the issues introduced in this chapter, such as the importance of political institutions, political culture, and U.S.–Latin American relations, will be addressed in greater depth in subsequent chapters.

Key Terms

Authoritarianism 36

Contested elections 37

Democracy 35

Military coup 47

Military regime 45

Personalist regime 47

Political culture 36

Political elites 60

Political institutions 53

Regime transitions 53

Bibliographic Recommendations

Nancy Bermeo. 2003. *Ordinary People in Extraordinary Times: The Citizenry and the Breakdown of Democracy.* Princeton: Princeton University Press.

Carles Boix, Michael Miller, and Sebastian Rosato. 2013. "A Complete Data Set of Political Regimes, 1800–2007." *Comparative Political Studies* 46(12): 1523–1554.

José Antonio Cheibub, Jennifer Gandhi, and James Raymond Vreeland. 2010. "Democracy and Dictatorship Revisited." *Public Choice* 143(1): 67–101.

Barbara Geddes, Joseph Wright, and Erica Frantz. 2014. "Autocratic Breakdown and Regime Transitions: A New Data Set." *Perspectives on Politics* 12(2): 313–331.

Stephan Haggard and Robert R. Kaufman. 1995. *The Politics of Democratic Transitions.* Princeton: Princeton University Press.

Scott Mainwaring. 2012. "From Representative Democracy to Participatory Competitive Authoritarianism: Hugo Chávez and Venezuelan Politics." *Perspectives on Politics* 10(4): 955–967.

Scott Mainwaring and Aníbal Pérez-Liñán. 2013. *Democracies and Dictatorships in Latin America: Emergence, Survival, and Fall.* New York: Cambridge University Press.

Web Resources

Center for Systemic Peace, Polity Project: http://www.systemicpeace.org/polityproject.html

The Economist Intelligence Unit, Democracy Index: https://www.eiu.com/topic/democracy-index

Freedom House: https://freedomhouse.org/

3

Guerrillas and Revolutions

On November 30, 2016, Colombia's House of Representatives ratified a peace agreement reached between the government and the country's main **guerrilla** group, the **Revolutionary Armed Forces of Colombia**, better known by its acronym, **FARC**. This accord marked the culmination of more than four years of negotiations and brought a violent conflict that had started in the early 1960s to an end. Over the course of the war, more than 220,000 people died, and around 5 million were displaced from their homes. The victims of the violent confrontation between guerrillas, paramilitaries, and the country's armed forces were mostly civilians, including thousands of children. The agreement was heralded as a major step in bringing Colombia closer to peace.

While today, very few leftist guerrilla groups remain active in Latin America, their presence was a major factor in the politics of the region for decades. Many Latin Americans (including many young college students) joined guerrilla groups, seeking to radically change their country's politics through violent means. Many others strongly opposed their tactics and instead pursued nonviolent ways to achieve political change. Ultimately, guerrilla groups contributed to the region's political instability. Their actions were most often met with harsh repression on the part of governments and, in some countries, they were also persecuted by illegal **paramilitary forces** and death squads. Leftist revolutionary movements were a source of serious concern for Latin American governments as well as for the United States (U.S.), which, for many years, saw these conflicts through the lenses of the Cold War.

This chapter examines the surge of leftist guerrilla movements in the post–World War II period. It explains the context that gave rise to such movements, underlines factors that facilitated or hindered the success of guerrilla movements, and contrasts the triumphant revolutions in Cuba and Nicaragua with the failed revolutions in El Salvador and Guatemala. The chapter ends with a review of the peace agreements between insurgents and the government in Colombia.

Guerrilla Movements in Latin America

The 1960s saw an explosion of armed revolutionary groups across Latin America. Such revolutionary fervor had a clear trigger: the Cuban Revolution. It was in its aftermath that most countries in the region experienced the emergence of guerrilla movements. A large number of left-wing militants, eager to follow the Cuban path, would eventually visit the Caribbean country to receive both revolutionary indoctrination and military training. During this time, relevant sectors of Latin American society became politically radicalized and embraced a romanticized view of the armed struggle.

Major guerrilla groups were characterized by a leftist, Marxist-inspired ideology. After the 1917 Bolshevik Revolution in Russia, communist parties began to emerge in many Latin American countries. Their appeal, however, had waned by the early 1960s. According to Jorge Castañeda, an academic who has conducted extensive research on Latin America's revolutionary movements, communist parties were discredited in the eyes of the young and the radical as a result of their submission to Moscow and accommodation to the governments in place.[1] In accordance with Moscow's dictates, these parties rejected armed confrontation to bring about revolutionary change and sought instead a peaceful path to socialism that included broad electoral coalitions. It was the Cuban Revolution, Castañeda notes, which brought renewed life to the radical left and convinced several of their militants to abandon party politics and join guerrilla bands.

The social and institutional context of the 1950s and 1960s seemed fertile for the spread of radical politics. Although improvements in economic development during the first part of the 20th century had brought about many social changes—including increases in literacy and political participation—governments appeared unable to bring about the deep social reforms that many expected. The region had the highest rate of income inequality in the world, and poverty remained widespread, particularly in the countryside. Land ownership was densely concentrated, and rural labor arrangements remained highly exploitative in several countries. Many Latin Americans had become skeptical of the idea that liberal democracy could offer an opportunity to achieve significant social reform. Military coups against reformist governments, such as the one that took place in Guatemala in 1954 against the government of Jacobo Arbenz, seemed to support the idea that democracies could not challenge the will of powerful economic elites. By the late 1960s, most Latin American countries were governed by repressive military governments that did not offer an electoral path for the left. One exception was Chile, where leftist parties engaged in political competition and, in 1970, elected Salvador Allende as president. However, this electoral experiment ended with a violent military coup in 1973 that deposed the socialist government, ushering in a military dictatorship that would rule the country until 1990.

Many political groups seeking radical reforms through armed struggle emerged in the period following the Cuban revolution. Table 3.1 lists the names of some of the best-known guerrilla groups and the year in which they were founded. While these organizations were primarily homegrown, the government of Cuba played an important role in training many of their members, assisting with logistical and even military support. For example, Cuba helped organize the landing of guerrilla forces in Panama (1959), the

TABLE 3.1 ● Examples of Guerrilla Organizations		
Country	Founding Year	Name
Argentina	1963	People's Guerrilla Army
	1970	Montoneros
	1970	People's Revolutionary Army (ERP)
Brazil	1966	Revolutionary Movement 8th October (MR-8)
	1967	National Liberation Command (COLINA)
	1967	National Liberation Action (ALN)
Bolivia	1966	National Liberation Army (ELN) of Bolivia
Chile	1965	Movement of the Revolutionary Left (MIR)
Colombia	1964	Revolutionary Armed Forces of Colombia (FARC)
	1964	National Liberation Army (ELN)
	1974	19th April Movement (M-19)
Dominican Republic	1959	Dominican Liberation Movement (MLD)
	1963	Revolutionary Movement 14th of June (MR1J4)
El Salvador	1970	Popular Forces of Liberation (FPL)
	1971	People's Revolutionary Army (ERP)
	1980	Farabundo Martí National Liberation Front (FMLN)
Guatemala	1962	Rebel Armed Forces (FAR)
	1972	Guerrilla Army of the Poor (EGP)
	1979	Revolutionary Organization of Armed People (ORPA)
	1982	Guatemalan National Revolutionary Unity (URNG)
Nicaragua	1961	Sandinista National Liberation Front (FSLN)
Peru	1962	National Liberation Army (ELN)
	1980	Túpac Amaru Revolutionary Movement (MRTA)
	1980	Shining Path
Uruguay	1965	Tupamaros
Venezuela	1962	Fuerzas Armadas de Liberación Nacional (FALN)

Dominican Republic (1959), Haiti (1959), and Venezuela (1967). For many years, Fidel Castro exerted tremendous influence on leftist movements across the globe. During the 1967 meeting of the Organization of Latin America Solidarity in Havana, Castro made headlines by giving a speech in which he publicly rejected the idea that elections and peaceful political competition could lead to revolutionary change, emphasizing that the only path forward in Latin America was guerrilla warfare. In that same year, his comrade and guerrilla icon, Ernesto Che Guevara, was killed in Bolivia, where he had gone to try to spur a revolution.

Several studies have addressed the reasons that individuals join guerrilla groups. A common answer points to grievances such as economic deprivation, inequality, and marginalization from politics. For instance, in-depth interviews with dozens of Colombian guerrillas revealed that the most common motivation expressed by these individuals were concerns about social and economic injustice and inequality.[2] But, as we know, joining guerrilla groups is risky and entails severe costs. Individuals who share the group's goals and want it to achieve its desired outcome would presumably enjoy the rewards associated with the group's success, regardless of whether they actively join the struggle. Moreover, the probability of success is most likely unaffected by an individual's effort. That being the case, joining a guerrilla group may seem irrational.

Academics have provided various explanations for why, despite this challenge, people still become part of armed revolutionary movements. Early works emphasized that participation in such hazardous endeavors hinged on selective incentives, such as gaining power, status, land, or money.[3] These studies tended to emphasize the importance of leaders—political entrepreneurs—who, after building a reputation for being capable and committed, use selective incentives to facilitate collective action.[4] These types of incentives have played a relevant role in recruitment into most Latin American guerrilla groups, such as the FARC in Colombia.

Scholars have also noted that the risks and costs of nonparticipation can be substantial and have underlined that an individual's consideration of personal security can be an important motivation for joining guerrilla groups.[5] In many instances, individuals joined because it helped them avoid violence perpetrated by other actors, such as paramilitaries, death squads, or the country's army. Indiscriminate repression in places such as El Salvador, Guatemala, and Nicaragua drove many to join revolutionary movements. Investigations have also revealed that some guerrilla groups, such as the FARC in Colombia, used intimidation and the threat of violence to forcibly recruit child soldiers.[6]

Other explanations have stressed the importance of belonging to communities. One perspective holds that the development of norms that encourage participation in group actions (i.e., doing one's fair share) are crucial because they foster participation when members consider success likely.[7] If individuals believe that enough members of their community will join the uprising, then they will find it in their interest to participate. Another perspective underlines the importance of the social networks that develop in communities with strong collective identities. According to this view, knowing that others in the community are participating in the insurgency, that contributors can be identified, and that effective social sanctions and rewards are in place promotes cooperation.[8]

Other studies explaining participation in guerrilla groups have underlined the psychological benefits derived from, among other things, a sense of duty to class, religion, humanity, or revolutionary brotherhood.[9] In her study of El Salvador, political scientist Elisabeth J. Wood argues that participation in insurgent groups hinged on the emotional benefits it provided to individuals.[10] Participating in an insurgency allowed individuals to express their defiance against long-resented authorities and their indignation at perceived injustices. According to her, "moral outrage, pride, and pleasure, along with more conventional reasons such as access to land, impelled the insurgency despite the high risks and uncertainty."[11]

Most guerrilla groups failed to recruit large numbers of followers and were either disbanded in a relatively short period of time or defeated by the respective country's armed forces. Counterinsurgency operations often received support from the U.S., which sought to suppress the spread of communist influence in the region. Beginning in 1961, the U.S. Army School of the Americas—located at Fort Gulick in the Panama Canal zone—provided counterinsurgency training to military personnel from Latin American countries. It eventually became highly controversial, as many of the graduates from this school went on to commit gross human rights violations in their respective countries. In 2001, the School of the Americas was shut down and replaced by the Western Hemisphere Institute for Security Cooperation.

There were two waves of guerrilla activity in Latin America: one in the mid-1960s, which spread across many countries but was relatively short-lived, and a second one in the 1970s, which was particularly intense in Central America (Nicaragua, El Salvador, and Guatemala), Colombia, and Peru. Sociologist Timothy P. Wickham-Crowley examined these events, seeking to understand what made some of these movements successful when most failed.[12] He concluded that three characteristics were crucial to the success of a guerrilla movement: (i) strong and sustained peasant support, (ii) military strength, and (iii) the ability to shift the support of the non-peasant population away from the incumbent government and to their movement.

According to Wickham-Crowley, peasant support for the guerrillas was most likely when they lacked ownership of the land where they worked (e.g., sharecroppers, migrant workers, and squatters) or when they were dislocated from their land. The balance of military strength between the guerrillas and government forces depended on external support, internal financing, and the nature of the regime in place. For example, U.S. support for counterinsurgency operations (such as in Guatemala during the 1960s) and military aid (such as in El Salvador during the mid-1980s) strengthened the position of government forces. The withdrawal of U.S. military support for the dictatorship of Anastasio Somoza Debayle and substantial international backing for the insurgency helped the Sandinistas defeat the Nicaraguan government in 1979. The shifting of mass loyalties in favor of the guerrillas was always difficult to achieve. Governments could weaken incentives to join guerrilla groups by allowing elections, legalizing political parties, declaring amnesties, or adopting reformist policies, such as land reforms. Guerrillas had greater difficulty winning popular support when they did not adopt relatively moderate programs or allies and when they shunned cross-class alliances.

The conditions favoring the emergence and success of guerrilla movements were also addressed by sociologist Jeff Goodwin.[13] He noted that guerrillas became strong in countries with exclusionary governments (i.e., with narrow constituencies) that avoided reformist policies and repressed political opponents. Similar to Wickham-Crowley, he believes that regime type matters.[14] More specifically, he argued that personalist regimes were less effective than military governments at confronting revolutionary challenges because their armies tended to have less competent fighting forces, their arbitrary practices often antagonized economic elites, and they were less likely to find democratization a viable strategy to decreasing support for insurgency groups. While most military officers can return to the barracks after democratization to continue their careers in the armed forces, leaders of personalist dictatorships and their inner cliques have few options besides exile, the prospect of which makes them cling to power.[15] According to Goodwin, the Sandinistas in Nicaragua were able to win the war primarily because they confronted a personalist dictatorship "that increasingly alienated large sections of the Nicaraguan bourgeoisie and political moderates."[16]

The rest of this chapter reviews some of the main events behind the Cuban and Nicaraguan revolutions, wherein guerrillas were able to seize state power, and the cases of El Salvador and Guatemala, wherein strong guerrilla movements ultimately failed to win the conflicts. Lastly, it addresses the peace process between the guerrillas and the government in Colombia.

The Cuban Revolution

The **Cuban Revolution** brought to an end the personalist dictatorship of Fulgencio Batista, a sergeant who became a prominent player in Cuban politics after leading a military coup in 1933. In the elections of 1940, Batista won the presidency for a four-year term and while in power cultivated the support of the country's armed forces. After being out of office for eight years, Batista decided to run again in the election of 1952, but that time around, he appeared unlikely to win. A few months before the presidential election was supposed to take place, he led a military coup that installed him as the country's ruler. Once in power, Batista ruled as an authoritarian, persecuting and jailing political opponents.

The U.S. government had a close relationship with Batista, who was viewed as a strong ally and a committed anti-communist. Economic links were also strong. At that time, U.S. companies played a prominent role in Cuba's economy, owning a substantial percentage of sugar plantations, cattle ranches, mines, public utilities, and railways.

About a year after the military coup that brought Batista to power, a group of opponents to the regime organized an attack on the Moncada military barracks. The leader of the insurrection was Fidel Castro, who, together with his brother Raúl and over a hundred recruits, fought to capture the weapons stored there, which they intended to use to trigger an uprising against the government. Fidel Castro was a lawyer and politician who had been active in the reformist Orthodox Party. After the 1952 coup, he began to organize a clandestine movement to depose Batista from power. The assault on the barracks failed, and the Castro brothers, along with many of their supporters, ended up in jail. While imprisoned, Fidel Castro renamed his political organization the **26th of July Movement** (**M-26-7**) to commemorate the attack on the Moncada barracks.

In May of 1955, a few months after winning a rigged presidential election boycotted by opposition parties, Batista decided to grant amnesty to Fidel Castro and the other members of the group responsible for the attack on the Moncada barracks. There are several reasons why he might have done so, such as appeasing political dissenters and amnesty groups, but what it reveals is that he felt sufficiently secure and did not consider Fidel Castro to be a serious threat to his rule. Later that year, as the government intensified its repression of political opponents, Fidel Castro and his brother Raúl decided to leave Cuba for Mexico, where they would organize to fight again.

In November of 1956, the Castro brothers and 80 other fighters sailed for Cuba to begin a guerrilla war against the Batista dictatorship. Among the insurgents were the Argentine Ernesto Che Guevara and the Cuban activist Camilo Cienfuegos, who had joined the revolutionary movement while in Mexico and who would become iconic guerrilla fighters. The battered yacht that transported the revolutionaries, called *Granma*, ran aground on the Cuban coast on December 2, 1956. The insurgents then proceeded to go inland, but government forces soon caught up with them and killed most of the fighters. The survivors fled to remote areas of the mountainous Sierra Maestra, where they reorganized the guerrilla force.

Over the next two years, the guerrillas grew in strength and succeeded in winning many supporters. The peasants of the Sierra Maestra were among the first to collaborate with the insurgents. A large portion of the peasants were squatters who lacked legal titles over their plots and were frequently targeted for eviction.[17] Fidel Castro promised them an agrarian reform that would provide them with security over the land where they worked.[18] The revolutionaries also found sympathy among Catholic priests, some of whom accompanied the guerrillas to the mountains.[19] When Fidel Castro was faced with a weapons shortage, President José M. Figueres of Costa Rica sent him a plane filled with armaments.

In urban areas, there were a variety of groups, mainly comprised of middle-class individuals, that engaged in political demonstrations and riots against the Batista regime. The urban branch of the M-26-7 movement, led in the Oriente province by Frank País, recruited many supporters, distributed propaganda, and prepared the ground for the arrival of Castro's forces to the cities. The Student Revolutionary Directorate, led by José Antonio Echeverría, engaged in violent acts against the government, including an attack on Batista's presidential palace. Another group, called the Civic Resistance Movement and led by Manuel Ray Rivero, also committed sabotage and other violent actions against the government. Both Frank País and José Antonio Echeverría were killed by government forces in 1957, but the urban armed opposition they helped to build continued to grow stronger.

In contrast, the Batista government was becoming progressively weaker. Repression increased, including the arbitrary detention of opponents, torture, and extrajudicial killings. A significant percentage of the middle classes began to withdraw their support for the government and to consider the rebel movement as a viable alternative. Exiles and members of the opposition gathered in places such as Miami and Caracas to strategize about how to confront the government. The Cuban army, which had quelled one internal uprising against Batista in 1956 and another in 1957, appeared ineffectual in their confrontation with the guerrillas, despite their greater numbers. Untrained recruits, outdated weaponry, and internal disunity made them vulnerable. Moreover, since the 1952 coup, Batista had transformed the armed forces into his own personal guard, corrupting the officer corps and diminishing their professionalism. Several rank-and-file soldiers ended up deserting to the guerrillas' cause.[20]

The U.S. government became increasingly reluctant to continue its support of Batista. It lobbied the Cuban government to end its suspension of constitutional guarantees and press censorship, which it did, temporarily. In March of 1958, after government repression intensified and Batista again suspended constitutional guarantees, the U.S. government decided to impose an arms embargo. Its reasons included the failure on the part of the Cuban government to create conditions for fair elections and the use of arms shipped by the U.S. in attacking domestic insurgents, which violated existing agreements. The embargo further diluted the readiness of the Cuban armed forces.

The M-26-7 guerrillas were successful in presenting themselves as ideologically rather moderate, despite having some known communists in their ranks, such as Ernesto Che Guevara and Raúl Castro. Batista tried to paint the guerrillas as communists, but Fidel Castro publicly rejected such accusations. The communist party of Cuba (the PSP) had, in fact, collaborated with Batista in the 1940s, opposed the actions of Castro's M-26-7 at the beginning of the insurrection, and only joined the battle when the armed struggle was almost over. Fidel Castro presented himself as a moderate, promising liberal-democratic reforms in addition to more radical social policies. Herbert L. Matthews, a *New York Times* journalist who had interviewed Fidel Castro in his hideout in the Sierra Maestra, described him as a man with "strong ideas of liberty, democracy, social justice, the need to restore the Constitution [and the need] to hold elections" and quoted him as saying, "Above all, we are fighting for a democratic Cuba and an end to the dictatorship."[21]

Fulgencio Batista finally left Cuba on January 1, 1959, following a series of military defeats. Opposition groups proceeded to take over the country's main cities, and Fidel Castro entered Havana on January 8. In the following weeks, thousands of individuals associated with the Batista regime were killed by firing squads. Massive rallies were organized in support of "revolutionary justice."

The new revolutionary government announced that it would rule by decree for about two years, after which, it hoped, the country would be ready for elections. Liberal lawyers Manuel Urrutia and José Miró were named as president and prime minister respectively, while Fidel Castro became the commander-in-chief of the armed forces. This arrangement did not last long. Five weeks later, Fidel Castro replaced Miró as prime minister and, in July of 1959, Osvaldo Dorticós replaced Urrutia as president. Both Miró and Urrutia had rejected the progressive radicalization of the revolutionary government and ultimately fled the country to live in exile.

During the first two years after the revolution, Fidel Castro strengthened his position within the government and began the implementation of major policy reforms. The government passed a law allowing for the expropriation of property belonging to individuals associated with the Batista dictatorship, later amending it to include the property of individuals guilty of counterrevolutionary activities. Expropriations and nationalizations of public utilities followed. A new land reform limited the size of landholdings and prohibited foreign ownership of sugar plantations. Expropriated land was to be redistributed to the peasants or put into the hands of state-run communes. The Cuban government then moved to expropriate land owned by U.S. sugar companies.

In early 1960, Cuba signed a pact with the Soviet Union that included a substantial loan in addition to sugar, trade, and oil agreements. When Soviet oil arrived in Cuba, the U.S. and other foreign companies refused to refine it. Castro retaliated by nationalizing the refineries (ESSO, Texaco, and Shell), which prompted President Eisenhower to slash the remaining quota of sugar imported from Cuba. The conflict escalated during August and September of 1960, when Castro moved to nationalize all U.S. businesses on the island, including U.S. banks. Over the following years, laws restricting private property rights continued to be passed, culminating with the virtual elimination of private property in 1968.

The Cuban government also began to curb press and individual freedoms. The target of the government purges now extended beyond former Batista supporters to include those in disagreement with the direction taken by the revolution. One of the first victims was Hubert Matos, a moderate guerrilla leader who had been named military governor of the province of Camagüey. Matos had complained to Castro about the increasing influence of communists in the revolutionary government before resigning from his appointment. Castro then publicly accused Matos of being a traitor and arrested him. After a five-day trial, Matos was sentenced to 20 years in jail. Matos's arrest followed the defection of Pedro Díaz Lanz, a former chief of the Revolutionary Air Force of Cuba, who became a vocal opponent of the influence of communists in the new government. When a group of students protested the visit of a Soviet diplomat in early 1960, they were quickly expelled from the University of Havana.[22] Then, in September, Castro announced the establishment of the infamous neighborhood watch committees, called Committees for the Defense of the Revolution. They would be in charge of monitoring counterrevolutionary activity, intelligence gathering, mobilizing against foreign incursions, and more mundane community activities.

The U.S. broke diplomatic relations with Cuba in January of 1961. By that time, thousands of Cubans had fled the island, dissatisfied with the course of the revolution. Nine months earlier, President Eisenhower had ordered the Central Intelligence Agency (CIA) to begin the training of Cuban exiles for a possible attack against Castro's government. That attack took place on April 17, 1961, a few months after John F. Kennedy had assumed the presidency. An exile force of around 1,200 men landed on the Bay of Pigs, armed with weapons provided by the CIA. The Cuban military quickly overpowered them and sank most of their ships. Around a hundred were killed and the rest were captured. The U.S. did not provide the air support that some expected, and the population of the island, still supportive of Castro, did not rise up in support of the exile force.

The failure of the U.S.–orchestrated attack had significant consequences. For instance, it heightened anti-American sentiment among the Cuban population. While Cubans resented the support given by the U.S. to Batista's government, the arms embargo of 1958 had helped to reduce their animosity. The failed invasion, however, prompted widespread anti-American demonstrations. It also helped to strengthen Fidel Castro's domestic position and weakened the incentives of the Cuban leadership to present themselves to the world as moderate reformists. The U.S.

government lost its ability to influence internal political developments in Cuba, and domestic opponents of the radical leftwing shift in Cuba became discredited. In December of 1961, Fidel Castro publicly declared that he was a Marxist-Leninist, thereby becoming the first openly communist head of government in Latin America.[23]

The failed invasion also strengthened the belief that Cuba needed to maintain a vigilant stance against the opponents of the revolution and that a future U.S. invasion was a very likely event. In early 1962, the Soviets and Castro discussed the idea of deploying ballistic missiles equipped with nuclear weapons into Cuba. Castro and the Soviets thought this would be a strong deterrent against a possible U.S. attack. On August 29, 1962, a U.S. spy plane flying over Cuba discovered evidence that the installation of Soviet missiles on Cuban soil had begun. This prompted the famous **Cuban Missile Crisis**, which pitted the U.S. against Cuba and the Soviet Union.

President Kennedy stated that the U.S. would not tolerate the deployment of offensive weapons in Cuba. He then proceeded to place military forces on the highest level of alert and ordered a naval blockade of Cuba. After a few tense days when nuclear war seemed to be a real possibility, the Soviets agreed to withdraw the weapons from Cuba in return for the promise that the U.S. would not invade the island. Fidel Castro resented having been excluded from the agreement reached by President Kennedy and Soviet leader Nikita Khrushchev and losing the offensive weapons. The resolution to the crisis ended up straining Cuban–Soviet relations.

Both the **Bay of Pigs invasion** and the Cuban Missile Crisis influenced subsequent political developments. For many, the failure of the CIA-backed exile force to bring down the government showed that a small country could defy the U.S. and emerge triumphantly. Revolutionaries elsewhere took notice. In addition, the alliance with the Soviet Union alienated moderate progressives in Latin America and frightened conservative forces. It made governments less likely to dismiss the actions of insurgent groups, no matter how small. Repression, often indiscriminate, became a typical response. Moreover, the U.S. now perceived Cuba as a Soviet beachhead in Latin America and considered the activities of pro-Cuba insurgent groups in the region as a matter of national security. This fostered political and military support for anti-communist regimes, many of which were dictatorships.

Among the left, a rising star from the Cuban revolution was Argentine Ernesto Che Guevara. In 1961, his book *Guerrilla Warfare* was published. The book described the lessons he had drawn from his experience fighting in Cuba and became an instant best-seller. Guevara noted that the Cuban revolution offered three central lessons for revolutionary movements in Latin America. The first was that a popular guerrilla force was capable of winning a war against a national army. The second was that insurgent groups could prime the conditions for a revolution; there was no need to wait until all the desirable conditions for a revolution were met. The third was that the armed confrontation should take place primarily in the countryside, not the urban centers. Soon after, many of the guerrilla groups that emerged elsewhere in the world became convinced of the idea that a small vanguard group could build enough support to prompt a revolution.

In the end, most guerrilla groups were defeated, and thousands of young Latin Americans died trying to bring about a revolution. Guevara himself would be captured and killed in Bolivia in 1967 after his small guerrilla band failed to win support from the local peasantry. Fidel Castro died of natural causes in 2016, with his early promise of democratic elections in Cuba never materializing. The only other successful guerrilla-led revolution in Latin America took place in Nicaragua. That is the topic of the next section.

The Nicaraguan Revolution

The revolution in Nicaragua brought to end a long-lived dictatorship led by the Somoza family. Anastacio Somoza García, the head of the Nicaraguan national guard and a former minister, first came to power after organizing a military coup in 1936. Three years earlier, he had orchestrated the assassination of Augusto Sandino, who was the leader of a nationalist rebellion against the 1927–1933 U.S. military occupation of Nicaragua. After the assassination of Anastacio Somoza García in 1956, his eldest son, Luis Somoza Debayle, became president. Following the death of Luis in 1967, his brother, Anastacio Somoza Debayle, became president. Either directly or through political figureheads, the Somoza family ran the country from 1936 until 1979, when the **Sandinista National Liberation Front (FSLN)** defeated the country's armed forces and captured the capital city of Managua.

The first Nicaraguan guerrillas entered the country from Honduras in 1959 and 1960. They were composed of only a few fighters and were defeated rather quickly by the National Guard. Survivors from those excursions and other individuals opposed to the Somoza regime gathered in Cuba to plan another attempt. In 1961, they formed a new guerrilla organization called the National Liberation Front that, two years later, morphed into the FSLN. Their members were profoundly inspired by the Cuban revolution, and several of them received military training on the island. Carlos Fonseca became the main leader of the FSLN, running the organization until November of 1976, when he was killed combating Somoza's forces. Fonseca, who was a former member of the Nicaraguan Communist Party (PSN) and who had spent most of the early 1970s living in exile in Cuba, sought to reconcile the nationalist ideals inspired by Sandino's fight with Marxist thought.[24]

The FSLN remained a relatively small force throughout the 1960s and, at some point in 1967, was almost wiped out by the national guard. The guerrillas had a difficult time gaining support among the peasantry and convincing other social groups in urban areas to shift their support to them.

Peasants' support for the FSLN began to grow in the early 1970s, particularly in the mountainous region of north-central Nicaragua. Wickham-Crowley notes that, as in Cuba, the areas of greater rural support for the guerrillas had a much-higher-than-normal proportion of squatters.[25] Displaced peasants living in the cities also assumed an important role in the urban uprising that preceded the downfall of the Somoza dictatorship.[26] The Association of Agricultural Workers (ATC), formed in 1978 and comprised of tens of thousands of members, helped to build a network of support for the guerrillas in the period before the fall of the Somoza regime.

Opposition to the government increased after a destructive earthquake hit the capital, Managua, in 1972, killing thousands of people and displacing about two-thirds of the city's residents. Somoza and his inner circle took advantage of the situation to capture lucrative contracts for rebuilding the city and stole significant portions of the foreign aid sent to the country.[27] This led to a significant backlash against the government and helped to move large sectors of the middle and upper classes to support the opposition.[28]

Government repression intensified during the 1970s, as the Sandinistas and other anti-Somoza groups became more active. In January of 1978, Pedro Joaquín Chamorro, the editor of the leading newspaper in Nicaragua and a vocal critic of the Somoza regime, was gunned down. The next day, tens of thousands rioted. Business organizations called for a two-week strike to protest the government's investigation of the crime and demanded Somoza's resignation. The government declared a state of siege and increased the repression of opponents. The death toll totaled approximately 3,000 lives.[29] One year later, Luis Medrano Flores, a prominent trade union leader, was assassinated by government soldiers as he handed out flyers encouraging people to attend religious masses in honor of Chamorro. The assassination of Chamorro bolstered the opposition to the regime, particularly among the urban middle classes.

After the mid-1970s, the Sandinistas—in particular, the "Tercerista" faction within the FSLN, which advocated alliances with middle and upper-class sectors against Somoza—became more successful at capturing international and domestic support. For example, in 1977, they promoted the formation of the so-called Group of Twelve, composed of a dozen prominent members of the establishment, which would go on to publicly advocate support for the FSLN. This group, which included businesspeople, lawyers, priests, and other professionals and intellectuals, helped to rally international opposition to the Somoza regime and worked to portray the FSLN as a moderate movement. In 1978, the Group of Twelve coalesced with the Democratic Liberation Union (UDEL; a political organization founded by the late Pedro Joaquín Chamorro), the Democratic Movement (formed by businessman Alfonso Robelo), the Social-Christian Party, and the Conservative Party to form the Broad Opposition Front (FAO). This front sought, unsuccessfully, to negotiate the resignation of Somoza. The Sandinistas also encouraged the formation of the movement People United, which was a collection of various unions, small leftist parties, student federations, and women's organizations. This group called for a popular uprising against the Somoza dictatorship.

Students also became actively involved in the Nicaraguan revolution. Several prominent leaders in the FSLN came from the student ranks. In the universities, the FSLN created the Revolutionary Student Federation, which would contribute to organizing and recruiting in urban areas. Anti-Somoza activism also extended to students in secondary schools.

Many progressive Christians gradually moved into the ranks of the FSLN. In 1973, a few Jesuit priests formed the Christian Revolutionary Movement, which was a left-wing organization supportive of the guerrillas. The hierarchy of the Catholic Church condemned the government's violent tactics, the use of torture, and the persecution of priests but did not side with the guerrillas. Once the FSLN defeated the Somoza government, three priests became part of the Sandinista cabinet: Ernesto Cardenal as minister of culture, Miguel D'Escoto as foreign minister, and Edgar Parrales as minister of social welfare.

As the Somoza regime weakened and opposition to the regime broadened, the U.S. government began to withdraw its long-standing support for the Nicaraguan dictatorship. In late 1978, it pushed for talks mediated by the Organization of American States to remove Anastasio Somoza from power and avoid a revolution that would install a leftist government and destroy the national guard.[30] This strategy failed. In early 1979, after increasing bilateral tension over human rights abuses, the U.S. cut all of its military and economic aid to the Somoza regime. The Organization of American States and the United Nations condemned Somoza, while several Latin American countries, such as Costa Rica, Venezuela, Panama, Colombia, and Cuba, provided some support for the Sandinistas.

The personalist regime of Somoza exacerbated the difficulty of finding a political solution. As noted earlier in this chapter, personalist regimes, as opposed to military regimes, seldom end with a negotiated transition to electoral democracy or a peaceful withdrawal from power. The dominant ruler and his inner clique have too much to lose by giving up control over the government and do not have many options besides exile. The kleptocratic character of the Somoza regime, particularly after the early 1970s, made things worse. As Goodwin remarks, Somoza's actions "drove elites and moderates into the revolutionary camp," and the personalist character of the dictatorial regime made it virtually impossible for a military coup to end his rule and stop the revolution.[31]

In many ways, the national guard operated as Somoza's personal force. Somoza kept the national guard relatively small to maintain better control over it; in the words of political scientist James Dunkerley, it was "large enough to seem ubiquitous in a small country and yet too small to develop an institutional ethic beyond loyalty to the commander."[32] According to Wickham-Crowley, Anastasio Somoza García removed any national guard officer who gained popularity, exhibited substantial personal ambition, or sought to professionalize the institution.[33] He also noted that the looting and theft of relief funds coming to the country after the 1972 earthquake severely weakened whatever legitimacy the national guard had left. In the late 1970s, when the fight against the insurgency became critical and supplies began to run out, many rank-and-file soldiers deserted.

In August of 1978, an FSLN commando took over the Nicaraguan National Palace while congress was in session. The Sandinistas captured a large number of prominent hostages and agreed to release them after payment of a substantial ransom, the release of several political prisoners, the broadcast of an FSLN document calling for a popular insurrection against the government, and safe passage for the hostage-takers out of the country. This event embarrassed the Nicaraguan government and emboldened the opposition.

The end of the Somoza regime accelerated after the three Sandinista factions, which had split in the aftermath of the death of Carlos Fonseca, reunified in March of 1979. By April, various guerrilla fronts had begun to push their way into the capital. The urban insurrection propagated and, in June, a general strike was called. On July 17, Anastasio Somoza Debayle finally resigned from power and fled to Miami. Two days later, the FSLN entered Managua, culminating the long struggle against the Somoza dictatorship.

The guerrilla insurrection that ended with the Nicaraguan revolution lasted two decades, resulting in approximately 35,000 fatalities in the final two years.[34] This was a much longer and deadlier conflict than in Cuba, where the death toll associated with the revolution has been estimated at around 5,000.

As in Cuba, the Nicaraguan guerrillas successfully built a multiclass coalition and defeated an increasingly isolated personalist dictatorship. The U.S., which had provided meaningful military and economic aid to the two countries, eventually withdrew support from the ruling dictators. Moreover, in neither case did the U.S. choose to intervene militarily to prevent the guerrillas from winning during their final offensive. Events following the guerrilla triumph in Nicaragua, however, differed in significant ways from what happened in Cuba.

Once the Sandinistas took control of the state, they established a provisional national reconstruction junta to formally lead the country, and a council of the state to act as a representative body. The FSLN dominated these organs, and the real power lay with its national directorate, which held veto power over policy decisions.

The new Sandinista government embarked on the difficult task of reactivating the economy and implementing deep social reforms. Soon after taking power, it confiscated around 2,000 farms belonging to the former dictator and turned them into state farms. Under pressure from the peasantry, an agrarian reform law was announced in 1981, which stated that the holdings of large landowners could be expropriated for land underutilization, sharecropping, or disinvestments. In addition, a decree established that the government could confiscate, without paying compensation, properties of any size that had been idle or abandoned for at least six months. Thousands of peasant families ended up with legal titles over land as a result of the agrarian reforms of the 1980s, while many of those whose lands were confiscated unsuccessfully tried to litigate, seeking restitution or compensation.[35] Large numbers of peasants also began working on state-run farms. The proportion of large and medium-sized private farms decreased markedly during the 1980s, but most of the land (about 60 percent) was still under private ownership.[36]

State involvement in the economy deepened with nationalizations in mining, forestry, fishery, banking, and foreign trade. These policies alienated moderates and conservatives who had been part of the broad anti-Somoza coalition. Many of them were already upset by the government's decision to postpone national elections until 1985. Non-Sandinistas held some positions in the appointed governmental organizations but, as a result of their lack of influence and policy disagreements, many of these sidelined politicians decided to resign.

The relationship with the U.S. began to sour as soon as Ronald Reagan assumed the presidency. The perception among the new administration in Washington was that the Sandinistas were too far to the left—a communist regime seeking to impose Cuban-style policies. In November of 1981, the U.S. president authorized covert support to the anti-Sandinista groups, labeled **Contras**, who were already gathered at the border with Honduras and receiving training from Argentine intelligence groups and the CIA. Reagan accused the Sandinistas of supporting the guerrillas in El Salvador and held them responsible for their crimes. The forces fighting the Sandinistas included the Nicaraguan Democratic Force (FDN), based at the Honduran border and composed primarily of former members of Somoza's national guard, and the Democratic Revolutionary Alliance (ARDE), based on the Costa Rican border and led by the ideologically moderate former Sandinistas commander, Edén Pastora. A group of indigenous peoples, mainly Miskitos who had been forcefully displaced from their homeland by the Sandinista government, also rose up in arms.

The U.S.–funded Contras engaged in several violent actions against the Sandinista government. In 1983, as the conflict escalated, the CIA became involved in the mining of Nicaragua's harbors. This event generated significant backlash within the U.S., where many questioned whether the Sandinistas actually posed a threat to U.S. interests. By 1984–1985, the Contras had failed to garner substantial support from Nicaraguans, were incapable of militarily holding territory, and had become involved in a number of human rights abuses, all of which contributed to the decision of the U.S. Congress to cut all aid to them. A political scandal, known as the **Iran–Contra Affair**, subsequently ensued. Senior members in the Reagan administration sold arms to Iran, which was prohibited by an arms embargo, to free U.S. hostages held in Lebanon and redirected part of the proceeds to fund the Contras, which was forbidden by Congress. The scandal led to the indictment of senior members in the Reagan administration and several convictions.

The Sandinista government responded to the escalation of the **Contra War** by calling for national elections to be held in November of 1984. The announcement was followed by a loosening of censorship and other press restrictions that the Sandinistas had put in place after their arrival to power. The harassment of opposition politicians also diminished as the day of the election approached. Daniel Ortega, who had been the most prominent leader of the Sandinistas since at least 1979, was the candidate of the FSLN. A handful of other small parties participated, but two prominent conservative candidates withdrew from the contest at the urging of the U.S. government. In the end, Ortega won the presidency with 67 percent of the vote in an election with an estimated turnout of 75 percent of the electorate.

Daniel Ortega's administration faced numerous challenges. The economic situation deteriorated, affected by the Contra War and economic mismanagement. Inflation skyrocketed, and budgetary constraints limited the reach of social programs. After the election, restrictions on the press resumed. In 1986, the government closed the main opposition newspaper, *La Prensa*, and the official radio station of the Catholic Church.[37] Both news outlets would reopen in 1987 as a result of regional negotiations undertaken by five Central American countries under the leadership of President Oscar Arias from Costa Rica. The agreement included provisions to promote peace negotiations with the Contras, protect human rights, end states of emergency, and conduct free and open elections.

Over the next two years, the government and the Contras would sign subsequent agreements to end the war and demobilize the insurgent forces. An agreement between the Miskitos and the government was reached in the latter part of the 1980s. The final death toll of the Contra War (1981–1989) was estimated to be somewhere between 30,000 to 43,000 fatalities.

The next presidential election, which took place in February of 1990, was supervised by a large number of international monitors, including the Organization of American States and the United Nations. Conservative parties agreed to participate and formed an alliance, called the National Opposition Union (UNO), to compete against the Sandinistas. To the surprise of many, the candidate of UNO, Violeta Chamorro (wife of slain newspaper editor, Pedro Joaquín Chamorro) was elected president with 55 percent of the vote in an election that had a turnout of 86 percent of eligible voters. The Sandinistas accepted defeat and turned the presidency over to the conservative coalition, which assumed power in April of 1990.

The transfer of power was a watershed event and provided evidence of the sharp difference between the path followed after the Nicaraguan revolution and the one followed after the Cuban revolution. After defeating Somoza, the Sandinistas did not embark in the widespread killing of former members of the regime. Instead, they organized a political party, competed in elections, and eventually transferred power to the opposition after losing at the ballot box. While individual rights and press freedoms were restricted, these policies were ultimately eased and did not come close to the draconic measures imposed by the Cuban regime led by Fidel Castro. The human rights record of the Sandinistas was poor but was still a marked improvement over the Somoza period and significantly better than that of neighboring El Salvador and Guatemala, which were engaged in their own fights against guerrillas. The next section addresses these conflicts.

Failed Revolutions in El Salvador and Guatemala

In El Salvador and Guatemala, the guerrillas became strong enough to pose a significant challenge to the governments, and the conflicts turned into bloody civil wars. However, both guerrilla movements failed to win their respective wars. The conflicts ended with the signing of peace agreements.

There are some fundamental differences between the conflicts in El Salvador and Guatemala and those in Nicaragua and Cuba. First, the guerrillas in the former countries confronted military rather than personalist regimes. As the conflicts escalated in the early 1980s, the armed forces withdrew from power and allowed semi-competitive elections to take place. Although the militaries acted autonomously from the civilian administrations and continued to exert indiscriminate repression, the political openings ultimately weakened the guerrillas. Progressive parties joined electoral contestation, and centrist Christian Democratic candidates won the presidency in both countries. These civilian regimes put in place nonviolent channels to voice grievances and participate politically, which negatively affected guerrilla recruitment and made the armed option less appealing to those seeking democratic and social reforms.

Second, the guerrillas in Nicaragua and Cuba successfully built multiclass coalitions to support their struggle. That did not happen in El Salvador or Guatemala—although Salvadorean guerrillas garnered comparatively greater support than those in Guatemala. Peasant groups, students, Christian activists, members of grassroots organizations, and (in the case of Guatemala) many indigenous people either joined the guerrillas or participated in political groups that supported them. However, as several scholars have noted, Salvadorean and Guatemalan elites did not embrace the revolutionaries.[38] In both countries, the landed elites remained highly cohesive and supportive of the military, and business elites consistently opposed the overtly Marxist guerrillas. In contrast to Nicaragua, there was considerably less urban support for the guerrillas in both Guatemala and El Salvador.

Third, the balance of military power was much more unfavorable to the Salvadorean and Guatemalan guerrillas. Government repression and the activities of death squads against those suspected of sympathizing with the guerrillas were far more extreme in El Salvador and Guatemala than in Nicaragua or Cuba. This indiscriminate repression weakened the guerrillas' military capabilities but helped them maintain support among sectors of the population that were victimized and outraged by the government's actions. Also crucial was the significant military and economic aid given by the U.S. to the respective governments. Increasing U.S. aid after the militaries of El Salvador and Guatemala announced their withdrawal from power helped the counterinsurgency efforts of the new governments.

El Salvador

The principal guerrilla force in El Salvador was the **Farabundo Martí National Liberation Front** (**FMLN**), formed in 1980 from five different guerrilla groups. The FMLN took its name from Farabundo Martí, a communist leader of the 1932 peasant uprising against the dictatorship of General Maximiliano Hernández Martínez, who was executed by the government after being captured. The oldest of its member groups was the Popular Forces of Liberation (FPL), which was established in 1970 by individuals who split from the Salvadorean Communist Party. The largest guerrilla group was the People's Revolutionary Army (ERP), which was formed in 1971 by former militants from the Communist and Christian Democratic parties as well as student groups. Meetings leading to the unification of the different factions took place in Havana, facilitated by the Cuban government.

Authoritarian regimes had governed El Salvador for decades. After the dictatorship of General Hernández Martinez (1931–1944), the armed forces continued to rule through a series of military-dominated political parties that competed in fraudulent elections. During the 1960s, right-wing death squads began to persecute social activists and politicians from opposition parties. Among those targeted were Christian Democrats, whose party had won the mayoral elections in the city of San Salvador. After the 1972 election, characterized by massive fraud, the military arrested, tortured, and sent into exile the main opposition candidate, the Christian Democrat Jose Napoleón Duarte, whom many considered the true winner of the electoral contest. He was accused of supporting a faction of young military officers who rebelled against the government's manipulation of the electoral results.

Repression increased markedly during the second half of 1970s, with security forces and death squads targeting political dissidents, including many religious activists and Catholic priests. According to Elizabeth J. Wood, many student and peasant activists, outraged by the violent repression, decided to join the guerrillas while others joined because "they had been identified as activists in opposition organizations and were therefore likely targets of government forces."[39]

In October of 1979, military officers in alliance with moderate civilian groups staged a coup. The new government junta announced elections to be held in 1982. At the same time, the military began a violent campaign against guerrillas and political dissidents, which led to over 22,000 people being murdered between 1979 and 1981.[40] Among the most prominent victims were the Catholic Archbishop of San Salvador, Oscar Romero, who was killed by a death squad while officiating mass in 1980, and three U.S. nuns and a lay worker, who were killed that same year by members of the Salvadorean national guard after being stopped at a military checkpoint. In January of 1981, the FMLN launched a major offensive, which ultimately failed to topple the government. The guerrillas then retreated to mountainous regions in the countryside. In December of 1981, a counterinsurgency unit of the Salvadorean military entered the village of El Mozote and slaughtered around 1,000 individuals, including a large number of children. The increasing violence prompted the resignation of some of the civilians who were part of the government.

Elections for a constituent assembly took place as scheduled in 1982. The assembly then selected a president from among three candidates nominated by the military. A popular election for the presidency took place in 1984. The elected president was Jose Napoleón Duarte of the Christian Democratic Party, who had returned from exile in the early 1980s to join the reformist military–civilian government that took power after the 1979 coup.

The U.S. government wanted to halt another leftist revolution and, to this end, stepped up its economic and military support for the government of El Salvador. During the Reagan administration, U.S. military assistance to El Salvador was, on average, about $107 million a year.[41] Thousands of Salvadorean soldiers were trained by the U.S. armed forces, including a substantial percentage of the officers' corps. The U.S. administration most often turned a blind eye to the human rights abuses committed by the Salvadorean security forces and the right-wing death-squads and publicly justified the government's crackdown on opponents. However, eventually, it put pressure on the Salvadorean military to halt such abuses and proceed with its political opening. In 1985, the U.S. Congress threatened to suspend all aid to the country if the military were to depose the newly elected president of El Salvador.[42]

The FLMN attempted another major offensive in 1989, after a presidential election brought to power a candidate from the right-wing Nationalist Republican Alliance (ARENA) party named Alfredo Cristiani. Amid fighting in the capital, a military unit entered the Catholic University and executed six Jesuit priests thought to be sympathetic to the guerrillas. This event made the government seem ineffectual and, to many, likely complicit.

Although the guerrillas failed to capture the capital, it became clear that the armed forces, despite significant U.S. aid, could not end the conflict militarily. The offensive also left the guerrillas weakened; not only had they suffered significant military losses, but it also became clear that their level of support among the population was not sufficiently broad. The FMLN had been losing members since the early 1980s, and some of their violent tactics had prompted repudiation from leftist groups engaged in the process of democratization. They used kidnappings and targeted assassinations to a greater degree than the Nicaraguan Sandinistas, which made the prospects of a multi-class alliance less viable. Among their victims were several elected mayors, the attorney general of El Salvador, captured civilians, and four off-duty U.S. Marines killed in 1985 at an outdoor cafe.[43] The FMLN also had greater internal conflicts, which, on occasion, turned violent.

By the late 1980s, a stalemate seemed to have developed. While, for most of the **Salvadorean Civil War**, the U.S. government pushed for a military defeat of the guerrillas, after the arrival of George H.W. Bush to the presidency in 1989, it began to advocate for a negotiated solution to the conflict.

A peace agreement between the guerrillas of the FMLN and the government of El Salvador began to be negotiated in 1990 and was finally reached in 1992. The United Nations played an instrumental role in mediating the peace talks. In the end, U.S. officials persuaded Salvadorean officials to accept significant concessions, while diplomats from Colombia, Mexico, Venezuela, and Spain worked for days to facilitate a compromise.[44] The agreement involved a ceasefire, disarmament, and demobilization of the guerrillas as well as provisions to reform the armed forces, the police, and the judicial system. Social programs to assist ex-combatants were also put in place. A truth commission was established to investigate the civil war and report on violations of human rights, and an amnesty law was agreed upon and then passed in 1993, addressing crimes committed by all sides during the civil war. The peace agreement also called for institutional reforms to guarantee free and fair elections and the legalization of the FMLN as a political party.

As in Nicaragua, the end of the war transformed the guerrillas into contenders in a civilian electoral democracy. In the subsequent presidential election of 1994, the FMLN candidate won 25 percent of the vote in the first round and 32 percent in the runoff. In the 2009 elections, the FMLN won the presidency of El Salvador for the first time.

Guatemala

In Guatemala, the first guerrillas emerged in the early 1960s. Leftist military officers, who had participated in a failed coup against the dictatorship ruling the country, organized the 13th of November Revolutionary Movement, named after the day of their 1960 insurrection. Not long after its creation, this guerrilla group joined a student organization and members of the communist Guatemalan Party of Labor (PGT) to form the Rebel Armed Forces (FAR). The guerrillas became active in mountainous areas in the southeast and jungle areas of the north as well as in the capital, Guatemala City. Their military strength, however, was somewhat limited.

Counterinsurgency operations began to take place soon after the emergence of the guerrillas. The election of a civilian president in 1966 did not lessen the conflict; the military continued to dominate politics and escalated its counterinsurgency efforts. After a series of kidnappings for ransom by the guerrillas, the U.S. helped to establish an urban task force to deal with the insurgents. U.S. helicopters were used in the stepped-up military campaign, and U.S. soldiers accompanied Guatemalan troops. In March of 1966, the Guatemalan security forces kidnapped, tortured, and killed the leader of the PGT and more than two dozen party militants. By 1967, the Guatemalan armed forces and their local associates had created death squads that carried out kidnappings, torture, and executions of real and alleged guerrillas and political dissidents, as noted in intelligence reports detailed by the U.S. Department of State.[45]

In 1968, the FAR assassinated the U.S. ambassador to Guatemala, John Gordon Mein, in what appeared to have been a botched kidnapping attempt.[46] That same year, the armed forces undertook a major offensive against the guerrillas, which resulted in the death of around 10,000 civilians.[47] The first phase of the insurgency (1962–1968) came to an end with the virtual defeat of the guerrillas.

In subsequent years, the armed forces and death squads continued to persecute and kill political dissidents and insurgent cells while the guerrillas carried out urban attacks. In 1970, the ambassador from West Germany was kidnapped and subsequently killed by members of the FAR. Death squads retaliated, killing a prominent leftist politician. At around that time, a new communist guerrilla group, the Guerrilla Army of the Poor (EGP), surfaced in the northern region of El Quiché.

By the end of the 1970s, the various guerrilla groups had reorganized, and their membership had begun to grow again. The main support came from peasant groups (e.g., landless and migratory peasants, as in El Salvador) rather than from the urban sectors. Government repression and violence by right-wing death squads, which had somewhat decreased in the mid-1970s, also began to climb. Many assassinations took place around El Quiché in the Mayan regions where guerrillas had become more active.

The conflict escalated exponentially in the early 1980s. The Sandinista victory in neighboring Nicaragua, the emergence of another guerrilla group called the Revolutionary Organization of Armed People (ORPA), and increased support for the guerrillas in Mayan areas worried President General Romeo Lucas García. The government responded with increasing violence against guerrillas and suspected political dissidents. As the conflict worsened, the guerrillas of the FAR, EGP, and ORPA coalesced with the PGT into an umbrella organization called **Guatemalan National Revolutionary Unity (URNG)**. While the UNRG succeeded in gaining substantial support in some rural areas, it was unable to break the cohesion of the elite and failed to gain the support of relevant portions of the urban middle classes or business groups.

In March of 1982, General Efraín Ríos Montt deposed General Lucas García in a military coup and proceeded to escalate the repression to unprecedented levels. Entire villages were massacred, and indigenous people became one of the primary targets of the counterinsurgency. Ríos Montt created civilian defense patrols to work alongside the military in the fight against the guerrillas. These civilian forces would become involved in many of the war's atrocities. The number of assassinations and "disappearances" peaked in 1982. A significant number of those killed were members of the Ixil indigenous community. Most of their villages were devastated, their farmlands burnt, and their livestock killed, and thousands became displaced.

At the end of 1983, another coup removed Ríos Montt from power and, the following year, there were elections for a constituent assembly. Presidential and congressional elections took place in 1985, leading to a new civilian president, Vinicio Cerezo, from the Christian Democratic Party. This political opening ended up weakening support for the guerrilla's insurgency strategy. Their number dropped from between 6,000 to 8,000 combatants in the early 1980s to around 3,000 in the late 1980s.[48] And while the Guatemalan armed forces continued their counterinsurgency campaign and remained highly influential politically, the overall level of repression and the number of murders of political dissidents dropped markedly in comparison to the early 1980s.

The first steps toward a negotiated peace were taken by the Guatemalan government in 1987, but the armed forces worked to impede progress and, by the end of the year, guerrilla attacks increased once again. Direct bilateral negotiations between the URNG and the government took place in 1991, but the process stalled. Then, in 1994, the United Nations began to mediate the process of reaching an agreement and, in December of 1996, a final accord was signed by the government of Guatemala and the URNG. The agreement concluded a civil war that had begun in the early 1960s and had caused tremendous hardships for the Guatemalan population.

The agreement included reforms to the military, police, and judicial branch as well as the elimination of the civilian defense patrols. The URNG agreed to demobilize its forces under the observation of the United Nations. In addition, the agreement provided for a constitutional reform that recognized the identity and rights of indigenous people (Maya, Garifuna, and Xica) and the multiethnic and multilingual character of the nation. It also established the United Nations Mission for the Verification of Human Rights, which oversaw the peace process in Guatemala until 2004.

An important aspect of the peace agreement involved the creation of the Commission for Historical Clarification (a truth commission), which was empowered to examine past human rights violations and acts of violence. However, the commission did not have the authority to take the perpetrators to court. In its final report, titled *Guatemala: Memory of Silence*, it was established that the **Guatemalan Civil War** that started in 1962 had caused over 200,000 deaths and displaced between 500,000 to 1.5 million people.

It also identified a total of 42,275 victims (including children), of which 56 percent had been arbitrarily executed. The study also found that 83 percent of these victims were indigenous Mayans and concluded that state forces and paramilitaries were responsible for 93 percent of the human rights violations and acts of violence documented in the report. Among the crimes reported were 626 massacres attributed to the Guatemalan armed forces. The report also highlighted various human rights violations committed by the guerrillas.

U.S. military aid and training for the Guatemalan security forces that committed the human rights violations were also discussed by the commission. In 1999, President Bill Clinton visited Guatemala and apologized for the U.S. role during the war. He said, "It is important that I state clearly that support for military forces or intelligence units which engaged in violent and widespread repression of the kind described in the report was wrong, and the United States must not repeat that mistake."[49]

The peace agreement transformed the URNG guerrillas into a political party. But unlike the Sandinistas in Nicaragua or the FMLN in El Salvador, the UNRG never received substantial electoral support nor did it capture the presidency. Nonetheless, it continued to participate in the electoral process and win seats in the national legislature.

Guerrillas and the Peace Process in Colombia

Colombia has had three main guerrilla groups: the FARC, the **ELN (National Liberation Army)**, and the **M-19 (the 19th of April Movement)**. The motives for the emergence of the guerrilla insurgency are likely the result of a combination of factors, including the violence that continued to affect rural areas in the aftermath of the 1948–1958 civil war, the political exclusion felt by the left in the semi-competitive context of the 1960s and early 1970s, the impact of the Cuban revolution, and socioeconomic conditions (e.g., rural poverty, social exclusion, displacements, land ownership) that triggered demands for deep reforms.

The most prominent Colombian guerrilla was the FARC, which was formed in 1964 by Manuel Marulanda and other communist fighters after escaping from a government raid on their rural community. Peasant enclaves under the control of communist groups had formed during the civil war that took place in the country between 1948 and 1958. During that civil war, typically known as *La Violencia*, the Conservative Party and its allies fought against the Liberal Party and its allies, with the Communist Party also becoming a target of violence. The war ended with a power-sharing pact between the Liberal and Conservative Parties, known as the National Front, which lasted from 1958 until 1974. After the war ended, several rural communities remained beyond the control of the national government, including some run by communist organizations. This is where the FARC originated. As with other peasant-based guerrilla groups, one of its main demands was land reform.

Until the early 1980s, the FARC remained a relatively small force that was active in a limited area of the country. But in the following years, it extended its operational area, and its membership increased significantly, reaching an estimated 18,000 fighters in the late 1990s.[50] Their expansion was partly the result of an increase in their economic resources—derived from kidnappings for ransom, extortion, and proceeds from the illicit drug trade—and the relative inefficacy of the government's counterinsurgency activities. Several scholars have found FARC violence to have been more prevalent in areas of weak state presence.[51]

The course of the conflict began to change under the presidency of Álvaro Uribe (2002–2010). The modernization of the armed forces, which had begun in the late 1990s, intensified. Better training, improvements in budgetary resources, increased police presence, and more effective counter-insurgency strategies turned the tide in favor of the government. The FARC suffered some significant losses among its top leadership, and the number of kidnappings, terrorist attacks, and homicides dropped sharply. The weakening of the guerrillas continued under Uribe's successor, President Juan Manuel Santos (2010–2018); under his leadership, the peace agreement with the FARC was finally reached. By the time the agreement was signed in 2016, the number of FARC fighters had dropped to about 8,000 individuals.

The second largest guerrilla group was the ELN, which was formed in 1964 by a group of communist activists and students who had trained in Cuba and were inspired by that country's revolution. One of the most prominent leaders of the ELN was the Catholic priest, Camilo Torres, who died in combat in 1966. By the early 1970s, the ELN had suffered signifi-cant defeats and was almost extinct. As with the FARC, its membership and areas of influence began to grow in the 1980s and rose significantly during the 1990s. By the end of that decade, the ELN membership peaked with between 4,000 and 5,000 fighters.[52] Their economic resources also came from kidnappings and extortions, which they would exert from the energy and mining companies working in their areas of influence. As with the FARC, their membership and areas of influence decreased significantly dur-ing the Uribe presidency.

Another prominent guerrilla group was the 19th of April Movement (M-19). It differed from the other two groups in that it was primarily an urban guerrilla group that advocated for a populist nationalism of the left, rather than a peasant-based guerrilla group with Marxist ideology. The group was formed by several leftist militants who believed that the presi-dential election of April 19, 1970, had been stolen from the populist can-didate favored by the left, the former dictator Rojas Pinilla, in favor of the establishment's candidate—hence its name, M-19.

In the mid-1970s, the M-19 began to kidnap businesspeople and family members of the country's elites. They kidnapped and killed the president of the Colombian Workers Confederation, José Raquel Mercado;

participated in various high-profile robberies; and attacked the embassy of the Dominican Republic, where they took 50 hostages, including several ambassadors. Their most famous action was an attack on the Colombian Palace of Justice, which culminated in the murder of 12 members of the Supreme Court. It was later revealed by a truth commission's investigation of these events that the attack had been financed by drug traffickers seeking to dispose of incriminating evidence that would have facilitated their extradition to the U.S. to face charges. In the mid-1980s, the M-19 had an estimated 2,000 fighters.[53]

In Colombia's complex conflict, another set of violent organizations played a prominent role: right-wing paramilitary forces. These groups emerged as self-defense forces in the early 1980s, organized by landowners, cattle ranchers, and others targeted by guerrillas and dissatisfied with government policies dealing with the insurgency. Several of these groups fused into the United Self-Defense Forces (AUC) in the mid-1990s. Several members of rural self-defense civilian forces, formed legally under the auspices of the government, joined the AUC after a ruling from the constitutional court severely limited their permitted activities. The paramilitaries were initially financed by regional elites but later resorted to illegal activities—mainly the drug trade. From the beginning, there were several links between paramilitaries and the drug cartels. Human rights organizations have also accused the government's security forces of complicity with the AUC.

The paramilitaries targeted not only actual and alleged guerrillas and their leftist sympathizers but also government officials, journalists, priests, academics, and social activists. Thousands of peasants were forcibly displaced by the actions of the AUC. It is estimated that by the end of the 1990s, most of the politically motivated assassinations in Colombia were caused by paramilitary forces.[54] By the time they entered peace negotiations with the government in 2003, the paramilitaries could boast of between 15,000 and 20,000 fighters.

Before moving on to discuss the **peace agreements** between the government and these armed groups, it is important to note a fundamental difference between the conflict in Colombia and those previously discussed in this chapter. Unlike in Cuba, Nicaragua, El Salvador, and Guatemala, the guerrillas in Colombia did not confront a dictatorial regime. While political competition during the National Front era was somewhat restricted as a result of the power-sharing agreement between the Liberal and Conservative Parties, contested elections have been the norm since 1958.

Peace Agreements

The first substantial pact between the government of Colombia and the FARC took place in 1984, when both parties agreed to a ceasefire. The agreement did not require the demobilization of forces or the renouncement of the armed struggle but gave members of the FARC the option to embrace electoral political competition. This led to the creation of a new political party, the Patriotic Union, formed by prominent members of the FARC and the Colombian Communist Party. In the presidential election of 1986, the Patriotic Union received only 4.5 percent of the vote, but in subsequent regional elections, 16 mayors and over 200 council members from the party won office. The ceasefire agreement between the FARC and the government fell apart in 1987, and violent confrontations restarted. The Patriotic Union continued to participate in elections, despite the assassination of many of its members by right-wing death squads, drug traffickers, and others associated with the country's security forces. For instance, the leader of the party and presidential candidate Jaime Pardo Leal was assassinated in 1987; its next presidential candidate, Senator Bernardo Jaramillo, was assassinated in 1990; several of its legislators and local candidates were killed in the late 1980s; and the last member of congress from the party, Senator Manuel Jose Cepeda, was assassinated in 1994. By the late 1990s, when the party virtually disintegrated, it was estimated that roughly 4,000 people associated with the Patriotic Union had been murdered.[55]

An accord between the M-19 guerrillas and the government of Colombia was announced in March of 1990. The group agreed to a ceasefire and demobilization of its guerrilla forces. It received a legal pardon for past crimes, guarantees for electoral participation, temporary economic assistance, and government protection. The M-19, together with other social groups, requested a constitutional reform, which occurred in 1991. The newly demobilized guerrilla group had 19 of their members elected to the constituent assembly in charge of rewriting the constitution and was awarded one of the three presidencies for the ensuing deliberations. Soon after signing the peace agreement, the guerrilla group transformed itself into a political party called Democratic Alliance M-19 (AD M-19). Its first presidential candidate, Carlos Pizarro, was assassinated on the orders of paramilitary leaders only a few weeks after the signing of the peace deal. Electoral support for AD M-19 waned during the 1990s, and the party eventually disintegrated. However, some of their leaders successfully continued their political careers as part of other leftist parties.

A significant next step in the Colombian conflict came in 2003, when the government entered into negotiations with the AUC paramilitary organization. These talks nearly fell apart the following year when rival paramilitaries killed the leader of the AUC, Carlos Castaño, and other top commanders. Negotiations were complex because existing legislation to benefit demobilized armed actors did not cover the heinous human rights violations committed against civilians by many of the paramilitaries. The legal framework that was developed allowed for some paramilitaries to benefit from amnesty, but those involved in the most severe violations, including the leadership of the AUC, were required to face trial. Legislation provided for reduced sentences (5 to 8 years) in exchange for providing information on the murders and forced disappearances they had committed, releasing the kidnapped individuals they held, and reparations to the victims. In

2008, the government of Colombia extradited 14 leaders of the AUC to the U.S. to face charges of drug trafficking because they had violated the terms of the peace agreement by continuing to engage in illegal activities.

In August of 2016, after four years of secret negotiations, the FARC and the Colombian government announced a new agreement. It was a complicated process with potential liabilities for both actors. On the one hand, the government worried about political costs, given that many Colombians distrusted the FARC and deeply resented their violent campaign, their involvement in drug trafficking, and the thousands of kidnappings they had undertaken. On the other hand, the FARC leadership worried about the safety of their members after disarmament, given their prior experience with the Patriotic Union, and had to convince their rank-and-file members to accept a deal at a time when they could not win significant policy concessions.

The accord included a plan for rural development and the distribution of some land for landless peasants. It also stipulated reforms to facilitate the entrance of new parties and security guarantees to prevent violence against politicians, the creation of a truth commission to investigate (but not prosecute) human rights violations, the creation of a special legal jurisdiction to prosecute crimes that do not qualify for amnesty, and reparations for victims of the conflict. It also guaranteed the FARC a minimum number of legislative seats for two electoral periods. Members from the United Nations and the Community of Latin American and Caribbean States were to be part of the monitoring and verification process.

President Juan Manuel Santos called for a referendum to approve the accord with the FARC. While the government, the Conservative and Liberal Parties, and various social and human rights groups campaigned for a *yes* vote, others, led by former president Álvaro Uribe, campaigned against the agreement, which they saw as too lenient with the guerrillas. To the surprise of most, the agreement was rejected: 49.8 percent voted in favor of it and 50.2 percent voted against it. The rejection of the agreement led to a process of renegotiation, which culminated with a series of amendments.

The changes clarified how the special courts dealing with the demobilized guerrillas would address cases related to war crimes and drug trafficking and established that these courts would operate for 10 years and that the judges serving in them would have to be Colombians. It also specified that guerrillas convicted of war crimes would serve time in restricted rural areas, required the FARC to declare and relinquish their assets to be used for reparations, and stated that the implementation of the agreement should not affect property rights guaranteed by the constitution. Finally, both chambers of congress approved the pact at the end of November of 2016. This time, the peace agreement was not subject to a popular vote.

The end of the conflict between the government of Colombia and the FARC guerrillas was heralded as a major accomplishment and was strongly endorsed by other Latin American countries. President Juan Manuel Santos was awarded the Nobel Peace Prize for his efforts on seeking such an agreement. In January of 2017, close to 7,000 guerrilla fighters proceeded to disarm and demobilize. That year ended with the fewest number of homicides since 1975.[56] In 2018, the FARC participated in national elections, which were the most peaceful in decades.

The momentum created by the accord also facilitated the beginnings of negotiations with the smaller ELN guerrilla group. In January of 2017, the government of Colombia and the ELN announced the start of talks to reach a peace agreement. However, talks broke down in early 2019, after the ELN undertook a car bomb attack on a police academy in Bogota, which killed 22 people and injured several others. The number of ELN fighters, which had dropped to about 2,500 in 2016, climbed in 2019 to about 4,000, mainly as a result of an influx of former FARC guerrillas who had rejected joining the peace process.[57]

Conclusions

This chapter addressed the emergence of guerrilla groups in Latin America and reviewed key aspects of the armed conflicts in Cuba, Nicaragua, El Salvador, Guatemala, and Colombia. It began with a discussion about the rationale for joining guerrilla movements and the factors that affect the success of such groups. It then moved to examine the Cuban revolution. There is a consensus among academics that this event had a profound political impact on the rest of Latin America and contributed to the spread of revolutionary movements across the region.

The armed revolutionary movements that began to emerge across the region in the late 1950s had a tremendous impact on Latin America. Some countries, such as the five discussed in more detail in this chapter, were profoundly altered by the resulting armed conflicts. Cuba continues to be ruled by the Communist Party, the offspring of Fidel Castro's M-26-7, which first came to power with the 1959 revolution. Nicaragua, the only other Latin American country where a leftist guerrilla force successfully defeated a sitting government, followed a different path than Cuba, but its politics also continue to be affected by the legacy of the revolution. Since the 2006 presidential elections, the FSLN has become the country's dominant party.

In El Salvador and Guatemala, the civil wars had a devastating effect on the population, but the peace agreements reached in the 1990s ended decades of state-led repression and facilitated a transition to competitive electoral politics. The conflict has lingered in Colombia for far longer than in other Latin American countries. It has had a profound effect on the workings of politics in the country as well as on the livelihood of a significant share of the population. Policies regarding how to deal with the insurgency have been some of the most contentious and publicly debated issues in the country for the last three decades.

This chapter delved into several factors affecting the likelihood that a guerrilla movement would win its war against the state. An important one was the impact of the international context, including the influence of the U.S. and the decisions made by its government, such as withdrawing support for Batista in Cuba and Somoza in Nicaragua and becoming engaged in the conflicts in El Salvador and Guatemala. The next chapter examines the relations between the U.S. and Latin America in greater detail.

Key Terms

Bay of Pigs invasion 75

Contra War 81

Cuban Missile Crisis 75

Cuban Revolution 70

Guatemalan Civil War 87

Guerrilla 65

Nicaraguan Revolution 76

Paramilitary forces 65

Peace agreements 90

Salvadorean Civil War 85

Bibliographic Recommendations

Jorge G. Castañeda. 1993. *Utopia Unarmed: The Latin American Left after the Cold War.* New York: Alfred Knopf.

Centro Nacional de Memoria Histórica. 2016. *BASTA YA! Colombia: Memories of War and Dignity.* Bogota: CNMH.

Jeff Goodwin. 2001. *No Other Way Out: States and Revolutionary Movements, 1945–1991.* New York: Cambridge University Press.

Ernesto Guevara. 1961 [2006]. *Guerrilla Warfare.* New York: Ocean Press.

Daniel Rothenberg (ed.). 2012. *Memory of Silence: The Guatemalan Truth Commission Report.* New York: Palgrave Macmillan.

Timothy P. Wickham-Crowley. 1992. *Guerrillas and Revolution in Latin America: A Comparative Study of Insurgents and Regimes since 1956.* Princeton: Princeton University Press.

Elisabeth Jean Wood. 2003. *Insurgent Collective Action and Civil War in El Salvador.* New York: Cambridge University Press.

Web Resources

Colombia's National Center of Historic Memory (*Centro Nacional de Memoria Histórica*): http://www.centrodememoriahistorica.gov.co

International Center for Transitional Justice, Guatemala Case Study: https://www.ictj.org/sites/default/files/subsites/challenging -conventional-truth-commissions-peace/guatemala.html

PBS, American Experience, Timeline Post-Revolution Cuba: https://www .pbs.org/wgbh/americanexperience/features/post-revolution-cuba/

4

U.S.–Latin America Relations

The relationship between Latin America and its most powerful neighbor, the United States (U.S.), has always been politically significant. The nature of this relationship has evolved over time, influenced by changes in the international context and foreign policy objectives. Unlike its southern neighbors, the U.S. belongs to a small set of countries that international relations theorists usually identify as "great" or "major" powers. These are countries that possess significant military and economic capabilities and exert influence beyond their geographical regions. Great powers are more likely than others to be involved in wars, militarized crises, and international disputes. While their interests spread globally, they tend to have spheres of influence in which they play more dominant roles.

For many years, direct military intervention and indirect political interference by the U.S. in the domestic affairs of Latin American countries were common. Most explanations for these actions underline security concerns or economic interests and occasionally domestic political factors. During the 19th century, the U.S. was guided by an aggressive and expansionist foreign policy that led to military confrontations with France, Britain, and Spain as well as a major war with Mexico and recurrent interventions in the Caribbean and Central America.[1] One of the major tenets of U.S. policy was the **Monroe Doctrine**, articulated by President James Monroe in 1823. It stated that the U.S. would not interfere in European affairs, that any intervention in the western hemisphere by European powers would be viewed as an act of aggression against the U.S., and that no other nation could establish a colony in this region.

The beginning of the 20th century brought about an even more assertive policy stance. What came to be known as the **Roosevelt Corollary to the Monroe Doctrine** (1904) stated that the U.S. might exercise "international police power" in Latin American countries that engage in "chronic wrongdoing," including failure to pay international creditors and recurrent internal disorder. This stance sought to preempt intervention by European powers, such as the naval blockade of Venezuela (1902–1903) undertaken by Britain, Germany, and Italy over the country's refusal to pay its debt obligations. It also came at a time when the U.S. was beginning to build the Panama Canal and wanted to assert its influence in the region. It was first implemented in 1905, when the government of the Dominican Republic, threatened by European collectors, asked the U.S. to protect its territorial integrity and invited it to assume responsibility for collecting custom-house receipts to pay foreign creditors.[2] In the following decades, the need to fulfill international financial obligations and the turmoil associated with internal unrest would be used as justifications for U.S. intervention in several Central American and Caribbean countries.

During the first decades of the 20th century, economic linkages strengthened. The U.S. became the principal destination for Latin American exports, most imports into the region came from the U.S., and U.S. firms began to establish subsidiaries in many Latin American countries. Some of the major U.S. corporations established in the region during this period included the United Fruit Company, Standard Oil, International Telephone & Telegraph, Anaconda Copper Company, General Electric, General Motors, and National City Bank. The bulk of foreign direct investment, as well as most development loans, came to Latin America from the U.S.

A shift away from military intervention as a tool of U.S. foreign policy in the region took place during the Great Depression. President Franklin Delano Roosevelt's new approach to Latin America came to be known as the **Good Neighbor Policy**. It emphasized the principle of nonintervention and deepening economic ties. Nevertheless, interference in domestic affairs did not entirely disappear. For instance, the U.S. indirectly supported the overthrow of nationalist presidents perceived to be favorable to the Axis powers in Panama (1941) and Bolivia (1944). Latin American countries, for the most part, supported the Allies during World War II, and several of them declared war on the Axis powers soon after the Japanese attack on Pearl Harbor. However, only Mexico and Brazil sent troops to the conflict.

The aftermath of World War II would again bring about a significant shift in U.S. foreign policy, with major consequences for Latin America. This is the focus of the next section, which discusses U.S.–Latin America relations during the **Cold War**. Another significant change began to take place in the late 1980s, as the Cold War came to an end and economic globalization deepened. The last two sections of this chapter address the aftermath of the Cold War and U.S.–Latin American relations in the early 21st century.

The Cold War

A new international order emerged following the end of World War II, structured by the rivalry between the U.S. and the Soviet Union. Western European countries allied with the U.S., while the Soviets and their local allies established communist governments across the Central and Eastern European countries they had occupied during the war. In 1949, the U.S. and its Western European allies formed the North Atlantic Treaty Organization (NATO), a military organization designed to provide collective defense. In 1955, the Soviet Union and its satellite states in Eastern and Central Europe organized their own collective defense organization, the Warsaw Pact, after West Germany joined NATO. The Cold War never devolved into a direct military confrontation between the two rival nuclear powers, but each used military force and indirect political influence to try to keep allies in power and to attempt the overthrow of governments considered to be either hostile or supportive of the rival pact. While the Soviet Union and the U.S. competed for influence across the developing world, each had areas considered to be under their own sphere of influence. Latin America was thought to be within the sphere of influence of the U.S., and preventing Soviet allies from emerging in the region was considered a matter of national security for American administrations during the Cold War.

The extent to which some of the targets of U.S. intervention in Latin America represented a real threat to its security is debatable. But for risk-averse administrations, preventing future threats in a not particularly costly manner often seemed justified. In Latin America, these interventions were frequently seen as favoring authoritarianism and preventing the establishment of progressive governments. It must be noted, however, that during the Cold War, the goal of promoting democracy and shunning dictatorial regimes took a back burner to security concerns. As senior diplomat and national security advisor Richard Hass noted, during this era, U.S. administrations paid little attention to the domestic nature of the allies they supported; "what mattered most was foreign policy orientation and whether the government was judged to be sufficiently anti-Communist."[3]

During the Cold War, the U.S. undertook direct military intervention in Latin America on two occasions, both in the Caribbean region. The first took place in the Dominican Republic in 1965, where a civil war had erupted following a coup that deposed Juan Bosch, the first democratically elected president of that country, from power. Bosch's progressive policies had antagonized the country's economic elites, the Catholic Church, and part of the military. But the U.S. remained supportive of the civilian-elected president, publicly condemned the coup, and (in its aftermath) announced the temporary suspension of economic and military assistance to the country.[4] The civil conflict erupted more than a year after the coup and led to a confrontation between two factions of the armed forces. The largest military faction supported the government installed after the coup and was backed by the country's elites, while the rebel camp included a smaller military faction and militants of Bosch's party, who were seeking his return to the presidency. As the violence escalated, the U.S. began the evacuation of American citizens using its armed forces. At that point, U.S. intelligence informed President Lyndon Johnson that Cuba's leader, Fidel Castro, was probably behind the uprising and that communists were actively involved in the fighting. A fundamental American objective in the Dominican Republic since the Kennedy Administration had been preventing a "second Cuba."[5] The U.S. ambassador reported that outsiders were likely playing a role in the conflict and warned that American lives were in danger. President Johnson then decided to send an occupying force with the stated goal of protecting American lives.

A month after the arrival of U.S. troops, an international force made up of members of the **Organization of American States** (**OAS**, led by Brazil) took over and began to oversee the implementation of the peace agreement reached by the warring factions. The occupation ended the following year, soon after a presidential election in which candidate Joaquín Balaguer defeated former President Juan Bosch. Later, evidence revealed that the intelligence information given to President Johnson had contributed to Washington's overestimation of the communist threat.[6] The involvement of communist factions in the conflict and their political influence appeared to have been exaggerated.[7]

The second military intervention by the U.S. in Latin America took place in 1983 in the tiny Caribbean island of Grenada. That country had been ruled by a left-wing government that came to power in a coup in 1979. Its authoritarian rulers had developed close links with the Cuban government, which had provided military assistance and had sent hundreds of its citizens—including military personnel—to work on an airport project. In addition, Grenada's government had signed a series of military agreements with the Soviet Union in 1982. The **Central Intelligence Agency (CIA)** had reported that Soviet access to Grenada "would have a significant impact on U.S. security interests, especially with regards to the Panama Canal and other lines of communication."[8]

The trigger for the invasion of Grenada was a coup by a radical left-wing faction within the government in October 1983, which led to the assassination of the prime minister and members of his inner circle. The invasion by U.S. forces began nine days after the coup. President Ronald Reagan publicly justified this action as a means to protect the lives of about 800 young U.S. citizens on the island attending medical school (it was thought they could be harmed or become hostages) and as a response to a request for intervention made by six members of the Organization of Eastern Caribbean States, Jamaica, and Barbados. But American officials appeared more concerned about Cuba's influence on the island and the potential use of the new airport as a Cuban or Soviet airbase. While the Cuban influence over the government of Grenada was real, the extent to which it represented a potential military threat to U.S. interest is debatable, and the actual threat to the American medical students was likely exaggerated.[9] U.S. troops left the country at the end of 1983, and the following year, elections made way for a new civilian government.

In three instances, the U.S. used the CIA to train and fund irregular forces seeking regime change. The earliest of these events took place in Guatemala in 1954. Between 1944 and 1954, Guatemala was governed by two reformist presidents, Juan José Arévalo and Jacobo Árbenz. Both presidents were reformist politicians who clashed with the country's elite over the social policies they sought to implement. After the Árbenz administration enacted a land reform program, large landowners and the United Fruit Company began to lobby the U.S. government, requesting its intervention to remove the sitting president. President Harry Truman dismissed these requests and helped to quash a plot by company officials to overthrow Árbenz.[10] The principal concern of the U.S. government was not Árbenz's agrarian policies but rather the influence of communists, which intelligence reports suggested were playing a significant role within the Guatemalan government.[11] The subsequent discovery of a shipment of Soviet-made arms from Czechoslovakia, which had been purchased by the Árbenz government, further cemented this narrative. President Dwight Eisenhower, who had assumed power in 1953, tried unsuccessfully to build international support for action against Guatemala.[12] President Árbenz, fearing an imminent intervention, declared a state of siege and began to repress political opponents. A CIA-trained and funded force entered Guatemala in June of 1954. The Guatemalan army refused to defend the government, and Árbenz was forced to resign. The overthrow of the government, which marked the end of the Good Neighbor Policy, would be followed by a repressive dictatorship and a long-lasting and violent civil war.

The other two instances during the Cold War in which the U.S. government utilized the CIA to train irregular forces to attempt regime change in a Latin American nation were discussed in the prior chapter. They included the financing and training of the forces that landed at the Bay of Pigs in Cuba in 1961, which sought to spur an uprising against the government of Fidel Castro, and the financing and training of anti-Sandinista Contra forces during the 1980s, which sought to depose the Sandinista National Liberation Front (FSLN) from power in Nicaragua. Both of these attempts at regime change were unsuccessful.

Aside from direct military interventions, the U.S. government interfered on several occasions in an indirect manner seeking regime change. In some of these cases, the role of the U.S. was not decisive, and the primary players were domestic actors. During this era of high political instability, coups and unscheduled government turnovers were not uncommon, and U.S. intelligence was, in most cases, aware of their likely occurrence. A well-known case of CIA involvement in the domestic affairs of a Latin American country took place in the early 1970s in Chile, a country with strong democratic traditions.

In 1970, Chileans elected Salvador Allende, a socialist, to the presidency. To many on the left, this event exemplified how a socialist government elected in free and fair elections could undertake deep social reforms within a democratic context. But the government held a minority of seats in the Chilean Congress, which limited the extent to which it could implement many of the radical reforms that it sought. Chilean politics became highly polarized under Allende's government, with major clashes between supporters of the government and the opposition. The economic establishment and foreign companies operating in Chile strongly opposed the nationalizations and expropriations undertaken by the government, and the main opposition parties denounced what they saw as violations of property rights, the bypassing of congress, and a disregard for judicial decisions. Furthermore, the closeness between the Allende administration and Cuba and the latter's involvement in training radical factions within Chile worried the U.S. government. The Chilean military appeared divided between a group that strongly opposed the Allende government and sought its overthrow and a legalistic faction that rejected the use of unconstitutional measures.

The conflict escalated in 1973. The Chilean Congress, with an opposition majority, accused the Allende administration of undertaking various unconstitutional actions, which the government denied. Finally, on September 11, 1973, the armed forces staged a military coup, which deposed the elected government and ushered in a 17-year dictatorship led by General Augusto Pinochet. The military regime undertook a violent campaign against the supporters of the previous government that resulted in widespread violation of human rights, including the imprisonment and execution of thousands of individuals.

The involvement of the U.S. in Chile followed two tracks.[13] The first path involved the covert use of propaganda during the presidential election against the front supporting Allende and, subsequently, the use of political pressure on members of the opposition so they would act in concert to deny Allende the congressional ratification he needed to become president.[14] The second path focused on covert CIA operations to foster a military coup that would prevent Allende from taking power. In this effort, the CIA became involved with a Chilean military faction in a botched kidnapping attempt that ended with the assassination of Army Commander René Schneider in December 1970. Both strategies failed.

The role of the U.S. in the 1973 coup that deposed the Chilean president is less clear, since declassified documents reveal no direct involvement aside from prior knowledge of the coup and the appearance of condoning the actions of the plotters. Unsurprisingly, given the far left and anti-American stances of the government, the U.S. antagonized the Allende administration in the international arena and sought to discredit it. Declassified information also reveals that after the 1973 coup, the CIA was involved in various propaganda projects seeking to build a positive image of the military dictatorship while discrediting the prior regime.[15]

During the Cold War, U.S. policy toward Latin America also involved economic and diplomatic initiatives. For instance, soon after assuming power, President John F. Kennedy proposed a major economic aid program for Latin America, which came to be known as the *Alliance for Progress*. The goal was to raise the standard of living for millions of Latin Americans and, in the process, reduce the appeal of communism. The ten-year program was put in place in 1961 and had an ambitious set of goals, which included economic growth targets, the elimination of adult illiteracy, improvements in income distribution, and the spread of democracy. The program was initially well-received, but its overall economic impact was limited, and the political goal of fostering democracies failed. Post-Kennedy administrations were not as keen about the program, and many Latin American governments were unwilling to undertake some of the policies (e.g., land reforms) sought in the original plan.

A significant diplomatic initiative involved the creation of the OAS. It was established in 1948, one year after a defensive military alliance between Latin America and the U.S., called the Rio Pact, was signed. The goal was to create an institution that would address interhemispheric affairs diplomatically, defend the territorial integrity and sovereignty of its members, and encourage cooperation. In practice, the OAS played a moderate role in the region during the Cold War. Latin American countries often perceived the organization as being dominated by U.S. interests,[16] while the U.S. often perceived it as unreliable and insufficiently committed to its own Cold War policies.

U.S. policy toward Latin America varied across administrations. President Kennedy, for example, was reluctant to use direct military intervention and thought that economic assistance, improved social conditions, and the promotion of democracy would ultimately be favorable to both the U.S. and Latin America. He nonetheless acted decisively to protect U.S. interests during the Cuban Missile Crisis.

The most relevant departure from the traditional Cold War zeal occurred under the administration of President Jimmy Carter. During the 1976 presidential campaign, Carter criticized the amorality of U.S. foreign policy, including the support given to Chile's dictatorship under Pinochet.[17] After assuming the presidency, he stressed cooperative multilateralism and made human rights an important component of his administration's foreign policy. The U.S. then worked with others to strengthen the Inter-American Commission on Human Rights and began to send human rights reports on each country to Congress. This latter move upset the military governments of Argentina, Brazil, El Salvador, and Guatemala, which retaliated by ending their agreements with the U.S. over military assistance.[18]

Aid to Argentina and Uruguay, both governed by military dictatorships involved in human rights violations, was cut in 1977. The Carter administration would later cut economic and military aid to Nicaragua after its ruler, Anastacio Somoza, refused to follow the recommendations of the OAS to negotiate a transition from power. In November of 1980, after the murder of four U.S. religious workers by right-wing death squads in El Salvador, Carter temporarily suspended all economic and military aid to that country.

One of the most significant achievements of the Carter administration was the renegotiation of the **Panama Canal Treaty**. The canal had been built by the U.S. in 1904 under a treaty that gave it a renewable lease to control its operation and five miles of land along either side of it. Animosity toward the U.S. over its control of the canal increased over time and, in 1964, led to a major riot in Panama and a brief break in diplomatic relations. Panama had long demanded a renegotiation, and seven Latin American countries had urged Carter to speed up discussions aimed at reaching an agreement.[19] The new Panama Canal Treaty, signed in 1977, required the U.S. to relinquish control of the canal on December 31, 1999, at which time the operation of the canal would shift to Panama. It also established the canal as a neutral water passage and gave the U.S. permanent authority to defend it if this status were to be threatened. The signing of this pact was very well-received across Latin America and, despite sharp criticism from many conservatives, was ratified by the U.S. Senate.

During the Carter administration, the problematic relationship with Cuba also came to the forefront. After assuming power, the president expressed his desire to improve relations with Cuba and begin bilateral discussions without preconditions. He nonetheless remarked that normalization of relations would require decreasing Cuban military involvement in Africa, releasing political prisoners, and a commitment to noninterference in the internal affairs of Latin American countries. The first direct diplomatic contacts since 1961 took place in 1977. They led to an agreement on maritime boundaries and fisheries as well as the establishment of U.S. and Cuban Interest Sections staffed by nationals of each country (before this, Switzerland and Czechoslovakia played the role of intermediaries). However, Fidel Castro refused to limit Cuba's military role in Africa and continued the build-up of forces under Soviet command in Ethiopia (around 17,000 in 1978). The following year, Cuba began training the army of Grenada after the leftist coup in the island and increased Cuba's assistance to the Sandinista guerrillas in Nicaragua. In the fall of 1979, revelations of a Soviet brigade stationed in Cuba further worsened bilateral relations and contributed to greater hostility between the U.S. and the Soviet Union, which would reach a low point after the Soviet invasion of Afghanistan four months later.

By the end of the Carter administration, an immigration crisis arose. It began when thousands of Cubans seeking asylum overran the tiny Peruvian embassy in Havana. Political dissidents then proceeded to seek refuge in other embassies. Castro, who had previously jailed dissidents seeking to leave the country, changed course and announced that those who wanted to leave the country would be allowed to do so. In what came to be known as the Mariel boatlift, close to 125,000 Cubans escaped to Florida.

When the time came for Carter to run for reelection, he had lost significant support among American voters. The president's overtures to the Soviets and the Cubans had not been reciprocated, revolutions in Nicaragua and Grenada had raised concerns about the effectiveness of nonintervention and multilateralism, and the handling of the 1979 hostage crisis in Iran had come to be seen by many as incompetent. Moreover, an oil shock in 1979 led to a shortage of gas, and inflation rose significantly, further weakening the president's chances of being reelected. In 1980, Ronald Reagan beat Jimmy Carter in a presidential election that would usher in a significant change in U.S. foreign policy.

President Reagan sought to change what he saw as major mistakes in U.S. foreign policy that had weakened America's prestige and power around the world. He pursued a hardline approach to further American interests that involved confronting the Soviet Union and fighting against the spread of communism. One of his first policy decisions was to drastically increase defense spending to levels that he expected the Soviets could not match. His support for the government of El Salvador, the training and funding of the Nicaraguan Contras, and the invasion of Grenada were all actions taken during Reagan's first term in office and fit well with his doctrine of confronting the spread of left-wing regimes. Within the U.S., he was a popular president who won reelection in a landslide, but within Latin America, Reagan's aggressive foreign policy was unpopular.

During Reagan's second term, a moderating shift took place. The coming to power of Mikhail S. Gorbachev in the Soviet Union began a period of historic change that would culminate with that country's disintegration. Once in power, Gorbachev introduced greater economic and political freedoms and promoted new foreign policy initiatives aimed at reaching a consensus with the U.S. government. Reagan welcomed these overtures and responded with accommodating policies that would culminate in major arms control agreements.

As the Cold War was coming to an end, the U.S. government embraced the political openness taking place in El Salvador and Guatemala and put pressure on the military of those countries to abstain from interrupting the process of democratization. The U.S. government also ended its earlier support for the Pinochet dictatorship in Chile, began to criticize him for human rights violations, and endorsed the process of democratization taking place in that country.

During Reagan's second term in office, a series of political scandals emerged, of which the most serious was the Iran–Contra scandal. This event, which involved the sale of arms to Iran in violation of an embargo and the subsequent channeling of funds to support the Nicaraguan Contras in violation of a congressional prohibition, culminated with the indictment of various officials and a drop in the president's public approval rating. The end of Reagan's term in office signaled the culmination of a long era of U.S.–Latin American relations that was affected to a great degree by the ongoing Cold War.

The Aftermath of the Cold War

George H. W. Bush assumed the presidency of the U.S. in January 1989 and, ten months later, the Berlin Wall fell. This event was followed by the breakup of the Soviet Union and the abandonment of authoritarian single-party government across communist Central and Eastern Europe. The end of the Cold War led to a realignment in U.S. foreign policy that would have significant implications for Latin America. Confronting the far left ceased to be a guiding principle, as the spread of communism was no longer considered a top national security concern. The most important crisis faced by President George H. W. Bush in Latin America surfaced during his first year in office and led to military intervention in Panama under a different rationale than in prior decades.

General Manuel Noriega, a former CIA informant, became the de facto leader of Panama in 1983 and orchestrated the election of a puppet government in the rigged elections of 1984. He became involved in international drug trafficking and money laundering and spearheaded the persecution and killing of political opponents. As bilateral relations deteriorated, Noriega got closer to Cuba and Nicaragua, and the U.S. imposed an economic embargo and fomented a coup. Latin American nations denounced both what they saw as excessive pressure on the part of the U.S. and Noriega's antidemocratic maneuvering.[20] Then, in 1988, a U.S. federal grand jury indicted Noriega on charges of drug trafficking.

After Noriega's chosen candidate lost in the Panamanian presidential election of May 1989, he nullified the election. The next day, his supporters violently attacked the opposition candidate and apparent winner, Guillermo Endara. The U.S. government then proceeded to expand its economic sanctions and ordered additional troops to its garrison in the Panama Canal.

On December 15, 1989, following an unsuccessful coup to depose Noriega, Panama's National Assembly and Noriega himself declared that American interference in the country's domestic affairs amounted to a state of war between both countries. The following day, four U.S. officers were stopped at a roadblock in Panama City and, after being surrounded by an angry crowd of Panamanians soldiers and civilians, decided to drive away. The Panamanian soldiers proceeded to open fire, killing one American and injuring another. The next day, President Bush approved an invasion of Panama with the goal of removing Noriega from power. In an address to the nation on his decision to use force, Bush underlined that Noriega, a dictator and drug trafficker, had declared a state of war with the U.S. and had publicly threatened the lives of Americans in Panama while his forces had attacked American soldiers. President Bush vowed to safeguard American lives, protect the integrity of the Panama Canal Treaty, and withdraw U.S. troops quickly after bringing General Noriega to face a U.S. court.

The military intervention in Panama began on December 20, 1989, and involved about 30,000 troops. After a few days in hiding, Noriega sought refuge in the Vatican diplomatic mission. He finally surrendered on January 2,

1990, and was flown to the U.S. to face criminal charges. The presumed winner of the 1989 election, Guillermo Endara, was sworn in as president and abolished the Panamanian military soon after. The intervention was opposed by Latin American nations, which unanimously voted in favor of an OAS resolution condemning the invasion and calling for the withdrawal of U.S. troops. The Mexican government declared that "fighting international crimes cannot be a motive for intervening in a sovereign nation."[21] Several other countries and the European Parliament denounced the intervention in Panama, but within the U.S., public approval of the president surged. Noriega was eventually convicted on eight counts of drug smuggling and racketeering in a U.S. court and sentenced to 40 years in prison (later reduced to 30 years). He was extradited to France in 2010, where he was found guilty of money laundering, and later to Panama, where he had been convicted in absentia of murder.

The invasion of Panama, although followed by the democratization of the country, strained relations between Latin America and the U.S. and reminded many of an earlier era of gunboat diplomacy. However, it also highlighted a collective failure on the part of Latin American nations.[22] As expressed by Venezuelan President Carlos Andrés Pérez in a speech at the OAS, Latin American countries shared some of the responsibility for the invasion as a result of their inability to act decisively in response to Noriega's disregard for constitutional norms and human rights.

In addition to Panama, President George H. W. Bush faced various foreign policy challenges during his term in office, such as the Tiananmen Square protests in China, an attempted coup against Soviet President Gorbachev, the beginning of the war in Yugoslavia, and most importantly, the first Persian Gulf War. Although the focus of American foreign policy was elsewhere, the U.S. also pursued some pro-democracy initiatives in Latin America. For example, it continued to support the process of democratization in El Salvador and Guatemala and helped to put pressure on the government of El Salvador to sign the peace accord that ended that country's civil war. In December 1990, the Bush administration cut off military aid to Guatemala after concluding that members of that country's military were involved in the killing of Michael Devine, an American citizen. After Peruvian President Alberto Fujimori dissolved the country's congress and detained opposition politicians, the U.S. government suspended all aid (except for humanitarian assistance) and voted with Latin American countries in the OAS to condemn the unconstitutional move. Also, in 1991, when the military deposed the elected president of Haiti, Jean-Bertrand Aristide, and threatened his life, the U.S. ambassador negotiated his release and the U.S. government and the OAS imposed sanctions on the country.

The conflict in Haiti worsened over time. The military rulers and their associates persecuted and killed opponents of the government, and the economic situation, made worse by **international sanctions**, became dire. This led to a large number of Haitians leaving the country and sailing toward the U.S. coast. During the 1992 campaign, President Bill Clinton promised to increase the pressure on the Haitian junta to restore democracy.

The following year, the military ruler of Haiti met with the special envoy of the United Nations and the OAS and agreed to give up power, but when the deadline to do so arrived, he refused. Further sanctions were imposed by the United Nations, the U.S., and other countries. Within the U.S. Congress, progressives (including the Congressional Black Caucus) pressured the Clinton administration to act. Then, on July 31, 1994, the United Nations Security Council passed a resolution authorizing its members to form a multinational force and use all necessary means to depose the military rulers of Haiti and return the elected president, Aristide, to power.

On September 17, 1994, two days before the scheduled arrival of a multinational force headed by the U.S., former President Jimmy Carter led a delegation to Haiti to negotiate with the military ruler. At the last moment, and after being shown a video of American warplanes headed for Haiti, the military leadership capitulated. This facilitated a peaceful entry of troops into the country. President Aristide returned to Haiti in October 1994 and, in March of the following year, command was transferred from the U.S.–led force to the United Nations Mission in Haiti.

The Haitian operation signaled a significant departure from Cold War–era interventions in Latin America. It was backed by a United Nations resolution—the first authorizing the use of force to restore democracy in a member nation—and, as a result of the agreement reached at the last moment, it became a peaceful peacekeeping occupation rather than an armed invasion to depose the military junta. Several Latin American countries, such as Mexico, Colombia, the Dominican Republic, Venezuela, Uruguay, and (unsurprisingly) Cuba, had publicly opposed the plan to militarily depose the Haitian junta. But after the agreement negotiated by Carter turned the operation into a peaceful occupation, some Latin American governments, such as those of Mexico, Colombia, and Argentina, expressed satisfaction with the outcome.

A major component of President Bill Clinton's policy toward Latin America involved building on the economic initiatives first advanced by his predecessor. The most important was the Enterprise for the Americas Initiative, proposed by President George H. W. Bush in April of 1990 with the goal of developing free trade agreements, expanding investment, and providing debt relief to some poor countries in the region. Negotiations with Mexico and Canada to create the **North American Free Trade Agreement** (**NAFTA**) began that same year and led to the signing of a draft treaty in 1992. President Bill Clinton subsequently added agreements on labor and environmental cooperation. NAFTA's implementation legislation passed the U.S. Congress with bipartisan support at the end of 1993, and the agreement went into effect on January 1, 1994. It would have a significant impact, boosting trade and investment and furthering economic integration among the three members.

The goal of promoting free trade fit well with the economic ideas in vogue in the 1990s. At that time, Latin America began to move away from the economic nationalism and protectionist policies that had characterized the region since at least the 1930s and toward more market-friendly policies. During this decade, a series of summits of OAS heads of government began to take place. The first Summit of the Americas occurred in Miami in 1994 and led to a declaration of principles, which included a commitment to promote democracy and economic prosperity, and the intention of working toward a Free Trade Area of the Americas (FTAA). During the 1990s, the region lowered tariffs, and intraregional as well as U.S.–Latin America trade increased. However, the impetus for the FTAA faltered after the gathering of heads of state in Miami. By the time the second summit took place in 1998 in Chile, it was clear that such an agreement was not going to emerge any time soon. Subsequent meetings brought little progress on this front.

During the Clinton administration, the signing of the peace accord that ended the Guatemalan civil war took place. The U.S., which had orchestrated the overthrow of the Guatemalan president in 1954 and provided training, aid, and political support to the governments that committed major human rights violations during the civil war, changed its position in the 1980s and began to condemn the crimes committed by the security forces and endorse the process of democratization. The U.S. played a constructive role in the negotiations to end the conflict. It appointed a special representative to the Friends Group assisting the United Nations in the mediating process, became involved in informal contacts with representatives of the guerrillas, and provided financial support to the Office of the Human Rights Ombudsman and to a project seeking to increase the independence of the judicial system. In 1999, President Clinton visited Guatemala and expressed regret for the support given by the U.S. to the security forces that engaged in violence and widespread repression, calling it a mistake that the U.S. should not repeat.[23]

The Clinton administration also played a relevant role in facilitating a resolution to the border dispute between Ecuador and Peru that led to a brief military conflict in early 1995. The long-running dispute between these two neighboring South American nations had led to a war in 1941, which ended with a peace treaty (the Rio de Janeiro Protocol) that included the U.S., Brazil, Argentina, and Chile as guarantors. Ecuador later challenged the agreement and established outposts in areas considered to be Peruvian, which led to military skirmishes in 1981 and then again in 1995. Diplomats and military representatives from the U.S. were instrumental in facilitating a resolution of the conflict.[24] Working with the other guarantors of the 1942 pact, they helped to put together a new peace accord between Ecuador and Peru, which was signed in 1998.

The U.S. also played a significant role in helping Mexico overcome a currency crisis in early 1995. After a series of unfavorable developments and misguided responses from the government, the country lost a massive amount of international reserves and the Mexican peso depreciated sharply. This led many to question whether Mexico could pay its short-term debt. The crisis was resolved after the U.S. organized and led a significant international rescue package and Mexico agreed to a strict program of economic reform.

At about the same time, the Clinton administration clashed with Colombia over the drug trade. Since the mid-1980s, the U.S. has conducted a controversial process by which it certifies whether a government in a major drug-producing or drug-transit country is cooperating in anti-narcotic efforts.[25] If a country is decertified during the **anti-drug certification process**, it risks losing U.S. foreign assistance and having the U.S. oppose loan requests in multilateral development banks. Officials in the Clinton administration decertified Colombia in 1995 due to poor cooperation but gave the country a temporary waiver for national security reasons. However, the following year, amid information that the electoral campaign of the Colombian President Ernesto Samper had been funded with drug traffickers' money, the Department of State decertified Colombia. This time, it led to a suspension of most economic assistance. In addition, the U.S. revoked President Samper's visa. In 1997, Colombia was decertified again, but no economic sanctions were put in place.

With the main goal of helping the Colombian government combat drugs and organized crime, President Bill Clinton signed into law a package of military and economic assistance called **Plan Colombia** in July of 2000. That year, a total of $1.3 billion in aid was allocated to the program and, over the next twelve years, the total funds would reach around $8 billion. The program was controversial. Human rights organizations, such as Amnesty International, criticized it, arguing that the Colombian government failed to protect human rights and colluded with violent paramilitary groups. But U.S. and Colombian officials regarded the aid as crucial in facilitating the government's fight against drug trafficking. Data from the United Nations show that after a steep increase in land under coca cultivation during the 1990s, a decreasing trend followed in the early 2000s.[26]

As the 20th century came to a conclusion, it seemed evident that a new era of U.S.–Latin American relations had started. Military coups were no longer common, most countries had ceased to perceive far-left guerrillas as a major security threat, and the end of the Cold War had eliminated a common justification for U.S. intervention. More generally, the strategic importance of Latin America to U.S. defense and security policies had declined. Most countries in the region had moved from dictatorship to democracy, economic nationalism and extreme protectionism had gone out of fashion, and the process of economic globalization had begun to change economic relations. Other issues, such as drug trafficking and free trade agreements, had become more important. In terms of the formulation of U.S. policy toward Latin America, these changes meant that some actors, such as the CIA and the Pentagon, were becoming less influential, while others, such as treasury, commerce, agriculture, the Office of the Special Trade Representative, the Export–Import Bank, and the Drug Enforcement Administration, were becoming more relevant.[27] The administration of President George H. W. Bush was the first to embrace this change, moving away from Reagan's fixation on leftist influence in Central America and promoting stronger economic linkages and new partnerships. This direction was also embraced by the subsequent administration of President Bill Clinton, who built on many of the initiatives started by his predecessor.

The Early 21st Century

With the new century came a sudden change in U.S. foreign policy priorities, a consequence of the terrorist attacks of September 11, 2001. President George W. Bush had begun his term in office in early 2001 by signaling interest in strengthening relations with Latin America. This was reflected in a meeting with Mexican President Vicente Fox soon after assuming power and during the subsequent Summit of the Americas, held in Canada. But the terrorist attacks, orchestrated by the Islamist terrorist group Al-Qaeda, changed the priorities of the U.S. government. The global "War on Terror" took center stage and relations with Latin America decreased in importance. The U.S. Congress authorized military action against those responsible for the attacks, including those that harbored them. Latin American governments expressed their solidarity with the U.S. and voted in the OAS to condemn the terrorist attacks of September 11. In October of 2001, the U.S. began its invasion of Afghanistan, where Osama bin Laden, Al-Qaeda's leader, had been operating with the complicity of the Taliban regime ruling that country.

As the conflict progressed, the Bush administration began to advocate the use of preemptive first-strike action against hostile states as well as against terrorist groups developing weapons of mass destruction (WMDs). Members of the U.S. government began to argue that the government of Iraq, led by Saddam Hussein, had developed a dangerous relationship with the Al-Qaeda terrorist group responsible for the attacks of September 11. In addition, the U.S. and British governments asserted that the Iraqi government remained in possession of large quantities of WMDs—even after many of its chemical weapons had been destroyed by the United Nations following the Persian Gulf War of 1990–1991—and was involved in secret plans to continue developing them. At the end of 2002, the United Nations restarted inspections to locate such weapons. In March of 2003, Chief Weapons Inspector Hans Blix reported that inspections were being conducted but cooperation had been somewhat reluctant,[28] and the director of the International Atomic Energy Agency reported that so far, they had not found any indication of a revival of a nuclear weapons program in Iraq.

The Bush administration insisted that Iraq possessed WMDs, argued that diplomacy and inspections were not working, and sought a resolution in the United Nations Security Council authorizing the use of force. The members of the Security Council disagreed about how to proceed. At that time, Chile and Mexico were in the council as temporary members.

As noted in the American press, those "were stressful days for the leaders of Chile and Mexico, caught between the demands of the remaining superpower and the overwhelming antiwar sentiments of their people."[29] Despite strong pressure exerted by the U.S. government, Mexico and Chile sided with France, Germany, and a majority of the members of the Security Council in opposing authorization for the use of military force. The U.S., Britain, and Spain, together with other allies, decided to proceed with an invasion of Iraq without the backing of a UN resolution. The war began on March 20, 2003.

The refusal of Chile and Mexico to back the U.S. in the Security Council angered the Bush administration, and many feared that it would lead to a backlash affecting policies relevant to both Latin American countries. However, this was not the case. President George W. Bush defended NAFTA and promoted a series of summits with the Mexican president and the Canadian prime minister to further cooperation on economic and security matters. He also pushed for immigration reform, including giving legal status to undocumented workers living in the U.S., which was an important policy priority for Mexico. The proposal for immigration reform was eventually defeated in Congress, despite strong support from President Bush. With regards to Chile, the most important issue on the agenda was a free trade agreement. After years of negotiations, the agreement was signed in mid-2003 and came into force at the beginning of 2004. It eliminated tariffs on 90 percent of U.S. exports to Chile and 95 percent of Chilean imports to the U.S., leading to a sharp increase in bilateral trade in subsequent years.

While the goal of creating a free trade area for the entire Western Hemisphere seemed unrealistic a decade after it was first proposed, the impetus for reducing trade barriers did not stop. The Bush administration successfully negotiated separate agreements with several Latin American countries. After the one with Chile, the U.S. signed free trade agreements with five Central American countries in May 2004, with the Dominican Republic in August 2004, with Peru in April 2006, with Colombia in November 2006, and with Panama in June 2007. These agreements worked to increase regional trade and promote economic integration.

Despite this success in the realm of trade relations, the international standing of the Bush administration weakened after the invasion of Iraq failed to uncover WMDs and revelations of abuses at Abu Ghraib prison by U.S. personnel became public. The election of several leftist governments in Latin America also contributed to an increase in anti-U.S. rhetoric in the region, most obviously from governments in Venezuela, Ecuador, and Bolivia. But it was in Haiti, again, where the next crises erupted.

The 2000 election, which resulted in Aristide's return to the presidency of Haiti, was boycotted by the opposition and preceded by the arrest of opposition candidates. International donors decided to withhold election assistance and refused to send election monitors. Extremely low turnout further eroded Aristide's legitimacy. Following the contest, political violence and harassment of opposition politicians continued to erode the country's human rights record. Pervasive corruption and misuse of public funds worsened the political situation. The U.S. then proceeded to freeze development assistance funds. The OAS, which had been involved in trying to mediate between the government and the opposition, passed a resolution in 2002 (with the agreement of Haiti's government) stating that legislative and local elections had to be held in 2003 and demanding the establishment of a new autonomous and independent electoral commission. Neither objective was accomplished, and the term in office of most legislators ended at the beginning of 2004 without elections having taken place to select their replacements. As a result, Aristide began to rule by decree.[30] The conflict escalated and, in February, an armed rebellion erupted in several cities around the country.

While rebel forces marched toward the capital, the Bush administration and the French government pressured Aristide to resign.[31] As armed dissidents were taking control of the national police headquarters, Aristide resigned and was flown out of the country by the U.S. military, which, in coordination with France, transported the Haitian leader to the Central African Republic. Aristide later claimed that he had resigned under duress and accused the U.S. and France of forcibly removing him from the country.[32] The U.S. government strongly rejected such claims. Following his departure on February 29, the chief of the Haitian Supreme Court was sworn in as president. Next, the United Nations passed a resolution authorizing an international force to restore order. The force was initially composed of U.S., French, and Canadian troops. A few months later, it was replaced by a peacekeeping force comprised of soldiers from several Latin American countries and led by the Brazilian army. In the end, the intervention prevented further bloodshed and tried to restore competitive elections, but it was also criticized by several observers who complained that the manner in which Aristide ended his presidency encouraged violent overthrows[33] and accused the Bush administration of working to oust the Haitian president.[34]

The arrival of Barack Obama to the presidency of the U.S. brought about policy changes as well as continuities from prior administrations. In the economic realm, no new free trade agreements were signed with Latin American countries, but some of those signed during the prior administration went into effect or were finally ratified during Obama's first term in office. The new administration also included some amendments to the free trade agreements signed with Colombia and Panama (both approved in 2011).

Following in the footsteps of the prior three presidents, Obama worked to strengthen bilateral relations with Mexico. In 2008, the **Mérida Initiative**, a security cooperation agreement between the countries, was signed into law. It sought to jointly address the problems of transnational organized crime and improve law enforcement cooperation as well as preventing arms and drug trafficking across the border. Also in 2013, the U.S. and Mexico began a series of cabinet-level meetings, called the High-Level

Economic Dialogue, to address mutual economic interests, improve coordination and transportation on the border, promote entrepreneurial activities, and cooperate on energy policy. On the issue of immigration, President Obama issued an executive order in 2012 that put in place Deferred Action for Childhood Arrivals (DACA), which allowed immigrants who had entered the country illegally as minors to be shielded from deportation. A later attempt by the government to expand DACA was stopped by the courts. These actions by the Obama administration were well-received by the Mexican government. Nevertheless, President Obama, like his predecessor, could not get a comprehensive immigration bill passed by Congress. In 2003, a related bill proposed by a bipartisan group of senators and endorsed by the president passed the Senate but was later defeated in the House of Representatives.

President Obama, similar to most other American presidents, also had to react to international crises. His first one in Latin America came in 2009, when the president of Honduras, Manuel Zelaya, was ousted from power by the military and sent into exile. Zelaya had been accused by the Supreme Court of violating the constitution in an attempt to hold a referendum to call for a constitutional assembly. The reform sought to end the prohibition on presidential reelection, allowing Zelaya to remain in power. The court responded with an arrest warrant for the president, but the military, instead of bringing him to trial, flew him out of the country. Then, the Honduran Congress, with the support of Zelaya's own party, voted to remove him from office and appointed the president of the chamber, Roberto Micheletti, as his replacement. Opposition to Zelaya in congress was not only rooted in what, for many, was an unlawful power-grab attempt by a sitting president but also in his closeness to the left-wing populist leader of Venezuela, President Hugo Chávez. For most observers and the international community, the illegal expulsion of Zelaya from Honduras amounted to a coup, although the country's Supreme Court and congress disputed that assessment. The United Nations and the European Union condemned Zelaya's removal from office, and the OAS voted to suspend Honduras's membership. President Obama called the coup illegal and a terrible precedent for the region.[35]

Subsequent diplomatic maneuverings became controversial. U.S. Secretary of State Hillary Clinton advocated for new elections and backed a mediation process led by Nobel Peace Prize winner and former president of Costa Rica, Oscar Arias. The talks eventually failed. U.S. officials then refused to formally call this crisis a "military coup" in order to avoid the automatic cutoff of all non-humanitarian aid. This move was widely criticized. Leaders of several Latin American countries publicly demanded that Zelaya be restored to the presidency, but the Honduran government refused and called for elections, which took place in November of 2009.

While the two major Honduran parties (the National Party and the Liberal Party) fielded candidates, a few independent candidates withdrew from the contest, alleging a lack of impartiality and their refusal to legitimize the de facto government that had organized it. The most well-known organizations dedicated to monitoring elections decided not to send observ-ers. The presidential election was won by Porfirio Lobos of the National Party in a contest *The New York Times* characterized as "clean and fair."[36] The U.S., Canada, Colombia, Costa Rica, Panama, and Peru recognized the new government, but most other Latin American countries refrained from doing so. However, by the second half of 2010, other Latin American coun-tries, such as Mexico, Chile, Guatemala, and El Salvador, had decided to restore diplomatic relations and recognized the Lobos administration. In May of 2011, the OAS overwhelmingly voted to restore Honduras's mem-bership. In the end, the Honduras crisis revealed important disagreements about how to respond to the overthrowing of a president and how to best proceed in promoting the restoration of democratic elections.

Disagreements were also evident in response to political developments in Venezuela. The arrival of Hugo Chávez to the presidency in February of 1999 brought about a drastic shift to the left in that country. Chávez, a classic populist and unabashed radical, won the presidency six years after failing to take over the country in a military coup. From the beginning, he embraced a vocal anti-U.S. rhetoric, reminiscent of the old Latin American far-left. His economic policies—widespread state intervention in the econ-omy, nationalization and expropriations of private enterprises, and trade protectionism—were geared toward reducing poverty and income inequal-ity, and his political reforms focused on centralizing power in the executive and eliminating checks and balances. Chávez received significant support from the Venezuelan population, particularly within low-income sectors of society. Yet, the upper classes, business interests, and a relevant portion of the middle class rejected Chávez's policies.

Relations between Venezuela and the U.S. rapidly deteriorated after Chávez assumed power. The Venezuelan president strengthened ties to countries deemed to be sponsors of terrorism, such as Iran, Iraq, and Libya; built an economic and military alliance with Cuba; scolded the U.S. for invading Afghanistan in 2001; and began to actively compete against the U.S. for influence in the region. Venezuela also strengthened economic and military ties with Russia and China. The U.S. criticized Chávez for crack-ing down on opponents and accused him of undermining democratic freedoms. In April of 2002, amidst increasing political violence and polar-ization inside the country, a faction of the Venezuelan military attempted a coup, which fell apart within a couple of days. The Bush administration blamed the Chávez government for what it saw as undemocratic actions that provoked the crisis leading to the coup. The U.S. National Endowment for Democracy had provided aid to various opposition groups, and declas-sified intelligence documents revealed that the U.S. government had infor-mation indicating a likely coup attempt was in the works.[37] However, there is no proof that it planned or organized the coup plotters.[38] Chávez did not initially blame the U.S. for the failed coup, but supporters of the left-wing president across Latin America attributed responsibility to the Bush admin-istration and, over time, so did the Venezuelan government.

Relations between Venezuela and the U.S. thawed briefly after Chávez's return to the presidency, but by 2004, they had already deteriorated. In 2005, Venezuela officially ended a military exchange program with the U.S., expelled U.S. military personnel, and suspended collaboration with the U.S. Drug Enforcement Agency (DEA). Chávez stepped up his condemnation of U.S. policies with personal insults against U.S. President George W. Bush and Secretary of State Condoleezza Rice. This incendiary anti-American rhetoric played well with his base, and many analysts believe that it was primarily directed at shoring up support among his domestic audience.

In 2006, Chávez further antagonized the U.S. government by publicly supporting Iran's uranium enrichment program, which the Security Council of the United Nations had demanded be stopped. Expropriations of assets belonging to various U.S. companies doing business in Venezuela, such as Cargill, ConocoPhillips, ExxonMobil, General Motors, and others, also strained bilateral relations. In 2010, Chávez prevented the appointed U.S. ambassador to Venezuela, Larry Palmer, from taking his post in Caracas. He had expelled the prior U.S. ambassador in 2008. In retaliation, the U.S. revoked the visa of the ambassador of Venezuela in Washington. Since that time, neither country has had an ambassador in the other's capitals.

After Hugo Chávez died in March of 2013, the presidency and most of the country's institutions remained in control of his political movement. Bilateral relations did not improve under the subsequent Venezuelan President, Nicolás Maduro. The expulsion of U.S. diplomats from Venezuela in late 2013 began a series of tit-for-tat expulsions that continued over the following years. Under President Maduro, economic mismanagement led to a tremendous recession, record-high inflation, shortages of food and medicines, and a rise in violent crimes. Support for the government plummeted and protests, which were sometimes violent, increased. In 2015, President Barack Obama issued an executive order imposing sanctions on a few Venezuelan officials for human rights abuses, demanded the release of political prisoners, and declared the country a national security threat. In December of that year, the Venezuelan opposition won a legislative majority in national elections. But soon after, the Supreme Court, controlled by the government, declared the decisions of the national assembly void. Opposition to the government mounted, and so did street protests. The government moved to violently repress anti-government gatherings, cancel regional elections, jail and proscribe opposition politicians, and ignore the actions of the national assembly.

In 2016, President Maduro named a general accused of drug crimes by the U.S. as the new minister of the interior. The following year, the new administration of President Donald J. Trump imposed sanctions on Venezuelan Vice President Tareck El Aissami, accusing him of involvement in drug trafficking. Criticism of Maduro's increasingly authoritarian rule became more vocal among Latin American countries.[39] In 2017, the secretary general of the OAS, Luis Almagro, accused the Venezuelan government of human rights violations and anti-democratic moves and urged the international body to consider imposing sanctions. In April of 2017, amid domestic unrest, the Venezuelan government announced that it was withdrawing from the OAS and blamed the U.S. and other Latin American nations for interfering in the country's domestic affairs.

The administration of President Trump proceeded to expand sanctions against the Maduro government. The target of these sanctions included more than 100 individuals and entities, including Maduro, the head of the army, members of the Venezuelan Supreme Court, Venezuela's state-owned oil company, and its central bank.[40] In January of 2019, President Trump recognized national assembly President Juan Guaidó as the interim president of Venezuela, in defiance to Maduro. Subsequently, 54 countries followed suit, including 13 Latin American countries. However, Maduro resisted the move and continued to violently repress political opponents. In August of 2019, the Trump administration imposed a total economic embargo on Venezuela, froze its assets, and threatened to impose sanctions to those engaging in business with the Maduro government.[41] In early 2020, the U.S. government imposed new sanctions against Venezuelan politicians aligned with Maduro.

The U.S. also had conflictual relationships with two other Latin American countries ruled by leftist governments allied with Venezuela: Bolivia and Ecuador. In Bolivia, the socialist leader of the coca growers' union, Evo Morales, assumed the presidency in 2006. U.S. officials were critical of Morales before and after the election. They were particularly concerned about his ties to Cuba and Venezuela, his opposition to U.S. anti-drug efforts, and the fate of U.S. investments in the country. They also questioned his commitment to respecting the democratic rights of the opposition. Morales was a vocal critic of U.S. foreign policy. In 2008, both countries expelled their respective ambassadors; Bolivia ejected the U.S. DEA from the country; and the U.S. decertified Bolivia for not cooperating with counternarcotic efforts, which ended U.S. trade preferences. In 2013, Morales expelled the **U.S. Agency for International Development (USAID)**, which had been assisting Bolivians since the 1960s. Bolivia remained a staunch ally of the Venezuelan government and consistently backed that country's denouncements of U.S. and foreign interference. At the end 2019, Bolivia's interim government appointed its first ambassador to the U.S. in 11 years; it followed the resignation of Morales from the presidency after widespread protests over election fraud.

Relations between the U.S. and Ecuador soured after President Rafael Correa came to power in 2007. Correa, similar to Morales in Bolivia, was highly critical of U.S. foreign policy and a close ally of Hugo Chávez. Soon after being elected, he closed a small U.S. airbase dedicated to anti-narcotic flights and passed a constitutional reform prohibiting foreign military bases on Ecuadoran soil. In 2011, Ecuador expelled the U.S. ambassador after the leaking of a diplomatic cable in which the ambassador mentioned pervasive corruption within the Ecuadorean police force and possible knowledge by President Correa. The U.S. reciprocated, expelling the Ecuadorian ambassador. Soon after, the U.S. Congress began moves to end Ecuador's trade benefits under the Andean Trade Promotion and Drug Eradication Act, which led to Correa withdrawing its country from the arrangement before being formally ejected. Both countries restored full diplomatic relations in 2012, but bilateral tensions continued. In 2014, after 53 years of working in Ecuador, USAID ended its activities in the country after Ecuador enacted new rules severely restricting its operation. Correa's third presidential term came to an end in 2017, after which relations between Ecuador and the U.S. improved.

Despite increasing tension with the leftist governments of Venezuela, Bolivia, and Ecuador, the U.S. government embarked on a historic rapprochement with Cuba. In December of 2014, President Barack Obama restored full diplomatic relations with the communist island, following 18 months of secret talks. In 2015, the U.S. embassy in Havana reopened after 54 years. The following year, President Barack Obama became the first president in almost a century to visit Cuba. In an unprecedented speech broadcast to the Cuban people, Obama called for greater freedoms, insisting that "citizens should be free to speak their mind without fear," "to organize and to criticize their government and to protest peacefully" without being detained, and "to choose their governments in free and open elections."[42] The rapprochement led to the loosening of travel and financial restrictions, but the long-standing trade embargo put in place by the U.S. Congress remained in effect.

After the arrival of Donald Trump to the U.S. presidency, relations with Cuba suffered a setback. The new president denounced the agreements signed by the prior administration and proceeded to reimpose some individual travel restrictions. In addition, the U.S. prohibited financial transactions with Cuban businesses linked to a military-run conglomerate. Then, in September of 2017, after more than twenty U.S. diplomatic staff in Havana suffered various ailments believed to be caused by acoustic (sonic) attacks, the administration withdrew more than half of its embassy staff. Cuba denied any involvement, and the U.S. did not accuse it of conducting such attacks but proceeded to expel fifteen Cuban diplomats from Washington. Then, in 2019, U.S. pressure on Cuba intensified after the Trump administration modified existing rules to temporarily allow American citizens to file lawsuits against businesses that operated on properties confiscated by the Cuban government after the 1959 revolution.

Two other major issues emerged during Trump's presidency. One was the renegotiation of NAFTA. Trump was a strong critic of the accord, which he believed disfavored U.S. interests. In 2018, member countries reached an agreement to replace NAFTA with a new treaty: **United States–Mexico–Canada Agreement (USMCA)**. After approval by the U.S. Congress, President Trump signed the new agreement into law in January 2020. Analysts tended to agree that the new pact was not too different from its predecessor, but its eventual economic implications will be known in the coming years.

The other issue was immigration. President Trump's anti-immigration rhetoric was evident during his presidential campaign, when he vowed to build a wall across the U.S.–Mexico border and increase deportations. By early 2020, however, only about 100 miles of the wall had been built, and the total number of deportations remained below the total number from the Obama administration. In a controversial move, the U.S. government began to apply a harsh border policy that, for a while, included separating children from the parents or guardians with whom they had crossed the U.S.–Mexico border. The number of poor Central American families fleeing poverty and violence in their countries increased substantially during Trump's term in office. The U.S. president sought to decrease the number of arrivals from Latin American countries by, among other things, putting pressure on Central American countries and Mexico. In 2019, after threatening to impose tariffs, ban travelers, and charge fees on remittances, the Guatemalan government agreed to require asylum seekers passing through on their way to the United States to first apply for protection in Guatemala.[43] After threatening to increase tariffs, Trump also reached an agreement with Mexico, which required that country to increase immigration enforcement and take in more migrants waiting for asylum hearings. Immigration from Latin America continued to be a subject of intense debate during the U.S. presidential campaign leading to the 2020 elections.

How Latin Americans View the United States

This chapter has examined many of the central issues influencing the relations between the U.S. and Latin America. The focus has been on intergovernmental relations and the strategic concerns of the U.S., but it is also revealing to explore what the citizens of Latin America think of the U.S., particularly during the most recent period. To this end, Table 4.1 summarizes the responses of public opinion surveys conducted across Latin America. The numbers show the proportion of people expressing that they have a good or very good opinion of the U.S. minus the proportion of people saying they have a bad or very bad opinion. The years when the surveys were conducted and the U.S. president (and term) at that time are shown at the top of the table.

The results highlight some interesting patterns. First, among Latin American citizens, the image of the U.S. is mostly very positive. On average, the proportion of respondents having a good or very good image of the U.S. is 45 points higher than the proportion of respondents having a bad or very bad image. Second, the data show that, over the period examined here, the highest opinion of the U.S. comes from countries in Central America and the Dominican Republic. This is the area of Latin America in which, historically, the U.S. has been most influential and where most of its 20th-century interventions took place. A significant share of these countries' trade is with the U.S., and migration from these countries to the U.S. is also substantial.

It is also clear that opinions have varied over time. For example, the average perception of the U.S. dropped markedly in 2003, the year of the U.S. invasion of Iraq. This is consistent with findings from other studies,

TABLE 4.1 ● Latin American's Opinions about the United States

Country	Bush I				Bush II				Obama I				Obama II		Trump I	
	2001	2002	2003	2004	2005	2006	2007	2008	2009	2010	2011	2013	2015	2016	2017	2018
Argentina	16	-17	-31	-30	-30	-55	-23	-27	33	25	12	13	14	24	7	4
Bolivia	52	20	2	1	7	5	16	3	37	31	36	11	9	28	5	4
Brazil	53	17	8	12	17	21	30	23	55	55	55	59	48	61	49	49
Chile	57	47	21	30	20	42	23	28	69	64	46	35	25	55	53	45
Colombia	58	62	44	53	46	49	50	49	64	68	66	53	51	61	62	49
Costa Rica	76	75	57	68	58	67	40	45	75	69	70	64	60	62	45	53
Dominican Republic			-	78	58	88	77	78	83	85	80	69	77	80	71	76
Ecuador	67	75	41	60	44	28	46	37	56	74	64	60	59	67	69	62
El Salvador	77	77	69	76	68	72	71	56	85	80	83	72	62	74	64	29
Guatemala	68	67	58	68	60	59	42	30	53	41	52	54	69	57	42	28
Honduras	80	83	68	72	77	71	66	63	72	71	81	72	73	77	65	47
Mexico	46	28	-16	-14	7	10	31	19	43	15	43	41	47	61	-3	-9
Nicaragua	82	75	51	51	50	64	67	53	65	58	46	53	40	59	44	53
Panama	58	85	69	71	74	85	77	48	77	72	66	79	51	72	58	60
Paraguay	64	44	7	30	13	17	23	34	48	47	66	68	36	72	52	53
Peru	60	59	44	52	49	45	42	35	56	60	61	50	52	65	47	23
Uruguay	32	17	2	-2	-8	26	17	-1	56	46	19	35	39	43	19	17
Venezuela	46	47	27	28	-6	-31	8	-9	37	33	20	22	12	35	23	28

Source: Latinobarómetro. [data available at http://www.latinobarometro.org]

such as those of the Pew Research Center, which show that favorable ratings of the U.S. dropped significantly in many countries around the world after the invasion of Iraq and remained low through 2008.[44] The evidence presented here also shows that views of the U.S. have worsened in the first two years of the Trump administration in comparison to the Obama administration. The decline has been particularly steep in the case of Mexico. Again, this change in Latin Americans' perceptions of the U.S. under President Trump follows more general worldwide trends.[45] Overall, the results presented here suggest that major foreign policy decisions have an impact on the views people have of the U.S. and show that most Latin Americans see the U.S. in a positive light, even when their government leaders adopt fiery anti-American rhetoric.

Conclusions

There is little doubt that the U.S. has had significant influence in Latin America. The political clout of the U.S. is a consequence of its economic and military power as well as its strategic interest in political developments in the region. Foreign policy decisions also have been influenced by more general guiding principles resulting from America's role in the world. From the end of World War II until the Soviet bloc began to unravel in 1989, the foreign policy of the U.S. was primarily guided by security concerns resulting from the Cold War. Until the 1970s, Marxism remained an appealing alternative for development among many Latin Americans. Preventing Soviet allies from emerging in the region was considered a matter of national security for American administrations. This chapter described how this Cold War zeal prompted direct military interventions in the Dominican Republic in 1965 and Grenada in 1983 as well as the training and funding of the irregular forces that intervened in Guatemala in 1954, Cuba in 1961, and Nicaragua in the 1980s. Economic and diplomatic initiatives during this period included the creation of the OAS after World War II and the Alliance for Progress in the 1960s.

The end of the Cold War and the related shift from a bipolar to a multipolar world led to a reassessment of priorities in U.S. foreign policy. This change had a profound impact on relations with Latin America. This chapter underlined how the last two military interventions in Latin America—in Panama in 1989 and Haiti in 1994—followed a very different rationale than previous ones during the Cold War. American presidents, beginning with George H. W. Bush, began to place significantly more weight on building economic ties, encouraging pro-market initiatives, and fighting drug trafficking than on fighting ideological foes. As noted in this chapter, the U.S. has signed free trade agreements with eleven Latin American since the early 1990s.

American presidents also must respond to foreign policy crises. Several were discussed in this chapter. We reviewed the involvement of the U.S. in helping to resolve the Mexican currency crisis of 1995 and the border dispute between Ecuador and Peru after military clashes in 1995 as well as the more controversial responses to the 2004 uprising in Haiti, the 2009 coup in Honduras, and the recurring crises in Venezuela. The era of U.S. military interventions in Latin America appears to be over, and diplomatic attempts at crisis management have become particularly relevant.

The future direction of U.S.–Latin American relations is uncertain. America has struggled to find an encompassing grand strategy since the end of the Cold War. From the early 1990s until 2016, successive American presidents have placed particular emphasis on deepening economic integration and coordinating crime-fighting initiatives. However, the arrival of Donald Trump to the presidency of the U.S. in 2017 called into question the continuation of prior initiatives. President Trump's rebuke of the free trade policies advanced by prior presidents and his confrontational approach have raised questions about the future direction of America's foreign policy in the region. Trump's trade and immigration initiatives and his proposal to cut foreign aid might sour relations with Latin American countries. The next few years should provide us with greater information to better evaluate America's new foreign policy priorities and its consequences in the region.

Key Terms

Anti-drug certification
    process 110
Central Intelligence Agency
    (CIA) 100
Cold War 98
Good Neighbor Policy 98
International sanctions 107
Monroe Doctrine 97
North American Free Trade
    Agreement (NAFTA) 108

Organization of American States
    (OAS) 100
Panama Canal Treaty 104
Roosevelt Corollary to the
    Monroe Doctrine 98
United States–Mexico–Canada
    Agreement (USMCA) 118

Bibliographic Recommendations

Hal Brands. 2010. *Latin America's Cold War.* Cambridge: Harvard University Press.

Nick Cullather. 2006. *Secret History: The CIA's Classified Account of Its Operations in Guatemala, 1952–1954,* 2nd edition. Stanford: Stanford University Press.

Richard Haas. 2017. *A World in Disarray: American Foreign Policy and the Crisis of the Old Order.* New York: Penguin Press.

Robert H. Holden and Eric Zolov (eds.). 2011. *Latin America and The United States: A Documentary History,* 2nd edition. New York: Oxford University Press.

David Scott Palmer. 2006. *U.S. Relations with Latin America during the Clinton Years.* Gainesville: University of Florida Press.

Robert A. Pastor. 2001. *Exiting the Whirlpool: U.S. Foreign Policy toward Latin America and the Caribbean,* 2nd edition. Boulder: Westview Press.

Web Resources

Central Intelligence Agency, General Report on CIA activities in Chile: https://www.cia.gov/library/reports/general-reports-1/chile/

Organization of American States: http://www.oas.org/en/

Oxford Research Encyclopedias, Latin American History, Diplomatic History: https://oxfordre.com/latinamericanhistory/

Institutions

Latin American Presidentialism

Constitutions provide a set of rules, rights, and fundamental principles that determine the structure of the state as well as the powers, limits, and responsibilities of the institutions of government. They are highly consequential, as they serve to organize politics and society and can help individuals coordinate their actions.

One of the fundamental issues in the creation of a constitution is how to design institutions that produce an effective central government that is sufficiently powerful but does not become a source of oppression. This dilemma was underscored by James Madison in *Federalist 51*: "In framing a government to be administered by men over men, the great difficulty lies in this: you must first enable the government to control the governed; and in the next place oblige it to control itself."[1] The solution he proposed involved institutions that combine the separation of powers with checks and balances. This entails different and competing branches of government that are both enabled and motivated to check each other's ambitions. The Constitution of the United States, signed in 1787, first established this unique set of institutions. One additional innovation introduced by the framers of the U.S. Constitution was the creation of a single chief executive elected by the citizens. This form of government came to be known as a *presidential republic*.

Most Latin American countries adopted the presidential form of government following their independence from Spain. Several countries in other parts of the world followed suit. But despite their widespread adoption, many scholars argue that **presidentialism** is fundamentally flawed. The debate over the merits and perils of presidential **constitutions** has been prominent in the comparative politics literature and, in particular, among

Latin American specialists. It is part of a larger argument about the role of institutions in bringing about democratic stability and economic growth.

The focus of this chapter is on Latin American presidentialism. The first section defines the presidential system of government and examines the main criticisms leveled against it. The next one reviews some provisions included in several Latin American constitutions that depart from the pure presidential form. The third section discusses how Latin American presidentialism differs from the prototypical U.S. version. The fourth and last section of the chapter focuses on presidential instability. Since the 1980s, many Latin American presidents have left or have been forced to leave office before the end of their term in office. These events have occurred without military intervention or a breakdown of democracy. The last section describes this phenomenon and examines the leading causes behind these presidential interruptions.

Presidentialism and Its Critique

The basic ideas underpinning the presidential form of government were initially advanced by James Madison, Alexander Hamilton, and John Jay in *The Federalist*, a collection of essays advocating the ratification of the U.S. Constitution. The presidential form of government combined the idea of separating the executive and legislative powers with checks and balances— that is, attributions that allow each branch to limit the power of the others. More precisely, *presidentialism* entails three defining features:[2]

1. a popularly elected president as the chief executive

2. fixed terms in office for the president and the legislative assembly

3. a president who names and directs the cabinet and has some constitutionally granted lawmaking authority

When first established, the election of a single chief executive chosen by a popular election was a significant innovation. Three Latin American countries—Argentina, Chile, and Paraguay—initially established an electoral college, elected by voters, to choose the president. These Latin American countries have since abolished this procedure, and now voters in all Latin American countries directly elect their respective presidents.

The second defining feature of presidentialism is a fixed term of office, which establishes that both the president and members of congress are elected for a constitutionally predetermined period of time. The president cannot dissolve the legislative branch, and members of congress cannot dismiss the president (except under some constitutionally prescribed **impeachment** procedure). Some have considered this trait of presidentialism as a source of stability, while others have viewed it as a source of excessive rigidity.

The last defining feature of presidentialism is executive authority. Presidents enjoy some constitutionally granted lawmaking power, which at a minimum comprises the ability to sign and veto legislation. Presidential prerogatives vary across countries and will be discussed further in this chapter, but even when circumscribed, they make the president a relevant player in the lawmaking process and promote executive-legislative bargaining. In addition, members of the cabinet are nominated by the president; the cabinet derives its authority from the president and not from congress.[3]

These attributes of presidentialism stand in contrast to the defining features of **parliamentarism**, its main alternative. In a parliamentary system, the head of government is the prime minister. The prime minister and the rest of the cabinet comprise the government, which is chosen indirectly by the legislative assembly, most often from among its members. Parliamentary systems do not have fixed terms of office: To remain in power, the government depends on the confidence of parliament, which can vote to dismiss it. Votes that can determine whether a government is dismissed are usually called *votes of confidence*. Many parliamentary countries also give the government the power to dissolve parliament and call for early elections.[4] This is why parliamentarism is sometimes described as a system of mutual dependence.

While in presidential systems the chief executive is both the head of government and the head of state, in parliamentary systems, the prime minister is only the head of government. The head of state is typically a monarch or a figurehead president.

The debate over which form of government is more conducive to democratic stability and good governance has a long history. Latin Americans debated it early in the 20th century and again, with particular intensity, at the beginning of the last wave of democratization. Most of the available evidence showed that presidential democracies were more likely to break down into authoritarianism than parliamentary democracies. But analysts have been in disagreement about the reasons behind this finding.

Many have blamed the inner workings of presidentialism for its instability. The best-known advocate of this perspective was the political scientist Juan J. Linz.[5] Critics such as Linz remark that the fixed terms of office that characterize presidentialism introduce an element of rigidity to executive-legislative elections: There is no mechanism to replace presidents who have lost the confidence of their parties or who have become highly unpopular. Because terms of office are fixed, **executive-legislative deadlock** cannot be easily overcome and may become particularly worrisome when confronting major crises or a highly polarized environment. Waiting for the next election may be considered too costly for some political actors, who may prefer to undertake unconstitutional actions to try to change an unfavorable situation. In other words, in the face of political stalemate, a president may be tempted to close congress (as Peruvian President Alberto Fujimori did in 1992); congress may tempted to use unconstitutional maneuverings to get rid of a president (as in the case of Ecuador in 1997); or frustrated political actors may knock on the barracks door to get the military to intervene.

A second related argument stresses that presidentialism offers few incentives for coalition formation, which is likely to exacerbate executive-legislative conflict.[6] Since presidents are not required to have the confidence of congress to remain in office, they are presumed to have few incentives to seek government coalitions with other parties. In addition, a direct election is likely to give presidents a sense of power and a popular mandate that work against power-sharing and coalition building. In the presence of multiple viable parties, as is the case in most Latin American countries, the chances that elections would produce presidents with a corresponding single-party majority in congress are diminished. Presidents that lack the support of a majority in congress, the argument goes, are likely to produce legislatively inefficient governments, which increase the chances of democratic breakdown.

A third criticism centers on the competing claims for legitimacy resulting from the direct election of members of congress and the president. Since both branches of government are independent and derive their power directly from voters, both can claim to represent the will of the people. As a result, critics claim, a conflict is always latent and can surface at any time. This is sometimes referred to as the problem of "dual democratic legitimacy."[7]

A related challenge centers on the two-dimensional nature of the presidency. An elected president is the head of government, which represents a clear political and partisan option. At the same time, the president is the head of state, which represents the nation. This dual role requires the president to switch from a ceremonial role embodying national unity to a political role seeking to advance a particular legislative program and confronting opponents. This is not always easy. As a result, people may think that a partisan president is betraying the unifier role demanded of a head of state, which can lessen the legitimacy of the presidency.

Critics of presidentialism, such as Linz, have argued that a parliamentary system of government could overcome most of the aforementioned challenges. First, it lacks the rigidity of presidentialism. The executive in a parliamentary system needs the support of a parliamentary majority to remain in power. Parliament can use a vote of confidence to dismiss a government, and a prime minister is often allowed (via a request to the head of state) to dissolve parliament and call for new elections. This institutional safety valve helps to relieve executive-legislative deadlock. Second, coalition formation is common in parliamentary countries, promoted by the government's need to have majority support to maintain power. When a majority party exists, it determines the composition of the executive. But if the largest party lacks a parliamentary majority, it is forced to bargain with other parties to craft a government acceptable to a majority of the members of parliament. This requirement fosters coalition building. Third, parliamentary systems also avoid the problem of dual democratic legitimacy, since it is parliament that chooses the executive, and the two-dimensional nature of the executive, since the head of government and the head of state are different individuals.

Critics of presidentialism have argued that many political crises confronted by Latin American countries could have been avoided or resolved less painfully if a parliamentary system had been in place. Consider the following examples from Chile and Venezuela. In 1970, Salvador Allende was elected president of Chile for six years after winning around 36 percent of the vote. His opponents had a majority in congress, rejected the government's policies, and accused the president of undertaking various unconstitutional actions. In this highly polarized conflict, there was no safety valve to provide a way out of the executive-legislative crisis. The conflict between the two branches of government ended with a military coup that took place in September of 1973. The breakdown of democracy in Chile might have been avoided, the argument goes, had a parliamentary system been in place. The opposition could have voted "no confidence" in the government and either replaced it with one acceptable to them or called for an early election, or Allende could have dissolved congress and called for a new election to legitimize his standing.

A more recent example comes from Venezuela. The country's descent into authoritarianism accelerated after the government party lost a parliamentary majority in congress in the elections of 2015. Executive-legislative deadlock paralyzed ordinary lawmaking and in the face of extreme political polarization, the executive began to govern around congress. This crisis intensified political violence and unconstitutional maneuvering on the part of the government. If Venezuela had a parliamentary system in place, the argument goes, the available institutional tools might have provided a democratic way out of this impasse.

Despite these arguments, many remain unconvinced that the inner working of presidentialism has made democratic breakdown more likely. Political scientist José Antonio Cheibub examined cross-national data from the second part of the 20th century and found no support for the view that presidential countries in which the executive lacks a congressional majority are more prone to democratic breakdown.[8] This finding seems to contradict the argument that executive-legislative deadlock makes the fall of democracy in presidential countries more likely. Studies have also shown that coalition making is not uncommon in presidential countries, as critics of this system of government have suggested. In fact, when presidents lack a single-party majority in congress, they are more likely to build a government coalition with other parties than not.[9] In contrast to the arguments of Linz and others, some have claimed that the main causes of democratic breakdown arise from extra-constitutional factors such as social divisions, political polarization, historical influences, or the economy.[10]

Presidentialism also offers some advantages over parliamentarism. Political scientists Matthew S. Shugart and John M. Carey emphasize three benefits.[11] First, the direct election of the president maximizes accountability. Voters can reward or punish the president (or the president's party) for the government's performance during the prior term in office. In parliamentary systems, the lack of direct elections for choosing the government weakens electoral accountability, particularly when the party system is very fragmented. Second, in presidential systems, voters are more likely to identify the potential government that would result from national elections than in parliamentary systems. As a result, presidential elections provide voters with a greater opportunity to make a prospective choice than elections under parliamentarism, which are often followed by lengthy bargaining and political maneuvering that make prior knowledge of which government will emerge less likely. Third, legislators in presidential countries are more independent from party leaders than under parliamentarism, which increases opportunities for bargaining and compromise. In other words, there are often a few legislators willing to cross the party line, which facilitates political accommodation. Under parliamentarism, the executive has coercive tools (e.g., the vote of confidence) to resist the initiatives of members of parliament and impose its will.[12]

A related argument about the merits of each constitutional type focuses on the provision of nationally oriented policies. Nationally cohesive parties help to aggregate interests in society and limit the incentives of locally oriented politicians to pursue pork barrel and patronage policies. Matthew S. Shugart notes that nationally oriented political parties are a prerequisite for parliamentary democracies to effectively provide national collective goods.[13] In their absence, he argues, presidentialism appears better suited for this task. Presidents, who are elected nationally, have both the motivation and the authority to pursue some collective goods policies that are national in scope. This can partially counteract the locally oriented tendencies of legislative parties. Given the lack of nationally oriented political parties in several Latin American countries, presidentialism might offer a distinct advantage over parliamentarism.

The academic debate over the merits and drawbacks of presidentialism is not over, but the chances that Latin American countries will switch their constitutional form of government in favor of parliamentarism are very low. Interestingly, Brazilians twice voted in referendums to decide whether to make this switch. The first time was in 1963 after the Brazilian Congress had introduced an amendment to the constitution instituting a parliamentary system of government. At that time, 82 percent of voters rejected the congressional reform. The second time was in 1993. On that occasion, 55 percent of the people voted in favor of presidentialism, and 25 percent voted in favor of parliamentarism.

One country that switched its constitutional form of government is Haiti, which, in 1987, moved from presidentialism to **semi-presidentialism**. This intermediate form of government, in place in France and several other countries in Europe and Africa, has three main characteristics. The first is a directly elected head of state, called a president, who has some relevant legislative powers. The second is a prime minister who serves as head of government. In Haiti, the prime minister is chosen by the president from among the members of the majority party in parliament (which may not be the president's party). If the largest party does not have a majority, then the Haitian president must reach an agreement with the heads of both chambers of parliament in the selection of the prime minister. The third characteristic is that the prime minister is subject to the confidence of a parliamentary majority (as in a parliamentary system).[14] While Haiti's goal in changing its constitution was to bypass some of the presumed perils of presidentialism, the country was unable to avoid political instability and military intervention in the subsequent years.

The definition of presidentialism given in this section reflects the "pure" version of this form of government. In several countries of Latin America, however, constitutional designers have experimented with variations that depart from the classic version of presidentialism. The next sections review some noteworthy distinctions implemented in various countries and elaborate on the differences between U.S. and Latin American presidentialism.

Constitutional Variations in Latin American Presidentialism

The prior section of this chapter discussed some essential characteristics of presidentialism and how it differs from parliamentarism. Within presidential countries, we also find relevant differences. Some of these procedural variations do not contradict the three basic traits of the presidential form of government underlined in the prior section. For example, Argentina, Bolivia, Colombia, Guatemala, Peru, Uruguay, and Venezuela have constitutional provisions that allow congress to censure and fire members of the cabinet. This prerogative is not inconsistent with the defining traits of presidentialism previously described. But in some of these countries, differences are more significant, which have led scholars to refer to them as *presidential hybrids* to distinguish them from the "pure" presidential form. This is most evident in Peru, Uruguay, and Venezuela, which allow motions to censure the cabinet that can trigger the dissolution of congress by the president. Table 5.1 summarizes these rules.

Peru's institutional structure deviates the most from the pure presidential type and has been considered by some scholars as being close to that of a semi-presidential country. The constitution of 1993, for example, established the position of cabinet chief. This official is in charge of coordinating the activities of the cabinet, acts as the government's spokesperson, and countersigns executive decrees. The cabinet chief is named by and can

TABLE 5.1 ● Distinct Attributes of Some Presidential Constitutions

Country	Who Can Be Censured?	Vote Threshold	Possibility of Confidence Motion	Possibility of Dissolution of Congress
Argentina	Only the cabinet chief	Majority vote	No	No
Bolivia	Individual ministers	Two-thirds of members	No	No
Colombia	Individual ministers	Majority of members	No	No
Guatemala	Individual ministers	Majority or two-thirds of members	No	No
Peru	Individual ministers or cabinet	Majority of members	Yes	Yes
Uruguay	Individual ministers or cabinet	Majority vote	No	Yes
Venezuela	Individual ministers or cabinet chief	Three-fifths vote	No	Yes

be fired by the president and has the responsibility of naming and removing other ministers with the agreement of the president. In addition, the Peruvian constitution of 1993 included a provision, also present in previous charters, which allows the (unicameral) congress to dismiss a member of the president's cabinet or the entire cabinet. For this to take place, a vote of censure needs to pass with the support of a majority of the members of congress. After the dismissal of two cabinets, the president has the power to dissolve congress and hold new elections.[15] Moreover, the Peruvian constitution allows the cabinet chief and individual ministers to introduce a motion of confidence linked to a bill. If congress rejects such a proposal, the individual minister making the motion (or the entire cabinet) must resign.

The constitution of Uruguay, enacted in 1967 and reformed several times after its inception, allows congress to censure ministers or the entire cabinet. Such a motion must garner a majority vote in one chamber of congress and then in a joint session of both chambers. If the vote of censure in the joint session passes with a two-thirds majority, the minister or ministers must resign. If the motion of censure passes with a majority smaller than two thirds, the president may veto it. After the veto, congress may override with a three-fifths majority, after which the minister or ministers must resign. However, if, following a veto, congress votes in favor of the motion of censure but does not reach the threshold required for an override, the president can prevent the minister(s) from resigning and proceed to dissolve congress.[16]

In Venezuela, the position of cabinet chief, called the *executive vice president*, was introduced in the 1999 constitution. This official is appointed by and can be fired by the president. The duties of the executive vice president include coordinating the activities of the cabinet, serving as a link between the executive and legislative branches, and managing personnel appointments in the state bureaucracy.[17] Venezuela's constitution indicates that members of the cabinet, as well as the executive vice president, can be dismissed by a vote of censure. Such action requires the support of a three-fifths supermajority in the country's (unicameral) congress. Moreover, the president can choose to dissolve congress if the executive vice president is dismissed three times over the course of one six-year presidential term.[18]

In Bolivia, Colombia, and Guatemala, members of the cabinet are also subject to a congressional vote of censure. For a minister to be fired, the Colombian constitution of 1991 requires a vote of censure to be passed with the support of a majority of the members of one of the two chambers of congress. In the case of Bolivia, the 2009 constitution requires a vote by two thirds of members in a joint meeting of both chambers of congress.[19] In Guatemala, the 1985 constitution stipulates that a vote to censure a minister must pass with the support of a majority of the members of congress, unless the president ratifies the minister, in which case the required threshold for dismissal becomes two thirds of members.

In Argentina, the position of cabinet chief was established by the constitutional reform of 1994.[20] The cabinet chief not only coordinates the activities of the cabinet and executes the national budget but is also a conduit between the executive and legislative branches, periodically reporting to congress. Although the president has the right to appoint and fire the cabinet chief, this individual can also be terminated via a majority vote in both chambers of congress following the approval of a motion of censure.

Another constitutional provision not commonly associated with a pure presidential system is the **recall referendum**, which can cut short the executive's term of office. This is ultimately the voters' decision. It is not uncommon to find this provision at the regional or local level or applicable to officials other than the president. But in Venezuela, Ecuador, and Bolivia, it can be used to remove a president from office.[21] The first step is to collect enough signatures to get the recall on the ballot. The minimum number of signatures required is 15 percent of registered voters in Ecuador and Bolivia and 20 percent of registered voters in Venezuela. The threshold that must be overcome for a recall referendum to pass varies: In Bolivia, it is the percentage of votes the president received when last elected; in Venezuela, it is the number of votes the president received when last elected; and in Ecuador, it is just a majority of voters.

Differences between U.S. and Latin American Presidentialism

There are significant ways in which Latin American presidentialism differs from the U.S. model. For the most part, presidents in Latin America are given greater authority over legislative matters than the U.S. president. This power is codified in various rules that equip the executive with institutional tools to influence policymaking. The next subsections summarize the workings of four of these instruments: the right to initiate bills; veto power; prerogatives to influence the legislative agenda; and **executive decree power**. Since these rules affect the bill-to-law process, the discussion not only informs us of differences between Latin America and the U.S. but also about the prerogatives presidents have at their disposal to enact their policy programs.

The Right to Initiate Legislation

The first step in getting legislation enacted into law is to draft a bill. While anyone may do this, the right to introduce a bill in the U.S. Congress is restricted to its members. Presidents do not have the right to initiate bills directly. To enact their programs, they require surrogates in congress to introduce and push forward particular bills. In Latin America, however, presidents have the authority to introduce bills directly. In fact, most major bills introduced in the legislatures of Latin America are drafted in the executive branch and subsequently introduced as presidential bills.

The relative allocation of policy expertise is one reason that highly complex bills originate inside the executive branch. Most Latin American legislatures have significantly fewer resources than the executive branch to draft such proposals; they frequently lack technical staff, sophisticated information-gathering resources, and internal funding. In addition, the relatively low reelection rates common to many legislatures in the region have hindered policy specialization and long-term commitments to improving the technical capacity of congressional committees.

Another reason for the relative importance of executive bills is that legislators from the government coalition usually expect the president to be the leading force pushing for the enactment of the party's legislative program. As a result, they tend to initiate other types of bills, usually less significant or more narrowly targeted.

Lastly, the importance of executive-originated bills is also the consequence of constitutional rules that give the president the exclusive right to initiate legislation in some specific policy areas. Several Latin American countries have rules that make the president the gatekeeper on certain legislative matters: No change may occur unless the executive introduces a bill on such a topic. For the most part, this presidential power is reserved for tax and spending legislation or administrative matters.

The process structuring the passage of the budget illustrates some of these salient differences between the U.S. and Latin America. In the U.S., the president sends a detailed budget request to congress, establishing executive spending priorities and recommending spending and tax changes, but the house and senate budget committees are the ones that eventually present the final budget resolution. While the president is an influential actor shaping the budget, the U.S. Congress ultimately holds the "power of the purse." If, for some reason, the federal budget is not approved by congress on time, there is no alternative budget that automatically goes into effect. Temporary legislative measures (continuing resolutions) may keep the government running, but if executive-legislative deadlock prevents this alternative path, the federal government may be forced to suspend some government activities funded by the appropriation bills. Also, the president cannot refuse to spend the appropriated money and has to request and receive the consent of congress before canceling or cutting appropriated amounts.

In Latin America, the passage of a budget bill is structured very differently. To start with, presidents are required to introduce the budget bill every year. Moreover, in some countries, such as Chile, Brazil, and Peru, only the executive branch can initiate spending legislation, and legislators face strict restrictions on the initiation of tax bills. Other countries, such as Colombia and Uruguay, restrict legislators from initiating spending bills but not tax-related proposals; others, such as Argentina and Costa Rica, do not significantly restrict the ability of legislators to initiate tax and spending bills.

Unlike the U.S., most Latin American countries have rules that favor the president in the event that congress fails to pass the budget bill by the beginning of the new fiscal year. One procedure, in place in Chile and Colombia, dictates that if such a scenario materializes, the original budget proposal sent by the president becomes law. Another procedure, in place in Argentina and Uruguay, establishes that in the absence of a budget bill, the previous year's budget must come into effect, usually accompanied by wide discretion to redistribute previously assigned funds. A third procedure, in place in Brazil, mandates the temporary enactment of the president's proposed budget until congress passes a new budget bill.

In addition, some Latin American countries give presidents broad discretion over the funds appropriated through the budget bill. For instance, Argentine presidents often redistribute funds from one purpose to another, and Brazilian presidents tend to selectively execute some appropriations and not others with the goal of influencing the behavior of individual legislators. The U.S. president is specifically prohibited from taking these actions with congressionally appropriated money.

Veto Power

All presidential constitutions give the executive the power to veto legislation. However, how much presidents can do with this power varies across countries in meaningful ways. According to the U.S. Constitution, the president has the authority to veto legislation passed by congress within ten days of the bill's passage. The president's veto applies to the entire bill passed by congress.[22] A vote of two thirds in both the House of Representatives and the Senate is required to override the president's veto and turn the bill into law. If congress does not act, or if it fails to reach the override threshold, then the bill is rejected and does not become law. As long as one third plus one of the members present in one chamber prefer the veto over the bill, the president's position will prevail. In practice, the possibility of an executive veto means that congress must consider the president's policy preferences as it labors to produce legislation.[23]

Latin American countries also give the executive the power to veto an entire bill, although the threshold for an override varies. In some countries, overriding the president's veto demands a two-thirds majority in each chamber (e.g., Argentina, Chile, the Dominican Republic, and Mexico), while in others, it requires a two-thirds majority in a unicameral congress (e.g., Costa Rica, Guatemala, and Honduras). In some places, the threshold is simply a majority of members in one (e.g., Nicaragua and Peru) or two chambers (e.g., Brazil and Colombia).[24]

What are the consequences of this variation in override thresholds? Consider this: In Argentina, presidents need the support of one third plus one of the members from one of the two chambers to prevent a bill from becoming law; presidents in Costa Rica need the support of one third plus one of the members from the single legislative chamber to do the same; presidents in Colombia need the support of a majority in one chamber to prevent a bill from passing; and presidents in Peru need the support of a majority from the single legislative chamber to achieve this goal.

Aside from variations in the threshold to override, other substantial traits make the executive veto in the U.S. and Latin America different. An important difference is the ability to issue **partial vetoes**. Aside from the power to reject an entire bill, as in the traditional **block veto**, most Latin American countries allow presidents to veto parts of the bill. Typically, presidents have broad authority over which part of the bill they are allowed to reject. In countries such as Argentina and Brazil, after a partial veto is exercised, the non-deleted parts of the bill become law, and the subsequent congressional debate is limited to whether or not to override the specific sections rejected by the president. In 1996, the U.S. Congress gave the president the power to exercise a line-item veto in appropriation bills (a more limited version of the partial veto), but the Supreme Court ruled that such delegation of power was unconstitutional.[25]

Many Latin American countries also give the president the power to issue **amendatory vetoes**, which allow modifications (amendments) in addition to deletions.[26] Congress can approve these changes introduced by the president by a majority vote, in which case they become law, or reject them. If it chooses the latter, then congress can try to override the veto and insist on the version of the bill it originally sent to the president.

In countries that allow amendatory vetoes, such as Chile, Costa Rica, El Salvador, Mexico, Peru, and Uruguay, presidents use this prerogative to introduce changes that essentially construct an alternative bill. If a congressional majority prefers the amended version returned by the executive over the original bill, it will vote to accept it. If congress cannot override the presidential veto, and a congressional majority prefers the amended version of the bill returned by the executive over the status quo, it will also vote to accept it. In short, the power to introduce amendments to vetoed bills gives the president significant leeway to influence the content of legislation. It should come as no surprise that in countries that allow this procedure, presidents are more likely to use amendatory than block vetoes.

To summarize, the executive veto is an important lawmaking tool. It affects legislative decision making at the last stage of the bill-to-law journey, and as a consequence, its influence permeates to earlier moves in the legislative process. As previously explained, most Latin American constitutions give the president greater discretion to affect legislation at the veto stage than the U.S. Constitution.

Legislative Agenda Setting

In the U.S. Congress, the legislative agenda is firmly controlled by the majority party, and the president lacks the formal authority to interfere in the day-to-day scheduling of bills. This is not the case in Latin America, where several presidents have powers to influence the legislative agenda. Let us consider the following three prerogatives: to declare bills to be of urgent consideration, to call extraordinary sessions of congress, and to participate in congressional debates.

Time is a scarce resource in congress. Many bills never see the light of day. For this reason, the ability to influence the scheduling of legislation is a particularly advantageous tool. In seven Latin American countries, presidents can compel congress to attend to a particular bill by attaching an urgency motion to it. Congress may reject such a bill or return it to a committee, but it must start debating it within a stipulated time. Deadlines vary across countries. For example, the Chilean constitution gives the president three types of urgency motions: an *immediate* motion that imposes a three-day deadline, a *suma* motion with a ten-day deadline, and a *simple* motion that allows a thirty-day deadline. Presidents in Brazil, Colombia, and Mexico also enjoy this prerogative, although without such short deadlines. Urgency motions are more compelling when the default outcome if congress does not act is the automatic passage of the bill. The constitutions of Ecuador, Uruguay, and Paraguay give the president this power.[27]

Most Latin American presidents also have the right to call extraordinary sessions of congress, where they can determine the congressional agenda. Many Latin American congresses have these special sessions every year. Presidents can use them to push bills of their choosing; however, congress retains the power to address or decline to address those items advanced by the executive.

Another salient difference between the U.S. and Latin America has to do with congressional debates. Many Latin American constitutions give the executive the right to take part in plenary debates. This prerogative, which has been in place since the early 19th century, allows the executive branch to send envoys to congress (typically ministers) to advocate, explain, and defend proposals on the plenary floor. In some countries, these representatives of the executive can even offer amendments to the bills being debated (but are not allowed to vote).

Decree Power

Latin American presidents typically have some powers to issue executive decrees. There are some similarities between these decrees and the executive orders permitted by the U.S. Constitution. In the case of the U.S., these executive directives have been used for several purposes, such as to reorganize executive agencies, change regulations, influence the interpretation and implementation of legislation, or set policy priorities.[28] Some famous directives put in place via executive orders include the internment of Japanese Americans during World War II, issued by President Roosevelt in 1942; the integration of the armed forces, issued by President Truman in 1948; the use of National Guard troops to help with the enforcement of desegregation in Little Rock's Central High School, issued by President Eisenhower in 1957; the deferment of deportations for people who came to the United States illegally as children, issued by President Obama in 2012; and the temporary ban on the issuance of new visas for citizens of seven Muslim-majority countries and for refugees, issued by President Trump in 2017. In general, federal courts have been reluctant to overturn executive orders but have done it on some occasions. For instance, in 1951, federal courts overturned President Truman's seizure of the steel mills, and in 1995, federal courts overturned President Clinton's order prohibiting federal contractors from hiring permanent replacements for striking workers.

In Latin America, executive decrees tend to have a greater reach than the executive orders of the American president. One common type is the **administrative decree**, which codifies ministerial decisions, such as the governing framework associated with public utilities. Another type is the **regulatory decree**, which specifies how a law is supposed to be implemented (i.e., the instrumentation of a [typically broad] piece of legislation). But the most controversial and far-reaching type is the **decree-law**, which gives the president much wider authority to legislate than the power associated with executive orders.

Four Latin American countries provide wide decree power to their presidents: Brazil, Colombia, Peru, and Argentina. In Brazil and Colombia, decrees take effect immediately and lapse after a certain period of time unless congress ratifies them. In Colombia, decrees must be preceded by a declaration of national emergency (something not uncommon in this country). In Peru and Argentina, decrees immediately become law and can only be nullified by a congressional act. In the case of Peru, such decrees are intended to be restricted to economic legislation. Although they are meant to be used in the context of an emergency, presidents have used them in various situations. Federal courts have the authority to nullify these decrees, and on several occasions, they have overturned them.

The fourth and final type is the **delegated decree**, which allows congress to temporarily cede authority to the president to legislate unilaterally on certain specified matters. While the U.S. Congress cannot delegate legislative powers to the president, it may assign some authority to the executive branch, such as food and drug regulation to the Food and Drug Administration, environmental regulation to the Environmental Protection Agency, or the collection of taxes to the Internal Revenue Service. In contrast, five Latin American countries have constitutional rules that allow congress to delegate legislative authority to the president: Argentina, Chile, Colombia, Peru, and Venezuela. For example, in February 2007, the Venezuelan National Assembly passed a bill delegating the authority to issue lawmaking decrees on health, education, housing, social security, and tourism to President Hugo Chávez for a period of 18 months. During that time, President Chávez issued 26 major new laws.

Presidential Instability

So far, this chapter has examined the main traits of the presidential form of government and some of the major institutional differences between presidentialism in the U.S. and Latin America. This section shifts our attention to presidential instability.

Despite holding institutionally powerful positions, many Latin American presidents have seen their term in office cut short. While military coups have become rare in Latin America, political crises have not disappeared. The numerous presidencies that have ended before the executive's stipulated term of office was completed have been particularly troublesome. Between 1985 and 2018, 20 Latin American presidents have fallen from power without military intervention or a breakdown of democracy. Table 5.2 presents a list of these presidential interruptions.

The circumstances that paved the way to the early end of these presidents' tenure vary. One mechanism at play has been impeachment. For example, in 2016, the Brazilian Congress ousted President Dilma Rousseff after an impeachment vote. The Senate, with 61 votes in favor and 20 against, convicted her on charges of breaking Brazil's budget law. She had

TABLE 5.2 ● Presidential Interruptions			
Country	Year	Name	Removal
Argentina	1989	Raúl R. Alfonsin	resigned/anticipated transfer of power
	2001	Fernando de la Rúa	resigned
	2001	Adolfo Rodriguez Saá	resigned
	2003	Eduardo A. Duhalde	resigned/anticipated elections
Bolivia	1985	Hernán Siles Zuazo	resigned/anticipated elections
	2003	Gonzalo Sánchez de Lozada	resigned
	2005	Carlos D. Mesa	resigned
Brazil	1992	Fernando A. Collor de Mello	impeached/resigned
	2016	Dilma Rousseff	impeached
Dominican Republic	1996	Joaquin A. Balaguer	resigned/anticipated elections
Ecuador	1997	Abdalá J. Bucaram	dismissed
	1997	Rosalía Arteaga Serrano	dismissed
	2005	Lucio E. Gutiérrez	dismissed
Guatemala	1993	Jorge A. Serrano Elías	resigned
	2015	Otto Pérez Molina	impeached/resigned
Peru	2000	Alberto K. Fujimori	resigned
	2018	Pedro P. Kuczynski	resigned
Paraguay	1999	Raúl A. Cubas Grau	impeached/resigned
	2012	Fernando A. Lugo	impeached
Venezuela	1993	Carlos Andrés Pérez	impeached

previously been impeached by the lower house of congress in a vote that had also surpassed the two-thirds required threshold. The rest of her term in office was served by the country's vice president. Paraguayan President Fernando Lugo was also toppled after an impeachment vote. In 2012, the country's Senate voted 39 to 4 to remove him from office, after the lower chamber had voted 76 to 1 to impeach him. Lugo was found guilty of poor performance in handling a deadly land dispute. He was replaced by the country's vice president, who served the rest of his term in office.

Both of these impeachments were highly controversial, and supporters of the deposed presidents decried the proceedings leading to the respective removals. In the case of President Rousseff, the Brazilian Congress impeached her for offenses that prior administrations also had committed but for which they were never indicted. Her trial occurred during a period of severe economic turmoil and amid a major corruption scandal involving many members of the Brazilian political and economic elite, including several closely linked to the governing party. In the case of President Lugo, the Paraguayan Congress impeached him, not for criminal acts, but for "poor performance of his duties," which is one of the three grounds given in the country's constitution to undertake such a process.[29] Supporters of the president complained that the Senate removed him from office the day after the lower chamber impeached him and thereby denied him due process. However, this was not a criminal trial but rather an impeachment proceeding under constitutional rules that give congress wide latitude to convict as long as it can muster the required supermajority.

Experts tend to agree that impeachment proceedings are always political and, in fact, both Rousseff and Lugo had lost the support of key congressional allies before their impeachments. Nevertheless, to move forward, the advocates of impeachment must follow specific rules established in the constitution.

Another presidential impeachment took place in Venezuela in 1993. The proceedings in that case followed a different path, stipulated in the Venezuelan constitution in place at that time. It started when the attorney general accused President Carlos Andrés Pérez of embezzling funds belonging to a presidential discretionary fund. After the Venezuelan Supreme Court decided that there were grounds to prosecute him, the Senate voted to strip the president of his immunity, a move that was akin to an impeachment. President Carlos Andrés Pérez was then removed from office by the Venezuelan Congress and later detained in 1994. The Supreme Court found him guilty of misappropriating government funds in May of 1996 and sentenced him to 28 months in prison.

A similar event took place more recently in Guatemala. In 2015, the federal prosecutor and the United Nations International Commission against Impunity in Guatemala (CICIG) asked for the impeachment of President Otto Pérez Molina, whom they accused of being a key player in a major corruption scandal. The Supreme Court decided that there were grounds to move forward with the accusation. After the dissemination of information implicating the president and massive street protests, the Guatemalan Congress voted unanimously to revoke the president's immunity. As in the Venezuelan case, this vote was akin to an impeachment. President Otto Pérez Molina challenged the legitimacy of this vote in the constitutional court but was unsuccessful. He subsequently resigned the presidency pending his trial and was arrested soon after.

In two other cases, Latin American presidents also resigned their posts before the end of the impeachment proceedings. Brazilian President Fernando A. Collor de Mello resigned in 1992 after the lower chamber of congress impeached him and just before the Senate trial. He was accused of involvement in influence peddling and racketeering. Paraguayan President Raúl A. Cubas Grau resigned in 1999 after the lower chamber of congress impeached him and just before the Senate trial. He was accused of involvement in the assassination of the country's vice president.

On some occasions, presidents were dismissed by congress by means that differed from the impeachment proceedings established in the constitution. Three of these controversial events happened in Ecuador.[30] The first one took place in 1997, when President Abdalá J. Bucaram was removed from office after being declared mentally incompetent to govern by a majority vote in the Ecuadorean Congress. This event occurred amid severe economic problems and widespread demonstrations against the president and without an official diagnostic of his mental condition. After the vote, Bucaram left the country to live in Panama, where he was granted political asylum.

The second such event occurred a few days later. After deposing Bucaram, the Ecuadorean Congress named Fabián Alarcón, the head of the chamber, as president. However, Bucaram's vice president, Rosalía Arteaga Serrano, challenged this decision in the constitutional court, arguing that she was supposed to assume the presidency. The court ruled in her favor, congress acquiesced temporarily, and she became president. However, two days later, the Ecuadorean Congress pushed for her dismissal and reinstalled the head of congress as the new president.

The third dismissal of an Ecuadorean president by congress took place in 2005. Amid violent protests and looting, President Lucio E. Gutiérrez declared a state of emergency and, seeking to appease his opponents, dismissed the Ecuadorean Supreme Court, which had been packed with his political allies. Protests continued to escalate, even after the emergency was lifted. This prompted congress to assemble and vote unanimously (60 to 0 in a 100-seat chamber) to oust the president on the grounds of abandoning his office.[31] Gutiérrez took refuge in the Brazilian embassy before being flown out of the country. Upon his return to Ecuador in October 2005, he was arrested on charges of subverting national security.

The most common type of early termination of a presidential term has not been impeachment or dismissal but formal resignation.[32] On three occasions—Argentina in 2003, Bolivia in 1985, and the Dominican Republic in 1996—presidents decided to call for early elections, and on one occasion—Argentina in 1989—the president chose to transfer power to the president-elect five months ahead of schedule.

The context surrounding the rest of the resignations vary. Twice in Argentina (both in 2001) and twice in Bolivia (2003 and 2005), presidents resigned due to protests and political pressure. In 1993 in Guatemala,

President Jorge A. Serrano Elías was forced to resign following his failed attempt to close down the country's legislature. And in 2000, Peruvian President Alberto Fujimori left the country amid a major corruption scandal and decided to resign while in Japan, where he remained in self-imposed exile. He was detained in Chile in 2005 and extradited to Peru in 2007, where he was convicted and sentenced to six years in jail for abuse of power. Two years later, he was convicted on charges of human rights abuses and sentenced to 25 years in jail. The next Peruvian president to resign amid a scandal was Pedro P. Kuczynski. He offered his resignation in March of 2018, after the release of videos showing some of his political allies trying to buy the support of opposition legislators before an impeachment vote. Kuczynski had already survived one impeachment vote a few months earlier. He was accused of wrongdoing in a corruption scandal revolving around bribes paid by a Brazilian construction company.

The most recent case of a presidential resignation took place in Bolivia in November 2019. This event is not included in Table 5.2 because disagreement remains about whether it classifies as a presidential interruption or as a military coup. The trigger to the crisis was the presidential election of October 20, 2019, in which President Evo Morales was seeking a fourth term in office. His candidacy was controversial. The country's constitutional and electoral courts, composed of loyalists, had allowed Morales to run for a fourth term despite a constitutional ban and a popular referendum against such reelection. The electoral contest was marred by irregularities, which prompted widespread protests, many of them violent. An independent international audit of the election concluded that there were "deliberate" and "malicious" efforts by election officials to rig the vote in favor of Morales.[33] As protests intensified and evidence of electoral fraud began to surface, many started to demand Morales's resignation. The president first announced that new elections would be held, but calls for his resignation multiplied. As violent confrontations intensified, the chief of the armed forces announced that the military had suggested to the president that his resignation would help to restore peace and stability. President Morales announced his resignation on November 10 and departed the following day for Mexico.

For some, the fact that Bolivia's army chief urged the president to resign amounts to a military coup.[34] It was immediately after this call that Morales announced that he was stepping down. However, according to many observers across the ideological spectrum, the president's resignation was the result of a popular uprising. The protests following the disputed election were widespread across the country, and many political and social organizations were calling for his resignation. Moreover, among those demanding that the president steps down were the miners' union and the Bolivian Workers' Center (the country's chief trade union federation), both former allies of Morales. The military's position, the argument goes, signaled their lack of confidence in the president and their unwillingness to repress the popular uprising to keep him in power.[35] From this perspective, the military's pronouncement might have accelerated events but was not a necessary condition; Morales was likely going to fall regardless, and the military did not take power after his resignation.

Causes and Implications of Presidential Interruptions

Several academics have examined **presidential interruptions**, seeking to understand the underlying causes and to derive some useful generalizations. Four explanatory variables have been underlined in various works: democratic longevity, the performance of the economy, congressional support for the president, and the incidence of street protests.

Political scientists Aníbal Pérez-Liñán and John Polga-Hecimovich have argued that after the 1970s, the spread of democracy in the region limited opportunities for military coups and made radicals in the opposition more likely to pursue constitutional mechanisms to oust presidents from office.[36] Evidence seems to suggest that whether these events end up with the ouster of a president or not is related to the country's democratic record. More specifically, in countries that have spent more time under democratic rule, presidents appear less likely to face an early termination of their term in office.[37]

The economy also appears to play a role. Several scholars have found that economic growth reduces presidential instability, while economic recessions make early terminations more likely.[38] More generally, political scientists Kathryn Hochstetler and Margaret E. Edwards have observed that attempts to remove the president ("challenges") are less likely to occur when the economy grows and in countries with higher levels of economic development.[39] This is consistent with the findings of the economic voting literature, which suggests that presidents are rewarded at the polls under favorable economic conditions.

Presidential support in congress also seems helpful in preventing early departures from power. Again, various scholars have found that a larger share of congressional seats for the president's party reduces the likelihood of a president being ousted (i.e., without a military coup or a breakdown of democracy).[40] When presidents hold a majority of congressional seats, they are better able to resist efforts to remove them from office.[41] However, not all minority presidents appear to be equally vulnerable. Political scientist Gretchen Helmke argues that among minority presidents, the likelihood of a crisis increases as the president's constitutional power grows.[42] According to her, minority presidents with robust formal powers have greater incentives to try to govern around congress, which increases the latter's incentives to oust them from power.

Lastly, it is important to emphasize that most of the presidential failures listed in Table 5.2 were preceded by significant street protests. Several political scientists have shown that an increase in the number of protests makes presidential interruptions more likely.[43] Interestingly, Kathryn Hochstetler and Margaret E. Edwards found that challenges to the president are more likely to lead to their ouster when the government uses deadly force against demonstrators.[44] An important and related point, advanced by Leiv Marsteintredet, is that popular pressure manifested in street protests is more critical to presidential failures when the issue at stake revolves around policies rather than illegal or unconstitutional actions attributed to the president.[45]

In conclusion, since the 1980s, we have observed more democratic stability, combined with more frequent nonmilitary presidential interruptions. These latter events raise questions about the proper functioning of Latin American presidentialism. Are the ousters from power discussed in this section good or bad for democracy?

On one hand, the fall of presidents who engaged in clearly antidemocratic behaviors or committed serious crimes may be seen as strengthening the rule of law and the country's democracy. For example, the fall of Guatemalan President Jorge Serrano Elías in 1993, after his attempt to close congress, can be construed as favorable to that country's nascent democracy. Similarly, the fall of Peruvian President Alberto Fujimori in 2000, after being implicated in the bribing of legislators and electoral manipulation, may also be seen as auspicious for democracy. Impeachment proceedings against President Fernando A. Collor de Mello in 1992 in Brazil and Otto Pérez Molina in 2015 in Guatemala, which came as a result of their involvement in major corruption scandals, may also be considered favorable to the rule of law.

On the other hand, some presidents have fallen in circumstances that reflect institutional weakness and questionable behavior by the president's opponents. In the anticipated transfer of power from Raúl R. Alfonsín to Carlos S. Menem in 1989 in Argentina, as well as in the resignation of Hernán Siles Zuazo in 1985 in Bolivia, presidents did not behave undemocratically nor did they become entangled in criminal scandals. In other instances, such as in the dismissals of Abdalá J. Bucaram and Lucio E. Gutiérrez in Ecuador, presidential improprieties that could have been met with formal impeachment proceedings were dealt with through constitutionally questionable proceedings. Many protests seeking to interrupt presidents' terms in office were not triggered by illegal or unconstitutional behavior on the part of the president but by opposition to policies advanced by the government and anger at a failing economy. As Aníbal Pérez-Liñán stated,

> There is no clear democratic principle to support the argument that protests should trump votes. . . . Why should the will of the people currently trying to oust the president prevail over the will of the people who cast votes in favor of the same president in the last election?[46]

Presidential instability has led some to once more advocate in favor of a switch from presidentialism to parliamentarism.[47] From their perspective, the latter regime type would allow challenges to the executive to be dealt with through legal procedures—such as **votes of no confidence**, parliamentary dissolution, or new elections—within a democratic constitutional framework. The rigidity embodied in the president's fixed term of office could be replaced by the flexibility of a parliamentary constitution. However, several of the presidential interruptions previously discussed followed legal procedures and successfully dealt with improper executive behavior within the established constitutional framework. None of the 20 cases of presidential interruptions listed in Table 5.2 gave way to a dictatorial regime. And a switch to parliamentarism would also imply a broader trade-off that would affect various other aspects of government, as noted earlier in this chapter.

Conclusions

Understanding Latin American politics requires familiarity with its political institutions. Presidential constitutions have played an essential role in structuring democratic politics in the region. This chapter has described the defining characteristics of presidential governments, explained how some Latin American constitutions veer from the pure presidential form, and identified the main differences between presidentialism in the U.S. and Latin America.

For many Latin American specialists, presidential constitutions have had detrimental consequences for democratic stability. This chapter has discussed the main criticisms leveled against presidential constitutions and why many have considered the parliamentary form of government a desirable alternative. It has also explained why some scholars disagree with the view that the inner workings of presidentialism are harmful to democratic stability and reviewed some potential advantages of presidential constitutions.

Military coups are no longer the norm, but over the last decades, many Latin American presidents have nonetheless fallen from power before the end of their stipulated term in office. While these so-called presidential interruptions have not given way to dictatorial regimes, they have raised questions about the ability of Latin American institutions to deal with the underlying conflicts triggering these crises. The last section of this chapter described the context of many of these incidents and the various ways in which presidents were removed from power. The chapter ended with a discussion of the factors that presumably increased the risks of presidential interruption and asked whether these events reflect fundamental weaknesses or strengths of the region's institutions. In the next chapter, we continue reviewing the institutional structure of Latin American presidential countries. The focus, however, shifts from the presidency to the legislature.

Key Terms

Constitutions 127

Executive decree power 136

Executive-legislative deadlock 129

Impeachment 128

Legislative agenda setting 139

Parliamentarism 129

Presidential interruptions 146

Presidentialism 127

Semi-presidentialism 132

Veto powers 138

Bibliographic Recommendations

José A. Cheibub. 2006. *Presidentialism, Parliamentarism, and Democracy*. New York: Cambridge University Press.

Juan J. Linz. 1990. "The Perils of Presidentialism." *Journal of Democracy* 1(1): 51–69.

Mariana Llanos and Leiv Marsteintredet (eds.). 2010. *Presidential Breakdowns in Latin America. Causes and Outcomes of Executive Instability in Developing Democracies*. New York: Palgrave Macmillan.

Scott Mainwaring. 1993. "Presidentialism, Multipartyism and Democracy: The Difficult Combination." *Comparative Political Studies* 26(2): 198–228.

Aníbal Pérez-Liñán and John Polga-Hecimovich. 2017. "Explaining Military Coups and Impeachments in Latin America." *Democratization* 24(5): 839–858.

Matthew S. Shugart. 2006. "Comparative Executive-Legislative Relations." In R. A. W. Rhodes, Sarah A. Binder, and Bert A. Rockman (eds.), *The Oxford Handbook of Political Institutions*. New York: Oxford University Press, pp. 344–365.

Web Resources

Comparative Constitutions Project: https://comparativeconstitutionsproject.org/about-ccp/

The Database of Political Institutions, Inter-American Development Bank: https://publications.iadb.org/handle/11319/8806

Virtual Library Miguel de Cervantes (constitutional texts in Spanish): http://www.cervantesvirtual.com/portales/constituciones_hispanoamericanas/

6

Legislatures in Latin America

Latin American legislatures used to be considered weak appendages to strong presidents. A popular textbook on Latin American politics written in the 1960s characterized most of the region's legislatures as inconsequential, overshadowed by the president, and "merely rubber stamps."[1] This is no longer the case. Legislatures are now much more autonomous than before and play a fundamental role in democratic politics.

During the 19th century, Latin American legislatures served as a forum in which elites could debate policies and find compromise, and as a result, they helped to lessen the violent disputes that characterized the decades after independence. As the right to vote was expanded to include the middle and working classes as well as women, the interests represented in legislatures began to widen to more closely reflect the societies of their respective countries.

During the 20th century, recurrent military interventions and long periods of authoritarian rule created inhospitable environments for the institutionalization of legislatures. Where democracy prevailed, such as in Chile, Costa Rica, and Uruguay, legislatures grew stronger and more effective at constraining the power of the executive. The process of democratization that spread across most countries in the region during the last decades of the 20th century signaled a new era, when most legislatures began to more forcefully play the central part given to them under the prevailing presidential constitutions.

Congresses are often evaluated according to their autonomy and effectiveness. **Legislative autonomy** refers to the ability of a congressional body to exercise its main functions independently of the president. The extent to which Latin American congresses act autonomously from the executive branch has been a matter of debate for several decades, but there is a growing consensus that, despite substantial cross-national variation, legislative autonomy has increased considerably since the last wave of democratization. Also important is the capacity of a congress to act effectively. **Legislative effectiveness** refers to the ability to coordinate on matters on which legislators agree and make decisions concerning matters in which they have differing and conflictive preferences. Several measures have been used to assess legislative effectiveness, such as the success rate of bills, the number of laws passed, and the capacity of members of congress to successfully amend executive proposals. In many respects, the region's legislative bodies have become more effective in the 21st century.

The first part of this chapter examines three of the most critical functions of legislatures: the representation of constituents and societal groups, the passage of legislation, and the exercise of oversight over the executive branch. The second part addresses the organization of legislatures. It analyzes various features associated with **bicameralism** and the committee system, including some relevant procedural rules. The third and last part of the chapter discusses the voting behavior of legislators.

The Legislative Branch

Legislatures are typically defined as organized, deliberative bodies with the authority to make laws. In presidential systems, the legislature is one of three classic branches of government, the other two being the executive and judicial branches. It is composed of members elected by the voters to represent their interests. In Latin America, these members are elected directly by voters, but during earlier periods, some were either appointed or selected by state legislatures. The overwhelming majority of legislators run for office as members of a political party.

Constitutions allocate a series of essential tasks to the legislative branch. Among the most important is the power to make laws. Also crucial is the responsibility to check the power of the executive. The rest of this section reviews the representational role of legislatures as well as these two essential functions. The discussion includes examples from various Latin American countries to illustrate both the importance of these activities and the differences we observe across the region.

Representation

Members of congress are expected to represent their constituents by promoting their interests and being responsive to their demands. To achieve this goal, they can initiate bills, introduce amendments to executive proposals, or advocate for or against particular government regulations. Legislators can also further the interests of their constituents by seeking the allocation of financial resources and public projects to their districts. Delivering speeches in congress is another activity available to legislators, which can be used to highlight constituent needs and demand action on their behalf. Assisting constituents by helping them solve some of the problems they confront when dealing with the government bureaucracy is also common. This activity is typically referred to as *casework*, and it involves such things as helping individuals apply for social benefits, helping businesses cut through red tape, and helping groups access government resources.

Why do legislators invest time and resources in representational activities? Many would answer that legislators do this because it helps them further their political careers, either by increasing their chances of reelection or by helping them compete for other elected or appointed offices. Admittedly, other reasons such as ideological commitment and advancing what they consider to be good public policy can also serve as strong motivators, but political scientists tend to argue that legislators engage in these various constituent-focused activities primarily for instrumental reasons.

Several studies have examined the representational role of Latin American legislators. Some focus on the types of bills introduced by legislators, seeking to find connections between the content of bills and constituency characteristics. For example, political scientists Brian Crisp and Rachael E. Ingall examine bill initiation in the Colombian Senate, where members are elected from one nationwide electoral district.[2] They find that geographically targeted bills are more likely to be initiated by legislators whose votes come mainly from geographically concentrated constituencies, while bills with a national focus are more likely to be introduced by legislators whose votes are dispersed across the whole country. In other words, senators seek to promote constituency interests by drafting bills dealing with matters associated with the geographical location of their core voters.

Other studies have focused on legislators' interest in bringing budgetary resources to their districts. For instance, in Brazil, electoral rules foster strong incentives for legislators to develop direct links with their constituents and behave in an individualistic rather than partisan manner. Studies have shown that presidents who lack majorities from their own party often win congressional support to advance their policy initiatives because they can control whether budgetary amendments targeted to legislators' individual districts are actually executed.[3] Brazilian legislators are persuaded to side with the president because obtaining these financial resources for their districts is important to advancing their political careers.

The case of Costa Rica, where reelection is prohibited, is illuminating. Despite being unable to run for reelection, Costa Rican legislators regularly engage in various time-consuming activities to advance the interest of their constituents, such as casework on behalf of individuals and lobbying the government to allocate public works to their district. They do so because such activities are electorally valuable to their parties, which can, in turn, help them obtain coveted appointments in the executive branch once their term in the legislature comes to an end.[4]

Members of congress also use speeches to advocate for the needs of their constituents. Many Latin American legislatures set aside a specific time during the legislative sessions when members can address matters of their choosing. Legislators tend to use these opportunities to highlight the specific needs of their districts and demand governmental action on their constituents' behalf. For instance, in Chile, career-oriented legislators know that it is to their electoral advantage to be responsive to the demands of district constituents and, as a result, they use their allocated speech time to highlight local needs, such as more medications to resolve shortages in public hospitals or better access to services provided by the government bureaucracy.[5]

The aspects of political representation discussed so far have involved activities that legislators undertake to advance the interests and demands of their voters. This type of advocacy on behalf of constituents is referred to as **substantive representation**. Another facet of political representation involves what political scientists and sociologists call **descriptive representation**. This refers to the extent to which representatives resemble their constituents and centers on the identifying features that legislators share with voters, such as gender, ethnicity, and race.

Despite significant advancements in gender equality over the last decades, the proportion of female legislators remains below their share of the population in most democratic countries. In Latin America, the proportion of female legislators has steadily increased since the 1980s. The improvement in the representation of women is partly the result of changes in the role of women in society as well as more specific changes in attitudes regarding women as political leaders. Institutional factors, such as electoral rules, have also been found to have an effect.[6]

One particular feature of the electoral system that has been credited with increasing the number of female legislators in Latin America and elsewhere is **gender quotas**.[7] The first country in the world to pass a law requiring all parties to have a specific percentage of female candidates was Argentina in 1991. It required that all political parties include at least 30 percent of women in the list of candidates to the Chamber of Deputies. Since that time, almost all Latin American countries have established some form of quotas requiring the nomination of a certain percentage of women to the legislature. Countries such as Bolivia, Costa Rica, Ecuador, Mexico, and Panama eventually passed reforms that raised the threshold to 50 percent. Table 6.1 provides information on Latin American legislatures, including whether they have established a gender quota for the election of their members.

Women's political representation has been the topic of several studies by Latin American specialists. For instance, Leslie A. Schwindt-Bayer analyzed the constituent-focused activities of female legislators in Argentina, Colombia, and Costa Rica and found that female and male legislators are quite similar in how they allocate resources to the district, present themselves to constituents, and explain their legislative work.[8]

However, her study also showed that female representatives undertook more hours of constituency service on behalf of female constituents and were more likely to participate in meetings, rallies, and other activities sponsored by women's groups. Studies from Argentina and Mexico show that increases in the number of female legislators led to many more bills on women's interests being introduced.[9] In her analysis of 18 provincial-level legislatures in Argentina, Tiffany D. Barnes found that female legislators tend to coalesce to promote shared interests and to raise awareness around issues that exert a disproportionate impact on women's lives.[10] In short, the available evidence from Latin America suggests that increases in the number of female legislators tends to improve women's substantive representation.

In addition to electoral quotas designed to guarantee the inclusion of women in legislative bodies, some countries have established other mechanisms to widen representation. Table 6.1 indicates which Latin American countries have adopted rules that reserve a predetermined number of congressional seats for ethnic minorities.

Colombia was the first Latin American country to create reserved seats for indigenous peoples: two in the Colombian Senate and one in the House of Representatives. In addition, Colombia also created two seats in the House of Representatives to be reserved for Afro-Colombians. These reforms were first implemented in 1991 and 1994, respectively. The next country to establish reserved seats for indigenous people was Venezuela. In its 1999 constitution, it guaranteed indigenous representation in the national assembly and implemented this mandate by reserving three legislative seats for these communities. When Bolivia reformed its constitution in 2009, it also sought to guarantee representation for the smaller indigenous communities. As a result, it incorporated seven reserved seats in the Chamber of Deputies for minority indigenous communities (including Afro-Bolivians) living in rural areas. Purposely, the new rules excluded the Aymara and Quechua indigenous communities, which encompass a majority of voters in several electoral districts. Peru passed an ethnic quota law in 2002, but it applies to regional and municipal elections and not to the national congress.

Another important feature related to political representation is **term limits** for legislators. Advocates of this policy tend to argue that limiting the number of terms a legislator can serve in congress enhances representation because high reelection rates and a chamber with numerous incumbents result in a membership that ignores the wishes of most constituents. Opponents of term limits disagree with this premise and underline the effect of elections in making legislators responsive to constituent interests. The evidence from the imposition of term limits across the United States (U.S.) states suggests that such reforms lead to legislators with less information, weak committees, leaders with less experience, policymaking with a short-term focus, and a shift in the balance of power in favor of the executive in terms of budgetary policy and oversight.[11]

TABLE 6.1 ● Latin American Legislatures							
Country	Chambers	Size of Body	Term in Office	Term Limits	Gender Quotas	Seats Allocated to Ethnic Groups	Settling Bicameral Differences
Argentina	Chamber of Deputies	257	4 years	No	Yes	No	Navette
	Senate	72	6 years	No	Yes	No	
Bolivia	Chamber of Deputies	130	5 years	Yes	Yes	Yes	Joint session
	Senate	36	5 years	Yes	Yes	No	
Brazil	Chamber of Deputies	513	4 years	No	Yes	No	Navette
	Senate	81	8 years	No	No	No	
Chile	Chamber of Deputies	155	4 years	No	Yes	No	Conference
	Senate	50	8 years	No	Yes	No	
Colombia	House of Representatives	163	4 years	No	Yes	Yes	Conference
	Senate	102	4 years	No	Yes	Yes	
Costa Rica	Legislative Assembly	57	4 years	Yes	Yes	No	~
Dominican Republic	Chamber of Deputies	190	4 years	No	Yes	No	Navette
	Senate	32	4 years	No	No	No	

Ecuador	National Assembly	137	4 years	Yes	Yes	No	?
El Salvador	Legislative Assembly	84	3 years	No	Yes	No	?
Guatemala	Congress	158	4 years	No	No	No	?
Honduras	Congress	128	4 years	No	Yes	No	?
Mexico	Chamber of Deputies	500	3 years	Yes	Yes	No	Navette
	Senate	128	6 years	Yes	Yes	No	
Nicaragua	National Assembly	92	5 years	No	Yes	No	?
Panama	National Assembly	71	5 years	No	Yes	No	?
Paraguay	Chamber of Deputies	80	5 years	No	Yes	No	Navette
	Senate	45	5 years	No	Yes	No	
Peru	Congress	130	5 years	No	Yes	No	?
Uruguay	House of Representatives	99	5 years	No	Yes	No	Joint session
	Senate	30	5 years	No	Yes	No	
Venezuela	National Assembly	167	5 years	No	Yes	Yes	?

Table 6.1 indicates which chambers in the region impose term limits on their legislators and the length of each term. Costa Rica and Peru are the only countries that prohibit the consecutive reelection of legislators. Mexico also had a similar restriction but, in 2013, it reformed its rules to allow members of the Chamber of Deputies to serve up to four consecutive terms and members of the Senate to serve up to two consecutive terms. Ecuador limits members of the only two terms (consecutive or not). The other Latin American countries do not have such restrictions. Interestingly, Bolivia imposed term limits in its 2009 constitution, restricting legislators to one consecutive reelection, but a 2017 decision by the country's Constitutional Tribunal eliminated this rule.

Latin American congresses exhibit varying degrees of careerism, but many of them have a large population of members serving their first term in office. The presence of so many newcomers is problematic, as a lack of experience is often associated with less policy expertise and inadequate oversight capability.

The legislative body with the highest rate of reelection in Latin America is the Chilean Congress, with most of its members having served prior terms in office. In other countries, such as Brazil, Uruguay, Colombia, and Panama, most members run for reelection, and the majority of those incumbents are reelected. In contrast, the legislatures of the other Latin American countries tend to have a much higher rate of first-time members. Consider, for example, the Argentine Chamber of Deputies. Since the return of democracy in the early 1980s, the average rate of legislators running for reelection has been less than 25 percent. While members of this chamber can be considered professional politicians, most are better characterized as amateur legislators.[12] Amateurism limits the role of the Argentine Congress in the production of public policy and its ability to effectively check the power of the executive branch.

Lawmaking

The second function of legislatures is lawmaking. Descriptions of the region's democratic institutions prior to the 1990s portrayed legislatures as being relatively weak in this dimension. The few exceptions were the Chilean and Uruguayan Congresses and the Costa Rican Legislative Assembly. But in 21st-century Latin America, the legislative branch of government has become a much more assertive player. This influence is revealed in various activities undertaken by legislators, most prominently in the initiation, amendment, delay, and rejection of bills.

Every year, Latin American legislators initiate a large number of bills addressing local and national issues and, to a lesser extent, matters of international scope. The total number of bills put forward varies from country to country and across chambers within countries. For example, according to a study of lawmaking in Latin America, the number of bills introduced each year by Chilean legislators is (on average) close to one per member, while in Argentina and Peru, the yearly average is greater than four per member.[13] As in other parts of the world, most bills fail to become law. The approval rate of bills introduced by legislators differs markedly across countries, oscillating from a low of around 5 percent in Argentina to a high of around 27 percent in Peru.[14] These numbers, however, can vary substantially across time.

If one moves from looking at the approval rates of bills to examining the total number of bills enacted into law, we find that in some countries, such as Colombia, Costa Rica, Mexico, and Peru, most laws originate as bills introduced by members of congress and not as presidential bills. In other countries, such as Chile and Uruguay, the share of laws that originate with members of congress is much lower than those that originate in the executive branch.

Most analysts of Latin American politics agree that major legislation is more likely to be initiated by the executive than by members of congress. However, legislators can still influence the content of such bills by modifying them before they become law. Evidence indicates that legislators successfully amend most major bills initiated by the president before they become law.[15]

The amending process provides an opportunity for legislators to impact the content of bills originating in the executive branch; however, they can also influence presidential proposals before they are introduced. Presidents know that they need congressional support for their bills to become law, which means that they must draft proposals that can gain enough backing to pass. How much presidents need to compromise when drafting a bill depends in part on the congruence of their preferences and those of members of congress. If the president's party is unified, holds a majority in congress, and has a similar policy position as the president, then executive-initiated bills are likely to correspond with congressional views. In such a context, there is not much need for ex ante compromise on the part of the president. But if both branches hold different positions, the president may avoid substantial amendments or a rejection by incorporating legislators' views into the bill during the drafting process. This is a more subtle way in which congress can influence policymaking.

Congress can also preserve policies in place (i.e., the status quo) by refusing to address a new proposal. It is noteworthy that the vast majority of bills that fail to become law never get a final passage vote on the chamber's floor: They expire or are archived after failing to get a committee report or because they are never scheduled for debate on the floor of congress. Time is a scarce resource in most legislatures, and it is not easy to successfully push a particular bill to the top of the agenda. Indeed, a significant percentage of the president's legislative program never becomes law because the related bills never move past the committee stage.

Scholars have attempted to categorize legislatures according to their institutional and policymaking roles.[16] Political scientists Gary W. Cox and Scott Morgenstern, for example, argue that legislatures in presidential countries may insert themselves into the policymaking process in two basic ways: *proactively*, which involves initiating and passing their own legislative proposals, or *reactively*, which involves amending and vetoing executive proposals.[17] They claim that Latin American legislatures are mostly reactive.

However, other studies have shown that Latin American legislators often act proactively. As noted in this section, in countries such as Colombia, Costa Rica, Mexico, and Peru, most laws are authored by members of congress; in others, such as Argentina, members of congress initiate a significant share of laws. Moreover, major legislation initiated by the executive is almost always amended in congress. Clearly, Latin American legislators influence policymaking in various ways, including amending and rejecting executive proposals as well as initiating laws. The relative weight of reactive versus proactive activities varies across countries, but both modes of action make Latin American legislators influential actors in the lawmaking process.

Oversight

The third crucial function of legislatures is **oversight** of the executive. Effective oversight can help deter corruption, restrain the power of the executive, and make governments more accountable. The ability to effectively accomplish this depends on the rules in place as well as the capacity of the membership of congress. The legislative branch is not the only institution that may exercise an oversight function; the judicial branch and other institutions, such as an audit office, a comptroller, or a public ombudsman, can also play important roles.

One prerogative available to the legislature to exercise its oversight function is the ability to call ministers or other high-ranking officials to answer questions on matters under their purview. Latin Americans call these summons ***interpelaciones***, which comes from the Latin word *interpellare*, meaning "to question." This procedure (with variations) is in place in most Latin American countries.[18] Some countries incorporated this provision into their constitutions long ago. For instance, Peru first required a minister to respond to a congressional summons in its constitution of 1860. The Chilean Congress also has been using this prerogative for a very long time. During the second part of the 19th century, it became a crucial congressional device to hold ministers in Chile accountable for their actions.

Members of congress can also exert oversight by requesting information from the executive. For example, in Mexico, the right of congress to ask written questions of the executive was introduced in the constitutional reform of 2008. Following the president's required annual report to congress about the activities of the government, the Mexican Congress can forward written questions to which the executive must respond within 15 days. It can also present written questions to bureaucrats in the federal government, who must respond within the same amount of time. In Chile, legislators can pass a resolution asking questions of the executive, which must be answered within 30 days. Individual deputies, with the endorsement of one third of the chamber, also may ask for particular information from the government, which must be provided within the same period of time. In El Salvador, the Legislative Assembly may pass a resolution requiring the government to produce information within a specific deadline.

Another way in which congress may exercise oversight is through investigative committees. Long ago, most Latin American congresses established rules that allow them to put in place such committees. These committees often have sufficient latitude to request information from the government and state-owned companies as well as to summon officials to be questioned by its members. Judicial investigations may take place simultaneously with the congressional inquiries, depending on the matter at hand.

The congressional support required to establish an investigative committee can vary significantly, which affects the ability of some parties to successfully investigate improprieties and of the government to prevent politically damaging inquiries. For example, the creation of an investigative committee requires the support of 35 percent of the congressional membership in Peru and two fifths of the membership in the Chilean Chamber of Deputies. In these two countries, such committees are frequently formed. It is harder to put in place such a committee in the Argentine Senate, which requires the support of two thirds of its membership.[19]

The topics addressed by the investigative committees vary substantially. For instance, in 2017, an investigative committee in the Uruguayan House of Representatives addressed allegations of illicit activities within the state's health care program. That same year, an investigative committee in the Costa Rican Legislative Assembly addressed apparent irregularities and improper political meddling in loans provided by the bank of Costa Rica. In 2016, a bicameral investigative committee was created by the Mexican Congress to investigate the events surrounding a bloody confrontation in the state of Oaxaca between teachers protesting educational reforms and federal police forces. Also that year, the Peruvian Congress put in place a committee to investigate allegations that a major Brazilian company had bribed officials to win government contracts.

The effectiveness of investigative committees is often called into question. One common critique is that legislators may not be impartial when the irregularities being investigated can be politically damaging to themselves, their party, or their president. For instance, when, in 2017, the Panamanian National Assembly set up a committee to investigate allegations of corruption in awarding public works, many expressed skepticism that legislators—some of whom had been involved in negotiating such contracts—could impartially scrutinize these activities.

Another aspect of the oversight activities of congress involves scrutiny of the national budget. Constitutions allocate to the legislative branch substantial authority to oversee the execution of the budget. But for the most part, Latin American legislatures have fallen short of adequately checking the actions of the executive in this area of policy. This is particularly evident with respect to the monitoring of executive compliance with approved budget rules. The executive's reassignment of expenditures during the execution of the budget, the recurrent use of off-budget expenditures, and the allocation of funds via executive decrees work to undermine legislative oversight.[20] Few internal financial resources, weak technical advisory capacity, and relatively amateurish committees hinder legislatures' budgetary oversight responsibilities.

Oversight activities in the area of national defense and security are also important. They have been the subject of a cross-national study undertaken by Transparency International, a reputed nongovernmental organization that examined 82 countries, including six in Latin America.[21] Countries were given scores based on five categories, including the role of the legislature in influencing the defense budget, debating and scrutinizing defense policy, overseeing intelligence services, and controlling defense procurement. According to their scores when assessing corruption risks in these areas, Brazil and Colombia ranked with the U.S. in the low-risk category; Argentina, Chile, and Mexico ranked in the moderate risk category; and Venezuela ranked in the very high-risk category.

Certain aspects of defense policy may be more easily scrutinized than others. Consider the case of Mexico, where the number of military personnel deployed to combat drug trafficking has increased dramatically since 2007. Even though the armed forces participated in major security operations in most Mexican states, the country lacked a legal framework to regulate the military's role in internal security until December of 2017. Numerous bills had been proposed on this matter and the secretary of defense had exhorted legislators to pass such a legal framework, but it took the Mexican Congress ten years to accomplish this task. This legal vacuum created difficulties for the operation of the armed forces and raised red flags about the ability of civilian authorities to investigate possible violations of human rights.

Lastly, it must be underscored that a capable membership and strong committees are crucial for congress to effectively exercise its oversight role. As noted earlier, an amateurish membership is unlikely to effectively oversee the actions of the executive branch or develop an appropriate regulatory framework. A professional membership within an institutionalized committee system is much more likely to take on these tasks effectively. In many of the region's legislatures, frequent membership turnover and few incentives for specialization work against accomplishing an effective oversight role.

Organization

Legislative organization refers to the offices and procedures that regulate the legislative process.[22] The work of legislators is structured according to a series of rules established in the constitution and the internal rules of procedure of each chamber. Other legal provisions and institutional norms also tend to affect the internal work of legislatures. These rules establish the various offices created to run legislative affairs, such as permanent committees and leadership committees, and their prerogatives. Because they allocate power to different actors and stipulate what needs to happen for a bill to become law, these institutional rules are highly consequential.

As legislative specialists have taught us, not all chambers are organized in the same manner. Some centralize power among a few elected leaders while others decentralize it among various committees. Some countries require the approval of two legislative chambers before a bill is sent to the president for approval while others have only one chamber. The rest of this section reviews the importance of bicameralism and the committee system as well as the impact of some consequential procedural rules.

Bicameralism

When thinking about legislative rules, it is important to distinguish between endogenous and exogenous rules. The former can be modified by the legislature itself, while the latter requires the agreement of actors outside the legislature. Exogenous rules tend to be very stable; they constrain the behavior of legislators in ways that cannot be easily changed. For example, the number of chambers and the rules to resolve disputes between chambers in a bicameral congress are usually stipulated in the constitution. Reforming the constitution to change these rules often requires the agreement of outside actors. Even in those cases where congress is permitted to undertake constitutional reforms by itself, supermajority requirements for passage, lengthy processes, and vested interests make reforming such fundamental rules very difficult.

In Latin America, nine countries have a bicameral congress. By adding a second chamber, constitutions require the agreement of two institutional bodies before a bill can be sent to the president. Having two chambers instead of one tends to make the passage of legislation more difficult. Advocates of a bicameral structure claim that it prevents abrupt changes in policy, providing a second check that can reduce arbitrary decisions and malpractices in policymaking.

Bicameral congresses can be classified according to the similarity of preferences between each chamber and the relative powers allocated to each one. The extent to which chambers have divergent preferences depends on such factors as the electoral rules, the size of the chamber, and the length of the mandate. If the members of each chamber represent different constituencies and are elected at different moments in time, they are more likely to have different inclinations. In all bicameral congresses in Latin America, the membership of the Senate is considerably smaller than the membership of the lower chamber. Table 6.1 indicates the size of each chamber and the length of a legislator's term in office, while the electoral rules are addressed in the next chapter.

In Latin America, the constitutions of Argentina, Brazil, and Chile tend to have the greatest number of mechanisms to enhance divergence between the upper and lower chambers.[23] In contrast, the constitutions of the Dominican Republic and Paraguay have institutional mechanisms that promote a high level of preference congruence between the upper and lower chambers.[24]

In general, there is less variation across bicameral congresses in the region in terms of the relative distribution of power between chambers. Arrangements considered to affect the degree of power symmetry include the ability to initiate, modify, and reject legislation as well as the ability to exercise oversight, influence executive appointments, and participate in the impeachment process.

Most analysts conclude that in Latin America, upper chambers are not significantly weaker than lower chambers, as is common in other regions of the world. Still, many countries give one chamber special prerogatives not enjoyed by the other. For instance, the constitution of Argentina establishes that tax bills must originate in the lower chamber. Bills introduced by the Brazilian president must originate in the lower chamber. In Bolivia, bills regarding the territorial organization of the country and decentralization policies must originate in the Senate. And in Mexico, international treaties signed by the president only need the approval of the Senate.

Also relevant is the method utilized to resolve differences when each chamber passes a different version of the same bill. Some countries have rules that favor one chamber over the other while others are rather neutral. Table 6.1 indicates the type of procedure employed to resolve inter-chamber differences in the nine bicameral congresses in the region.

Among these bicameral congresses, only Chile and Colombia utilize **conference committees** to resolve disagreements on the content of a bill. These committees, composed of members of both chambers, are tasked with working out differences and presenting a final version of the bill. In Chile, the conference committee must be composed of an equal number of deputies and senators, while in Colombia, there is no such requirement and, on some occasions, one chamber has a larger delegation.[25] The legislative literature characterizes conference committees as powerful entities because their proposals to both chambers are voted up or down, without the possibility of further amendments.

Two countries, Bolivia and Uruguay, utilize a joint session of both chambers to resolve inter-chamber differences. In Bolivia, the joint session decides the final version of the bill by a majority of those present. Given the relative size of each chamber, the lower chamber (130 members) has a significant advantage over the upper chamber (36 members). In Uruguay, the final version of the bill needs the support of two thirds of legislators to pass, which lessens the advantage of the larger lower chamber.

In the other five countries—Argentina, Brazil, the Dominican Republic, Mexico, and Paraguay—bills are shuttled from one chamber to the other to try to resolve the differences in the respective versions of the bill. This mechanism is usually called the *navette*. This procedure may favor one of the two chambers. In Argentina and Brazil, the chamber of origin (i.e., the one that first passed the bill) has an advantage over the revising chamber. In Paraguay, it is the revising chamber that has an advantage. And in Mexico and the Dominican Republic, no chamber is advantaged by the rules.[26]

Surprisingly, the constitutions of Chile and Paraguay allow one chamber to pass a bill even after the other chamber completely rejects it.[27] In Paraguay, a bill rejected by the revising chamber may still pass if the chamber of origin votes in favor of it a second time. If this happens, the revising chamber can only kill this bill by rejecting it again—but this time, by two thirds of its membership. The rules are more complex in Chile because they involve the president. There, the executive can ask a chamber to reconsider a bill (a) rejected by the revising chamber, (b) proposed by the conference committee and rejected by one of the chambers, (c) unable to come out of the conference committee with an agreement, or (d) initiated by the executive and rejected by the chamber of origin. In these cases, if one of the two chambers passes the bill with the support of two thirds of votes and the other does not reject it with two thirds of votes, it is considered passed.

To sum up, bicameralism can have consequential effects on lawmaking and representation. It makes the passage of legislation more difficult and provides a second check that can prevent bad policies from being enacted into law. In Latin America, the relative allocation of powers does not differ much between chambers, and the rules in place tend to promote substantial heterogeneity in the composition of each chamber. Similar powers and divergent preferences make agreement between both chambers arduous. The greater the distance between the preferences of each chamber, the more likely they will disagree on the content of bills. When disputes emerge across chambers over different versions of a bill they want to pass, constitutional rules specify how to resolve them. This section reviewed these dispute mechanisms and highlighted whether one chamber has an advantage over the other.

Committees and Procedural Rules

Many of the internal rules that organize the daily work of legislatures and assign power to various offices are put in place by the legislators themselves. This is why many congressional procedures are considered endogenous. Some legislative specialists consider endogenous rules to be less constraining than exogenous ones because if members of congress no longer approve of those rules, they can choose to change them. Others disagree, maintaining that these internal rules are nonetheless enforceable because negotiating and implementing changes to them is difficult and costly.

A system of permanent or standing committees is a salient feature of all legislatures. This arrangement, usually codified in the internal rules of each chamber, entails a division of labor whereby each committee has authority over some specific policy jurisdictions. Other offices, such as select committees (created temporarily to address a specific subject), investigative committees (created temporarily to investigate a specific issue), and leadership committees are also standard.

Political scientists have underlined different reasons for establishing a system of committees. Informational theories argue that uncertainty about the consequences of legislation creates incentives for developing a committee system that promotes policy specialization and takes advantage of the skills that legislators already have.[28] Giving committees some relevant powers—such as the authority to make proposals to the chamber and to prevent certain bills from moving forward—is meant to encourage their members to specialize.

Another explanation stresses that the need to organize stems from the limited time available to address the large quantity of issues members of congress want to tackle. Inside legislative bodies, "time is a scarce resource."[29] According to this perspective, allocating certain powers to a committee system and other offices helps legislators coordinate to overcome bottlenecks. Giving committees power over the flow of bills facilitates the passage of legislation.

There are two main sources of committee power: One has to do with the prerogatives given to the committee by the rules of procedure; the other has to do with the capability of its members. The strength of committees and the professionalization of its membership are important research topics among legislative specialists.

One relevant source of committee power is its ability to review bills and report back to the chamber as to whether they should be passed, amended, or rejected. After a bill is introduced in congress, it is usually forwarded to one or more committees to be examined. Committees may be able to kill a bill by recommending its rejection or by never reporting on it in the first place. If a majority of the chamber or its authorities want to debate a bill a committee does not wish to report, they often have mechanisms to bypass the committee. In a few countries, presidents with the power to declare a bill "urgent" can use this prerogative to force a bill out of committee and onto the floor of the chamber for a vote.

Bills reported to the plenary of the chamber often include amendments introduced during the committee stage, but legislators not in the committee can also propose some of their own. In most legislatures, committees are given some advantages to defend their version of the reported bill. For instance, when a bill is debated on the floor of congress, a representative of the committee is usually given a prominent role in the discussion. In addition, some legislatures (such as those of Brazil, Chile, Mexico, and

Argentina's lower chamber) have a pre-filing requirement for amendments, which means that legislators seeking modifications usually need to present the related amendments before the bill's debate.[30] This rule gives committees the opportunity to assess the impact of such amendments and, if deemed necessary, respond with their own counterproposal.

In the U.S., committees may be given the authority to present bills under "closed rules," which prohibit amendments. This practice, which strengthens the power of committees, is not a common feature of Latin American legislatures. However, there is an exception: The conference committees used in Chile and Colombia to resolve bicameral disputes must present their proposals to the chamber under this take-it-or-leave-it procedure.

Congressional committees are also strengthened by experienced legislators and a stable membership. In several chambers in the region, legislators frequently switch committees throughout their term in office, which lowers incentives to specialize. Discontinuity in committee membership is associated with lower expertise, absenteeism, and infrequent meetings.[31]

For example, in Costa Rica, legislators are not only forbidden from running for reelection but are also frequently forced to rotate committee assignment.[32] In Argentina, low levels of reelection and incentives to pursue political careers at the provincial level give legislators few incentives to specialize or promote constituency service, which leads to a weak and amateurish committee system.[33] In their study of the committee system in the Brazilian Chamber of Deputies, Carlos Pereira and Bernardo Mueller note that "although there tends to be a stable core within each committee, the total composition tends to vary as frequently as from one meeting to another."[34]

The capabilities of committees are further weakened by norms that force frequent rotation in positions of authority, such as committee chairs. This rotation is common even in legislatures that have a relatively low turnover of members and are otherwise considered rather strong and well-institutionalized, such as the Chilean Chamber of Deputies or the Uruguayan House of Representatives. In Colombia, the yearly rotation of committee chairs and other chamber authorities is stipulated in the country's constitution.

The assignment of legislators to many committees also makes specialization less likely, although this is not very common. According to data provided by the Inter-American Development Bank, legislators in Latin America are assigned, on average, to two committees.[35] In some chambers, such as the Costa Rican Legislative Assembly and the Uruguayan House of Representatives, members are assigned to only one committee. However, in Argentina and the Dominican Republic, legislators are assigned to an average of more than three committees.

Congresses also tend to have leadership committees comprised of representatives from each party delegation. In many legislatures, such as the Argentine, Brazilian, Chilean, and Mexican lower chambers, these party leadership committees help to craft the congressional agenda. This prerogative gives them significant influence in deciding when and whether particular bills are debated and voted by the membership of the chamber. These leadership committees usually make these decisions in consultation with the chamber authorities, such as the president of the chamber.

In short, all congresses have permanent committees that play a notable role in the passage of legislation. Most bills that pass are amended during the committee stage, and many bills that die never make it out of committee. While congressional committees in Latin America are not as powerful as those in the U.S. Congress, they still possess substantial authority to affect the passage of legislation. One weakness, however, is the prevalence of rules that discourage specialization. Committees composed of members with low expertise on the policy areas they must address are more prone to make mistakes, less able to check the power of the executive, and more likely to rely on the dictates of legislative party leaders.

Legislative Voting Behavior

Voting is an important part of a legislator's job. It is how bills, resolutions, procedural motions, and other important decisions are passed on the floor of congress. In many instances, these votes are recorded, although some countries do this much more frequently than others.[36]

Several studies analyze these recorded votes, usually called **roll-call votes** by legislative specialists. There is a great deal of useful information that can be extracted by examining the votes that legislators cast. We can evaluate the unity of different parties or coalitions; uncover the influence of particular political actors, such as presidents, governors, or party leaders; examine whether electoral rules drive differences within or across countries; map the ideological positions of legislators and parties; or explain the choices individual legislators make on some specific highly salient votes.

In general, members of the same party tend to vote together. Why is this common? One reason is that members of the same party tend to share similar policy preferences. The ideological cohesiveness of parties may result from a process of self-selection—people with similar preferences joining the same party—or because voters or leaders weed out those members who hold preferences dissimilar to those of their parties. Another reason is that party leaders use their resources to compel legislators to act in a unified way. Leaders can influence the fate of bills, renominations, appointments, and other perks of office that legislators want. Therefore, they can pressure legislators to toe the party line.

Institutions can also create incentives for or against party unity. Electoral rules have long been found to influence the unity of parties in congress. The details of electoral rules are addressed in the following chapter, but one important finding worth stressing here is that party unity tends to be lower when electoral rules provide incentives for legislators to behave independently from the leadership and when they promote intra-party competition.

Cross-national evidence also suggests that the voting unity of parties tends to be higher in parliamentary than in presidential countries.[37] Some believe this is the consequence of institutional traits present in parliamentary constitutions, such as the vote of confidence, which pressures government parties to act together. Others, however, believe that this is the consequence of institutional traits common in presidential constitutions, which give the executive influence to steer opposition legislators away from their parties in order to vote in favor of government proposals.[38]

Presidents can also use their power to boost the unity of government parties, even in countries where electoral rules foster disunity. As noted earlier in this chapter, Brazilian presidents use their power over the execution of budgetary amendments targeted to legislators' districts to counteract some of the individualistic incentives derived from that country's electoral rules and enhance the unity of the government coalition in congressional votes.[39]

Governors may also influence the voting behavior of legislators. In federal systems, such as those of Argentina, Brazil, and Mexico, governors and other regional elites tend to control important resources and exert significant influence over political careers at the subnational level. Members of congress often continue their political careers at the local level, becoming mayors, state legislators, or members of the regional bureaucracy.

Roll-call votes can also reveal the influence of legislative leaders. Party leaders are "hired" to advance the legislative goals of the party, help pass bills sought by a majority of its members, and prevent the passage of bills the party opposes. When a party or coalition holds a majority of seats in the chamber, it also controls the office in charge of scheduling bills for a floor vote, which should help advance the legislative goals of the party.

Patterns of voting on the floor of congress can help illuminate whether the leadership of the majority party or coalition effectively controls the scheduling of bills.[40] One way to do this is by examining whether the majority party is "rolled" on legislative votes. A party is rolled when a bill passes despite most members of the party voting against it.[41] If the leaders of the majority party in charge of scheduling bills exercise gatekeeping power, then they should prevent the passage of bills opposed by the majority of the party's congressional membership. Studies have shown that in Argentina, the majority party is almost never rolled, while opposition parties often are.[42] In Chile, the evidence shows that parties in the majority coalition are rarely rolled, while parties in the opposing coalition frequently are.[43] The evidence from Brazil, where governing coalitions are less unified than in Chile, is mixed for the period prior to the mid-1990s.[44] However, more recent evidence shows that government parties are infrequently rolled.[45]

Characteristics of individual parties have also been associated with their voting behavior. For instance, more established and durable parties are more likely to have built valuable reputations, which are worth maintaining through voting unity. This is the argument advanced by John Carey, who presents cross-national evidence that party longevity increases voting unity in roll-call votes.[46]

One common measure of party unity is the Rice Index, which measures the proportion of legislators siding with the majority of their party. The values range from 0 (indicating a 50–50 split) to 100 (indicating unanimity). For example, data from the 2000s shows that the average Rice Index was 92 in Argentina (2005–2007), 88 in Chile (2002–2006), 81 in the United States (2003–2004), 76 in Brazil (2003–2006), and 76 in Peru (2001–2006).[47] These numbers seem to indicate that in places such as Peru and Brazil, where party systems are less institutionalized (more electorally volatile and organizationally weak) party unity tends to be lower. However, there is significant variation within countries, which suggests that individual party traits may play a more significant role in explaining unity in legislative votes than party system characteristics.

Some sophisticated techniques also allow legislative specialists to condense the information provided in hundreds of roll call votes into a map, where each legislator is represented by one ideal point. Sometimes the information can be accurately represented in one dimension, with legislators' ideal points ordered along one line according to the similarity of their voting choices. Other times, the information is more accurately represented in a two-dimensional map. Specialists can then look at this map to try to infer what those dimensions represent. This approach can illuminate how parties align on legislative votes as well as the relative cohesion within each party.

For example, when this technique is applied to the case of Chile, the information provided by the roll-call votes can be accurately captured in one dimension, which reflects the ideological positions of the different parties as well as the division between the country's two main coalitions. This is shown in Figure 6.1, which maps the position of 120 members of the Chamber of Deputies in one dimension (ranging from 1 to -1). Each dot represents one legislator's ideal point. Ideal points of legislators from the center-left alliance appear in gray, while ideal points of legislators from the center-right alliance appear in dark gray.[48] When this technique is applied to the case of Argentina, the information provided by the roll-call votes can also be accurately captured in one dimension, but in that instance, it primarily reflects the division between the government and the opposition rather than the ideological ordering of parties. Findings from the Brazilian congress also reveal the primacy of the government–opposition dimension.

FIGURE 6.1 ●   Ideal Points Derived from Roll-Call Votes from Chile's Chamber of Deputies

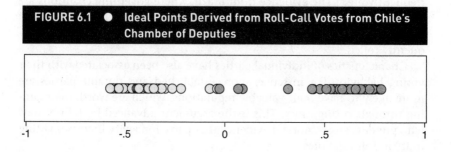

| -1 | -.5 | 0 | .5 | 1 |

Conclusions

Any informed observer of contemporary Latin America must recognize the relevance that legislatures play in national politics. This chapter began by reviewing the main functions of the legislative branch of government: representation, lawmaking, and oversight. It discussed various ways in which legislators seek to represent the interests of their constituents, such as drafting bills targeted to specific groups, seeking to influence budgetary allocations, engaging in casework on behalf of particular voters, and using speeches for advocacy purposes. It also explained the concept of descriptive representation and illustrated the ways in which various Latin American countries have sought to increase their number of female legislators. The potential consequences of term limits for legislative representation were also discussed.

The chapter then argued that Latin American legislatures play a salient role in the lawmaking process. Members of congress initiate a substantial number of bills, and although most do not pass, members of congress still draft a large number of the country's laws. In a few countries, most laws actually originate with members of congress rather than with the president. While it is still true that most major bills are proposed by the president, the available evidence shows that members of congress successfully amend most of these proposals before they become law.

Oversight of the executive branch is one legislative function where there is substantial room for improvement. This is important to restrain the power of the president and make governments more accountable. Latin American legislators engage in numerous activities related to this task, such as summoning members of the cabinet, requesting information from the executive branch, setting up investigative committees, and scrutinizing the national budget. In Latin America, effective oversight over the executive branch is often undermined by inexperienced legislators and the short supply of specialized committees.

The second part of the chapter focused on legislative organization. First, it examined bicameralism, discussing the rationales for it and the way political scientists have usually classified congresses with two chambers. The various ways in which bicameral congresses resolve disputes between chambers and whether rules favor one chamber over the other were also examined. Next, it addressed the committee system, including the reasons for establishing a system of permanent committees and the sources of committee power. The discussion of the importance of legislative organization further illuminated the relevance of procedural rules for the workings of Latin American legislatures.

The chapter concluded with a discussion of the voting behavior of legislators. Voting records capture the choices legislators make on the floor of the chamber and, as a result, reveal important aspects of politics. This section illustrated how scholars have used legislative votes to, among other things, evaluate the influence of legislative leaders, measure party unity, and map the positions of individual legislators. Studies of legislative votes have shown that presidential countries have a greater tendency toward party disunity than parliamentary countries, but they have also noted that presidents can use the resources at their disposal to foster congressional support for government proposals.

As noted in this chapter, electoral incentives play a relevant role in gaining an understanding of the representational activities of legislators as well as their voting behavior. The next chapter of this book focuses on the electoral rules in place in the region. Together with this and the prior chapter, it should improve our understanding of how political institutions work in Latin America and how rules influence who gets elected to congress and the presidency.

Key Terms

Bicameralism 152	Legislative organization 163
Descriptive representation 154	Legislatures 152
Gender quotas 154	Oversight 160
Legislative autonomy 151	Substantive representation 154
Legislative effectiveness 152	Term limits 155

Bibliographic Recommendations

Eduardo Alemán and George Tsebelis (eds.). 2016. *Legislative Institutions and Lawmaking in Latin America*. New York: Oxford University Press.

Gary W. Cox and Scott Morgenster. 2001. "Latin America's Reactive Assemblies and Proactive Presidents." *Comparative Politics* 33(2): 171–189.

Mariana Llanos and Detlef Nolte. 2003. "Bicameralism in the Americas: Around the Extremes of Symmetry and Incongruence." *The Journal of Legislative Studies* 9(3): 54–86.

Carlos Pereira and Bernardo Muller. 2004 "The Cost of Governing: Strategic Behavior of the President and Legislators in Brazil's Budgetary Process." *Comparative Political Studies* 37(7): 781–815.

Sebastian M. Saiegh. 2010. "Active Players or Rubber Stamps? An Evaluation of the Policymaking Role of Latin American Legislatures." In Carlos Scartascini, Ernesto Stein, and Mariano Tommasi (eds.), *How Democracy Works. Political Institutions, Actors, and Arenas in Latin American Policymaking.* Washington, DC: IDB Harvard University Press.

Leslie A. Schwindt-Bayer. 2010. *Political Power and Women's Representation in Latin America*. New York: Oxford University Press.

7

Elections and Electoral Rules

Elections are a necessary condition for democracy. They have not always been fair and, for many years, large sectors of the population were not eligible to vote. But it is a great achievement that today, most countries in the region hold free and fair elections and embrace universal suffrage. Many Latin Americans fought and paid dearly for the right to cast a vote.

In the 19th century, when elections began to be held across the region, most people did not vote. Electoral participation was typically limited to the elites, and most adults were excluded from voting as a result of various legal impediments. Many countries also lacked procedures to ensure a secret ballot. The political struggle to eliminate restrictions based on wealth and literacy, to implement procedures to guarantee a secret ballot, and to extend the right to vote to women took many decades. Most of these reforms were implemented in the 20th century and succeeded in making Latin American democracy more inclusive. Several countries went on to pass legislation making voting compulsory to ensure a high electoral turnout.

Electoral systems also evolved over time. In the late 19th century and early 20th century, most Latin American countries had **majoritarian electoral systems** allocating a disproportionally large share of congressional seats to the parties winning the most votes, thereby penalizing minor parties. Eventually, most of those countries abandoned such systems in favor of **proportional representation** rules, which provide a closer correspondence between the share of votes received in an election and the share of congressional seats won. Rules for electing presidents also changed, although less drastically. Initially, most countries used **plurality rule**, which awarded the presidency to the candidate who received more votes than anybody else. Several countries continue to use this means of choosing their chief executive. But by the end of the 20th century, several countries had switched to rules that required a second round of voting if the top vote-getter failed to receive a sufficiently large share of votes in the first round. For the most part, electoral reforms worked to create a more favorable context for the emergence of multiple parties representing many different interests.

The details of electoral systems are of consequence. The political science literature has shown that different electoral rules are associated with different outcomes. They affect who gets elected, the conduct of campaigns, the behavior of voters and politicians, the fragmentation of party systems, the direction of public policies, and the incentives of members of the government. It is therefore important to know the mechanics behind the various electoral systems and the main rationale for choosing one method over another. A thorough understanding of the region's political institutions is unlikely without knowledge of the electoral rules in place and the pros and cons associated with each of them. This is the goal of this chapter.

The first part focuses on suffrage rights, explaining the most common restrictions to the right to vote and reviewing when they were finally abolished. This is followed by a discussion of **compulsory voting**. Latin America is a region in which mandatory voting is common, although not every country enforces such requirements. The rest of the chapter examines electoral rules. It addresses the rules for electing presidents, together with the most common advantages and disadvantages of each method. This is followed by a discussion of the rules used to elect members of congress. The countries of Latin America exhibit relevant variations in their electoral systems, differences that are associated with dissimilar political outcomes. These are addressed in the last section of this chapter.

Suffrage Extensions

In the Americas, as in Europe, the beginnings of representative government were characterized by legal restrictions that circumscribed political rights to wealthy males. Women and poor males were excluded from political participation. It took a long time for universal suffrage to become the norm.

The idea of curbing political rights was common during the 19th century. At that time, voter registration was controlled by the government and, in most countries, voting was public, not secret. Up until the 20th century, the most common restrictions in place had to do with wealth, education, and gender. Income qualifications typically required voters to be taxpayers, earn a specific salary, own property, or have a profession. Literacy restrictions were also prevalent and prevented poor and indigenous people from voting. Most countries eliminated wealth restrictions before those related to literacy. Table 7.1 shows some of the limits to universal suffrage common until the mid-20th century.

TABLE 7.1 ● Restrictions to Universal Suffrage				
Country	**1875**	**1990**	**1925**	**1950**
Argentina	Gender	Gender	Gender	Universal
Bolivia	Literacy + Wealth + Gender	Literacy + Wealth + Gender	Literacy + Wealth + Gender	Literacy + Wealth + Gender
Brazil	Wealth + Gender	Literacy + Gender	Literacy + Gender	Literacy
Chile	Literacy + Gender	Literacy + Gender	Literacy + Gender	Literacy
Colombia*	Literacy + Gender	Literacy + Wealth + Gender	Literacy + Wealth + Gender	Gender
Costa Rica	Wealth + Gender	Wealth + Gender	Gender	Universal
Dominican Republic	Gender	Gender	Gender	Universal
Ecuador	Literacy + Gender	Literacy + Gender	Literacy + Gender	Literacy
El Salvador	Literacy + Wealth + Gender	Gender	Gender	Universal
Guatemala	Literacy + Wealth + Gender	Literacy + Wealth + Gender	Literacy + Wealth + Gender	Universal
Honduras	Wealth + Gender	Gender	Gender	Gender
Mexico	Gender	Gender	Gender	Gender
Nicaragua	Wealth + Gender	Gender	Gender	Gender
Panama	~	~	Gender	Universal
Paraguay	Gender	Gender	Gender	Gender
Peru	Literacy + Wealth + Gender	Literacy + Wealth +Gender	Literacy + Wealth + Gender	Literacy + Gender
Uruguay	Literacy + Wealth + Gender	Literacy + Wealth +Gender	Gender	Universal
Venezuela	Gender	Gender	Gender	Universal

*Colombia's federal constitution (1863) gave states the rights to decide who could vote. While some areas had universal suffrage, other areas imposed literacy restrictions.

Wealth restrictions were established early on in several countries. The classic argument for restricting the right to vote based on wealth was articulated by Sir William Blackstone, a famous legal scholar and conservative politician in 18th-century Britain, who observed that "the true reason of requiring any qualification, with regard to property, in voters, is to exclude such persons as are in so mean a situation that they are esteemed to have no will of their own."[1] According to Blackstone, if "these persons had votes, they would be tempted to dispose of them under some undue influence or other."[2]

To many 19th-century politicians in Latin America, restrictions based on wealth and literacy made sense.[3] For example, José María Químper, a Peruvian politician and cabinet minister, argued during the Constitutional Convention of 1867 that restricting the right to vote to taxpayers (at that time, a small portion of the population) was an obvious decision because "the one who does not contribute to carrying the burdens of society should not enjoy the benefits that it conveys to its members."[4]

Even in countries that adopted universal adult male suffrage early on, such as Argentina, arguments in favor of restricting the right to vote were common. Consider, for example, the position advanced by Dr. Aditardo Heredia, an Argentine politician advocating for suffrage restrictions during a constitutional debate in the province of Buenos Aires in June of 1885.[5] Speaking on the floor of the convention, he argued that a voter needed a certain level of education and social status to cast an informed and free vote, independent of the dictates of others. Furthermore, he maintained that many Argentine voters who had such qualifications had chosen not to vote because they felt that under the permissive rules in place, their vote would have been drowned by those of the unprepared masses.

In several countries, indigenous people were one of the main groups excluded from voting as a result of literacy restrictions. The unease many politicians felt about giving indigenous peoples the right to vote is exemplified by the stance taken by Manuel Vicente Villarán, a well-known jurist who became minister of justice in Peru in the early 20th century. At a time when politicians debated literacy restrictions, he argued that giving voting rights to indigenous people would only serve to increase the electoral power of those regions of the country populated "by the most ignorant inhabitants" and to heighten the influence of the rural patrons who usually dominated them.[6]

While public arguments in favor of wealth and literacy restrictions often underlined the irrationality or lack of independence of poor voters, more instrumental reasons typically motivated the advocates of such exclusions. The extension of the right to vote to the economically disadvantaged had the potential to threaten the political power and economic benefits enjoyed by the elites. Adopting broader suffrage implied a more equal distribution of political influence.

One of the early advocates of universal suffrage was the politician Manuel Murillo Toro, twice president of Colombia, who argued passionately against wealth and literacy restrictions in the mid-19th century. While recognizing some potential pitfalls due to the undue influence of powerful interests on economically vulnerable voters, he argued that the right to vote should not be subject to any arbitrary qualification test because it was an individual's inherent prerogative as a member of the community.[7] Moreover, he believed that repeated voting educated individuals in such a manner that, over time, it reduced the ability of the elites to manipulate the political choices of disadvantaged individuals. Others went on to argue that universal suffrage was desirable because it promoted equal protection of individuals' interests. Those advocating for voting rights also considered the elimination of these restrictions morally justified since all individuals were subject to the laws and policies imposed by the state.

The first Latin American countries to eliminate literacy restrictions on voting were Argentina, Mexico, and Costa Rica, during the 1850s. The Dominican Republic, Paraguay, El Salvador, Nicaragua, and Honduras followed, eliminating such constraints before the end of the 19th century. This is shown in Table 7.2, which lists the year in which literacy restrictions were legally abolished.

The last country to eliminate literacy restrictions was Brazil in 1985. At that time, close to one fourth of Brazilian adults were considered to be illiterate. Other countries where this restriction had lingered for many decades were Peru, which abolished it in 1979, and Ecuador, which abolished it in 1978. In both countries, this impediment worked to exclude many indigenous people from exercising the right to vote. Chile, another late reformer, got rid of literacy qualifications for voting in 1970.

The right to exercise a free vote was also hampered by the slow adoption of rules ensuring a secret ballot. During the 19th century, several countries included such provisions in their legal framework, but many others were ruled by politicians disinclined to undertake such reforms. Arguments that the secret vote would protect individuals from undue influence and retaliation did not convince everyone. For instance, Carlos Pellegrini, who was president of Argentina in the period 1890–1892, argued that the secret vote presupposed a rational vote, which he believed the masses of illiterate voters could not be expected to exercise. Thus, for him, the secret vote was inadvisable under universal adult male suffrage. Moreover, Pellegrini argued that instead of protecting voters who lacked political independence, the secret vote would upset current laws "to give a shield to civic cowardice."[8] However, despite opposition from some politicians, by the middle of the 20th century, all Latin American countries had adopted provisions favoring the secret vote.

Extending the right to vote to women was also a complicated matter. At the beginning of the 20th century, no Latin American country had enfranchised women. Some of the arguments in favor of the status quo stressed that women were already represented by their husbands, that voting might place women in competition with men, that most women did not want to vote, or that it would shift a woman's attention from the home and motherhood to the dirty realm of politics. While these ideas now seem absurd

TABLE 7.2   ● Suffrage Extensions

Country	Abolition of Literacy Restrictions	Adoption of Secret Vote	Adoption of Women's Suffrage
Argentina	1853	1912	1947
Bolivia	1952	1839	1952
Brazil	1985	1932	1932
Chile	1970	1890	1949
Colombia	1936	1853	1954
Costa Rica	1859	1925	1949
Cuba	1901	1901	1934
Dominican Republic	1865	1844	1942
Ecuador	1978	1861	1929
El Salvador	1883	1950	1939
Guatemala	1945	1945	1945
Honduras	1894	1894	1955
Mexico	1857	1857	1953
Nicaragua	1893	1893	1955
Panama	1904	1920	1945
Paraguay	1870	1911	1961
Peru	1979	1931	1955
Uruguay	1918	1918	1932
Venezuela*	1946	1946	1946

*In Venezuela, literacy restrictions were introduced by the constitution of 1936.

Sources: Adam Przeworski. 2009. "Conquered or Granted? A History of Suffrage Extensions." British Journal of Political Science 39(2): 291–321; Dieter Nohlen (ed.). 2005. Elections in the Americas: A Data Handbook, Volumes I and II. New York: Oxford University Press; Brian Loveman. 1998. "When You Wish Upon the Stars: Why the Generals (and Admirals) Say Yes to Latin American 'Transitions' to Civilian Government." In Paul Drake and Mathew D. McCubbins (eds.), The Origins of Liberty: Political and Economic Liberalization in the Modern World. Princeton: Princeton University Press, pp. 115–145.

and archaic, they were not uncommon in the patriarchal societies of the early 20th century. A few politicians on the left of the ideological spectrum had a more instrumental reason to oppose women's suffrage: They thought it would strengthen conservative parties because women would be likely to follow the guidance of the Catholic Church.

Many women defied the status quo and began to organize themselves to demand equal rights, including the ability to vote. One early advocate of women's rights was Hermila Galindo, a journalist and vocal supporter of the Mexican revolutionary leader, Venustiano Carranza. During the constitutional convention of 1917, she appealed to the sense of justice of the all-male delegation and requested that women be granted the right to vote.[9] Although she failed to convince the delegates to adopt this reform, she was instrumental in persuading Mexican President Venustiano Carranza to pass a family relations law, which gave women a variety of new rights, such as equal custody rights over their children, the right to receive alimony following separation from their spouse, and the ability to file a lawsuit.

The first Latin American country to extend the right to vote to women was Ecuador in 1929. The events leading to this change began when Matilde Hidalgo, the first woman to receive a medical degree in Ecuador, tried to vote during the legislative elections of 1924. When challenged, she correctly argued that the legal codes in place at the time did not expressly prohibit women from voting. Hidalgo's actions triggered a legal consultation that affirmed her right to vote and culminated with the incorporation of women's suffrage into the 1929 constitution.

Uruguay, Brazil, Cuba, and El Salvador followed with their own reforms soon after Ecuador. Most other Latin American countries extended the right to vote to women in the 1940s and 1950s. The last Latin American country to extend the right to vote to women was Paraguay in 1961.

Compulsory Voting

Many would agree that voting is a citizen's duty. However, making voting mandatory is controversial. Only a small percentage of the world's democracies have such a requirement in place. One region where compulsory voting is prevalent is Latin America. Most of the laws imposing that obligation were initially passed during the first half of the 20th century.

Compulsory voting tends to increase voter turnout, which reduces the costs parties must bear to mobilize their supporters to the polls. The reasons for the adoption of such a legal requirement most often had to do with the strategic consideration of parties in government. Incumbents faced with a growing opposition resorted to compulsory voting to rally their potential supporters to the voting booth.[10] During the early 20th century, the advocates of compulsory voting were mostly on the right of the political spectrum and concerned that the mobilization of working-class voters would affect their political future. Today, the advocates of compulsory voting tend to be on the left of the ideological spectrum.

Proponents of compulsory voting usually underline three beneficial consequences. First, they note that by increasing turnout, compulsory voting enhances the legitimacy of the elected representatives. Lower turnout may lead to governments elected by a minority unrepresentative of the voting population, which can threaten the legitimacy of the political system. Second, they postulate that compulsory voting fosters political equality because it primarily increases the participation of the economically disadvantaged, who would otherwise be less likely to influence the elected representatives.[11] There is some evidence that mandatory voting in Latin America has made individuals with low levels of education more cognitively engaged in politics.[12] Third, they assert that voluntary voting makes political polarization more likely by increasing the relative influence of the hard-core partisans that voluntarily show up to vote. Mandatory voting would presumably reduce polarization by making voters who are less attached to political organizations and less committed to specific policies more likely to participate in elections.[13]

Besides these reasons, which stress favorable outcomes, some proponents of compulsory voting argue that individuals have a civic duty to vote. *Civic duties* refer to citizens' responsibilities as members of a community and involve activities that enhance the welfare of society. Some believe that citizens have a responsibility to help preserve democracy and to prevent the rise of unaccountable governments. Democracy requires that people vote, and the outcome of elections affects people's lives and liberties. If people are to enjoy the benefits of belonging to a free democratic society, the argument goes, they must contribute to the collective decision-making process that makes it possible. If voting is conceived as a democratic duty rather than as a right, then voting may be considered a task necessary to preserve political liberty.

Despite these arguments, many remain unconvinced. Opponents of compulsory voting typically raise four objections. First, they believe that governments compelling citizens to vote is a basic infringement of individual freedom. A right is not an obligation and must be protected against state intrusion; the state's coercion of individuals to register and cast a vote against their will is an excessive restraint on individual liberty. Second, they argue that the right to vote is akin to that of free speech: Compulsory voting violates an individual's right to not go to the polls, which is a form of speech—a signal of dissatisfaction with the available candidates, a protest against the political system, or perhaps mere indifference. Third, compulsion may be justifiable if the failure to vote imposed substantial costs on others, but this is not the case since nonvoters do not impose a cost on voters and, most likely, increase the influence of those who choose to vote.[14] Fourth, several analysts have contended that voluntary voting makes the typical voter more informed and educated than the typical nonvoter. According to this view, compulsory voting would tend to make the typical voter more misinformed, leading to lower-quality government.[15] Rather than promoting moderate and rational politics, mandatory voting would likely increase the number of voters who are uneducated and intolerant and could promote greater support for fringe anti-system parties.

The debate over the merits and drawbacks of compulsory voting remains alive in Latin America. In the last few years, proposals to either introduce or eliminate compulsory voting were debated in places such as Chile, Colombia, Mexico, Peru, and the Dominican Republic.

Currently, four Latin American countries have voluntary voting laws: Chile, Colombia, Nicaragua, and Venezuela. The last one to adopt voluntary voting was Chile in 2012, which changed a law that established voluntary registration and mandatory voting for those registered to one requiring automatic registration and making voting voluntary. The reform passed with wide support in congress and among the population. Politicians on the center-left expected that the establishment of automatic registration would increase their share of potential voters, while those in the center-right believed that their supporters would be more likely to turn out to vote under the voluntary provision.[16]

There is another group of countries in which rules are ambiguous: Many analysts interpret constitutional provisions to mandate voting, but there are no legal sanctions for failing to do so. This is the case in Costa Rica, El Salvador, Guatemala, Panama, and the Dominican Republic. In the case of Costa Rica, for example, the constitution explicitly states that voting is an obligation. In El Salvador, Guatemala, Panama, and the Dominican Republic, those countries' constitutions mention voting as both a right and a duty. But since no legal sanctions are in place, these countries have de facto voluntary voting.

In another nine countries, constitutional provisions establish compulsory voting and there are some legal provisions that mention penalties. But even within this group, sanctions are not always enforced. For example, in Mexico, Honduras, and Paraguay, voting is mandatory, but nonvoters are not penalized. In contrast, sanctions are more often enforced in Argentina, Bolivia, Brazil, Ecuador, Peru, and Uruguay. If a nonvoter chooses not to pay the set monetary penalty (which is usually low), then other sanctions, such as a prohibition to apply for government jobs or the inability to obtain government-issued documentation, may be applied.

Rules for Electing Presidents

Latin American countries use three different types of electoral rules for choosing presidents, which are listed in Table 7.3. The first is *plurality*. Under this rule, the candidate that receives the most votes is elected president. The winner is not required to get a specific share of the vote, only more votes than each of the other candidates. This was the most common rule for electing presidents in the early parts of the 20th century. Currently, six Latin American countries use plurality rule for choosing the president.

The second electoral rule is **majority runoff**. Under this rule, a candidate needs to receive more than 50 percent of the vote to win the presidency. If no candidate passes the 50 percent threshold, a second election, known as

TABLE 7.3 ● Presidential Election Rules				
Country	Rule	Threshold (Percent)	Length of Term	Consecutive Term of Reelection
Argentina	Runoff with reduced threshold	> 45 or 40 + 10 lead	4 years	Yes, once
Bolivia	Runoff with reduced threshold	> 50 or > 40 + 10 lead	5 years	Yes, no limits
Brazil	Majority runoff	> 50	4 years	Yes, once
Chile	Majority runoff	> 50	4 years	No
Colombia	Majority runoff	> 50	4 years	No
Costa Rica	Runoff with reduced threshold	> 40	4 years	No
Dominican Republic	Majority runoff	> 50	4 years	Yes, once
Ecuador	Runoff with reduced threshold	> 50 or > 40 + 10 lead	4 years	Yes, once
El Salvador	Majority runoff	> 50	5 years	No
Guatemala	Majority runoff	> 50	4 years	No
Honduras	Plurality	none	4 years	Yes, no limits
Mexico	Plurality	none	6 years	No
Nicaragua	Plurality	none	5 years	Yes, no limits
Panama	Plurality	none	5 years	No
Paraguay	Plurality	none	5 years	No
Peru	Majority runoff	> 50	5 years	No
Uruguay	Majority runoff	> 50	5 years	No
Venezuela	Plurality	none	6 years	Yes, no limits

a *runoff*, is held between the top two vote-getters. In the second round, the candidate with the most votes is elected president. Because there are only two candidates in the second round, the winner always gets more than 50 percent of the valid vote. This is the most common method of electing presidents in Latin America.

The third type of electoral rule is a modified version of the majority run-off, which is called **reduced-threshold runoff** or *qualified runoff*. Under this rule, there is a specific threshold (lower than 50 percent) of the vote that the top candidate needs to pass to win the presidency in the first round. If the candidate with the most votes does not pass this required threshold, there is a runoff election among the top two vote-getters. This rule is in place in four Latin American countries.

Rules regarding the specific threshold required to win in the first round and avoid a runoff election vary across these four countries. In Costa Rica, a candidate needs more than 40 percent of the vote to win in the first round. In Argentina, a candidate needs more than 45 percent of the vote or at least 40 percent of the vote with a minimum difference of 10 percent over the runner-up. In Bolivia and Ecuador, a candidate needs more than 50 percent of the vote or more than 40 percent of the vote with a minimum difference of 10 percent over the runner-up.

In Latin America, as in the rest of the world, the trend has been to move from a plurality rule to a runoff system. Critics of plurality rule point out that this method can lead to presidents who are elected with relatively low levels of electoral support and who therefore lack a clear popular mandate. Under plurality rule, it is possible for a candidate to win more votes than the others and still be disliked by a majority of the electorate. Furthermore, a particularly "bad" candidate—one who can be beaten in a pairwise competition by each of the other candidates—can still become president by winning a plurality of votes.[17] Advocates of majority runoff claim that requiring the winner of the presidential election to get more than 50 percent of the vote in the first or second round of voting not only increases the legitimacy of the elected president but also prevents such "bad" candidates from being elected.

Advocates of plurality rule argue that their preferred method of electing presidents is simple and avoids the costs of conducting a second election. Moreover, they contend that runoff rules usually lead to more candidates and greater fragmentation of the party system than does plurality rule.

Why would runoff systems lead to more candidates and parties than plurality rule? Under plurality rule, presidential candidates from small parties are discouraged from participating in the election because they have low chances of getting more votes than the other contenders—voters typically do not want to waste votes on candidates who have a negligible probability of winning, and parties are reluctant to spend resources in a futile run for office. However, under majority runoff, presidential candidates from small parties may play a pivotal role in the election of a president even if they do not end up among the top two vote-getters. This is because the two candidates going to the runoff election usually reach out to others who can help them win in the second round, so a good showing in the first round can make otherwise marginal candidates politically relevant. These candidates from smaller parties can make policy or office demands to the second-round contestants in exchange for publicly calling on their supporters to vote for one of them. There is some evidence that runoff rules result in a more fragmented party system, which several consider problematic for the functioning of presidential regimes.[18]

Supporters of runoff systems counterargue that the greater number of candidates in the first round of voting gives voters more opportunities to actually choose the one who best aligns with their preferences. This is likely to increase the legitimacy of the system, as voters with diverse preferences are more likely to go to the polls. There is some tentative evidence showing that under runoff electoral systems, voter turnout is higher.[19]

Another potential advantage of runoff elections is that the two-candidate competition in the second round tends to draw competitors toward the center. This is likely to prevent extremist candidates from winning and makes the election of moderate presidents more likely.[20] It also encourages interparty bargains and consensus building in support of candidates running in the second electoral round. Political scientist Josep M. Colomer showed that Latin America presidents elected under runoff systems are more likely to obtain the support of the median voter than presidents elected under plurality rule.[21]

While in most instances where a runoff takes place the candidate with the most votes in the first round ultimately wins in the second round, in about a quarter of the cases, the runner-up wins the presidency in the runoff election. Recent examples include Juan Manuel Santos in 2014 in Colombia, Mauricio Macri in 2015 in Argentina, and Pablo Kuczynski in 2016 in Peru.

Presidential Reelection Rules

Latin American countries also differ with respect to the length of the term given to the president and, more importantly, with regards to the possibility of running for reelection. Information on these two variables appears in Table 7.3. As the table shows, all but two countries have presidential terms equal to four or five years. Only in Mexico and Venezuela are presidents elected for a six-year term. Differences regarding the possibility of presidential reelection are starker.

Before the last wave of democratization, most Latin American countries banned presidents from seeking reelection. This ban on reelection was supposed to prevent already-powerful presidents from perpetuating themselves in office. It was a check on the power of the president. When presidents lack sufficiently robust countervailing institutions, such as strong and independent legislatures and judiciaries, unlimited reelection may promote tyrannical tendencies.

When presidential reelection is possible, the incumbent's advantage may diminish the fairness of the election and weaken the electoral chances of the opposition. Incumbents may use public resources to sway potential supporters, intimidate opponents, coerce interest groups, bend campaign rules, or build a personality cult. Political scientists Javier Corrales and Michael Penfold examined 125 elections in eighteen Latin American countries and found that candidates who stood for reelection tended to win by much larger margins (with regards to the runner-up) than winners in elections featuring only nonincumbents.[22] Moreover, they found that incumbents usually won with even wider margins in countries with weaker democratic institutions.

Opponents of **presidential term limits** argue that consecutive reelection promotes accountability. Presidents who intend to run for office again know that voters will judge them based on their record. This expectation is supposed to promote responsiveness to the electorate. Presidents have an incentive to perform well in office in order to convince voters that they deserve another term.

Other arguments in favor of presidential reelection focus on the rights of voters and officeholders. From this perspective, if voters wish to reelect a president, prohibiting it restricts their choice. Less persuasive is the argument that any type of presidential term limit constitutes unequal treatment because it restricts the individual officeholder's right to run for office.

Currently, ten Latin American countries prohibit consecutive reelection of the president. Of these, four countries prohibit reelection altogether: Colombia, Guatemala, Mexico, and Paraguay. In six countries, nonconsecutive reelection is allowed. In Chile, El Salvador, Peru, and Uruguay, former presidents may run again after sitting out one term. In Costa Rica and Panama, former presidents are eligible to run again after sitting out two terms.

Presidents may run once for reelection in four countries: Argentina, Brazil, Ecuador, and the Dominican Republic. In Argentina and Brazil, presidential reelection was prohibited until the 1990s, when both countries changed constitutional rules to allow for the possibility of two consecutive terms. Former presidents may run again for a third time after sitting out one term. In Ecuador, a new provision establishing a limit of two terms for the president was approved by voters in a referendum in 2018. This reversed the prior ban on presidential term limits, which former President Rafael Correa had spearheaded in 2015. The Dominican Republic reformed its constitution in 2015 to allow presidents the opportunity to run once for consecutive reelection.

Lastly, four Latin American countries allow unlimited reelection of the president: Bolivia, Honduras, Nicaragua, and Venezuela. In Venezuela, the reform was proposed by President Hugo Chávez and approved by voters in a popular referendum that took place in 2009. Interestingly, the removal of presidential term limits in the other three countries came as the result of judicial decisions. The constitutional commission of the Nicaraguan Supreme Court overturned a ban on reelection in 2009, and the national assembly finally eliminated term limits for the president in a constitutional reform that passed in 2014. The Supreme Court of Honduras declared the ban on reelection unconstitutional in 2015. The Constitutional Tribunal of Bolivia declared the clause establishing presidential term limits unconstitutional in 2017, despite a 2016 popular referendum in which voters rejected unlimited reelection.

Constitutional clauses regarding presidential term limits continue to be hotly debated in many Latin American countries. For example, in 2017, riots broke out in Paraguay during protests against a bill seeking to lift the ban on presidential reelection. Many of the reforms banning or allowing presidential reelection have been passed in the last few years, and it is unclear whether they will stand the test of time.

Rules for Electing Members of Congress

Electoral rules can be broadly divided into three main types: majoritarian, proportional, and mixed systems. Majoritarian formulas tend to amplify the share of seats for the leading party and penalize minor parties. By boosting representation of the largest party, majoritarian rules seek to create working legislative majorities. The main rationale is that effective governance is more likely when one party has a legislative majority. Preventing a fragmented congress and promoting single-party governments are supposed to further effectiveness.

The most common majoritarian rules are plurality and runoff rules (both previously discussed in the context of presidential elections). In the case of single-member districts (i.e., where only one legislator is elected per district), majoritarian rules promote the representation of local interests and make the personal reputations of candidates important to voters.

The guiding principle of proportional representation is that the distribution of congressional seats should be based on the share of the vote received by each party. This rule favors the incorporation of minor parties into the legislature. Because a variety of interests are more likely to win representation, it increases the probability that minority preferences will be taken into account. Advocates of proportional representation believe that a close correspondence between the share of votes and the share of seats is fundamentally fair.

Mixed-member formulas combine both majoritarian and proportional rules to elect members of the same legislative chamber. Some representatives are elected under majoritarian rules and others are elected under proportional rules. While the goal is to combine the best of both worlds, there is an ongoing debate about whether this objective is really achieved, with some arguing that the behavioral consequences of one of the rules extend to members elected under the other rule (a so-called contamination effect).

The different formulas utilized for electing legislators in Latin America are summarized in Table 7.4. These electoral rules also vary with regards to the number of tiers, the type of lists utilized, and the number and size of districts. Before discussing the consequences of these rules, this section reviews the main traits of each formula.

Proportional Representation

Proportional representation is the most common type of rule utilized in Latin America. Under this rule, each party presents a list of candidates

TABLE 7.4	●	Rules for Electing Members of Congress		
Country	Chamber	Electoral Rule	Tiers	List System
Argentina	Chamber of Deputies	Proportional Representation	One	Closed
	Senate	Incomplete List	One	Closed
Bolivia	Chamber of Deputies	Mixed (SMD + PR)	Two	Closed
	Senate	Proportional Representation	One	Closed
Brazil	Chamber of Deputies	Proportional Representation	One	Open
	Senate	Plurality	One	~
Chile	Chamber of Deputies	Proportional Representation	One	Open
	Senate	Proportional Representation	One	Open
Colombia	House of Representatives	Proportional Representation	One	Open (optional)
	Senate	Proportional Representation	One	Open (optional)
Costa Rica	Legislative Assembly	Proportional Representation	One	Closed
Dominican Republic	Chamber of Deputies	Proportional Representation	One	Open
	Senate	Plurality	One	~
Ecuador	National Assembly	Proportional Representation	Two	Open Free List
El Salvador	Legislative Assembly	Proportional Representation	One	Open Free List
Guatemala	Congress	Proportional Representation	Two	Closed
Honduras	Congress	Proportional Representation	One	Open Free List
Mexico	Chamber of Deputies	Mixed (SMD + PR)	Two	Closed
	Senate	Mixed (Incomplete List + PR)	Two	Closed

(Continued)

TABLE 7.4 ● (Continued)

Nicaragua	National Assembly	Proportional Representation	Two	Closed
Panama	National Assembly	Hybrid (semi-proportional or mixed)	One	Open
Paraguay	Chamber of Deputies	Proportional Representation	One	Closed
	Senate	Proportional Representation	One	Closed
Peru	Congress	Proportional Representation	One	Open
Uruguay	House of Representatives	Proportional Representation	One	Open (Double Simultaneous Vote)
	Senate	Proportional Representation	One	Open (Double Simultaneous Vote)
Venezuela	National Assembly	Mixed (Plurality + PR)	Two	Closed

for each district, the votes cast in an electoral district are aggregated by party, and seats are allocated to parties according to their share of the district vote. For example, consider the case wherein ten seats are allocated to a district. If Party A gets 60 percent of the district vote and Party B gets 40 percent of the district vote, then Party A should win six seats and Party B should win four seats.

Proportional representation systems vary according to various features. One of those is the manner in which voters select candidates from the lists presented by the different parties. In closed-list systems, voters choose party lists composed of candidates who were ranked by their party before the election. So, following the earlier example, the six candidates elected from Party A should be the ones the party ranked one through six in its list of ten candidates for the district (candidates ranked seven to ten were not elected). With regards to Party B, the four candidates elected were the ones the party ranked one through four in its list of ten candidates for the district (candidates ranked five to ten were not elected). Under **closed-list proportional representation**, voters cannot alter the ranking of candidates within each party list.

Proportional representation with closed lists is used in seven chambers: Argentina's Chamber of Deputies, Bolivia's Senate, Costa Rica's Legislative

Assembly, Guatemala's Congress, Nicaragua's National Assembly, and Paraguay's Chamber of Deputies and Senate.

Proportional representation elections can also be conducted under open lists, which allow voters to cast a preferential vote. In open-list systems, voters are allowed to show preferences for particular candidates. Under the most common type of open list, voters can indicate their preference for one or more candidates within one party list.[23] Votes in the district are aggregated by party, and seats are allocated to parties according to their share of the district vote. Next, the seats won by each party are allocated to its candidates based on the individual preference votes that each candidate of that party received in the particular district. So, voter preferences rather than a prearranged ranking determine the allocation of the seats won by a party.

Open-list proportional representation is used in seven chambers: Brazil's Chamber of Deputies, Chile's Chamber of Deputies and Senate, Colombia's House of Representatives and Senate, the Dominican Republic's Chamber of Deputies, and Peru's Congress. For example, in Chile, voters have to choose one candidate from a party's list. In the lower houses of Brazil and the Dominican Republic, voters may select one candidate from a party's list or simply choose a party.[24] In Peru, voters can select one or two candidates within a party list or choose a party. In Colombia, parties decide whether they want to present closed or open lists, but most choose to run with open lists. When presented with an open list, Colombian voters may select one candidate from the party's list or choose a party as a whole.

Uruguay uses an alternative version of the open list called the double simultaneous vote (DSV). It differs from the version previously described in that each party (*lema*) presents various sub-lists (*sublemas*) of ranked candidates in each district. These sub-lists are made up of candidates from different factions of the same party. Voters pick a party and one of its sub-lists. Votes are aggregated by party, and seats are allocated to parties according to their share of the district vote. Then, the seats won by each party are distributed to each party's sub-list according to their share of the party vote. Under this rule, voters choose a party and indicate their preference for one of its many factions. However, they cannot alter the ranking of candidates presented by the sub-list they choose.

Another version of the open list is called the *free list* or *panachage*. It gives voters the ability to pick candidates from different party lists (up to the number of seats assigned to the district). Votes are aggregated by party, and seats are allocated to parties according to their share of the party vote. The seats won by each party are then apportioned to its candidates according to their individual votes. So the difference from the typical open list is that voters are not restricted to choosing candidates from within one party list; they can choose one candidate from one party and another candidate from a different party (but all have to be candidates running in the same district).

Proportional representation with a free list system is used to elect legislators in the unicameral congresses of Ecuador,[25] El Salvador, and Honduras. In these three countries, a voter can choose as many candidates as there are seats in the district. So, for instance, a voter in a district that elects five legislators can choose up to a total of five candidates, who do not need to belong to the same party list.

Some electoral systems include more than one *tier*, which refers to the level at which votes are translated into seats. For instance, in Guatemala, Nicaragua, and Ecuador, there are two overlapping tiers of electoral districts, both using proportional representation. One of the two is made up of a national district covering the entire country. This means that voters elect legislators from both a local district and a second, more extensive, national district. In Guatemala and Nicaragua, both tiers use closed lists, while in Ecuador, both tiers use the free list system.

Majoritarian Rules: Incomplete List and Plurality

Majoritarian rules are used to elect senators in Argentina, Brazil, and the Dominican Republic. The two types of majoritarian rules in place in the region are the **incomplete list system** and plurality. Because these electoral rules disproportionally favor parties with a large share of the vote, they are considered majoritarian. In Argentina, voters elect three senators per district using the incomplete list system. Rules require that voters choose a party, which presents a list with two candidates. The party with the most votes in the district wins two seats. The party coming in second in the district wins one seat, which goes to the candidate ranked first in that party's list.[26]

Plurality rule is used to elect senators in Brazil and the Dominican Republic. In the Dominican Republic, elections take place in single-member districts (as in the case of the United States House of Representatives). It means that voters choose one candidate from among those competing in the electoral district, and the candidate with the most votes wins the seat. Plurality rule is sometimes called *first past the post*.

The case of Brazil is somewhat different. Three senators represent each of the 27 electoral districts, but they do not run all at the same time. Senators serve eight-year terms, with staggered elections taking place every four years. In one electoral cycle, one third of the Senate seats are filled. In each district, a party can nominate one candidate and only one senator is elected. As a result, the electoral rule is plurality in single-member districts, as in the Senate of the Dominican Republic. In the other electoral cycle, two thirds of the Senate seats are filled. This time, there are two open seats per district and parties nominate two candidates for each. Voters now cast two votes for two different candidates in the district, and the top two vote-getters win the two seats.[27] In this case, voters do not need to choose two candidates from the same party.

Mixed-Member Electoral Systems

Another type of electoral rule in place in Latin America is the **mixed-member electoral system**. This type of rule combines the distribution of seats by a majoritarian system and by proportional representation. The most common combination is plurality rule in single-member districts and proportional representation with closed lists. This is the type of mixed-member system in place in the lower chambers of Bolivia and Mexico.

In Bolivia, voters have two votes to elect members of the Chamber of Deputies. With one vote, they choose one deputy to represent a single-member district. This election takes place under plurality rule, so the candidate with the most votes in the district wins. The other vote is to choose several candidates in a larger multimember district. This election takes place under proportional representation with closed lists.[28] Therefore, in Bolivia, there are two overlapping tiers of electoral districts. The first tier is composed of 63 single-member districts, plus an additional seven special single-member districts allocated to indigenous groups. The second tier is composed of nine multimember districts that elect between two and fourteen deputies each.

In Mexico, voters also elect legislators to the Chamber of Deputies from two tiers, one composed of single-member districts (using plurality rule) and another one composed of multimember districts (using proportional representation). In the case of Mexico's lower chamber, the first tier is composed of 300 single-member districts, while the second tier is comprised of five multimember districts that elect 40 deputies each. One relevant difference to Bolivia is that Mexican voters only have one vote, which counts both to elect a deputy from a single-member district and to elect a party list in the larger multimember district. So, in the case of Mexico, voters cannot choose one party in the multimember district and a candidate from a different party for the single-member district.

The Mexican Senate uses a similar mixed-member electoral system but utilizes the incomplete list (in three-member districts) instead of plurality rule in single-member districts. In this first tier, there are 32 districts, each electing three members, and parties present lists of two members per district. The party that has the most votes in the district elects two members and the party that comes in second elects one member. The second tier is composed of one national district that covers the entire country. There are 32 seats allocated to this national district, and the rule for distributing seats is proportional representation with closed lists. As in the lower chamber, there are two overlapping districts and voters cast one vote.

The Venezuelan National Assembly uses a mixed-member electoral system, which has two tiers and gives voters the right to cast two votes. The first-tier districts include 87 small districts that elect one, two, or three candidates each. Here, voters are given as many votes as there are seats to be filled in the district. When it is a single-member district, the method is as previously outlined: A voter casts one vote for one candidate, and the candidate with the most votes wins. However, when the number of seats to be filled in the district is greater than one—for example, three—then voters cast three votes for three different candidates (they do not need to all be from the same party), and the top three vote-getters win the seats. Close to one fourth of the lower-tier districts elect more than one legislator each.

The second tier in the Venezuelan election is composed of 24 multi-member districts that elect members using proportional representation with closed lists, with voters choosing between two and three members per district. In comparison to other countries using mixed-member electoral systems, the number of legislators elected in each of the upper-tier districts is very low, which leads to rather disproportional results.

Lastly, there is a fourth country, Panama, which uses an unusual rule to elect members of its National Assembly. Some consider it a hybrid with similarities to the mixed-member system, while others consider it a semi-proportional rule. The chief difference with the pure mixed-member system is that it has only one tier of districts (rather than two overlapping ones). Basically, the country has 26 single-member districts that elect one legislator each using plurality rule and 13 multimember districts that elect between two and seven legislators each using open-list proportional representation.

The Consequences of Congressional Electoral Rules

Social scientists have long been interested in the consequences of electoral rules. Their impact is the consequence of both the mechanics behind each method and the way voters react to such rules. For instance, under certain electoral rules, the translation of votes into seats makes it difficult for minor parties to win seats, which in turn makes voters who would be initially inclined to support such parties reluctant to follow through because they do not want to feel that they are wasting their votes.

Ultimately, electoral rules entail a trade-off between a variety of desirable attributes. Some electoral rules lead to a close correspondence between the share of votes and the share of seats that each party receives, while others are more likely to reduce the fragmentation of the party system. Electoral rules can give voters the ability to hold individual representatives accountable for prior performance or, instead, stress collective accountability by making voters more likely to reward or punish entire party organizations. Party unity can be enhanced or hindered depending on the method used for choosing legislators. In short, choosing the electoral rules of a country often requires deciding between multiple and competing objectives.

A crucial feature of electoral rules that affects the outcomes discussed in the rest of this section is the **district magnitude**. Electoral districts or electoral circumscriptions are the territories from which representatives are elected. In many countries, electoral districts correspond with territorial boundaries, such as states, provinces, or departments. Some countries have a national district that covers the entire territory. District magnitude is the number of seats assigned to a district at election time. So, if the number of members to be elected in a district is five, that district has a magnitude equal to five.

In some countries, district magnitude does not vary from one electoral district to another, but in others, we find wide variations. For example, in Brazil, the state of Amazonas has a district magnitude equal to eight, while the state of Rio de Janeiro has a district magnitude equal to 53, and the state of São Paulo has a district magnitude equal to 70.[29]

The Relationship between Share of Votes and Share of Seats

One important criterion to evaluate electoral rules is proportionality: how close the share of seats allocated to parties after an election is to the share of votes each party received during the election. To many, this relationship reflects on the fairness of the electoral rule.

The type of electoral formula in place affects the proportionality of seats to votes. Many studies have shown that proportionality is greater under proportional representation rules than under plurality rule.[30] Plurality rule boosts the number of seats distributed to large parties and penalizes small parties, which leads to disproportional results. Proportional representation rules reduce the bias in favor of large parties, which reduces disproportionality. This is one of the reasons why, during the 20th century, many countries decided to switch from majoritarian formulas, such as plurality rule, to proportional representation.

In countries using proportional representation electoral rules, disproportionality varies with district magnitude. A district that allocates many seats is likely to produce more proportional results. In contrast, where district magnitude is small, disproportionality increases. Thus, there is a negative association between district magnitude and level of disproportionality.[31]

One commonly used measure of disproportionality is the Least Squares Index proposed by Michael Gallagher.[32] This is constructed in four steps. First, for each party, the difference between the percentage of votes received and the percentage of legislative seats won is squared. Second, these numbers are added together. Third, the sum is divided by two. And fourth, the square root of that number is taken. The resulting number captures the deviation from perfect proportionality, with high numbers reflecting greater disproportionality.

The relationship between electoral formula, district magnitude, and disproportionality can be illustrated by focusing on a handful of Latin American cases. These cases vary from very low to very high district magnitude. First, we have the Colombian Senate, which uses proportional representation and has one national district with magnitude equal to 100.[33] Second, we have the Paraguayan Senate, which uses proportional representation and has only one national district with a magnitude equal to 45. Third, we have the Costa Rican National Assembly, which uses proportional representation and has seven districts where the mean district magnitude (MDM) equals 8.1 (it ranges from 4 to 19). Fourth, we have the Panamanian National Assembly, which has a total of 39 districts and where the MDM equals 1.8. As noted before, Panama has an unusual system, with 26 single-member districts that use plurality rule and 13 multimember districts that elect between two and seven legislators each using proportional representation. Lastly, we have the Senate of the Dominican Republic, which uses plurality rule in 32 districts and each district has a magnitude equal to 1. Figure 7.1 shows the Disproportionality Index and the MDM for each of these five chambers.[34]

As the figure shows, levels of disproportionality are much higher in the Senate of the Dominican Republic, which uses plurality rule, than in the other four chambers. It also reveals that as district magnitude increases, the Disproportionality Index goes down. In the Senate of Colombia, which has a very high district magnitude, there is a very close correspondence between the share of votes and the share of seats.

Differences in the level of disproportionality resulting from these rules are also reflected in the number of seats won by the largest party. For example, in Colombia, the largest party received 20.1 percent of the votes and 20.6 percent of the seats (a difference of 0.5 points); in Paraguay, it received 38.5 percent of the votes and 42.2 percent of the seats (a difference of 3.7

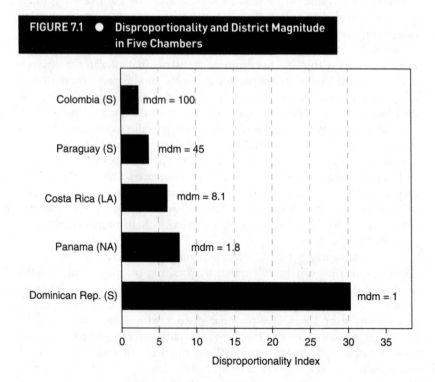

FIGURE 7.1 ●   Disproportionality and District Magnitude in Five Chambers

Disproportionality Index

points); in Costa Rica, it received 25.7 percent of the votes and 31.6 percent of the seats (a difference of 5.9 points); in Panama, it received 33.7 percent of the votes and 42.3 percent of the seats (a difference of 8.6 points); and in the Dominican Republic, it received 41.8 percent of the votes and 81.3 percent of the seats (a difference of 39.5 points). This example shows how the relative boost in the number of seats allocated to the largest party is associated with district magnitude and electoral formula.

Institutional designers seeking to create working legislative majorities for the largest party should find plurality elections in single-member districts particularly useful, while those advocating for a close correspondence between the share of votes and the share of seats should find proportional representation with high district magnitude well-suited to achieving this goal. The Senates of Colombia and Paraguay are good examples of chambers in which there is a close association between votes and seats. There, minor parties have a much higher chance of winning legislative representation than in the Senate of the Dominican Republic, which uses plurality rule.

These results have shown that the degree of disproportionality is closely associated with electoral rules (plurality versus proportional representation) and district magnitude. It should be noted, however, that levels of disproportionality usually vary within countries from election to election and are also affected by other features not discussed here, such as the mathematical formula used to translate votes into seats (e.g., highest-divisor or quota methods) and rules that impose a minimum threshold of votes to win legislative seats.

The Personal Vote versus the Partisan Vote

Electoral formulas also have a significant effect on the incentives legislators have to campaign based on a personal reputation. Politicians are motivated to build a personal reputation when the prospects of advancing their political careers are improved if voters know and think highly of them. What political scientists call the **personal vote** refers to contexts where politicians pursue votes based on their individual popularity rather than on the reputation of their party.

However, under certain electoral formulas, the party label is crucial; in many places, voters choose parties, not individual candidates. A candidate's party label offers a recognizable shortcut for voters, which reduces the information costs associated with deciding how to cast a vote. If politicians believe that the reputation of their party is decisive for their electoral prospects, they are more likely to collaborate to enhance the value of the party label. In contexts where the partisan vote is important, candidates are less likely to run on their personal traits and more likely to campaign as members of a team.

Incentives to seek a partisan vote are associated with different outcomes than are incentives to seek a personal vote. In situations where the partisan vote is important, legislators from the same party are more likely to behave in a unified fashion in congressional votes.[35] They are also more likely to provide nationally oriented public goods and less likely to spend funds on inefficient localized projects.[36] Studies have also shown that party-centered electoral rules tend to increase electoral turnout,[37] which is assumed to be the result of parties' greater inclination to encourage individuals to vote.

Under personalized voting systems, legislators are expected to build stronger linkages with their constituents, which promote individual accountability. Electoral rules that promote the personal vote have been associated with more frequent contact between legislators and their constituents than those that promote a partisan vote.[38] Constituency service is more likely because it has a greater utility to career-oriented legislators. Evidence also suggests that under personalized voting systems, candidates are more likely to have individual connections (local roots) to the districts where they are nominated, such as lower-level electoral experience or being native to the district.[39]

Electoral rules can be classified according to their incentives to cultivate a personal or a partisan vote. The classic article on the subject was written by political scientists John M. Carey and Matthew S. Shugart.[40] The basic idea is that the incentives of the electoral rules are based on such characteristics as the structure of the ballot, the pooling of votes, the type of votes cast, and district magnitude. The impact of these variables can be illustrated with examples from the electoral rules previously discussed.

Consider proportional representation formulas, which involve competition between party lists. Under closed-list proportional representation, parties present a list of ranked candidates that voters cannot alter (*ballot*); voters cast a single vote for one party (*votes*) and each vote counts as a vote for the party (*pooling*). According to the Personal Voting Index, the extent to which proportional representation with closed lists creates incentives for a personal vote is wholly determined by district magnitude. When district magnitude is high, then the partisan vote is dominant, but if district magnitude is low, the personal vote is more important. For example, in Argentina, 16 out of the 24 electoral districts have a magnitude equal to 2 or 3. In those districts, the personal vote is very important. In contrast, the province of Buenos Aires has a district magnitude equal to 35, which makes voters more likely to care about the party label than the personal characteristics of the candidates appearing in the lengthy party lists.

In short, under closed-list proportional representation, district magnitude is the key determinant of the personal vote. In districts that elect very few legislators, a voter is more likely to know the candidates and their personal attributes are more likely to matter, whereas in districts that elect many legislators, the partisan vote is most important.

The impact of district magnitude on the personal vote is supposed to be the opposite when the electoral rule is open-list proportional representation, which, as we know, allows voters to show a preference for particular candidates (*ballot*). Under open-list proportional representation, candidates want voters to choose their party (because votes are pooled at the party level) and to select them as their preferred choice. That is, a candidate has to convince voters to vote for him or her rather than for another candidate in the same party list. As a result, candidates not only compete against candidates from other parties but also against other candidates from the same party. This creates incentives to cultivate a personal reputation to attract preference votes. High district magnitude increases the number of co-partisans against which candidates compete, which according to many specialists on electoral rules, increases the incentives to cultivate a personal vote.[41] While parties may successfully craft these open lists in ways that ameliorate intra-party competition,[42] incentives to cultivate a personal vote are usually high when open lists are combined with high district magnitude.

As noted before, open lists vary by country. Where voters are required to choose one candidate (e.g., Chile), personal vote incentives are supposed to be higher than when voters have the option of choosing either a party or a candidate (e.g., Brazil's Chamber of Deputies) or have more votes for multiple candidates (e.g., Peru). They are also said to be higher than where voters have multiple votes that can be distributed across different party lists (i.e., the free list variation in place in Ecuador, El Salvador, and Honduras) than when these multiple votes must be allocated to members of one party.

In terms of personal vote incentives, elections under the incomplete list system (e.g., the Argentine Senate) are akin to elections with low magnitude closed-list proportional representation. The personal vote is even more important where plurality rule in single-member districts is in place (e.g., the Dominican Republic Senate). However, it should be noted that these two rules are supposed to generate fewer incentives to cultivate a personal vote than elections under open-list proportional representation, where competition among candidates from the same party is the norm.

To summarize, this section discussed what political scientists mean by personal vote and the outcomes typically associated with rules that promote such incentives. As noted, Latin American countries have various electoral rules in place that differ significantly with respect to the value given to candidates' personal reputations. This aspect of electoral rules affects the orientation of political campaigns, the behavior of legislators, and whether voters primarily reward or punish individual politicians or political parties. These are some of the reasons that many social scientists have spent a great deal of time researching the connection between electoral rules and the value politicians place on personal reputation.

Conclusions

The electoral system is a fundamental part of the institutional structure of a nation. When Latin American countries began to hold elections, exclusionary rules that prevented the participation of most members of society were standard. Over time, more inclusionary rules became the norm, and electoral participation increased. This chapter began by reviewing the process of suffrage extension and discussing common arguments in favor of and against expanding the franchise. It also presented information about when literacy restrictions were abolished, when the secret vote was adopted, and when women won the right to vote. These reforms significantly changed the nature of electoral competition.

Increasing the share of individuals who are permitted to vote does not guarantee that most eligible voters will exercise this right. For some, choosing not to vote is a form of free speech, while others consider it neglecting one's duty. Voter turnout is often associated with the health of a country's political system, but imposing rules that make voting mandatory is controversial. This chapter discussed the case for compulsory voting and the objections to such a requirement. It also reviewed the different rules in place across Latin America. Many nations in the region have recently engaged in public debates over the benefits and drawbacks of mandatory voting and discussed altering their respective legal codes on this matter.

Aside from who can or should vote in an election, the rules that determine how a vote is counted are highly consequential. Understanding how rules for electing presidents and legislators work is important to identify the incentives that shape the behavior of politicians. And, as this chapter made clear, it also affects the choices faced by voters.

Some Latin American countries use plurality to elect presidents while others use runoff rules. The difference is not trivial. This chapter discussed how these rules vary and how they affect competition for the nation's highest office. It also addressed the controversy surrounding presidential reelection. Many countries have put in place some form of term limits, with a few prohibiting presidential reelection altogether. Others have gone in the opposite direction, raising some questions about the potential erosion of institutional checks on presidential power. This continues to be a hotly debated topic in the region, with significant political consequences.

The last part of the chapter examined the rules for electing members of congress and some relevant outcomes associated with those rules. The rules can be grouped into three main categories, but there is substantial variation within each. The details of each country's electoral system were presented first, including information about the number of districts, electoral tiers, and district magnitude. Next, the chapter focused on the relationship between the share of seats and the share of votes and the incentives for cultivating a personal vote. Both topics, which have generated a substantial amount of research, illuminate the significant consequences of electoral systems for political representation and legislative behavior.

In conclusion, understanding the mechanisms behind electoral rules and their potential outcomes improves our understanding of political institutions in Latin America. Learning about the process of suffrage extension makes us appreciate how republican institutions and the representation of societal interests have evolved over time, making Latin American countries more politically inclusive. So far, we have examined presidential and legislative institutions as well as electoral rules; in the next chapter, we proceed with our analysis of the region's institutions by examining the judiciary.

Key Terms

Compulsory voting 176
District magnitude 194
Majoritarian electoral systems 175
Majority runoff 183
Mixed-member electoral
    systems 192

Personal vote 197
Plurality rule 175
Presidential term limits 187
Proportional representation 175
Reduced-threshold runoff 184

Bibliographic Recommendations

Jason Brennan and Lisa Hill (eds.). *Compulsory Voting: For and Against.* New York: Cambridge University Press.

John M. Carey and Matthew S. Shugart. 1995. "Incentives to Cultivate a Personal Vote: A Rank Ordering of Electoral Formulas." *Electoral Studies* 14(4): 417–439.

Miguel Carreras. 2016. "Compulsory Voting and Political Engagement (Beyond the Ballot Box): A Multilevel Analysis." *Electoral Studies* 43: 158–168.

Josep M. Colomer. 2004. "The Americas: General Overview." In Josep M. Colomer (ed.), *The Handbook of Electoral System Choice*. New York: Palgrave Macmillan, pp. 81–109.

Javier Corrales and Michael Penfold. 2014. "Manipulating Term Limits in Latin America." *Journal of Democracy* 25(4): 157–168.

Cynthia McClintock. 2018. *Electoral Rules and Democracy in Latin America*. New York: Oxford University Press.

Web Resources

Election Passport, Electoral Systems in Latin America: http://www.electionpassport.com/electoral-systems/latin-america/

Institute for Democracy and Electoral Assistance, Electoral System Design Database: https://www.idea.int/data-tools/data/electoral-system-design

Political Database of the Americas, Electoral Systems and Data: http://pdba.georgetown.edu/Elecdata/elecdata.html

8

The Judiciary

The judicial branch of government plays an essential role in the functioning of presidential countries. When it falters in its obligations and abdicates its role as guardian of the constitution and individuals' rights, democracy and the rule of law suffer greatly. In 20th-century Latin America, military governments and unconstrained presidents often worked with a complaisant and deferential judiciary. As democracy began to consolidate across the region, the relevance of the judiciary as an independent institutional actor began to grow. It is now common for the region's courts to decide on the constitutionality of presidential decrees and legislative statutes, tackle corruption cases involving high-ranking officials, adjudicate over executive-legislative disputes, and take action to protect the fundamental civil and political rights of individuals.

Democracy has also brought new challenges. Too often, politicians try to manipulate the courts, use appointments and impeachments to influence the behavior of judges, and avoid complying with judicial rulings. **Judicial crises**—wherein one of the political branches threatens to alter or succeeds in altering the composition of the high court via impeachment, forced resignation, **court-packing**, or other mechanisms[1]—have occurred repeatedly over the last decades. Political scientist Gretchen Helmke counts 44 such crises in Latin America between 1985 and 2008.[2]

The role of the judiciary in Latin American presidentialism and, more specifically, the authority of high courts and the methods of selecting and dismissing judges as well as their tenure in the bench have been the focus of intense debate within the region. Many of the constitutional reforms undertaken in Latin America over the last decades targeted the design of judicial institutions. Some countries created new **constitutional courts**, others amended the functions of their existing high courts, and many expanded the list of rights available for judicial enforcement.

The authority of the courts and their degree of autonomy from the president and congress are of vital importance. This chapter examines both topics as well as the public's perception of the judiciary. Learning about the rules that structure the workings of high courts and how the political context influences judicial behavior should further our understanding of Latin American politics. The rest of this chapter is organized into three sections. The first defines the concept of **judicial independence** and discusses how institutional rules and the political context might induce judicial autonomy. The second focuses on **judicial authority**, describing different aspects of the judicial process that influence the formal powers of constitutional courts. Examples from six Latin American countries are used to illustrate institutional features associated with both independence and authority. The third and last section of this chapter reviews public and expert perceptions of the judiciary, including public trust and expert assessments of judicial independence across all Latin American countries.

Judicial Independence

It is important to begin our discussion of judicial independence by defining this somewhat ambiguous term. *Independence* refers to the autonomy of the court. Judges are independent when they make decisions sincerely according to their own ideas of what the law requires, without undue political or private pressures conditioning such decisions. Hence, independence requires that judges have a significant level of autonomy from the executive and legislative branches.

Ideally, judicial independence requires that judges impartially adjudicate the cases before them without being concerned about a potential backlash from other institutions. But in practice, judges are seldom isolated from external pressures or political constraints. As was aptly summarized by three well-known political scientists, "It is easy to conceive of courts that are at the polar ends of complete independence and utter dependence, at least in hypothetical terms; but in reality, most courts occupy a middle ground on this continuum."[3]

Political actors often try to influence the decisions of courts. Examples abound. For instance, in 2014, the national congress of Honduras sacked four members of the Supreme Court after they voted in favor of a provisional ruling that declared a police reform law unconstitutional because it appeared to violate police officers' right to due process. Congress fired the judges in a 4 a.m. vote after an investigation that took less than 24 hours and without giving the judges a chance to defend themselves.[4] The dismissals occurred one day before the full Supreme Court was scheduled to make a final decision on the fate of the controversial law.

Another infamous example comes from Venezuela during the presidency of Hugo Chávez. In December 2009, Judge María Lourdes Afiuni, following Venezuelan law, granted the temporary release of a government critic accused of corruption who had spent close to three years in detention waiting for a trial. He subsequently fled the country. This event led President Chávez to denounce the judge as a "bandit" and call for her to be given a 30-year prison sentence. She was then arrested by intelligence officers and spent over a year in jail in pretrial detention, where she was physically abused. The provisional judge who ordered the arrest had publicly stated that he would never betray his commander, President Hugo Chávez.[5] In March 2019, she was sentenced to five years in jail for corruption. After intense international pressure, the Venezuelan government released Judge Afiuni and 21 other political prisoners in July 2019, after almost ten years of confinement.[6]

On several occasions, Latin American presidents seeking to control the high courts have pushed for the resignation of adversarial judges or the packing of courts with political loyalists. This happened during the presidencies of Carlos Menem in Argentina, Evo Morales in Bolivia, Lucio Gutiérrez in Ecuador, and Hugo Chávez in Venezuela, to name a few. In the early 1990s, when Argentine President Carlos Menem, with the support of his allies in congress, moved to increase the number of Supreme Court justices from five to nine, he not only appointed a group of loyal jurists with little experience but he also maneuvered to have a former partner in his brother's law firm appointed chief justice. In 2004, Ecuadorian President Lucio Gutiérrez, with the support of congress, replaced five of the seven members of the electoral court, eight of the nine members of the Constitutional Tribunal, and 27 of the 31 members of the Supreme Court. This triggered a political crisis that, months later, would end with the president being deposed from power.

Scholars have been debating the conditions that favor an independent judiciary for a very long time. Montesquieu famously argued in 1748 that liberty requires that the powers of judging be separated from the legislature and the executive.[7] Separation of powers laid the foundation for judicial independence. Other institutional mechanisms can also help foster an autonomous judicial branch. In 1779, John Adams advocated for constitutional provisions that would prevent the executive from dismissing members of the Supreme Court and the legislative branch from manipulating their salaries.[8]

Constitutional designers have struggled to find an institutional framework conducive to judicial independence. Recent works on Latin American courts have emphasized the importance of four mechanisms aimed at promoting judicial independence: **appointment rules**, tenure guarantees, removal proceedings, and clauses specifying the number of judges in higher courts.[9] These institutional instruments seek to prevent undue influence on the appointment process as well as unwarranted pressures after the judges are seated. The following subsections discuss these mechanisms and provide examples from six Latin American countries: Argentina, Bolivia, Brazil, Chile, Mexico, and Peru.

Appointment Rules

Judicial independence is enhanced when neither the executive nor the legislative branch has unilateral control over the appointment process.

In most countries, the appointment of judges requires the involvement of more than one actor. When two institutional bodies participate in the process (e.g., the executive and congress), usually one nominates the candidate while the other gives its consent. That being the case, both need to reach an agreement. This is known as a *cooperative appointment procedure*.

Increasing the number of participants in the appointment process is thought to improve the autonomy of the judiciary by preventing judges from being obligated to meet the preferences of a single actor.[10] By including multiple actors in this process, appointees are also more likely to be mainstream judges. However, the involvement of various actors in the appointment process may lead to disagreements over the suitability of the potential candidates, in which case, the vacancies may not be filled. Therefore, increasing the number of actors with the power to veto judicial appointments is likely to promote judicial independence but may also make deadlock more likely.

An alternative mechanism is to give two or more bodies unilateral power to appoint a share of the court's judges. Each institutional actor decides, often alone, whom to appoint to fill some of the vacancies. This is known as the *representative appointment procedure*. Its goal is to promote impartiality by preventing one institutional actor from controlling the composition of the court. It may also help to incorporate a mix of judges who have different backgrounds. Key political actors are guaranteed the power to select some of the judges and are assured that rival actors will not dominate the appointment process. While this mechanism can lead to a court that is representative of the preferences of the main political actors, it can also reduce the independence of individual judges by making them agents of the particular institution that appointed them.

Another mechanism gives the judicial branch the power of self-appointment. This procedure enhances independence from the executive and legislative branches of government but makes for appointees who are more likely to be co-opted by judges from higher courts. It can foster professionalism but may decrease accountability and promote conformity with the judicial establishment.

Some countries utilize yet another mechanism that gives judicial councils the power to appoint judges (usually in conjunction with other actors such as congress and the executive). The composition of these councils often includes judges, members of the bar association, and academics as well as government and congressional appointees. This mechanism has become very popular in the last decades, although it is more commonly used for selecting lower court judges rather than those of high courts.

Cooperative and representative mechanisms sometimes include high courts or judicial councils as one of the institutional actors involved in the appointment process. When multiple actors are involved in the appointment process, the inclusion of a judicial council or a high court is intended to enhance judicial independence in comparison to mechanisms that only include the president and congress.

Judicial appointments may also be decided directly by voters. Popular elections can enhance accountability and reduce the perception that judges are too far removed from ordinary citizens. However, judicial independence requires that judges make decisions that are often unpopular; hence, direct elections may negatively affect the impartiality of judicial decisions. This method can also lead to candidates with low qualifications and little professional expertise. To try to prevent this, a prior screening mechanism to choose eligible candidates may be put in place. Another criticism is that elected judges may be beholden to the interest groups that contribute to their electoral campaigns. This is why candidates for judicial positions are sometimes forbidden to have partisan affiliations or from campaigning altogether.

Lastly, it must be noted that the size of the majority required to nominate or appoint a judge also matters. In some countries, institutional bodies (such as a chamber of congress, a judicial council, or a higher court) decide appointments by a simple majority vote. Increasing the level of consensus is thought to promote more competent and moderate candidates. When rules require a supermajority vote (e.g., two thirds of members), judicial independence is usually enhanced.

Latin American countries use a variety of procedures to appoint judges to their higher courts. In Argentina, the process involves the president and the Senate. The president nominates a candidate and the Senate must approve it by a two-thirds vote of those present; otherwise, the position remains vacant until a new candidate reaches the required support.

In Mexico, the appointment of Supreme Court justices also involves the president and the Senate. To fill a vacancy, the president nominates three candidates, and the Senate must choose one of them by a two-thirds vote of those present in the session. The Senate can also reject such candidates by a majority vote, in which case, the president must send another list of three candidates. If the Senate cannot agree to appoint or reject the proposed candidates or if it rejects the two lists proposed by the president, the position is filled unilaterally by the president from the list of proposed candidates. In practice, this means that the president can fill a supreme court vacancy with his preferred candidate as long as he has the support of a Senate majority and, under some circumstances, with the support of just over one third of senators. It also means that deadlock cannot lead to the vacancy going unfilled.

In Brazil, Chile, Bolivia, and Peru, the supreme court, which is the country's highest appellate court, lacks the power of judicial review. This authority resides with a constitutional tribunal, which is a separate institutional body. Many European countries have a similar institutional design, which establishes a separate and autonomous constitutional court.

The highest appellate court in Brazil is the Superior Court of Justice, while the constitutional court is the Supreme Federal Court. The president nominates candidates to both courts, who then need the approval of a majority of senators to become instated. In the case of the Superior Court of Justice, the president selects a nominee from a list of three potential candidates presented by the court itself.[11] As a result, the president has less discretion in choosing judges for the Superior Court of Justice than in selecting those for the Supreme Federal Court.

The appointment of judges to the Chilean Supreme Court involves three actors: the president, the Senate, and the Supreme Court. The first step is for the court to present a list of five potential candidates to the president. Next, the president nominates one of the five candidates to the Senate, which needs to approve the nomination by a vote of two thirds of its membership for the vacancy to be filled.

Appointments to the Chilean Constitutional Tribunal follow the representative procedure, which gives different institutional actors the power to name a share of the court's judges. Three members are appointed by the Chilean Supreme Court, three are appointed by the president, and four are appointed by congress. The Chilean Senate must approve its two appointments with the vote of two thirds of its membership. The other two appointees are nominated by the Chamber of Deputies and must be confirmed by a vote of two thirds of the membership in each chamber of congress.

Bolivia is the only country where high court judges are elected directly by voters. Judges to the Supreme Court and the Constitutional Tribunal are elected by popular vote from a list of eligible candidates selected by a two-thirds vote in a joint session of the two chambers of congress.[12] These candidates compete in nonpartisan elections where they cannot publicly campaign. Voters choose nine judges (plus an additional nine alternates) for each of the two courts.

The appointment of judges to the Peruvian Constitutional Tribunal remains exclusively in the hands of the country's unicameral congress. Each appointment requires the vote of two thirds of the members of congress. Supreme court and lower court judges are elected by a judicial council, which decides appointments by a vote of two thirds of its members. The Peruvian judicial council (*Consejo Nacional de la Magistratura*) is composed of seven members elected for five years: one elected by the Supreme Court, one elected by public prosecutors, one elected by the bar association, two elected by other professional associations, one elected by the presidents of public universities, and one elected by the president of private universities.[13]

Table 8.1. summarizes these appointment procedures. The first column indicates the country and the ten different courts discussed in this section. The second column lists the different institutional actors involved in the appointment process, and the third column notes the required threshold when a congressional vote is required to make the appointment effective.

Length of Tenure

Another critical factor influencing judicial independence is the length of time of judicial appointments. There are different views on this issue. James Madison (in *Federalist 51*) and Alexander Hamilton (in *Federalist 78*)

TABLE 8.1 ● Rules for Appointing High Court Judges and Length of Tenure			
Country	Actors Involved	Threshold in Congress	Length of Tenure
Argentina			
Supreme Court	President & Senate	Supermajority	Lifetime
Bolivia			
Supreme Court	Congress & Voters	Supermajority	6 years
Constitutional Tribunal	Congres & Voters	Supermajority	6 years
Brazil			
Superior Court of Justice	President, Senate, & Court	Majority	Lifetime
Supreme Federal Court	President & Senate	Majority	Lifetime
Chile			
Supreme Court	President, Senate, & Court	Supermajority	Lifetime
Constitutional Tribunal	President, Congress, & Court	Supermajority[i]	9 years
Mexico			
Supreme Court	President & Senate	Supermajority[ii]	15 years
Peru			
Supreme Court	Judicial Council	~	Lifetime[iii]
Constitutional Tribunal	Congress (unicameral)	Supermajority	5 years

[i] The supermajority vote regarding appointments to the Constitutional Tribunal applies only to congressional nominations but not to those made by the president or the court under the representative procedure.

[ii] Mexico requires a supermajority, but it may be circumvented (as explained in the text).

[iii] A review conducted after seven years in office could result in early dismissal.

famously argued for the permanent tenure of Supreme Court judges, which they thought would eliminate all sense of dependence on those who appoint them and, as a result, promote impartiality. Many judicial scholars in Latin America have agreed with this perspective.

Lifetime appointments also have their share of critics. Some argue that they may create incentives for politicians to constrain the power of judges and to resort more frequently to judicial impeachments. Political scientists Gretchen Helmke and Jeffrey Staton argue that valuable lifetime appointments (with the guarantee of high lifetime salaries) may lower judicial independence by making judges more likely to comply with the wishes of those politicians who can dismiss them.[14] According to this perspective, shorter appointments can make judges less concerned about being removed from the bench and, as a result, promote impartial behavior even under the threat of impeachment.

But how long should the appointments last? Many experts on the judiciary have argued that short appointments ultimately reduce judicial independence by creating incentives to please those institutional actors who can help judges secure coveted jobs after their term in office is over.[15] Most agree that judicial independence is enhanced when the length of tenure is longer than that of the appointers.[16] Information on the length of term for judicial appointments to the high courts of Argentina, Bolivia, Brazil, Chile, Mexico, and Peru is summarized in the last column of Table 8.1.

Members of the Supreme Court in Argentina and Chile and members of both the Superior Court of Justice and the Supreme Federal Court in Brazil have lifetime appointments but face mandatory retirement when they reach the age of 75 years. In the case of Argentina, Supreme Court judges who reach that age can stay for an additional five years if they are once again nominated by the president and endorsed by a supermajority vote in the Senate. Members of the Peruvian Supreme Court have lifetime appointments in principle, but the judicial council that appoints them must ratify them in their position after seven years in service, at which time it may opt for their dismissal.

In Mexico and Bolivia, and the Constitutional Tribunals in Chile and Peru, judges are elected for a specific number of years. Members of the Mexican Supreme Court are appointed for 15 years and cannot be reelected. In Chile, members of the Constitutional Tribunal are elected for nine years and are also required to retire when they reach 75 years of age. Members of the Bolivian Supreme Court as well as members of the country's Constitutional Tribunal are elected for six years. Supreme Court judges cannot be reelected, while judges of the Constitutional Tribunal may once again become eligible after standing down for a period equal to their term in office.

Members of the Peruvian Constitutional Tribunal are appointed for five years, the shortest term among the high court judges in the six countries discussed here. Moreover, the length of their appointment is equal to the term in office of the president and members of congress.

Removal Proceedings

The procedure for dismissing judges is an additional factor that may influence judicial independence. Even when tenure is secured, as in the case of lifetime appointments, judges may be forced to resign. When judges fear arbitrary dismissal by political actors, judicial independence is threatened.

As with appointments, the larger the number of actors involved in the process of disciplining high court judges and the greater the majority required for dismissal, the greater the potential for judicial independence. If the disciplinary process includes actors other than congress and the president, such as judicial councils, independence should also be enhanced.

The procedures in place to dismiss judges vary significantly across Latin America. For Supreme Court judges in Argentina, Bolivia, Chile, and Mexico and Constitutional Tribunal judges in Bolivia, the process of dismissal involves both chambers of congress. In Argentina, members of the Supreme Court can be dismissed for committing crimes or for improper performance of their duties, which requires a vote by two thirds of members present in the Chamber of Deputies and a subsequent vote by two thirds of members in the Senate.

In Bolivia, members of the Supreme Court and the Constitutional Tribunal may be dismissed for illicit activities. The process requires an initial majority vote of the members present in the Chamber of Deputies and a subsequent conviction in the Senate by a vote of two thirds of the members present. In Chile, members of the Supreme Court may be dismissed for gross dereliction of duty. The process first requires a vote by the majority of those present in the Chamber of Deputies and then a vote by a majority of members in the Senate. In Mexico, members of the Supreme Court may be impeached for violations of the constitution or federal laws. The process requires a vote by a majority of members in the Chamber of Deputies and a subsequent vote by two thirds of the members present in the Senate.

In Brazil, members of the Supreme Federal Court can be fired by the Senate for committing improper activities, which, according to the law, includes negligent behavior as well as exercising political/partisan activities and engaging in behavior incompatible with the dignity of the office. Dismissal requires a vote by two thirds of senators present in the respective session. Members of the Superior Court of Justice accused of ordinary or so-called responsibility crimes are tried by the Supreme Federal Court.

In Peru, members of the Supreme Court and the Constitutional Tribunal may be dismissed for constitutional violations and crimes, including infractions that endanger the proper functioning of the state apparatus and those that significantly lessen the confidence in the judge. For the dismissal to take place, a vote by two thirds of the members of the unicameral congress is required.[17]

Lastly, members of the Chilean Constitutional Tribunal cannot be dismissed, except in cases in which a member of the tribunal has been formally charged with a crime or misdemeanor and the appellate court of the city of Santiago finds that there are grounds for prosecution. If such an event occurs, then the rest of the members of the Constitutional Tribunal can vote to dismiss the accused judge.

Table 8.2 summarizes information on how high court judges in Argentina, Bolivia, Brazil, Chile, Mexico, and Peru may be removed from the bench. The last column also indicates whether the size of the high court is constitutionally determined, which is the topic of the next subsection.

Size of Higher Courts

One other institutional trait that is considered to influence judicial independence is whether the constitution stipulates the number of

TABLE 8.2 ● Rules for Removing High Court Judges and Whether the Size of the Court Is in the Constitution			
Country	Actors Involved	Removal Threshold in Congress	Size of Court in Constitution
Argentina			
Supreme Court	Congress	Supermajority in each chamber	No
Bolivia			
Supreme Court	Congress	Majority and then supermajority	No
Constitutional Tribunal	Congress	Majority and then supermajority	No
Brazil			
Superior Court of Justice	Supreme Federal Court	~	Yesⁱ
Supreme Federal Court	Senate	Supermajority	Yes
Chile			
Supreme Court	Congress	Majority in each chamber	Yes
Constitutional Tribunal	Courts	~	Yes
Mexico			
Supreme Court	Congress	Majority and then supermajority	Yes
Peru			
Supreme Court	Congress (unicameral)	Supermajority	No
Constitutional Tribunal	Congress (unicameral)	Supermajority	Yes

ⁱThe constitution only establishes the minimum number of judges in the Superior Court of Justice.

members in the supreme court and the constitutional tribunal. When the specific number of judges in the court is written into the constitution, it is more difficult for political actors to modify the rules to pack the court with friendly appointees. If such a provision is in place, a constitutional amendment must be passed to change the size of the court. However, if it is only a matter of law, then it can be changed more easily, which facilitates court-packing by political actors.[18]

Several Latin American countries have established the size of high courts in their constitutions. For instance, in Mexico, the number of members of the Supreme Court is established in the constitution. In Chile, both the number of members of the Supreme Court and the number of members of the Constitutional Tribunal are set in the constitution. In Brazil, the number of members of the Supreme Federal Court is established in the constitution, but in the case of the Superior Court of Justice, the constitution only sets a minimum number. In Peru, the number of members of the Constitutional Tribunal is determined by the constitution, but the number of members of the Supreme Court is determined by a judicial council (*Consejo Ejecutivo del Poder Judicial*) composed of members of the judicial branch and a representative of the bar association.

In contrast, the number of members in the high courts of Argentina and Bolivia is determined by law, which allows the president and congress to more easily modify the size of these tribunals. For example, in 1990 in Argentina, under the presidency of Carlos Menem, a law was passed to increase the number of judges from five to nine. This change allowed the government in power to pack the high court with its appointees. In 2006, another law changed the number of judges back to the original five. In Bolivia, the number of judges in the Supreme Court and the Constitutional Tribunal can also be modified by the passage of legislation. In 2017, for example, a new law increased the number of members in the Bolivian Constitutional Tribunal from seven to nine.

The Political Context

So far, this chapter has discussed four mechanisms that may help to promote the independence of the judiciary. Surely there are other features that also matter, such as whether funding for the judicial branch (salaries and budget) can be manipulated by the government to pressure judges,[19] but the four aforementioned procedures are most often considered crucial and thoroughly illuminate the institutional variations found across Latin America.

Several studies on judicial independence have also underscored the importance of the political context. One prominent argument postulates that fragmentation of partisan power shapes the incentive structure facing judges. More specifically, when the presidency and congress are not controlled by the same party, sanctioning judges is more difficult, and as a result, members of the judiciary are more likely to act independently.[20]

In addition, the lack of a unified government makes it more likely that one of the elected branches may protect judicial independence by vetoing actions that would overturn high court decisions.[21] In contrast, under a unified government, the risks of reprisal.and override are greater, which can make judges less likely to oppose government policies or to curb presidential excesses.

Several political scientists have found support for the argument that political fragmentation (i.e., the lack of unified government) increases the likelihood of judicial independence in presidential countries. For example, Rebecca Bill Chávez, John A. Ferejohn, and Barry R. Weingast described various historical episodes in Argentina and the United States in which the lack of unified government prevented presidents from packing the court with friendly appointees or using the impeachment process to remove judges for political reasons.[22] Their study supports the idea that fragmentation of power among the elected branches enables the emergence of an independent judiciary. Druscilla Scribner also tackled this topic in an analysis of judicial decisions in Argentina and Chile.[23] She showed that on matters affecting executive power,[24] judges are more likely to rule against presidents who lack majority support in both chambers of congress.

In Mexico, the Supreme Court was subservient to the ruling party (i.e., the Institutional Revolutionary Party [PRI]) for most of the 20th century. A significant reform in 1994 strengthened the power of the Supreme Court, giving it greater powers to interpret the constitution, including in cases of constitutional controversies involving different levels and branches of government. Julio Ríos Figueroa examined judicial decisions on constitutional matters made by the court following the 1994 reform and found that political fragmentation in the elected branches of government increased the probability of rulings against the former dominant party.[25]

The potential problems of one-party dominance on judicial independence are also evident in the case of Bolivia. As noted before, the country adopted direct elections to choose high court judges but gave congress the authority to select nominees. In both the 2017 and 2011 judicial elections, the judicial candidates were unilaterally selected by the leaders of the ruling party (i.e., the Movement Towards Socialism), which controlled a large majority in both chambers of congress. Unsurprisingly, the country's Constitutional Tribunal has ruled in favor of the government on most occasions, going as far as to strike down the term limits established in the constitution to allow the president, Evo Morales, to run for a fourth term in 2019.

Another contextual factor that several judicial analysts consider important in influencing judicial autonomy is the pressure emanating from societal forces. One view underlines the effect of public opinion on political actors. According to this perspective, citizens may provide cover to judges when politicians believe that they will be punished for retaliating against the judiciary in response to adverse rulings.[26] So, media coverage and public support for the judiciary may enhance judicial independence by promoting politicians' compliance with judicial resolutions.[27]

Public opinion and interest groups may also exert direct pressure on the courts. The monitoring of judicial proceeding by nongovernmental organizations, televised trials, and public demonstrations surrounding high-profile cases may help to lessen bias in favor of politically powerful defendants and improve accountability.[28] This may be particularly important in Latin America, where political elites have long been considered by many to be above the law.

While judicial independence requires that the public mood not undermine the impartiality of the court, in reality, judges are not immune to public opinion. Going against the public mood too often can undermine the legitimacy of the court. Judges who care about the public standing of the court may be less inclined to challenge federal laws that have broad public support. In addition, rulings that satisfy popular positions are more likely to result in compliance from public officials and the public, which is important to the judiciary. The correlation between judges' rulings and public opinion may not be the result of judges' strategic incentives; sometimes they are the consequence of judges changing their views as a result of the same developments that foster changes in mass public opinion.[29]

One event that highlights the public pressures sometimes faced by high courts took place in Brazil on July 5, 2018. On that day, the country's Supreme Court had to decide whether the ex-president, Luiz Inácio Lula da Silva, would be sent to prison while he continued to appeal a lower court corruption conviction. Lula was one of the most influential politicians in Brazil, the leader of the largest party in the country, and the leading candidate in the forthcoming presidential elections. Moreover, most of the judges in the Supreme Court had been nominated either by him or by his successor, Dilma Rousseff, a co-partisan and vocal Lula supporter. Before ruling on this matter, the court received a petition signed by over 5,000 prosecutors and judges demanding that the justices uphold a prior ruling that allowed the jailing of defendants after their first appeal has been rejected (as was the case here). The court also received another petition signed by over 3,600 private lawyers and public defenders supporting the former president's petition to remain free until the Supreme Court reviewed the lower court conviction. Supporters and detractors of the former president demonstrated in many cities across the country, while many politicians (and even the head of the army) issued public statements regarding the case. In the end, the Supreme Court ruled 6–5 against the former president, who was subsequently jailed.

Judicial Authority

The power of the judiciary not only depends on its independence from the elected branches of government but also on its formal authority. As noted earlier in this chapter, most analysts agree that Latin American courts have increased their scope of authority since the late 20th century. The specific prerogatives allocated to high courts, however, differ in significant ways across the region.

This section of the chapter examines the constellation of prerogatives allocated to the different constitutional courts. Judicial authority matters because it affects the kind of issues that constitutional courts can address and the consequences of such rulings. While many significant issues—such as the protection of property rights, disputes between federal and state governments, and the validity of new legislation—may fall under the purview of a constitutional court, the conditions under which courts may address particular controversies, who has legal standing to bring a case to the court, and the effects of court decisions vary significantly from country to country.

Instruments of Judicial Authority

Before describing the specific characteristics of judicial authority in several Latin American countries, it is important to define and explain a series of prerogatives that affect the decision-making power of courts. Following Julio Ríos Figueroa's analysis of Latin American constitutional courts, the types of legal instruments in place can be categorized according to five relevant characteristics: type, timing, jurisdiction, access, and effects.[30]

Type refers to the kind of claims that can be brought before the court. Constitutional questions may be addressed by the court only in the context of *concrete* legal cases, or they may be addressed in the *abstract*. For a concrete review to take place, there must be a real case or controversy. This means that only after a law is in effect or a specific action related to such law has already taken place can the court find it unconstitutional. Abstract review can take place in the absence of an actual case. Therefore, the court may review a piece of legislation before an actual injury or violation of constitutional rights has occurred. Under abstract review, the court may interpret the constitutionality of a text in response to the demand of some specific political actors, such as members of congress or the executive.

Timing refers to the moment when **constitutional review** may take place. When a constitutional review can only take place after a law has been adopted, it is called *a posteriori* (or *ex-post*). If the constitutional review can take place before a bill is formally enacted, it is called *a priori* (or *ex-ante*). According to this definition, concrete review may only take place a posteriori, while abstract review may take place both a priori or a posteriori.

Jurisdiction indicates whether the process of constitutional review may or may not take place only in one court. Jurisdiction is said to be *centralized* when there is only one court with judicial review authority, while it is *decentralized* (or *diffused*) when more than one court may exercise such a review. In the case of centralized jurisdiction, other courts must refer constitutional controversies to the single constitutional court. In contrast, when jurisdiction is decentralized, judicial review may take place in lower courts. As a result, more than one court can interpret the constitution and rule an act unconstitutional. When abstract review is possible, it takes place under a centralized jurisdiction. That is, cases reviewed in the abstract are assigned to the single constitutional court rather than to lower-court judges. In addition, when there is a priori review, jurisdiction is always centralized. However, when courts review concrete cases, the jurisdiction may be centralized or decentralized.

Next, we have the matter of *access*, which refers to who can bring a claim. In some countries, access is *open*, which means that citizens have legal standing to bring a claim to the court. Other countries have a *restricted* system, which only allows specific institutional actors—usually federal and state governments, congress, a predetermined number of legislators, or a tribunal—to raise cases for constitutional review. In those cases wherein the constitutional court may address a priori matters, access is always restricted.

The four instruments discussed so far lead to six distinct combinations (identified as I through VI), which are summarized in Figure 8.1. The first two describe procedures that are concrete and centralized, the third describes a procedure that is concrete and decentralized, and the last three describe procedures that are abstract and centralized.

Lastly, the *effects* of the judicial decisions taken by constitutional courts can be classified as **erga omnes** (valid for all) or as **inter partes** (valid only for the parties involved in the case). Consider a case brought to the court by an individual who claims her rights were violated by a new pensions law. If the effects of the court's decisions are limited to inter partes, then its ruling affects the application of the pensions law only for the specific plaintiff in this case. If instead, the effect of the court's decisions is erga omnes, then the ruling affects how the new law applies to all individuals affected by it.

Decisions in concrete types that have a centralized jurisdiction (i.e., Combinations I and II in Figure 8.1) can be inter partes or erga omnes. Concrete types that have a decentralized jurisdiction (i.e., Combination III) are usually inter partes, at least until they reach the supreme court, when

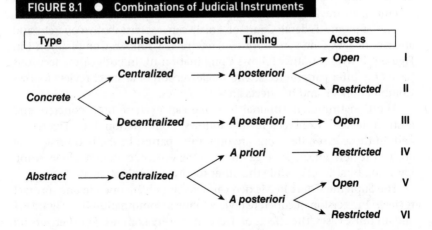

FIGURE 8.1 ● Combinations of Judicial Instruments

Type	Jurisdiction	Timing	Access	
Concrete	Centralized	A posteriori	Open	I
			Restricted	II
	Decentralized	A posteriori	Open	III
Abstract	Centralized	A priori	Restricted	IV
		A posteriori	Open	V
			Restricted	VI

decisions in some instances may become applicable to all. Abstract types (i.e., Combinations IV, V, and VI) are always centralized and erga omnes.

The instruments influence the authority of constitutional courts as well as their behavior. For example, Julio Ríos Figueroa has argued that abstract and restricted access (Combinations IV and VI) are suitable instruments for settling political disputes between different institutional actors but not very effective for enforcing rights, while concrete types (particularly Combination III) are better for enforcing rights.[31]

Judicial Authority in Six Latin American Countries

The legal instruments described above are helpful in evaluating the authority of the different constitutional courts. Courts for which decisions have only inter partes effects have less authority than those which can issue erga omnes decisions. Courts that have concrete but no abstract review have less authority than those which have both concrete and abstract review. Courts with restricted abstract review may be considered weaker than those in which access to abstract review is also open. More avenues for review (i.e., more combinations) strengthen the court. Let us now summarize the prerogatives of six different constitutional courts in Latin America.[32]

The Supreme Court of Argentina has only concrete review authority, which follows Combination III in Figure 8.1. Decisions taken by the Argentine Supreme Court are inter partes, not erga omnes. Although not expressly stated in the constitution, the decisions of the Supreme Court of Argentina sometimes evolve into binding precedent.[33]

The Constitutional Tribunal of Bolivia can exercise both concrete and abstract review. One version of concrete review follows Combination II in Figure 8.1 and, in those cases, the effects of decisions are erga omnes. Another version of concrete review follows Combination III and, in those cases, the effects of decisions are inter partes. One version of abstract review follows Combination IV and another follows Combination VI. In both instances, abstract decisions have erga omnes effects.

The Supreme Federal Court of Brazil can exercise both concrete and abstract review. One version of concrete review follows Combination I in Figure 8.1, while another follows Combination III. In both cases, decisions have only inter partes effects. The single version of abstract review follows Combination VI, and its effects are erga omnes.

The Constitutional Tribunal in Chile can exercise both concrete and abstract review. Concrete review follows Combination I in Figure 8.1 and, in those cases, decisions are only inter partes. In the two versions of abstract review, effects are erga omnes. One version of concrete review follows Combination IV, while the other follows Combination VI.[34]

The Supreme Court in Mexico can exercise both concrete and abstract review. One version of concrete review follows Combination II in Figure 8.1 and, in those cases, the effects of decisions are erga omnes. Another version of concrete review follows Combination III and, in those cases, the effects of decisions are inter partes. The Mexican Supreme Court can also exercise abstract review along the lines of Combination VI, which has erga omnes effects.

In Peru, the Constitutional Tribunal can exercise both concrete and abstract review. One version of concrete review follows Combination II in Figure 8.1, and the other version of concrete review follows Combination III. In both cases, the effects of decisions are inter partes. This court can also exercise abstract review along the lines of Combination VI and, in this case, rulings have erga omnes effects.

What do these institutional instruments tell us about the formal authority of these constitutional courts? Restricting ourselves to these prerogatives, the Argentine Supreme Court emerges as the weakest of the group. It can only exercise concrete review, and its decisions do not have erga omnes effects. The relative authority of the other courts depends on whether we focus on abstract or concrete review.

In terms of abstract review, the Constitutional Tribunals in Chile and Bolivia have greater authority than the constitutional courts in Brazil, Mexico, and Peru, which have a single abstract procedure.[35] As noted earlier, scholars have underlined that abstract procedures are particularly suitable for resolving disputes between institutional actors.

In terms of concrete review, the court in Chile has only one procedural avenue (similar to Argentina), whereas those in Bolivia, Brazil, Mexico, and Peru have two. The Peruvian and Brazilian courts seem more constrained than those of Bolivia and Mexico because when they rule on concrete cases, the effects can only be inter partes.

Some judicial scholars have argued that in addition to the instruments discussed so far, the court's ability to enforce rights is also related to the number of rights enumerated in a country's constitutional text. For example, Daniel M. Brinks and Abby Blass argue that the court's scope of authority is also determined by the kinds of issues that are entrusted to the court's jurisdiction.[36] They believe that the number of civil, political, economic, social, and cultural rights included in the constitution chart the potential field of judicial intervention. From this perspective, the relative power of the constitutional court on this substantive area increases with the number of individual rights (and group rights) expressly stipulated in a national constitution. Among the six examples discussed in this section of the chapter, the constitution of Bolivia stands out for its long list of individual and group rights.

Also relevant are legal actions called *amparos* or *tutelas*, which are extraordinary legal proceedings that allow individuals or entities to petition the court to protect their constitutional rights in the face of blatant and illegal actions by government actors or other authorities or by their failure to act at all.[37] Amparos originated in Mexico in the mid-1800s and have since expanded to most Latin American countries (except Cuba and Haiti). While the details regarding the application of the amparo vary across countries, they are considered a vital instrument to protect citizens' rights from being trampled or neglected by public officials. For instance, the Constitutional Tribunal of Colombia issued major rulings in cases stemming from tutelas that improved access to health care (in 2008), legalized same-sex marriage (in 2016), and ordered administrative and judicial authorities to implement reforms to protect women who are victims of violence (in 2017).[38] Their frequent use across the region, however, has raised some concerns about the ability of courts to process them promptly and the potentially negative consequences of overloading courts with this type of petition.[39]

Perceptions of the Judiciary

So far, this chapter has reviewed the institutional framework that affects the authority and independence of high courts. In addition, it noted that the political context interacts with the rules in place to influence the behavior of the courts. One crucial element of the political context is the perception that members of the public have regarding the judiciary. When courts are seen as legitimate and citizens respect them, political actors are more cautious in their attempts to retaliate against unfavorable rulings and are more predisposed to comply with the courts' decisions. This is an important reason why judges care about citizens' perceptions of the **judiciary's legitimacy**. Moreover, public support for the courts strengthens the rule of law and influences public support for democracy.

For the most part, the public's perception of the judiciary is not very favorable. For example, data provided by the Latin American Public Opinion Project (LAPOP) for the years 2016 and 2017 revealed to what extent people believe that their country's courts guarantee a fair trial.[40] The average score for the region, based on a 7-point scale running from 1 (not at all) to 7 (a lot), is 3.4, with only modest variation across countries.[41] This low score highlights citizens' concerns with the impartiality of their countries' justice system. Studies have shown that such negative perceptions have been present for many years.[42]

Also illuminating is the proportion of the public that reports having been asked to pay a bribe to the courts. The question, part of the same 2016–2017 LAPOP survey, first asked whether an individual had any dealings with the courts in the prior twelve months and, if the answer was yes, whether or not they were asked to pay a bribe. The results, which vary significantly across countries, show that on average, over 9 percent of Latin Americans who had interacted with the court system were asked to pay a bribe.

In Bolivia, around 30 percent of those who had interacted with the court system reported having been asked to pay a bribe. This is a troubling statistic. A significantly large proportion of respondents in Mexico (25 percent), Paraguay (18 percent), and Venezuela (18 percent) also reported having been asked to pay a bribe. The country in which respondents reported the fewest incidents of bribery in the court system is Costa Rica (less than 1 percent). Low percentages were also reported in Uruguay, Brazil, Argentina, and Chile.

Many comparative studies of the judiciary have examined the public's confidence in the judicial branch. These analyses try to explain variations in individuals' trust of the courts and their potential implications. For example, political scientists Ryan Salzman and Adam Ramsey found that individuals who express greater support for a democratic form of government and the rule of law are also more likely to express confidence in the courts.[43] In contrast, those who prefer a powerful president relative to other government institutions and those who perceive higher levels of corruption among public officials tend to have less confidence in the country's courts. In her study of interbranch crises in Latin America, Gretchen Helmke found that public trust in the judiciary reduces the likelihood that the elected branches would initiate or threaten to initiate an attack on the judiciary to forcefully restructure its composition.[44]

Results from worldwide surveys have shown that Latin Americans have lower confidence in the judicial system than individuals in most other regions of the world.[45] In Latin America, public confidence in the judiciary has been low—under 40 percent on average—since at least the mid-1990s. Figure 8.2 shows the proportion of people who have "a lot" or "some" trust in the judiciary, according to the answers provided to various Latinobarómetro surveys from 1995 to 2018.

Respondents in some countries, such as Uruguay, Costa Rica, and Brazil, have consistently expressed higher-than-average trust in the courts, while respondents in other countries, such as Peru and Ecuador, have expressed comparatively low levels of trust in the courts.

Most surveys have shown low levels of public confidence in the courts, which is often interpreted as indicative of a fundamental legitimacy problem.[46] But not everyone agrees. Some believe this is not an appropriate measure of legitimacy. For example, political scientists Amanda Driscoll and Michael J. Nelson argue that confidence measures tend to capture short-term satisfaction with the political regime rather than institutional legitimacy.[47] The latter concept represents an individual's willingness to accept the decisions and coercive authority of courts, irrespective of whether they agree or not with its decisions. As such, the commonly used confidence questions employed in most surveys may not be particularly apt to capture institutional legitimacy. These scholars prefer to focus instead on an alternative survey question that asks whether presidents could be justified in dissolving the supreme court. Answers to this alternative question show that a substantial percentage of respondents across Latin America express an unwillingness to tolerate fundamental changes to the institutional integrity of the high court, which these scholars interpret as reflecting a reasonably high level of institutional legitimacy.

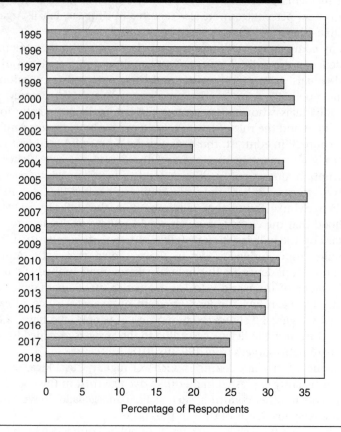

FIGURE 8.2 ● Public Trust in the Judiciary, 1995–2018

Source: Latinobarómetro Data Bank, surveys for 1995-2018.

Experts' Assessments

Surveys of country experts are another insightful tool to evaluate the performance of the judicial branch. There are various organizations that poll academics, businesspeople, and other experts to get an informed assessment of the functioning of political institutions. One organization that has gathered significant data across countries and over time on a variety of institutional features is the Varieties of Democracy (V-Dem) project, headquartered in the department of political science at the University of Gothenburg, Sweden.

Among the many institutional indicators offered by the data set compiled by the V-Dem project, one focuses on the independence of the judicial branch. It seeks to identify autonomous judicial decision making by asking whether the court adopts the government's position, regardless of its genuine view of the case. The specific question posed to the country experts asks,

When the high court in the judicial system is ruling in cases that are salient to the government, how often would you say that it makes decisions that merely reflect government wishes regardless of its sincere view of the legal record?

The answers are captured by an ordinal scale that goes from 0 to 4, where 0 = always, 1 = usually, 2 = about half of the time, 3 = seldom, and 4 = never. The results for 20 Latin American countries covering the period 1985 to 2018 appear in Figure 8.3.

In general, expert evaluations of the independence of the region's constitutional courts present a somewhat positive outlook. Currently, courts are perceived to be more independent than in the 1980s, when many Latin American countries transitioned from authoritarianism to democracy. But time trends and rankings vary significantly across countries.

FIGURE 8.3 ●   Judicial Independence, 1985–2018

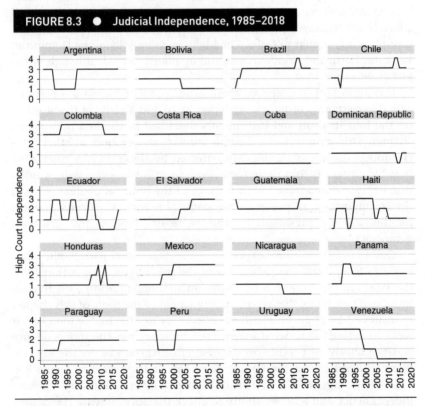

Source: Michael Coppedge, John Gerring, Carl Henrik Knutsen, Staffan I. Lindberg, Jan Teorell, David Altman, Michael Bernhard, M. Steven Fish, Adam Glynn, Allen Hicken, Anna Lührmann, Kyle L. Marquardt, Kelly McMann, Pamela Paxton, Daniel Pemstein, Brigitte Seim, Rachel Sigman, Svend-Erik Skaaning, Jeffrey Staton, Steven Wilson, Agnes Cornell, Lisa Gastaldi, Haakon Gjerløw, Nina Ilchenko, Joshua Krusell, Laura Maxwell, Valeriya Mechkova, Juraj Medzihorsky, Josefine Pernes, Johannes von Römer, Natalia Stepanova, Aksel Sundström, Eitan Tzelgov, YitingWang, Tore Wig, and Daniel Ziblatt. 2019. V-Dem [Country-Year/Country-Date] Dataset v9, Varieties of Democracy (V-Dem) Project. https://doi.org/10.23696/vdemcy19.

The highest-ranked court over this entire period is the Colombian Constitutional Tribunal, despite having experienced some fluctuation over time. The constitutional courts in Costa Rica and Uruguay are also ranked high in terms of independence and have not experienced any change in their scores over this period. Four countries show a positive trend, increasing the independence of their high courts over time and ending with a favorable ranking. These are Brazil, Chile, El Salvador, and Mexico. The ranking of the high courts in Argentina, Guatemala, and Peru exhibited some fluctuation over time, but similar to the others, end with a relatively favorable score.

The high courts in Ecuador, Panama, and Paraguay end 2018 with a higher score than in the mid-1980s, but lag overall behind those in the previously mentioned countries. In the rest of the countries, constitutional courts are not seen as independent by country experts.

Cuba's court has the worst record of the region over the entire period, lacking any independence from the executive branch. The constitutional courts in the Nicaragua and Venezuela culminate the period with the lowest possible score, similar to Cuba. The high courts in Bolivia, the Dominican Republic, Haiti, and Honduras also end up poorly ranked, although not as low as the other three.

It is important to note that there is no apparent correlation between expert assessments of judicial independence and a ranking based solely on the four institutional instruments described in the first part of this chapter. This finding has led some scholars to question whether judicial independence is significantly affected by these de jure rules. One possible answer is that these formal rules cannot be evaluated in isolation because they interact with features of the political context, such as the fragmentation of power in the political branches, citizens' support for the judiciary, presidential authority, regime type, or the quality of democracy.

One source that utilizes expert assessments together with public opinion data to evaluate the judiciary and the rule of law cross-nationally is the World Justice Project, a nongovernmental organization. One item in its Rule of Law Index that is particularly salient to the topic of this chapter measures whether governments are effectively limited by the judiciary. It seeks to determine to what extent "the judiciary has the independence and the ability in practice to exercise effective checks on the government."[48] Results from the 2019 Rule of Law Index appear in Figure 8.4. The scores range from 0 to 1, with higher numbers indicating a greater independence and a better ability to check the government. The dashed vertical line indicates the mean score for the Latin American countries listed in the figure.

Interestingly, there is a high correlation between this ranking of judicial constraints on the powers of government and the prior ranking on

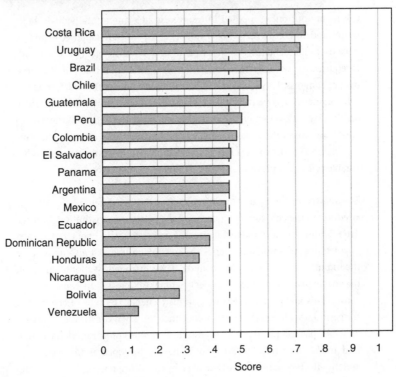

FIGURE 8.4 ●   The Judiciary's Ability to Check Government Powers, 2019

Source: World Justice Project, Rule of Law Index, 2019.

judicial independence. Countries with more independent judiciaries are better at checking the power of the executive. The countries whose judiciaries rank highest in terms of their ability to constrain the executive are Costa Rica, Uruguay, Brazil, and Chile, which are also among those having the highest scores in terms of independence. Likewise, those ranked lowest in terms of their ability to constrain the executive—Venezuela, Bolivia, Nicaragua, and Honduras—are poorly ranked in terms of judicial independence.[49]

To summarize, public opinion surveys and expert opinions add valuable information about how the judiciary is perceived and evaluated. The data presented here complement the earlier examinations of institutional features to give a more complete picture of Latin American courts and show relevant cross-national variations that help us identify underperforming courts and countries that have managed to build better-functioning judiciaries.

Conclusions

Courts are not only supposed to resolve disputes among individuals, businesses, and different levels of government but they also are supposed to protect citizens' fundamental rights. In a separation of powers systems, the judiciary is required to guard against possible transgressions undertaken by the president or congress. This is one reason why the autonomy of the courts from the other branches of government is so essential. As former Supreme Court Justice Sandra Day O'Connor noted, "Judicial independence is tremendously hard to create, and easier than most people imagine to destroy."[50] Elected politicians routinely attack the courts to try to score points with the public, change unfavorable rulings, or prevent inquiries into improper behavior.

The analysis of the Latin American judiciary presented here paid particular attention to the autonomy of judges and the powers of constitutional courts. After defining judicial independence, the first part of this chapter explained how various rules might influence the court's autonomy. It also underlined the importance of the political context. The subsequent section focused on the mechanisms that affect the decision-making process in constitutional courts. This included a review of legal instruments: the type of claims that the court may address (abstract and/or concrete), when constitutional review may take place (a priori and/or a posteriori), matters of jurisdiction (centralized and/or decentralized), who can bring a claim (open and/or restricted), and the effects of judicial decisions taken by constitutional courts (erga omnes and/or inter partes). Together, the first two parts of this chapter informed us about the institutional framework that structures judicial behavior.

The perception that the general public and country experts have of the courts was the focus of the last section of the chapter. It reviewed evidence that indicated whether citizens believe that their country's courts guarantee a fair trial and trust the judiciary. Lastly, the chapter presented two indicators based on experts' assessments, one measuring judicial independence over a period of more than 30 years and another one evaluating the court's ability to check the power of the government. We noted that these indices are highly correlated, allowing us to group countries according to the autonomy and strength of their respective courts.

The analysis presented in this chapter complemented the previous ones on the executive and legislative branches of government and furthered our understanding of the workings of Latin American presidentialism. The scholarship on judicial institutions is vast; this review highlighted some of the most critical themes within this literature. The next part of this book shifts our attention from political institutions to public policies and social actors.

Key Terms

Appointment rules 205
Constitutional courts 203
Constitutional review 216
Court-packing 203
Judicial authority 204

Judicial crises 203
Judicial independence 204
Judiciary's legitimacy 220
Tenure 208

Bibliographic Recommendations

Daniel Brink 2012. "'A Tale of Two Cities': The Judiciary and the Rule of Law in Latin America." In Peter Kingstone and Deborah J. Yashar (eds.), *Routledge Handbook of Latin American Politics*. New York: Routledge, pp. 61–75.

Daniel M. Brinks and Abby Blass. 2018. *The DNA of Constitutional Justice in Latin America: Politics, Governance, and Judicial Design*. New York: Cambridge University Press.

Gretchen Helmke. 2017. *Institutions on the Edge: The Origins and Consequences of Inter-Branch Crises in Latin America*. New York: Cambridge University Press.

Gretchen Helmke and Julio Ríos Figueroa (eds.). 2011. *Courts in Latin America*. New York: Cambridge University Press.

Julio Ríos-Figueroa. 2007. "Fragmentation of Power and the Emergence of an Effective Judiciary in Mexico, 1994–2002." *Latin American Politics and Society* 49(1): 31–57.

Lydia Tiede and Susan Achury. 2019 "Challenging Authorities' (In)action vi Amparos." In Susan Sterett and Lee Walker (eds.), *Research Handbook on Law and Courts*. Cheltenham, UK: Edward Elgar Publishing.

Political Attitudes, Policies, and Outcomes

PART II

Political Attitudes,
Policies, and
Outcomes

9

Political Culture

During the early 20th century, a large percentage of Latin American citizens believed that restrictions to the right to vote were simply common sense. At around the same time, many members of the political establishment believed that a centralized form of government that concentrated power in a national leader was appropriate to bring about political order and development. These political attitudes, many would argue, hindered the emergence of democratic institutions and inclusive political participation. Likewise, levels of **tolerance** among present-day Latin Americans and their views regarding such matters as social inequality and environmental challenges affect their political preferences. Moreover, individual traits such as age and education have been shown to have a significant effect on individuals' attitudes and political behavior.

Political thinkers from Aristotle and Jean-Jacques Rousseau to the social scientists of the mid-20th century who brought to the forefront the scientific study of **political culture** have strived to understand the connection between attitudes, behavior, and political outcomes. Such research is central to the work of many academics who specialize in the politics of Latin America. The greater availability of public opinion data in the last couple of decades has facilitated the study of political attitudes and fostered illuminating debates about the region's political culture.

While earlier chapters discussed how institutions structure political decision making in Latin America, this one shifts our attention to the political attitudes of its citizens. It is divided into three parts. The first focuses on a paradigmatic topic within this field of study: public support for democracy. It discusses the presumed relationship between support for democracy and democratic stability and its linkage to satisfaction with the way democracy works. In addition, it explains why answers to questions about the desirability of authoritarian practices and tolerance can help to uncover democratic attitudes. The second part centers on trust and examines two different aspects of that quality: **confidence in institutions** and **interpersonal trust**.

Several authors have underlined that in comparison to citizens in developed countries, Latin Americans have comparatively low levels of both. This section illustrates the differences across nations and discusses the individual traits associated with levels of trust. Lastly, the chapter addresses political ideology and the self-placement of individuals along the left–right spectrum. This section shows the relative weight of the different ideological groupings across countries in the region and examines the extent to which individuals' self-identification correlates with policy preferences typically associated with positions along the **left-to-right dimension**. Overall, the chapter provides a comprehensive introduction to some of the central issues that characterize the study of political culture in Latin America.

Support for Democracy

In 1963, Gabriel Almond and Sidney Verba published a groundbreaking book in the field of political culture titled *The Civic Culture*.[1] It is considered to be the first systematic study of the relationship between cultural traits and democracy. *Political culture* refers to the beliefs, values, and attitudes shared by people in a society, which give meaning to various political processes and shape political behavior. Almond and Verba defined it as citizens' psychological and subjective orientations toward politics. The theory elaborated in their book postulated that certain beliefs of the population, which they called *civic culture attitudes*, have a significant effect on the emergence and stability of democratic regimes. This book fostered numerous studies that examined the causes of different political attitudes and the relationship between attitudes and political outcomes.

A critical premise of *The Civic Culture* was that the success of democracy requires a substantial share of the population to support the principles of democratic government. This idea has been embraced by many scholars and policymakers alike, even if it has been somewhat reformulated over time. For example, Ronald Inglehart, a renowned expert in political culture, argues that overt support for democracy seems a necessary but not sufficient condition for countries to transition from authoritarianism to democracy; however, he believes that the long-term stability of democracy is unlikely unless democracy has strong support from the public.[2] Along the same lines, Larry Diamond, an expert on democratization, observes that "democratic consolidation is most evident and secure when support for democracy is not only unconditional but also widely shared by all major political groups and tendencies."[3] Focusing on the effects of political culture in Latin America, political scientists John A. Booth and Mitchell A. Seligson contend that public support for democracy, together with support for institutions and a favorable assessment of the government's economic performance, work to enhance the stability of democracy.[4]

A public commitment to democracy is supposed to make governments more likely to survive crises without facing a regime breakdown. Widespread rejection of authoritarianism as a form of government should lower the chances that it becomes a viable option when a country faces difficult times; it increases the costs of undertaking antidemocratic actions.

While early studies of the civic culture saw political attitudes as an important cause of the emergence of democracy, subsequent studies began to argue that the relationship may also go in the other direction: Democratic longevity is likely to affect political beliefs. For instance, economists Nicola Fuchs-Schündeln and Matthias Schündeln examined data from 104 countries over time and found that preferences for democracy increase as people spend more time living under a democratic regime.[5] In their book on public opinion and democracy in Latin America, John A. Booth and Patricia Bayer Richard also found that a longer experience with democracy affects public support for **democratic norms**.[6]

One common means of evaluating citizens' attitudes toward democracy is through public opinion polls that ask individuals whether they support democracy. Many cross-national surveys have sought to measure democratic norms. Figure 9.1 shows the results of a survey conducted in Latin America and the United States (U.S.) by the Latin American Public Opinion Project (LAPOP) in 2016 and 2017, which asked respondents whether they agreed with the following statement: "Democracy may have problems, but it's better than any other form of government." Answers to this question have been rescaled to go from 0 (not at all) to 100 (a lot).

FIGURE 9.1 ● Democracy Is Better Than Any Other Form of Government, 2016–2017

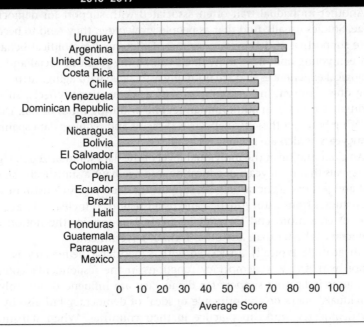

Source: AmericasBarometer, LAPOP, 2016–2017 surveys.

The average score for the 20 countries, indicated by the dashed vertical line, was just over 62. The highest average score based on this survey question corresponded to Uruguay, the country that Booth and Bayer Richard called the most culturally democratic in Latin America,[7] followed by Argentina, the United States, and Costa Rica. The lowest scores were reported in Mexico, Paraguay, and Guatemala.

The ordering of countries based on this question is highly correlated with their long-term patterns of democracy—for instance, with data on years of democracy derived from the Mainwaring and Pérez-Liñán data set described in Chapter 2 of this book.[8] This result is consistent with the findings of Booth and Bayer Richard on democratic norms in Latin America.[9]

At the individual level, studies have consistently found a significant association between support for democracy and education. Education promotes norms of **political tolerance**, makes people more likely to recognize the importance of extending individual freedoms, and fosters a greater acceptance of political diversity. As Seymour Lipset noted long ago in his classic work on the prerequisites for democracy, "The higher one's education, the more likely one is to believe in democratic values and support democratic practices."[10] The argument that education nurtures democratic norms has a long history in the social sciences, and cross-national evidence has validated this association in many different contexts. Consistent with prior works, a study of 38 nations conducted by the Pew Research Center found that individuals with higher levels of education were more likely to have favorable attitudes toward democracy than those with less education.[11]

Another individual trait often associated with support for democracy is age. Studies usually find that as people grow older, they tend to become more supportive of democratic regimes. Differences in political behavior between young and older individuals can be the result of social and psychological experiences that are normally associated with aging, such as settling down and raising a family, as well as generational effects, such as having lived under an authoritarian regime or during times of war. Differentiating between these two effects is difficult and requires data spanning many years, which are not always available.

An examination at the individual-level of the data summarized in Figure 9.1 reveals that both years of education and age have a statistically significant and positive association with support for democracy. Consistent with prior studies from Latin America and other regions,[12] increases in age and years of education tend to result in greater support for the notion that democracy is better than any other form of government.

An attitude typically associated with support for democracy is satisfaction with the way democracy functions in the respondent's country. Responses indicating support for democracy are influenced not only by individuals' views on the principle or ideal of democracy but also by the way democracy works in practice in their countries. When statistically examining individuals' support for democracy using the LAPOP data (summarized in Figure 9.1), the results not only show a positive association with age and education but also with satisfaction with the way democracy works. That is, those respondents who more positively evaluate the way democracy works in their country are also more likely to express support for that form of government.

Overall, the levels of support for democracy were greater than the levels of satisfaction with the way democracy works in practice. In the 2016–2017 surveys conducted by LAPOP, Uruguayans appeared to be the most satisfied with the way democracy works in their country, while Brazilians ranked lowest. Of course, responses to these questions are highly contingent on the political context. For instance, the survey of Brazil took place months after the impeachment of President Dilma Rousseff, during an investigation that uncovered an unprecedented web of corruption involving many well-known political figures and following two years of economic decline.

Many political observers have noted the contrast between the positive image that democracy now has all over the world and the cautious support it received during most of the 20th century when authoritarian forms of government were more popular. Global support for democracy now extends to countries whose governments fail to meet the basic standards of democracy. While some interpret this as evidence that support for democracy fails to bring about democratization, others point out that even if it is not sufficient, support for democracy is helpful to bring about such change and, most importantly, necessary to the consolidation of democracy once it is achieved. However, if democracy means different things to different people, then it may fail to capture the concept of a liberal democracy that most academics have in mind when discussing political outcomes. As political scientists Ryan E. Carlin and Matthew M. Singer note, "Many citizens express support for 'democracy' in abstract terms but reject concrete democratic freedoms, values, and norms."[13]

One way to try to circumvent different interpretations of democracy is to focus on survey questions that measure respondents' support for institutions and practices that we associate with democracy.[14] Table 9.1 presents answers to two such questions from the LAPOP surveys conducted during 2016 and 2017.[15] The first one asks, "Do you believe that when the country is facing difficult times, it is justifiable for the president to close congress and govern without it?" The second question asks, "Would a coup and military takeover of government be justified if there is a lot of crime?" The answers, shown in Table 9.1, indicate the percentage of respondents who answered affirmatively to each question.

Overall, support for an executive coup, which is what "closing congress and governing without it" actually represents, was rather low. In most countries, fewer than a quarter of respondents endorsed such a course of action. Support was lowest in Uruguay, Argentina, Venezuela, and Colombia. However, in Peru, close to 38 percent of respondents considered an executive

Country	When the country is facing difficult times, it is justifiable for the president to close Congress and govern without it	If there is a lot of crime, a coup leading to a military takeover of government is justifiable.
Argentina	11.3	28.2
Bolivia	24.8	37.8
Brazil	19.3	37.4
Chile	23.0	37.2
Colombia	15.3	33.0
Costa Rica	18.9	40.3
Dominican Republic	19.2	35.3
Ecuador	21.8	39.8
El Salvador	16.4	34.5
Guatemala	24.4	49.4
Haiti	30.0	28.9
Honduras	19.7	37.5
Mexico	17.1	48.3
Nicaragua	19.9	26.7
Panama	22.8	32.9
Paraguay	28.7	46.6
Peru	37.7	55.4
Uruguay	8.7	25.4
Venezuela	13.1	34.5
United States	16.6	23.3

TABLE 9.1 ● Justifying Authoritarian Takeovers, 2016–2017

Source: AmericasBarometer, LAPOP, 2016–2017 surveys.

coup to be justifiable when the country is facing difficult times. Perhaps more surprising is the high proportion of respondents who thought that a military coup is justifiable when there is a great deal of crime. The average of the national totals was around 37 percent. The highest percentage was from Peru, where just over 55 percent of respondents approved of a military takeover in such a context. In both Guatemala and Mexico, almost half of the respondents expressed support for a military coup in the presence of extensive criminal activity. Increases in levels of education and age are associated with lower support for these types of authoritarian undertakings, a finding that is consistent with previous ones about individuals' support for democracy.

The responses to these questions about a military or an executive coup are evidence that authoritarian tendencies are still prevalent among a substantial share of the region's population. As we would expect, those respondents who considered an executive or a military coup justifiable were significantly less likely to agree with the idea that democracy is better than any form of government. However, some of those giving high marks to democracy believed that an authoritarian takeover might be acceptable during difficult times or when facing a significant amount of crime. This apparent inconsistency, which is not altogether uncommon, exemplifies why some political analysts prefer to use questions such as these over those seeking overt support for democracy to measure the proportion of individuals who embrace democratic norms.

Another aspect of political attitudes that has traditionally been linked with democratic norms is tolerance. Acceptance of the rights of members of the opposition, dissidents, and individuals from marginalized groups is considered an essential component of democratic principles. One approach to measure tolerance, used in several studies on Latin America, investigates individuals' answers to questions regarding the acceptability of people who speak poorly of the country's system of government.[16] To this end, we build a score based on answers to questions that ask whether critics of the political system should be allowed to vote, conduct peaceful protests, run for office, and express their views on television. Figure 9.2 presents an index that runs from 0 (strong disapproval) to 100 (strong approval) based on the average responses to these questions about regime critics, which were asked in the 2016–2017 LAPOP survey. The dashed vertical line indicates the average country score.

Overall, responses to these questions reveal only moderate levels of tolerance for regime critics. The lowest-ranked countries were Colombia, Peru, and El Salvador, while the highest-ranked were the United States, Brazil, and Uruguay. It is interesting to note that among Latin American countries, there was less cross-national variation on these scores than in the responses regarding authoritarian takeovers discussed previously.

Academics have long debated how to accurately quantify tolerance, with some arguing that tolerance is best measured by asking people whether they support the rights of those whom they dislike. This approach is not always easy, since it often requires respondents to identify groups they dislike and to subsequently ask them about their tolerance for those specific groups. Even doing this can be problematic because individuals dislike groups with differing degrees of intensity, and some refuse to identify groups they dislike. These challenges can result in poor indicators.

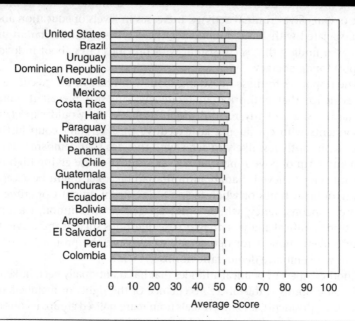

FIGURE 9.2 • Tolerance for Citizens Who Speak Poorly of the Regime, 2016–2017

Source: AmericasBarometer, LAPOP, 2016-2017 surveys.

Another way to attempt to measure tolerance is to evaluate attitudes toward a group that a significant part of the population dislikes. Ronald Inglehart argued that rejection of homosexuality remains widespread, which makes attitudes toward homosexuals a useful litmus test of tolerance.[17] He found that tolerance of homosexuality is a considerably stronger predictor of stable democracy across the world than any of the items that measure explicit support for democracy. John A. Booth and Patricia Bayer Richard showed that Latin Americans are less willing to accept gays as neighbors than to accept other outgroups as neighbors.[18] Despite significant advances in such fronts as marriage rights, violence against lesbian, gay, bisexual, and transgender (LGBT) persons in Latin America remains high.[19] In short, investigating attitudes regarding the political rights of this group is a promising avenue to uncovering levels of tolerance among the population.

Figure 9.3 summarizes answers to the following question asked by the 2016–2017 LAPOP surveys: "How strongly do you approve or disapprove of homosexuals being permitted to run for public office?" The answers were recoded to run from 0 (strong disapproval) to 100 (strong approval).

According to this measure, the most tolerant countries were Uruguay, United States, Chile, and Brazil, in that order. The least tolerant, starting from the bottom, were Haiti, Guatemala, El Salvador, and Paraguay. There was much more variation across countries in the responses to this question

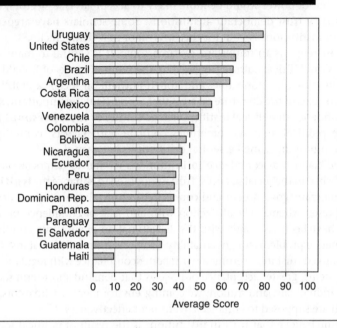

FIGURE 9.3 ● Tolerance for Gay Persons Running for Office, 2016–2017

Source: AmericasBarometer, LAPOP, 2016-2017 surveys.

than to the questions on tolerance for people who speak poorly of the country's system of government. Interestingly, the ordering of countries based on this question is highly correlated with their long-term patterns of democracy, just as it was with responses about support for democracy.

At the individual level, both education and age are again significant predictors of political tolerance. In terms of education, more years of schooling are associated with greater tolerance toward citizens who speak poorly of the country's regime as well as toward gay persons. However, increases in age are associated with lower levels of tolerance toward both of these groups. Younger Latin Americans are more tolerant than older ones, particularly with regards to gay persons. So, while the more educated are more likely to support democracy, oppose authoritarian pathways, and exhibit greater tolerance, older Latin Americans differ in terms of the last measure: They are less tolerant, despite their greater tendency to support democracy and oppose authoritarian options.

Confidence in Institutions and Interpersonal Trust

One important strand of the literature on political culture has focused on trust. In early work on civic culture, democratic values were thought to require that individuals be law-abiding, politically active, and positively oriented toward political authority. Accordingly, citizens should not only support democracy but also have confidence in the country's institutions. Those out of power would be more likely to accept adverse electoral results when they trust democratic institutions. Some scholars have argued that trust in institutions is vital for the survival of new democracies.[20]

Trust remains an important research topic. It is central to many of the studies on political culture triggered by the seminal works of Ronald Inglehart on self-expression values and Robert Putnam on social capital.[21] There are two areas of the literature on trust that are particularly important: studies of confidence in political institutions and studies of **interpersonal trust**. While political analysts sometimes conflate both factors, contemporary research has underlined essential distinctions between them.

The claim that confidence in institutions is vital to democracy is well-established in the social sciences. Trust is supposed to enhance the **legitimacy** of democratic government and connect citizens to the institutions designed to represent them.[22] Dissatisfaction with and lack of confidence in institutions have been associated with the delegitimation of authority and thought to generate problems for governability.[23] Reports from influential institutions have linked trust in government with better compliance with regulations and tax systems, greater acceptance of policies that demand short-term sacrifices from individuals, and a more welcoming environment for investors, all of which are supposed to enhance government effectiveness.[24]

Some believe that trust in institutions is the result of political socialization, while others see it as the consequence of institutional performance. The former perspective views it as a complex social process that can take decades or generations to develop, while the latter perspective views it as being able to develop more quickly as a result of good economic and governmental performance. William Mishler and Richard Rose have argued that institutional theories do a better job of explaining political trust in the new democracies that emerged in post-communist societies than cultural theories rooted in political socialization.[25] This is consistent with the findings of Gabriela Catterberg and Alejandro Moreno, who examined **survey data** from 26 countries (including four from Latin America) and concluded that confidence in institutions is associated with a country's ability to increase or maintain individuals' economic well-being.[26]

Contradicting the premise that confidence in institutions is a crucial trait of democratic citizens, several studies have shown that political trust in established democracies declined significantly after the 1960s. For example, the percentage of people in the U.S. who "trust the government in Washington always or most of the time" dropped from around 70 percent in the 1960s to less than 40 percent in the 1990s and less than 30 percent after 2005.[27] Significant declines were also found in other advanced industrial democracies. Some interpreted this change as dangerous for the health of democratic institutions, but others saw it as the result of changing expectations among the public prompted by socioeconomic development.[28]

According to this view, rising economic and physical security contributed to the emergence of a new set of values characterized by the rejection of traditional authority and growing skepticism. The allegiant orientations described in *The Civic Culture* had given way to a "new assertive form of citizenship," with higher expectations regarding government performance, and a greater willingness to challenge political elites and criticize governments.[29] The evidence appeared to show that in the U.S., decreases in public trust in institutions were particularly salient among the more educated and the young.[30] According to political scientist Pippa Norris, this surge of critical citizens revealed dissatisfaction with government performance among younger and more sophisticated generations rather than dissatisfaction with democracy as a form of government.[31]

The lack of public trust in government institutions is commonplace in Latin America, and there is evidence that distrust in national governments has been growing. Some see this as a worrying trend, usually echoing the concerns expressed by analysts of the older and more economically developed democracies some time ago. For example, *Latin American Economic Outlook 2018*, produced by the United Nations Economic Commission for Latin America and the Caribbean (ECLAC) and the Organization for Economic Cooperation and Development (OECD), maintains that rising mistrust risks intensifying the disconnect between people and public institutions and damaging social cohesion.[32] It goes on to argue that trust in government institutions is critical for the success of public policies and to guarantee renewed economic growth.

The limited historical data make it impossible to study long-term trends in institutional trust in Latin America; we do not know if trust in political institutions was higher during the 1960s than at the beginning of the 21st century. While this precludes in-depth analyses of changing trends over the last decades, scholars can still examine individual and institutional factors associated with confidence in institutions in more recent years. Table 9.2 presents information from the 2016–2017 LAPOP surveys that measured individuals' confidence in the executive, congress, and political parties. Individual responses have been rescaled to go from 0 (none) to 100 (a lot). The numbers indicate the average for each country.

The results show that in almost all the countries, confidence in political parties is lower than confidence in congress or the executive. Interestingly, confidence in the executive and confidence in congress are, on average, higher in Latin America than in the U.S., an established democracy and a wealthy country.

At the individual level, we find that trust in political institutions is associated with education, economic well-being, and perceptions of corruption. Individuals who are more educated tend to have less trust in institutions. This result is consistent with findings from the U.S. Also, the better an individual's reported economic situation, the higher his or her trust in institutions is. There is also evidence that individuals who believe that

TABLE 9.2 ● Confidence in the President, Congress, and Political Parties, 2016–2017			
Country	Executive	Congress	Political Parties
Argentina	39.6	46.5	29.5
Bolivia	51.8	49.1	28.9
Brazil	21.5	29.7	18.0
Chile	43.9	31.9	20.2
Colombia	33.2	37.1	23.7
Costa Rica	40.3	50.4	33.2
Dominican Republic	62.3	45.6	29.2
Ecuador	53.3	49.0	33.6
El Salvador	36.7	43.7	31.1
Guatemala	44.4	41.4	26.6
Haiti	56.6	27.1	24.5
Honduras	41.5	43.7	30.7
Mexico	26.3	43.6	22.7
Nicaragua	62.4	56.3	42.0
Panama	35.7	33.6	24.1
Paraguay	31.1	37.5	27.7
Peru	37.6	30.2	23.1
Uruguay	50.7	51.8	37.3
Venezuela	28.2	53.1	33.4
United States	36.1	36.8	29.1

Source: AmericasBarometer, LAPOP, 2016–2017 surveys.

politicians are corrupt tend to express lower trust in institutions. The effect of age is not consistent across the three different indicators.

The second strand of studies on trust focuses on interpersonal trust. Scholars from various academic disciplines have studied the causes and consequences of individuals' trust in other people, with most agreeing that trust between people facilitates cooperation. Interpersonal trust is thought to help people solve collective action problems and, according to many economists, lower costs associated with economic transactions, such as the costs of negotiating and enforcing agreements.[33] Several studies have argued that interpersonal trust is important for democracy.[34] Inglehart showed that it is closely linked with stable democracy.[35] Political scientists have associated interpersonal trust with political participation, membership in voluntary associations, welfare state support, confidence in institutions, and perceptions of corruption, among other variables. However, establishing causality has been difficult, so while some scholars see these variables as outcomes of interpersonal trust, others see them as the causes of it.

In the 1990s, when large cross-national studies were becoming more widespread, scholars began to note the comparatively low levels of interpersonal trust prevalent across Latin America. For some, this constituted an impediment to the development of civil society, threatened democratic stability, and revealed the shallow social foundations of Latin American democracy.[36] Others were less pessimistic and believed that years of continuous democracy would ultimately generate high levels of interpersonal trust.[37]

Several political scientists interested in political culture in Latin America have sought to uncover the consequences of trusting other people. For instance, Abby Córdova examined the effect of interpersonal trust on citizen support for reducing inequality, finding that individuals with high levels of interpersonal trust are more likely to favor policies designed to reduce economic inequality.[38] Interestingly, she also found that among the wealthy, who are generally opposed to such policies, higher levels of interpersonal trust have a strong effect on boosting support for anti-poverty policies. Other empirical studies have shown that those who do not trust their fellow citizens are more likely to believe that the political system is corrupt,[39] to conclude that elections cannot be trusted,[40] and to hold antidemocratic norms.[41] Those with higher levels of interpersonal trust appear more likely to express support for political institutions[42] and participate more frequently in political activities.[43]

Table 9.3 presents data on interpersonal trust from two different cross-national surveys. The first is the Latinobarómetro, which asked respondents, "Generally speaking, would you say that you can trust most people or that you can never be too careful when dealing with others?" This is similar to the question asked in other surveys, such as the General Social Survey from the U.S. National Opinion Research Center. The percentage of individuals indicating that they trust most people appears in the second column of the table. The second question is from the LAPOP survey, which asked respondents, "Now speaking of the people from around here, would you say that people in this community are very trustworthy, somewhat trustworthy, not very trustworthy, or untrustworthy?" The percentage of respondents who answered this question and expressed that people in their community were very or somewhat trustworthy is shown in Column Three, while the percentage of those who answered this question and expressed that people in their community were not very trustworthy or untrustworthy is shown in Column Four.

TABLE 9.3 ● Interpersonal Trust

		People in this community are	
	Most people can be trusted	Very trustworthy or somewhat trustworthy	Not very trustworthy or untrustworthy
Country	2017	2016–2017	2016–2017
Argentina	19.3	71.6	28.4
Bolivia	10.4	46.0	54.0
Brazil	6.8	36.8	63.3
Chile	20.3	66.1	33.9
Colombia	15.7	62.9	37.1
Costa Rica	10.6	69.9	30.2
Dominican Republic	11.3	56.1	43.9
Ecuador	23.2	55.2	44.8
El Salvador	16.6	58.7	41.3
Guatemala	12.4	58.7	41.3
Haiti	~	37.6	62.4
Honduras	12.2	63.5	36.6
Mexico	13.8	57.2	42.8
Nicaragua	14.0	60.9	39.1
Panama	11.3	54.4	45.6
Paraguay	8.9	69.0	31.0
Peru	13.1	46.8	53.3
Uruguay	19.1	75.9	24.1
Venezuela	8.9	54.6	45.4
United States	~	80.1	19.9

Sources: Latinobarómetro Data Bank, 2017 survey (column 2); AmericasBarometer, LAPOP, 2016-2017 survey (columns 3 and 4).

The first question is more general than the second, since it asks whether "most people" can be trusted. These results reveal relatively low levels of trust. In Ecuador, which exhibited the highest proportion of people expressing trust in most of their fellow citizens, the average was around 23 percent. Chile, Argentina, and Uruguay follow next, with averages around 20 percent and 19 percent. The lowest rate was from Brazil, where less than 7 percent of respondents expressed that most people can be trusted. Venezuela and Paraguay also exhibited low levels of trust. The regional average was close to 14 percent. This was much lower than the average for OECD countries, where about 36 percent of respondents expressed trust in others.[44]

The second question focused on trusting members of the respondents' community. It captured a narrower context than the previous question. As expected, responses to this question revealed a much higher level of trust than responses to the previous one. The lowest levels of interpersonal trust were in Brazil and Haiti. Respondents in Bolivia and Peru also seemed to have relatively low levels of interpersonal trust. These are the only four countries where the share of respondents expressing that people in their community were untrustworthy or not very trustworthy was higher than the share of people expressing that these people were very trustworthy or somewhat trustworthy. The Latin American countries with the highest levels of interpersonal trust according to this measure were Uruguay, Argentina, and Costa Rica. Respondents in the U.S. expressed a much higher level of interpersonal trust than the Latin American average.

In terms of individual-level traits, the LAPOP surveys revealed that older individuals and those with more years of education had higher levels of interpersonal trust. There was also evidence of lower levels of interpersonal trust among individuals who have been victims of crime and those who are facing economic hardship.

In conclusion, trust is an important research area in the field of political culture. Many cross-national analyses have found that Latin Americans exhibit relatively low levels of both confidence in institutions and interpersonal trust. For some, these findings are highly problematic because they reflect a fundamental weakness of Latin America's political culture, which can undermine democracy. Others are more cautious about the negative impact of low levels of confidence in institutions, which they link to temporal evaluations of government performance and to a generational change that has spurred more skeptical and critical individuals. The persistence of low levels of interpersonal trust is more difficult to explain; perhaps they will increase if living conditions in the region improve. Crime victimization and economic hardship seem to lower trust in members of the respondents' community. The results presented in this section also show that older individuals tend to express higher levels of interpersonal trust and greater confidence in institutions. Those who are more educated are also more likely to express higher levels of interpersonal trust but tend to show lower confidence in institutions. These results are consistent with previous studies on political attitudes. The lack of historical data on Latin Americans' attitudes regarding confidence in institutions and interpersonal trust makes analyzing long-term patterns impossible. This is problematic for examining the relationship between democratic consolidation and trust. It remains possible that democratic stability will, in the future, boost trust among Latin Americans.

Ideological Positions

Another important aspect of individuals' political beliefs is their ideology. This is the topic of this last section. **Ideology** refers to a set of beliefs according to which individuals evaluate the political context and guide their political stances. Ideologies are typically composed of some established principles about such things as the role of government in the economy, the consequences of free markets, the primacy of individual liberties, or the implementation of income redistribution policies. Some individuals hold ideological views comprised of a rather sophisticated set of principles, while others structure their political views around more simple elements. Most often, political scientists identify ideology with a cohesive set of political ideas and beliefs or a particular package of policies. There are also those who do not hold fixed political principles and are more predisposed to adopting different (and sometimes opposing) positions depending on various contextual factors.

A complex political ideology embodies a series of core principles that are consistent over a range of substantive issues. They involve ideas about the organization of society as well as policy prescriptions. Some well-known political ideologies include communism, socialism, liberalism, and conservatism. Each of these is constructed from a long list of elaborate principles that form an internally coherent view of politics. Most individuals are unlikely to be familiar with the various details of complex political ideologies, and the extent to which they embrace such rigid and internally cohesive principles is debatable. However, most individuals identify themselves with a few core principles that can be placed along the left-to-right dimension.

The notion of *left* and *right* has its origins in the French National Assembly of 1789, where conservative monarchists sat to the right of the king, and liberals and radicals sat to his left. While it is not possible to neatly rank all dominant ideologies along one dimension, the left-to-right political spectrum provides a useful shortcut to contrast some core principles. It plays an important role in organizing some basic political ideas that help differentiate parties and candidates for office.

One central distinction between left and right has to do with the idea of inequality. According to political scientists Juan Pablo Luna and Cristóbal Rovira Kaltwasser, "Whereas the right conceives inequalities as natural and difficult (or even inconvenient) to eradicate, the left conceives most inequalities as socially constructed and as a target for progressive social change."[45] The role of the state with regards to social inequalities—promoting interventionist government policies to counteract them or seeing them as natural and outside the scope of desirable government action—is one important component of the left–right divide. That is why many interpret the **left–right dimension** with preferences regarding economic redistribution. Others, such as Inglehart, also believe that the left–right division captures economic preferences but define this axis in broader terms by arguing that it distinguishes between those who favor (left) and those who oppose (right) state intervention in the economy.[46]

Many individuals associate ideologies such as socialism and conservatism with positions along the left–right dimension. But there are political positions that do not align as well with this dimension and are better thought of as distinct lines of conflict, such as authoritarian versus democratic or religious versus secular. These issues, for example, divide parties on both the right and the left of the political spectrum. Other political ideologies, such as nationalism and populism, also have both left and right manifestations, as is the case with some economic ideas, such as free trade.

Political elites often make use of *left* and *right* terms to convey their positions to voters. In some Latin American countries, political parties on the right of the political spectrum have been somewhat reluctant to associate themselves with these labels.[47] This is perhaps the consequence of the connection that many make between right-wing ideology and the despotic military governments that ruled many of the countries in this region during the late 20th century.

The extent to which individuals' self-placement along the left–right dimension corresponds to coherent policy beliefs is an exciting research topic. A few scholars have examined this linkage among Latin American voters. For instance, Elizabeth Zechmeister and Margarita Corral found that in most countries in Latin America, self-placement along the left–right dimension does not necessarily correlate with expectations regarding individuals' preferences for state intervention in the economy.[49] They provided some evidence that among more educated individuals, there is a greater correlation between left–right positioning and the expected preferences for state intervention in the economy than among individuals with less education. Nina Wiesehomeier and David Doyle also investigated the linkage between left–right identification and political beliefs, finding some support for the expected association between attitudes toward inequality and left–right positions, although the differences did not appear to be substantively large.[49]

To illustrate the left–right self-placement of Latin Americans, Table 9.4 presents information from LAPOP surveys conducted in 2016–2017. Individuals ranked themselves on a 10-point left-to-right scale from which we derive five categories: left (1 and 2), center-left (3 and 4), center (5 and 6), center-right (7 and 8), and right (9 and 10). The table also shows the proportion of individuals who chose not to respond or replied that they did not know.

The first relevant result worth highlighting from Table 9.4 is that on average, about 89 percent of respondents in Latin America can place themselves along the left-to-right dimension. It goes from a high of just over

TABLE 9.4 ● Left–Right Self-Placement, 2016–2017						
	Left	Center-Left	Center	Center-Right	Right	Don't Know/ No Answer
Argentina	10.0	14.1	38.8	15.7	7.3	14.1
Bolivia	12.8	16.3	36.4	13.2	9.9	11.4
Brazil	17.8	21.4	25.4	13.8	13.8	7.9
Chile	12.4	13.7	38.0	9.5	6.8	19.6
Colombia	13.4	15.5	37.2	13.4	14.7	5.8
Costa Rica	16.6	17.0	31.9	16.5	9.6	8.5
Dominican Republic	24.2	14.1	12.6	13.2	29.6	6.2
Ecuador	13.4	16.4	31.2	15.4	14.9	8.7
El Salvador	14.1	10.3	34.6	13.5	16.7	10.8
Guatemala	17.1	18.4	26.5	14.9	17.0	6.1
Haiti	22.7	9.5	12.1	8.1	25.1	22.6
Honduras	16.6	11.4	21.4	12.6	23.4	14.7
Mexico	17.2	20.0	27.7	14.5	10.0	10.6
Nicaragua	22.6	10.0	18.9	12.6	23.1	12.8
Panama	19.3	16.7	30.8	11.2	16.2	5.8
Paraguay	21.3	16.6	19.8	13.4	14.5	14.5
Peru	12.3	19.1	34.8	15.7	11.4	6.8
Uruguay	13.1	19.7	34.2	15.8	9.4	7.9
Venezuela	14.7	10.0	28.2	13.6	22.7	10.8
United States	9.4	19.7	29.9	20.7	20.2	0.3

Source: AmericasBarometer, LAPOP, 2016-2017 surveys.

94 percent in Colombia and Panama to a low of around 77 percent in Haiti. This finding reveals that a very high proportion of Latin Americans self-identify on the left–right spectrum, which is consistent with similar conclusions from earlier studies.

When focusing on the actual placement of individuals along this dimension, we find that in all countries, the median respondent (as well as the average) self-identifies as a centrist. In most Latin American countries, the largest group is the centrist, with about 28 percent of respondents. The exceptions are the Dominican Republic, Haiti, and Nicaragua, where those placed on the far left and the far right outnumber centrists, as well as Honduras, where those on the far right outnumber centrists, and Paraguay, where those on the far left outnumber centrists.

The countries with the highest proportion of people placing themselves on the left and center-left are Brazil, the Dominican Republic, and Paraguay. Comparatively fewer people place themselves on the left and center-left in Argentina, El Salvador, and Venezuela.

The countries with the highest proportion of people placing themselves on the right and center-right are the Dominican Republic, Venezuela, and Honduras. The fewest proportion of respondents placing themselves on the right and center-right are in Chile, Argentina, and Bolivia.

The largest proportion of centrists are in Argentina, Chile, and Colombia, which have a comparatively smaller share of respondents identifying as leftists or rightists. In contrast, citizens in the Dominican Republic and Nicaragua appear particularly polarized, with large numbers of leftists and rightists and comparatively few centrists.[50]

The comparison between Latin America and the U.S. is rather interesting. Almost all respondents in the U.S. place themselves on the left–right spectrum as opposed to 89 percent in Latin America. The proportion of those identifying as centrists is not much different in either place, and the share of those identifying with the center-left or the left is only slightly higher in Latin America. However, the share of respondents placing themselves on the right or center-right is much higher in the U.S. (close to 41 percent) than in Latin America (on average, just over 29 percent).

While many respondents are willing to select a position along the left–right dimension, the extent to which individuals hold policy preferences that coincide with the usual interpretation of these ideological labels remains debatable. Some studies have shown at least a partial coincidence between individuals' positioning and hypothesized policy preferences, but others have failed to find a strong linkage or consistent issue attitudes. To examine this topic, we can look at the connections between individuals' self-placement along the left–right scale and their answers to some specific policy questions.

The LAPOP survey used to illustrate left–right self-identification also included questions that reflect preferences over issues traditionally thought to differentiate between left and right ideologies. One question asked whether the state or the private sector should own the most important enterprises and industries of the country; another asked whether the government should implement policies to reduce income inequality between the rich and the poor. Based on the core definitions of left and right provided by the academic literature, we should expect that those to the left would tend to support state ownership of major enterprises and industries and approve of government policies designed to reduce income inequality. In contrast, those on the right should tend to reject those positions. Table 9.5 shows the average response to these two questions by each of the five ideological groups.[51] The range of possible answers goes from 0 (no support for state ownership/no support for redistributive policies) to 100 (strong support for state ownership/strong support for redistributive policies).

Preferences over state ownership of the most important businesses and industries in the country did not align with each of the left-to-right groupings as one might anticipate. The typical respondent was positioned somewhere around the middle of the distribution, and there was relatively little difference across the different ideological groupings in terms of their responses to this question. Moreover, those individuals positioned on the right of the ideological spectrum were somewhat more likely to support state ownership of business and industries than individuals positioned on the left and the center-left. This is the opposite of what we would have expected based on traditional characterizations of policy preferences and ideological leanings. Uruguay was an exception; there, ideological leanings and preferences for state ownership aligned as expected.

TABLE 9.5 ● Policy Preferences and Left–Right Self-Placement, 2016–2017				
	The state should own the most important businesses and industries in the country.	The state should implement policies to reduce inequality between the rich and the poor.	I support same-sex marriage.	I believe that economic growth should be prioritized over environmental protection.
Left	50	72	31	49
Center-Left	50	73	39	46
Center	50	73	39	45
Center-Right	51	71	36	51
Right	54	71	28	58

Source: AmericasBarometer, LAPOP, 2016-2017 surveys.

Answers to the question regarding state involvement in reducing income inequalities also revealed relatively small differences between each of the left-to-right groupings. Overall, the typical respondent was rather supportive of government action to reduce inequality, and differences between the ideological groupings were minimal. Those positioned on the center and center-left were somewhat more likely than those on the right and center-right to support government policies to reduce inequality, but the difference was substantively very small. And, on average, those positioned at the left differed very little on this topic from those positioned on the right.

It is worthwhile to examine this issue further to see if other preferences better differentiate these left–right groupings. Table 9.5 presents answers to two additional items from the LAPOP surveys: support for same-sex marriage and to what extent economic growth should be prioritized over environmental protection. For these two questions, the possible answers go from 0 (strong disagreement with same-sex marriage/environmental protection should be prioritized) to 100 (strong agreement with same-sex marriage/economic growth should be prioritized).

The responses to the surveys showed rather low levels of support for same-sex marriage among Latin Americans. Differences among the ideological groupings were larger in comparison with the answers to the prior two questions. Those who identified with the center and center-left of the ideological spectrum were significantly more supportive of same-sex marriage than others. Interestingly, the average score on this question for those on the left of the ideological spectrum was statistically indistinguishable from the average score of those on the right and lower than the average score for those on the center-right.

The last column summarizes the preferences of respondents regarding the prioritization of economic growth over environmental protection. Here, the difference between those identifying with the left and those identifying with the right was significant. Those on the right were much more likely than those on the left to prioritize economic growth over environmental protection. In fact, the most substantial difference concerning the answers to this question was between those who identified with the center and those who identified with the right, with centrists being the most supportive of environmental protection.

It is also worth noting that other factors, such as religiosity and support for abortion when the mother's health is at risk, did not correspond with conventional expectations about the positions of the different ideological grouping either. The assessment on the first matter is based on an analysis of the ideological leanings of those respondents who answered that religion is very important in their lives. Those identified with the right expressed the highest level of religiosity (as expected) but not too much higher than the level of religiosity expressed by those identified with the left. There was little difference in regards to this topic between those on the left and those on the center-right. Individuals who identified with the center and the center-left were the ones who expressed the lowest levels of religiosity.

When individuals were asked whether they believed abortion was justifiable if the health of the mother was at risk, most Latin Americans answered in the affirmative. However, differences between those who identified with the left and those who identified with the right were not significant. Those individuals most supportive of this statement were those who identified as centrists.

To summarize, the focus of this section of the chapter has been on the left–right divide in Latin America. The analyses based on survey responses revealed several interesting findings. Most Latin Americans readily identified with positions along the left–right dimension and, in all countries, the median respondent was a centrist. In about three fourths of countries, the largest grouping was made up of self-identified centrists. Overall, the percentage of those positioned on the left and center-left was slightly higher than the percentage of those positioned to the center-right and right.

Concerning the policy preferences revealed by individuals identified with the different groupings, the analysis presented here revealed a low correspondence with the ideological principles associated with the usual definitions of *left* and *right*. On average, those on the left were not much different from those on the right in terms of their policy preferences on reducing inequality between the rich and the poor or supporting same-sex marriage, and were somewhat less likely than those on the right to support state ownership of business. Rightists clearly prioritized economic growth over environmental protection and expressed a higher level of religiosity than others. Centrists were particularly supportive of environmental protection and same-sex marriage and, more than others, believed abortion was justified when the mother's health was at risk.

Conclusions

Political attitudes and beliefs affect the policy preferences of individuals, which in turn influence political outcomes. This chapter addressed three key components of what social scientists call political culture: support for democracy, trust, and ideological positioning. It discussed what some thought would be the ideal political culture conducive to a stable democracy and some of the potential criticisms of such views. In addition, it illustrated how Latin American countries differ in terms of their attitudes about these critical issues and how they compare with the beliefs prevalent in the U.S.

The findings presented here showed that Latin Americans' support for democracy as a form of government is positively associated with their satisfaction with the way democracy works in their country as well as with individual traits, such as their education and age. Because democracy may mean different things to different people, we examined beliefs regarding authoritarian episodes, such as scenarios potentially justifying executive or military takeovers. Results confirmed that most Latin Americans appear committed to democracy, although significant cross-national differences are evident. Less positive were results regarding individuals' tolerance. For the most part, Latin Americans appeared to exhibit rather low levels of tolerance toward critics of the political regime and gay persons running for public office. At the individual level, more education was correlated with greater tolerance while increases in age were correlated with lower tolerance.

With regards to trust, which social scientists have associated with a host of positive outcomes, the findings also highlighted important cross-national differences. While confidence in institutions is rather low across the region, it is not lower than in the U.S., a developed country with a long history of democracy. The discussion also noted that academics disagree about the causes and implications of low confidence in institutions. Results regarding interpersonal trust reveal that the more educated tend to have greater levels of interpersonal trust, while younger individuals exhibit lower levels of interpersonal trust.

Lastly, the chapter examined the ideological leaning of Latin Americans. In most countries, moderates made up the largest group, but a few exhibited a polarized context in which extremists comprise the largest share of the population. In addition, the findings cast doubt on a simple and straightforward association between ideological self-identification and policy positions. In many instances, the expected differences between supporters of the left and the right were either not manifested or substantively small.

The topics addressed in this chapter not only provided an illuminating picture of the political beliefs of Latin Americans but also complemented previous chapters focused on the institutions that structure the behavior of citizens and political elites. Analyses of political culture and institutional analyses usually proceed in separate tracks, but a comprehensive understanding of the politics of Latin America requires an awareness of both strands of research. The next chapter continues our examination of the politics of the region by addressing the topic of corruption.

Key Terms

Confidence in institutions 231
Democratic norms 233
Ideology 246
Interpersonal trust 231
Left–right dimension 232

Legitimacy 240
Political culture 231
Survey data 240
Tolerance 231

Bibliographic Recommendations

John A. Booth and Patricia Bayer Richard. 2015. *Latin American Political Culture: Public Opinion and Democracy.* Los Angeles: CQ Press.

Ryan E. Carlin. 2006. "The Socioeconomic Roots of Support for Democracy and the Quality of Democracy." *Revista de Ciencia Política* 26(1): 48–66.

Ryan E. Carlin and Matthew M. Singer. 2011. "Support for Polyarchy in the Americas." *Comparative Political Studies* 44(11): 1500–1526.

Mollie J. Cohen, Noam Lupu, and Elizabeth J. Zechmeister (eds.). 2017. *The Political Culture of Democracy in the Americas, 2016/17: A Comparative Study of Democracy and Governance.* Latin American Public Opinion Project (LAPOP), Vanderbilt University.

Abby Córdova. 2011. "The Role of Social Capital in Citizen Support for Governmental Action to Reduce Economic Inequality." *International Journal of Sociology* 41(2): 28–49.

Nina Wiesehomeier and David Doyle. 2012. "Attitudes, Ideological Associations and the Left–Right Divide in Latin America." *Journal of Politics in Latin America* 4(1): 3–33.

Web Resources

Latin American Public Opinion Project (LAPOP): https://www.vanderbilt.edu/lapop/

Latinobarómetro: http://www.latinobarometro.org

Pew Research Center, Latin America: https://www.pewresearch.org/topics/latin-america/

Corruption

In September of 2018, the former president of El Salvador, Elías Antonio Saca, was sentenced to 10 years in prison after pleading guilty to embezzlement and money-laundering charges. During the trial, Saca confessed to a variety of corrupt activities, including using government funds to pay $100,000 a month to advertising firms that would, in turn, spend 80 percent of that amount at radio companies that he owned and using funds from an executive branch account to pay his wife a monthly stipend of $10,000. He also confessed that several members of his cabinet and other government officials regularly received illegal bonuses and that many millions of dollars had been illegally diverted to his political party, the Nationalist Republican Alliance (*Alianza Republicana Nacionalista* [ARENA]).[1] Saca's successor, President Francisco Flores, was himself facing charges of diverting 15 million dollars in donations for earthquake victims to his party and personal accounts when he died in early 2016.[2]

In March of 2018, Peruvian President Pedro Pablo Kuczynski resigned his post after videos surfaced showing some of his close allies offering legislators public works contracts in exchange for help in defeating a second impeachment vote against him.[3] Peru's prior president, Ollanta Humala, was arrested a year earlier and remained in pretrial detention for nine months after being implicated in a corruption scandal and accused of money laundering. At the same time, another former president of Peru, Francisco Toledo, was accused of taking a $20 million bribe from a Brazilian construction company and remained in the United States fighting an extradition request.[4] Also implicated in this scandal was former President Alan Garcia, who killed himself in early 2019 when authorities tried to arrest him. All the while, President Alberto Fujimori, who ruled Peru in the 1990s, remained in jail serving a 25-year sentence after being convicted of bribery and human rights abuses.

Several other Latin American presidents and prominent government officials have been involved in high-profile **corruption scandals**. One of the most debated cases of the late 2010s involved Lula da Silva, the former president of Brazil, who was heralded with advancing policies that drastically reduced poverty in this country and remained a highly popular figure in progressive circles in Latin America and elsewhere. In July of 2017, Lula da Silva was found guilty of corruption and money laundering and subsequently sentenced to 12 years in prison. From jail, he sought to run for the presidency again and remained a top contender until August 2018, when the highest electoral court in the country ruled that he could not stand for office.

Corruption in Latin America is not circumscribed to political elites; businesspeople, low-level bureaucrats, and members of the security forces, among others, are also frequently entangled in corruption scandals. There is a consensus that corruption is detrimental to economic development and the workings of democracy. It tends to lower public confidence in institutions, politicians, and civil servants. In addition, it negatively impacts the economic well-being of vulnerable social sectors of the population and the quality of public services. Ordinary citizens regularly name corruption as one of their top concerns.

This chapter examines corruption in Latin America. It seeks to explain why it has a tremendous impact on the lives of Latin Americans and how it has affected politics in the region. It is organized into four parts. The first begins by defining the concept and proceeds with a discussion of the causes and consequences of corruption. The second part reviews efforts to combat corruption. The third presents alternative measures of corruption, discusses their differences, and describes how individual countries and the region fare in such rankings. It shows how perceptions of corruption vary significantly across countries. The last part of the chapter reviews a few major corruption scandals and asks whether these events reveal advances in the rule of law or whether they have unintentionally undermined democracy in the region.

Corruption

When asked to identify the type of activities that fall under the umbrella of corruption, most citizens across the world tend to agree. Theft and embezzlement by public officials and the bribery of such officials by private actors are considered to be corrupt practices everywhere. However, there is less consensus among academics and policymakers about how to properly define this concept. The most widely used definition of corruption is that of the World Bank: the abuse of public office for private benefit.

This characterization centers on the actions of public officials. When officials embezzle funds that they are supposed to manage by diverting public money to themselves or their families, they are engaging in corrupt acts. This is also the case when public officials steal government property, such as vehicles, technical equipment, or relief materials intended for victims of natural disasters. Other forms of corruption, such as bribery, usually involve the interaction between public officials and private actors. A classic example is when a private company bribes a government official to win a public contract. Another one is overbilling for services contracted by the government in exchange for kickbacks to the public officials involved in negotiating or monitoring such contracts. Government officials demanding bribes to issue licenses to provide utility services or exploit natural resources is another example of a rather prevalent corrupt act. And, as noted in Chapter 8, the bribing of corrupt members of the judiciary by citizens who need to interact with the court system is also not uncommon.

Small-scale corruption by low-level public officials often involves the payment of bribes. Examples range from police officers asking for bribes to disregard traffic violations to bureaucrats asking for bribes to issue driving permits or passports to hospital workers asking for bribes to provide better medical care to education officials asking for bribes in exchange for diplomas or a spot in a top school.

Activities commonly understood as corrupt acts go beyond bribery and theft. They also include obstruction of justice, extortion, fraud, money laundering, misuse of privileged information, violations of campaign finance regulations, and influence peddling.[5] Defining corruption as the abuse or misuse of public office for private gain does not imply that officials committing such an act must enrich themselves in the process. These persons may benefit indirectly, for example, when the act favors members of their family, party, or clique.

The misuse of public office is not so easy to operationalize.[6] A legalistic definition can be problematic because some corrupt activities may not be outlawed. For example, it was not until 1977 that the United States made it illegal for American companies to pay bribes abroad (in several countries, gift-giving to public officials is not unlawful). Equating misuse with violations of the public interest is also difficult because of the ideological and normative connotations associated with defining what the public interest entails. It is not uncommon for public officials accused of corruption to argue that their alleged misdeeds were done to further the public interest.

An alternative is to follow public opinion to establish what misuse is. Some are skeptical of a universal understanding of misuse of public office and believe that using public opinion to measure corruption leads to ambiguous results. However, cross-national public opinion polls tend to support the view that there is a common understanding of corrupt practices. Economist Oskar Kurer observes that similar "actions or practices are identified as corrupt even in environments where cultural relativity theory predicts them to be morally acceptable."[7] This point is important because most of the available cross-national measures of corruption are based on individuals' perceptions of corruption.

Some scholars have associated corruption with partiality and, therefore, injustice. Political scientists Bo Rothstein and Aiysha Varraich, for instance, associate it with favoritism in the exercise of public power.[8] They go on to link other related concepts, such as clientelism and patronage, with corruption. **Clientelism** refers to the distribution of selective benefits in exchange for electoral support, while **patronage** is more narrowly defined as the exchange of public employment for electoral support. While these scholars recognize that clientelism and patronage do not always imply corruption, they believe that these phenomena go hand-in-hand.

This connection is most obvious in the case of vote buying. In many Latin American countries, anecdotes of party brokers distributing material benefits in exchange for votes in an upcoming election are abundant. The types of benefits that are distributed range from food, mattresses, construction materials, and children's toys to money. For example, a national survey conducted during the 2018 national election in Mexico found that 33.5 percent of the respondents were offered the opportunity to sell their votes.[9] A survey conducted in Honduras during the 2013 election revealed that about 10 percent of respondents admitted they had received money or gifts in exchange for their vote, while 49 percent reported seeing politicians or party members distributing gifts or favors in exchange for votes.[10]

While vote buying is usually illegal, some forms of patronage are not. In many countries, it is customary for the government to staff a large part of the bureaucracy with appointees loyal to the party in power. However, the prevalence of patronage as a form of selecting public officials is likely to create conditions favorable to the emergence of corruption. When civil service regulations are skewed to allow the appointment of unqualified but politically loyal individuals to positions in the bureaucracy, the potentially harmful consequences are evident.

Now that the conceptual issues surrounding the definition of corruption have been introduced, we shift our attention to the causes and consequences of corruption as well as to the efforts to combat it. It should be noted at the outset that distinguishing between causes and consequences is not an easy task; what some see as causes others see as consequences, and empirical analyses often cannot identify the direction of causality.

The Causes of Corruption

Several studies have tried to identify which factors make corruption more likely. As expected in this ongoing research endeavor, some findings are more robust than others. The most important factors influencing corruption typically underlined in the specialized literature are democracy, institutions, natural resources, press freedom, poverty, and cultural factors.[11]

Democracy is thought to reduce incentives for corruption. More specifically, political competition and alternation in power are supposed to create incentives for politicians to eschew corrupt activities and to increase the likelihood that such activities are exposed and punished. Accountability and checks and balances should work to deter corrupt behavior. However, some have argued that democracy can also create incentives for corrupt activities, such as vote buying.

The evidence that levels of democracy lower corruption is inconclusive. While several studies have found democracy to reduce corruption, others have shown that this link is insignificant once we control for other effects, such as income.[12] Moreover, some political observers have cast doubt on the notion that transitions to democracy in Latin America led to significant reductions in corruption.[13]

Rather than current levels of democracy, what appears to decrease the likelihood of corruption is its longevity and stability.[14] This finding is consistent with many accounts that describe corruption as increasing in newly democratized countries and then decreasing as democracy consolidates.[15] Regime stability is important because new democracies need time to build transparent and accountable institutions, which are vital to control corruption.[16]

The quality of institutions has also been underlined by many as a significant factor influencing levels of corruption. Strengthening the rule of law, for instance, is expected to improve efforts at fighting corruption. It typically consists of reforms that enhance the courts' ability to enforce the law impartially and provide prosecutors with the necessary tools to investigate and charge corrupt officials. The likelihood of being caught and convicted influences individuals' decisions to engage in corrupt activities. Additionally, high levels of regulation are thought to increase opportunities for public officials to be bribed by private agents seeking to avoid red tape. Statistical analyses have found evidence that increasing the rule of law decreases the likelihood of corruption [17] and that high levels of government regulation increase the likelihood of corruption.[18]

Several studies have also argued that abundant mineral wealth increases corruption when countries have weak institutions. There are several reasons for this. One is that linkages between politicians and their constituents are weaker, in large part because these resource-rich countries tend to have much lower rates of taxation, which makes citizens less inclined to demand accountability and to monitor government spending. Another reason is the lack of **transparency** associated with these industries. Companies engaged in exploiting oil and gas often provide inadequate financial statements and keep payments made to governments secret.[19] The large financial flows associated with the oil and gas sector increase the incentives of public officials to seek bribes and other benefits from those companies trying to do business in the country. In addition, the significant financial resources available to governments in these countries tend to increase the use of patronage to build political support among critical sectors of the population. Countries are better equipped to avoid these problems if they established strong institutions before becoming economically reliant on revenues from mineral resources.

Corruption scandals in the Venezuelan, Brazilian, and Ecuadorian state oil companies fit these expectations. For instance, in late 2017, an anti-graft crackdown in Venezuela led to the arrest of two former oil ministers and presidents of the state oil company (Petróleos de Venezuela, S.A. [PDVSA]), six top executives of CITGO (the Venezuelan-owned and United States–based refinery), and many other oil managers and officials. The alleged offenses included misuse of insider information, bribery, embezzlement, money laundering, and conspiracy. In Brazil, the state-owned Petrobras company was involved in a 10-year corruption scandal that came to light in early 2014, which included kickbacks to oil officials and overpricing various projects and purchases. According to Brazilian prosecutors, the Petrobras scheme siphoned $2.1 billion, with much of that money going to politicians to assist in the funding of electoral campaigns and into Swiss bank accounts.[20] In 2016, Interpol issued a detention order for Ecuador's former oil minister, Jorge Pareja, who was on the run after being accused of bribery as part of an investigation into corruption in the country's state-run oil company, Petroecuador.[21] Eventually, the former official was found guilty of bribery, embezzlement, influence peddling, and other crimes and sentenced to serve many years in jail and pay a hefty fine.[22]

Another significant factor in curbing corruption is freedom of the press. When media outlets can operate freely, journalists are better equipped to uncover and report corruption scandals. By reporting cases of corruption, the press helps to reduce the incentives of public officials and businesses to engage in such behavior. In Latin America, journalists have been instrumental in uncovering major corruption scandals in places such as Argentina, Brazil, Guatemala, Mexico, Peru, Panama, and Venezuela. Cross-national studies have found support for the proposition that press freedom has a significant effect on reducing levels of corruption.[23]

Corruption is also thought to be more prevalent in low-income countries. As economists Cheryl W. Gray and Daniel Kaufmann note, in poor countries, economic deprivation and low salaries motivate public officials to increase their income while the institutional and political context usually creates many opportunities to engage in corrupt activities.[24] Public officials with broad discretion, high levels of economic regulation, poorly defined and ever-changing rules, ineffective judiciaries, and restricted political competition make many of these countries ripe for corruption.

Scholars have also linked cultural factors with levels of corruption. One argument is that countries with high levels of interpersonal trust tend to have lower levels of corruption. Political scientist Robert Putnam distinguished between "bonding" trust (trust in friends and people similar to us) and "bridging" social capital (trust in those who are different from ourselves).[25] Measures of interpersonal trust capture the bridging or moral trust aspect of society. While strong bonds among an in-group may help sustain corruption,[26] high levels of interpersonal trust should work to deter it: They lead to empathy, cooperation, and respect for moral codes and the law.[27] Studies have found that increases in interpersonal trust tend to reduce levels of corruption.[28]

The factors highlighted here are not the only ones thought to affect levels of corruption. Scholars have also emphasized the impact of different religions, colonial heritage, the participation of women in the labor force, and trade restrictions, to name a few. Multiple causes of corruption, as will be noted further in this chapter, complicate efforts to combat it.

The Consequences of Corruption

Public dissatisfaction with corruption is evident across most countries of the world. Aside from the moral outrage that it usually generates, corruption leads to tangible negative consequences for society. This section reviews five outcomes associated with higher levels of corruption: less private and foreign investment, decreases in government spending on education, increases in income inequality, erosion in confidence in public institutions, and a favorable context for criminal activities.

Corruption hurts both private and foreign investment. When investors decide whether or not to allocate funds for a project, they must consider the additional costs of bribing public officials to win contracts, permits, and licenses and to avoid excessive time delays and red tape. These additional costs tend to lower the profitability of investments. Furthermore, corruption erodes the security of property rights, which in turn increases the risks of investments. Empirical evidence from cross-national studies has confirmed the negative impact of corruption on both private and foreign direct investment.[29]

Government services, such as education, are also negatively affected by corruption. Corruption can lower the impact of education spending and shift public spending away from this area. Even when education is provided at low or no cost by the government, people may end up paying illegal bribes to obtain services. Bribes associated with admissions to educational institutions, provision of textbooks, and passing examinations are thought to hurt educational achievements.[30] But for the most part, more lucrative bribes are easier to collect in other markets characterized by low competition and highly specialized goods. Economist Paolo Mauro argues that more corrupt countries choose to spend less on education because it does not offer as many profitable opportunities for public officials as other components of government spending do.[31] He finds that corruption significantly lowers expenditure on education.

Corruption is also thought to increase income inequality. It is well-connected individuals in influential positions who tend to benefit the most from corruption.[32] Corruption fosters tax evasion and lax enforcement of tax laws, which usually favor wealthy sectors of the population.[33] In addition, it hinders the provision of social services and tends to divert resources away from infrastructure investments designed to assist the poor.[34] Moreover, as the World Bank notes, "the burden of petty corruption falls disproportionally on poor people."[35] Impoverished people are more likely to be shaken down for bribes than the middle class or the rich because they are often powerless to complain; usually, public officials are more fearful of the potential repercussions arising from trying to extort money from wealthier individuals.[36]

While global studies have found that higher corruption is associated with higher income inequality,[37] the evidence from Latin America is inconclusive. In recent times, such as in Brazil under the Lula da Silva administration and Argentina under the Cristina Fernández de Kirchner administration, countries appeared to have experienced both a significant reduction in income inequality and an increase in corruption. While some studies focused on this region have shown that corruption indeed leads to increases in inequality,[38] others have failed to uncover a significant link.[39]

Another way in which corruption hurts the region is by lowering confidence in institutions. As noted in the previous chapter, trust in institutions is thought to strengthen the legitimacy of governments, the stability of democracy, and the connection between citizens and representatives. In contexts of high corruption, citizens are more likely to perceive institutions as biased and ineffective. Studies have found that in countries where corruption is perceived to be widespread, confidence in public institutions is low, and within those countries, respondents who report personal experiences with corruption tend to have less confidence in public institutions.[40] Evidence from Mexico shows that corruption lessens individuals' trust in public institutions which, in turn, fosters a propitious environment for corrupt behavior, thereby creating a vicious circle that perpetuates corruption and low levels of trust.[41]

Lastly, it should be noted that corruption and crime tend to coincide. According to the United Nations World Drug Report, "Corruption is the great enabler of organized crime."[42] Corrupt public officials facilitate illegal activities such as the trafficking of persons, the manufacturing and trafficking of drugs, money laundering, and smuggling. Corruption also weakens the deterrence capacity of judicial institutions and the security forces. Indices of public sector corruption correlate strongly with the prevalence of organized crime.[43]

In summary, corruption has a pervasive impact on the economy and social fabric of Latin American countries. It hurts economic development and the delivery of social services, lowers confidence in political institutions, fosters an environment where criminal activities can flourish, and potentially aggravates income disparities among the population. This is why combating corruption is so essential.

Efforts to Combat Corruption

Countries around the world, often with the support of civil society and international organizations, have sought to respond to the demands for anti-corruption measures with a variety of tools. The list of possible strategies to fight corruption is long and varied. Not a single measure appears to be sufficient in of itself, but attacking the problem with comprehensive and complementary measures can make a difference.

A well-designed legal framework not only dissuades individuals from engaging in corrupt activities but also increases the chances of detecting such violations when they occur. This requires mechanisms that encourage individuals to report corrupt activities and protect whistleblowers from retaliation. Other legal reforms often advocated by specialists include policies to increase transparency, promote integrity and accountability in public procurement, and improve the civil service.

Transparency policies improve the capacity of the public to monitor public officials, thereby reducing opportunities for engaging in corruption. They facilitate access to information about the financial transactions and decisions taken by governments. Information portals that offer ready availability of documents detailing budgetary and other financial information are a useful step in this direction. Freedom of information laws can facilitate access to government records, while rules requiring the monitoring and reporting of how budgets are executed can improve fiscal transparency. Incorporating off-budget revenues and expenditures, which are especially vulnerable to corruption, into the budget can improve legislative scrutiny.[44] Also important is establishing an independent audit office with broad access to government information.

Mexico's 2015 General Transparency and Access to Information Law, which standardized access to information at the federal and state levels, is an excellent example of a significant reform in this area. Among other things, it expanded the type of entities required to disclose financial information; required comprehensive record-keeping by public officials; allowed the right to make an anonymous request for information; limited the ability of public officials to deny access to such information; and made obligatory the wide dissemination of information, such as the qualifications and salaries of senior officials, procurement procedures, contracts granted, and performance-monitoring reports.[45]

As noted in a prior section of this chapter, a free press plays a crucial role in disseminating information about government activities and investigating allegations of corruption. A legal framework that prevents public officials from retaliating against journalists and media organizations for exercising their profession is also critical to combat corruption.

Public procurement—government acquisitions of goods and services—is an area where opportunities for corruption are usually plentiful. The building of bridges, dams, and roads and contracting for water and power supply involve large amounts of money. Many of the major corruption scandals in Latin America have to do with public contracts. Ensuring real competition in the bidding process, establishing effective oversight mechanisms, and improving transparency can reduce corruption in public procurement.[46] Transparency can be improved by requiring public disclosure of the need for the contract, the bidding process, the rationale for the award decision, and auditing reports. Involving various stakeholders in the procurement process, such as end users, civil society, and the private sector, can also help.

Several Latin American countries have put in place initiatives to reduce corruption in public contracting, such as electronic procurement platforms and freedom of information legislation. For instance, in 2004, the Brazilian Office of the Comptroller General (CGU) established the Transparency Portal, an online tool that citizens can use to track and monitor the financial implementation of government programs. The portal is a resource helpful to civil society groups and journalists investigating acts of corruption and is regularly used by specialists from the CGU to identify irregularities in public spending.[47] Chile is another country that has put in place various transparency reforms. In 2008, it passed the Law on Transparency and Access to Public Information, which provides citizens with free access to information on the use of public funds, including documentation about the public procurement process.

Also important is putting policies in place to reduce the corruption of civil servants. While the exact relationship between civil servants' salaries and corruption remains unsettled, there is growing agreement that poverty-level wages and sudden declines in salaries are likely to increase corruption.[48] Frequent auditing and periodic rotation of assignments for public servants can help to prevent the development of bureaucratic linkages with criminal groups.

Reforms that seek to decrease the importance of political connections and institute a professional criterion for recruitment and promotion in the civil service are also critical.[49] Several Latin American countries have attempted to reform their civil service, seeking to improve its efficiency and reduce corruption. In the 2000s, Chile, Uruguay, and Peru adopted new legislation seeking to professionalize the senior civil service cadre. But not all reforms attain their desired goals. For example, the Dominican Republic passed an ambitious law in 2008 designed to reduce the use of patronage and political contacts in staffing the civil service and to promote meritocratic standards, performance evaluations, and transparent remunerations. While the law succeeded on several fronts, progress regarding meritocratic recruitment and promotion of personnel remained elusive.[50] It proved challenging to commit parties in government to eschew the use of political appointments and nepotism in favor of impartial merit-based procedures.

To fight corruption, it is also critical to have effective enforcement of the law. This requires capable, well-funded, and impartial judges, prosecutors, and investigative agencies. The United Nations Convention against Corruption, for example, has called for the establishment of specialized and independent anticorruption law enforcement bodies. In addition, rules that require judges and prosecutors to declare their assets and those of their families, both upon taking office and at the time of their departure, and an independent body to monitor such disclosures and the assets of judges and prosecutors during their terms in office, should help to reduce incentives to engage in corrupt behavior.

Another useful tool is to allow for the greater use of plea bargains, which can help prosecutors understand and dismantle sophisticated criminal organizations.[51] Plea bargains were crucial in uncovering widespread government corruption in Brazil and Argentina. In 2013, Brazil passed a new law expanding the employment of plea bargains and allowing their use in cases involving organized crime. The same year, the country passed another law modifying leniency agreements related to economic crimes. Brazilian prosecutors and the police have considered both tools essential in investigating corruption in the state oil company, Petrobras—first uncovered in 2014—as well as in other major corruption scandals. Argentina modified its limited plea bargain provision in 2016 with a new law that expanded its use to cover acts of corruption. Plea bargains were instrumental in investigating the "Notebook" corruption scandal of 2018, which revealed collusion between Argentine government officials and businesses engaged in fraudulent public procurement schemes and illegal campaign contributions.

Reforms that professionalize the police are also helpful. They typically include improvements in the areas of recruitment, training, and oversight. Interpol's Global Standards to Combat Corruption in Police Forces/Services suggests, among other things, putting in place rules that oblige police officers to report corruption and that protect those who do so; requiring full disclosure of the income, assets, and liabilities of those who perform policing functions; making police corruption a severe criminal offence; mandating that the proceeds of corruption be forfeited; and establishing mechanisms to encourage participation by civil society in activities designed to prevent corruption in the police forces.[52]

Latin American governments have a poor record when it comes to police reforms. Even when implemented, they are often reversed after a short period of time. For example, in the early 2000s, government officials in Honduras attempted to terminate many police officers thought to be involved in various corrupt acts. After some progress, the courts stopped their efforts and the officers were soon reinstated. Then, some of the officials advocating the reforms were themselves fired. In 2012, a new effort to reform the police led to new investigations, which subsequently revealed that a very large number of police officers had failed to pass polygraph tests designed to uncover whether they had participated in illegal activities or received money from organized crime.[53] Despite evidence of widespread police corruption, that cleanup effort ended in 2014 without having much progress. Another reform was then started in 2016, after evidence implicated the director of the police and other officers in several crimes, including the 2009 murder of antidrug czar Julián Arístides González. Over the next two years, close to 5,000 police officers were fired and the murder rate dropped significantly. While the new body in charge of reforming the police made some relevant progress, confidence in its ability to succeed was weakened in early 2018 when the press revealed that an intelligence report had uncovered linkages between the new police chief and a drug cartel.[54]

Efforts to combat corruption are doomed to be incomplete if they fail to tackle the influence of money in politics. While private financing of political campaigns is a legitimate instrument, it can usher in opportunities for corrupt activities. Repeated corruption scandals associated with electoral competition have made that clear. Promoting transparency in campaign finance can deter corruption and help uncover illegal acts.

Over the last two decades, many Latin American countries have put strict campaign finance regulations in place. Standard regulatory practices include setting limits on contributions and banning contributions from foreign governments, government contractors, and anonymous sources. In addition, corporate donations for political campaigns have been banned in several countries, such as Brazil (2015), Chile (2016), Costa Rica (2009), and Mexico (1996). In Argentina, such contributions were prohibited in 2009, but in practice, they did not go away, which was one reason why congress in 2019 passed a new law allowing them once again. The new regulations, however, outlawed donations made in cash and contributions from government contractors (e.g., companies that have public work contracts or sell services to the government).

Campaign finance regulations require governments to invest resources in ensuring compliance, but too often, the electoral authorities in charge of monitoring the financing of political campaigns lack enforcement capacity. Kevin Casas-Zamora, a former OAS official, concludes that the central problem regarding campaign finance "is the limited interest in enforcing existing legislation and the correspondingly weak capabilities to do so."[55]

Because stringent limits on contributions can unintentionally promote questionable and corrupt practices, many countries have opted for a public system of campaign finance, shortening the official period for campaigns, and restricting campaign advertising.[56] The first two countries in the world to establish public financing of political parties were Uruguay and Costa Rica; it is now common throughout Latin America. In 2017, for instance, the Brazilian congress approved a bill that instituted a public campaign fund that allocates money and free television time primarily based on the number of congressional seats held by each party. This complements a previously existing fund that distributes money to parties according to their number of registered voters.

Political corruption has also been linked to laws that prevent the detention and jailing of legislators and members of the government. Many countries in Latin America give government officials and legislators partial immunity from prosecution. In some instances, the prosecution can proceed if a high court or the legislature (depending on the country and the type of official involved) votes to lift the immunity. In other cases, the legal case may proceed but unless the immunity is lifted, the accused cannot be incarcerated. When first put in place, these laws sought to protect politicians from politically motivated attacks and attempts at censoring them for exercising freedom of speech. However, by shielding politicians from investigation and prosecution, such immunity creates incentives for abusing elective office and engaging in corrupt acts. Transparency International, for instance, has called for lifting political immunity for corruption cases. Along the same lines, Jorge Díaz, the attorney general of Uruguay, has called for reforming immunity laws so corruption offenses can be investigated and prosecuted without eliminating provisions that protect politicians from being prosecuted for their opinions.[57]

There are many anecdotes about the detrimental use of parliamentary immunity. For example, in September of 2010, Julio César Godoy, a Mexican politician accused of laundering money for a drug cartel, walked into congress after months as a federal fugitive and claimed the seat he had won in the prior year's election.[58] Immediately, he was shielded from prosecution as a result of the parliamentary immunity conferred to him by being a member of congress. That same year, the Brazilian Congress passed a bill, dubbed the Clean Record Act, making a candidate who was convicted of a serious crime, was forced out of their political positions due to corruption, or resigned to avoid impeachment ineligible to hold public office for eight years. Based on this law, the courts barred 300 candidates from the ensuing elections. In 2018, Brazil's top electoral court cited this law to disqualify former President Lula da Silva, who was in jail convicted of corruption, from running for reelection.

Lastly, it should be noted that international cooperation can also play an important role in the fight against corruption. It encourages public dialogue, helps to disseminate information, and legitimizes efforts to implement anti-corruption reforms.[59] Latin American countries have adopted a series of international agreements designed to combat corruption and increase transparency. The first was the **Inter-American Convention Against Corruption**, which came into force in 1997. It sought to promote cooperation among countries to improve the prevention, detection, and punishment of corruption. The accord inaugurated a process of mutual evaluation in which a committee of experts reviews how states are implementing various anti-corruption recommendations. Model laws, legislative guidelines, and best practices are discussed and evaluated, and country reports inform about the implementation of the recommendations formulated to each country.[60] In addition, Latin American countries have ratified the United Nations Convention Against Corruption, the first internationally binding treaty against corruption, which was approved in 2003. Most Latin American countries also have signed the Open Government Partnership agreement, launched in 2011 to promote transparency and fight corruption in collaboration with civil society organizations.

Measuring Corruption

Understandably, corruption is difficult to measure with certainty. Perpetrators try to keep their acts secret, and comprehensive information is scarce. There are many different types of corrupt activities, and some

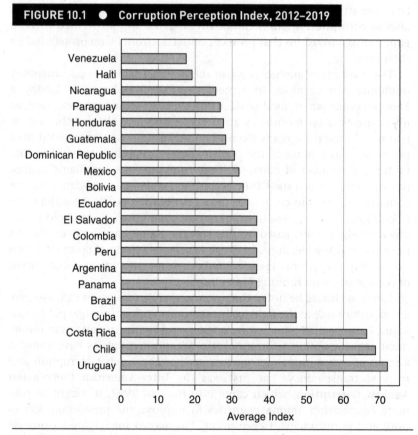

FIGURE 10.1 ● Corruption Perception Index, 2012–2019

Source: Transparency International, indices for 2012 to 2019.

elude detection more easily than others. In some cases, governments are not keen on divulging data about corruption in their countries. Despite these challenges, the assessment of corruption has improved significantly since the late 20th century. There are now several measures that provide a good picture of the prevalence of corruption across countries; these have been used to evaluate the causes and consequences of corruption and the effectiveness of anti-corruption measures. However, it is still important to remember that the available measures only imperfectly capture the actual prevalence rates of corruption.

The best-known indicators are the **Corruption Perception Index** (**CPI**; compiled by the anti-corruption organization, Transparency International) and the **Control of Corruption Index** (**CCI**; compiled by the World Bank). Both are perception-based indicators. The first relies on expert assessments and surveys of business elites and focuses on corruption in the public sector, while the second also includes data from citizen surveys and assesses the ability to control corruption in both the public and private sectors. By relying on broad perception-based indicators that combine various sources, they reduce the potential for bias.

These indicators have not been immune from criticism. Some people disagree with the way they aggregate and weight the types of information they collect, believe that differences in the conceptualization of corruption across countries weaken the reliability of the indicators, and consider a single overall score per country insufficient. However, it is generally agreed that these indicators do very well at capturing a country's overall perceived level of corruption in a manner that is comparable over time. And, as noted earlier in this chapter, conceptual challenges have been disputed by those who argue that for the most part, citizens tend to understand corruption similarly across different countries.

The average CPI for each Latin American country for the period 2012–2019 appears in Figure 10.1. The index ranges from 0 (high levels of corruption) to 100 (low levels of corruption).[61] The worst-ranked countries are Venezuela, Haiti, and Nicaragua. At the other end, we find Uruguay, Chile, and Costa Rica, which exhibit the lowest levels of perceived corruption. Latin America scores worse than Western Europe and the United States but better than sub-Saharan Africa and Eastern Europe and Central Asia.

The prior section of this chapter underlined that transparency is an essential tool in the fight against corruption. Transparency is meant to deter corruption by improving the capacity to monitor public officials, fiscal policies, public procurement, and campaign activities as well as by promoting accountability and integrity. The World Justice Project elaborates an open government indicator that captures the notion of transparency quite well. It has four components: public availability of laws and government data, the right to access government information, instruments for civic participation, and complaint mechanisms.

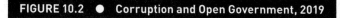

FIGURE 10.2 ● Corruption and Open Government, 2019

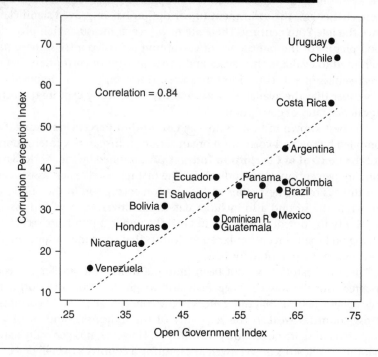

Source: Transparency International (https://www.transparency.org), and World Justice Project (https://worldjusticeproject.org/).

Figure 10.2 plots the 2019 CPI data and the Open Government Index for the same year. The dashed line shows the linear prediction from statistically regressing the Open Government Index on CPI and the correlation between both variables appears on the left part of the figure.

As the figure shows, there is a strong association between transparency and corruption. Countries with more robust transparency mechanisms tend to have lower levels of perceived corruption than those where transparency mechanisms are lacking, as expected, based on the studies reviewed previously in this chapter. The correlation coefficient between the CPI for 2019 and the Open Government Index for the same year is 0.84, which is very high, considering that 1 indicates the strongest possible agreement between the two variables.

The other widely used index of corruption, the CCI from the World Bank, provides a very similar ranking of Latin American countries than the CPI from Transparency International. Both indices rank Uruguay, Chile, and Costa Rica as the least corrupt countries in the region, and Venezuela and Haiti as the most corrupt. The correlation coefficient between the CPI and CCI is close to 1, indicating an almost perfect association between both measures.

FIGURE 10.3   ●   Corruption and Rule of Law, 2018

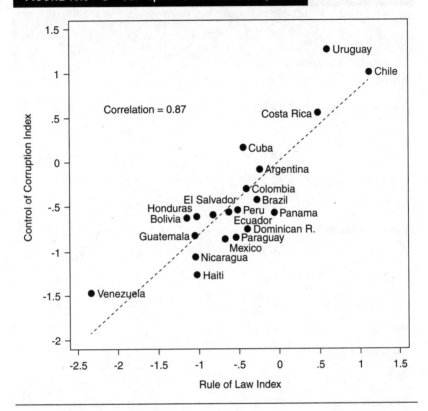

Source: World Bank, Worldwide Governance Indicators.

Corruption perception has also been linked to the rule of law. This association is shown in Figure 10.3, which plots the World Bank's CCI and Rule of Law Index for 2018. The indicator of the rule of law captures "perceptions of the extent to which agents have confidence in and abide by the rules of society, and in particular the quality of contract enforcement, property rights, the police, and the courts, as well as the likelihood of crime and violence."[62] The country scores derived from both of these indicators range from approximately -2.5 to 2.5, with positive values reflecting comparatively high scores (i.e., low corruption and a favorable estimate of the rule of law).

As the figure shows, Latin American countries that rank low in the Rule of Law Index tend to exhibit high levels of corruption. The correlation coefficient between these two variables is 0.87, which indicates a strong association. In countries with high marks on features associated with the rule of law—such as Chile, Uruguay, and Costa Rica—corruption perceptions are comparatively low. At the other end of the spectrum, we find countries—such as Venezuela—where the lack of the rule of law coexists with high levels of corruption to render a troubling social environment.

TABLE 10.1 ● Survey of Business Leaders, 2017–2018				
Country	Irregular Payments and Bribes	Diversion of Public Funds	Government Favoritism	Government Transparency
Argentina	3.3	2.4	2.6	3.6
Bolivia	2.7	1.8	1.8	3.4
Brazil	3.1	1.8	2.3	3.1
Chile	5.5	4.3	3.6	4.6
Colombia	3.3	2.1	2.2	3.8
Costa Rica	4.3	3.6	3.4	4.6
Dominican Republic	3.0	1.8	1.7	3.8
Ecuador	3.3	2.2	1.8	3.3
El Salvador	3.2	2.1	1.8	3.2
Guatemala	3.7	2.3	2.4	4.0
Haiti	2.3	2.2	2.1	2.7
Honduras	3.4	2.5	2.4	3.7
Mexico	3.2	2.2	2.0	4.0
Nicaragua	3.0	2.8	2.0	3.6
Panama	3.8	2.8	2.6	4.1
Paraguay	2.8	2.0	2.2	3.7
Peru	3.4	2.5	2.3	4.1
Uruguay	5.5	4.3	4.0	4.8
Venezuela	2.3	1.3	1.5	2.3

Source: World Economic Forum, *The Global Competitiveness Report, 2017-2018*, available at https://www.weforum.org/reports/the-global-competitiveness-report-2017-2018. Data for Bolivia comes from the 2016-2017 report.

Other types of perception-based indicators focus only on the views of the business sector. For example, the Executive Opinion Survey carried out by the World Economic Forum examines the views of business leaders around the world. Since such indicators do not capture the views of ordinary citizens, they are less likely to reflect the prevalence of **petty corruption**. However, they can be illuminating about the type of **grand corruption** affecting economic development.

Table 10.1 presents the results to four questions included in the Executive Opinion Survey conducted by the World Economic Forum. The first asks, "In your country, how common is it for firms to make undocumented extra payments or bribes connected with (a) imports and exports, (b) public utilities, (c) annual tax payments, (d) awarding of public contracts and licenses, (e) obtaining favorable judicial decisions?" In each case, the answer ranges from 1 (very common) to 7 (never occurs) and the number reported is the average score across the five components. The second asks, "In your country, how common is illegal diversion of public funds to companies, individuals, or groups?" The answer ranges from 1 (very commonly occurs) to 7 (never occurs). The third asks, "In your country, to what extent do government officials show favoritism to well-connected firms and individuals when deciding upon policies and contracts?" The answer ranges from 1 (show favoritism to a great extent) to 7 (do not show favoritism at all). The fourth question asks, "In your country, how easy is it for companies to obtain information about changes in government policies and regulations affecting their activities?" The answer ranges from 1 (extremely difficult) to 7 (extremely easy).

The results of this survey of business leaders show a close correspondence with the two measures of corruption perception previously discussed. Business leaders tend to provide high marks for Uruguay, Chile, and Costa Rica and give Venezuela the lowest score in every category. The questions reported in this survey ask about the perception of corruption and related activities of individuals who frequently interact with public officials but do not ask directly about their involvement or personal experience with corrupt acts.

Another way to measure corruption is through surveys that ask respondents about their actual knowledge of corrupt activities. These are called *experience-based indicators*. They provide a measure of corruption based on individuals' actual experiences rather than on their perceptions. These indices are also subject to criticism. One challenge is getting people and businesses to admit that they have engaged in illegal activities. Other potential drawbacks may include the inability to verify the information disclosed and difficulties in capturing various types of corruption.

The surveys conducted by Latinobarómetro ask citizens about their actual experiences with corruption. Table 10.2 summarizes information on the percentage of respondents who admitted having paid a bribe or given a gift out of all those who had contact with the respective public service entity during the prior 12 months. The first column refers to those who had contact with the police; the second to those who sought services from state utility providers (water, sanitation, or electricity); the third to those who sought to obtain documentation (identification, birth certificate, driver's license, passport, voter identification, or state permit); and the fourth to those who had contact with a clinic or public hospital.

These reports of personal experiences with corruption are quite revealing. For instance, they show that bribes and gift-giving are particularly high among those seeking attention in public hospitals and

TABLE 10.2 ● Public Services Corruption, 2016				
Pecentage of individuais who paid a bribe or gave a gift to				
Country	Police	Utility Providers	Agency Document	Hospital
Argentina	16	7	9	10
Bolivia	18	16	20	21
Brazil	6	10	7	7
Chile	7	6	11	15
Colombia	21	15	18	24
Costa Rica	13	13	16	19
Dominican Republic	22	29	27	34
Ecuador	13	16	16	22
El Salvador	18	18	21	24
Guatemala	24	20	18	18
Honduras	18	18	25	21
Mexico	33	35	40	41
Nicaragua	10	9	10	22
Panama	20	16	18	29
Paraguay	11	9	20	22
Peru	20	16	21	30
Uruguay	12	9	14	16
Venezuela	42	43	34	32

*Source:*Latinobarómetro, 2016 survey.

clinics. Around 41 percent of Mexicans, 34 percent of Dominicans, and 32 percent of Venezuelans seeking attention in public hospitals and clinics report having to pay a bribe or give a gift to access services. Reported figures are also high when describing access to other types of public services. For example, the proportion of individuals who sought documentation and reported giving bribes or gifts is about 40 percent in Mexico, 34 percent in Venezuela, and 27 percent in the Dominican Republic. Among those who sought services from state utility providers, bribing and gift-giving was reported by around 43 percent of Venezuelans, 35 percent

TABLE 10.3 ● Private Firms' Experience with Corruption				
		Percentage of firms		
Country	Year of Survey	Experiencing at Least One Bribe Payment Request	Expected to Give Gifts to Secure Government Contracts	Expected to Give Gifts to "Get Things Done"
Argentina	2017	9.3	12.9	6.8
Bolivia	2017	9.1	13.8	19.2
Brazil	2009	11.7	32.9	12.5
Chile	2010	1.3	1.0	0.7
Colombia	2017	6.6	14.7	10.8
Costa Rica	2010	8.7	7.2	3.7
Dominican Republic	2016	12.3	23.2	15.3
Ecuador	2017	5.9	20.5	4.4
El Salvador	2016	4.2	15.2	5.5
Guatemala	2017	2.8	0.2	8.5
Honduras	2016	8.7	4.1	10.9
Mexico	2010	17.6	34.9	11.6
Nicaragua	2016	6.5	2.3	10.0
Panama	2010	7.1	~	30.5
Paraguay	2017	13.8	34.2	8.2
Peru	2017	17.6	23.1	13.6
Uruguay	2017	2.4	0	2.0
Venezuela	2010	10.3	69.1	23.7

Source: World Bank, Enterprise Surveys.

of Mexicans, and 29 percent of Dominicans. Bribing and gift-giving among those who contacted the police was about 42 percent in Venezuela, 33 percent in Mexico, and 24 percent in Guatemala. According to these surveys, the participation of individuals in activities related to public service corruption is lowest in Brazil, Chile, Argentina, Nicaragua, and Uruguay.

Another experience-based indicator of corruption comes from the Enterprise Surveys carried out by the World Bank.[63] These are firm-level surveys of a representative sample of the country's private sector. Table 10.3

summarizes results that indicate the percentage of firms that reported paying at least one bribe, that were expected to give gifts to secure a government contract, and that were expected to give a gift to "get things done."

According to these firm-level surveys, bribe requests are highest in Peru, Mexico, and Paraguay. Gift-giving to secure government contracts is most prevalent in Venezuela, Mexico, and Paraguay, while gift-giving to "get things done" is most prevalent in Panama, Venezuela, and Bolivia. According to these three measures, the least corrupt countries are Chile and Uruguay. Guatemala also scores very well on the first two questions, and Costa Rica scores very well on the last one. Some regional variations are striking: No firms reported giving gifts to secure contracts in Uruguay, while in Venezuela, 69 percent of firms reported giving gifts in such instances.

The two experience-based indicators focus on different types of corruption, as can be inferred by the types of questions asked. While the Latinobarómetro surveys sought to capture individual-level experiences when interacting with public service providers, the World Bank surveys were intended to assess firm-level experiences when interacting with government officials. Together, they illuminate the different facets of public corruption. For example, the results show that Brazil ranks low in terms of individual corruption experience with public service providers but rather high in the area of businesses interacting with government officials.

Experience-based and perception-based indices coincide in the rankings of some countries but not others. For instance, both types of measures coincide in ranking Chile and Uruguay as countries with low levels of corruption, and Venezuela as one where corruption is pervasive. Costa Rica also ranks well in both perception-based and experience-based indicators, although much better in the experience of businesses than in that of individuals dealing with public services. But for some other countries, the assessments differ. Nicaragua and Guatemala fall into this category. They are perceived as countries with comparatively high levels of corruption, but experience-based indicators tend to place these countries in a better position.

In conclusion, several reputed organizations have gone to great lengths to capture levels of corruption across countries and over time. Both perception and experience-based indicators have advantages and drawbacks, but together, they illuminate important aspects of this complex problem. Measuring corruption not only allows us to discern among countries in terms of their performance but also provides essential information with which to study the causes and consequences of corruption. This information is also necessary to help design appropriate policies to combat corruption. This part of the chapter has also shown that there is significant variation across Latin American countries in terms of the prevalence of corruption.

Corruption Scandals

The vast number of major corruption scandals that surfaced during the second decade of the 21st century prompted a debate about their implications for the future of democracy in the region. On the one hand, some see these events as democracy enhancing.[64] From this perspective, these cases reflect improvements in judicial institutions; they have triggered new anti-corruption legislation and greater international collaboration to detect and punish perpetrators. Many corrupt politicians and businesspeople have been found guilty and are serving prison terms. Moreover, these scandals have helped to legitimize **anti-corruption efforts**. Latin American governments are currently more transparent, and there are better legal tools to prevent, investigate, and punish corrupt activities.

On the other hand, some believe that corruption scandals may undermine democracy in the region. They think these events are likely to lower confidence in institutions and foster disillusion with the workings of democracy.[65] Because corruption in political circles is widespread in many countries but only some cases are prosecuted, these anti-corruption efforts may be perceived as evidence of selective prosecution. However, as Jorge G. Castañeda, Mexico's former foreign minister remarked, "Whatever the drawbacks and dangers of the current anti-corruption drive in the region, they are preferable to the alternative: an intolerable status quo."[66]

It is critical to understand the magnitude of grand corruption and why these events have mobilized so many citizens in Latin America to protest corruption and demand justice. In some cases, these incidents have triggered a significant political backlash against those implicated in the malfeasances and their associates. The rest of this section describes some prominent scandals.

Odebrecht

Latin America's largest construction conglomerate, Brazilian-based Odebrecht, has been at the center of one of the most significant corruption cases in history. At its peak, the company had tens of thousands of employees in 21 countries. Among other things, it built refineries, power plants, dams, and airports. In June of 2015, its chief executive, Marcelo Odebrecht, was arrested as a result of an investigation into corruption at the state oil company, Petrobras. The following year, he was found guilty of 11 charges of bribery and 40 counts of money laundering and sentenced to 19 years in jail. The sentence was subsequently reduced to 10 years after he signed a leniency deal in exchange for providing evidence to authorities and paying a nearly $2 billion fine. Dozens of Odebrecht executives have since been arrested. In December 2016, the company pleaded guilty to bribery charges in a United States court, which resulted in a $2.6 billion fine.

Odebrecht executives confessed to paying around $788 million in bribes to officials in 12 countries, including Argentina, Brazil, Chile, Colombia, the Dominican Republic, Ecuador, Mexico, Panama, Peru, and Venezuela.[67] For over a decade, they bribed public officials, various politicians, and other individuals to gain contracts and lucrative benefits. In Brazil, they funneled illegal campaign contributions to the most relevant political parties and bribed politicians, members of the government, and executives of state-owned companies. Together with other companies, they engaged in bid-rigging to win public projects, many from Petrobras. Brazilian prosecutors also alleged that Odebrecht paid $3.8 million for an apartment and land for an institute as a bribe to President Lula da Silva, an accusation supported by the testimony of his former finance minister, Antonio Palocci.[68] Lula da Silva was convicted of corruption and money laundering in a separate case involving another construction company.

In Peru, four presidents were caught in corruption scandals linked to Odebrecht. Former President Ollanta Humala and his wife were detained in 2017 after being accused of receiving $3 million in illegal campaign funds from Odebrecht and conspiring to hide it. That same year, a Peruvian judge ordered the arrest of former President Francisco Toledo, who was accused of receiving a $20 million bribe from Odebrecht in exchange for public-works contracts during his administration. He was in the United States at the time his arrest was ordered and did not return to his country. In March of 2018, Peruvian President Pedro Pablo Kuczynski resigned his post just prior to an impeachment vote related to accusations that he concealed information about payments that Odebrecht had made to his consulting company, some of which took place when he was a member of Toledo's cabinet. Eight months later, former President Alan García entered the Uruguayan embassy in Lima and requested asylum, hours after being banned from leaving the country while under investigation for bribes allegedly received from Odebrecht. García committed suicide in April of 2019 after the police entered his home to arrest him on corruption charges.[69]

In the Dominican Republic, prosecutors accused several politicians, including a former public works minister and the director of the national water authority, for links to a bribery scheme connected to Odebrecht. It is believed that the company paid $92 million in bribes to obtain public works contracts in that country. The company also admitted to paying $49 million in bribes in Panama. Panamanian prosecutors revealed that Odebrecht paid the two sons of former President Ricardo Martinelli millions of dollars in bribes.[70] They have also accused three former government ministers, a party treasurer, and several politicians and businesspeople of being involved in criminal activities linked to the Brazilian company in Panama, including money laundering and illegal financing of political campaigns. Corruption investigations continue in the Dominican Republic, Panama, and several other countries; many politicians, public officials, and businesspeople linked to Odebrecht are expected to face criminal charges.

The CICIG and the Anti-Corruption Fight in Guatemala

In Guatemala, the fight against corruption has been led not only by local prosecutors but also by the United Nations–backed International Committee against Impunity in Guatemala (CICIG), which was established in 2007 to help fight against criminal networks. The CICIG was instrumental in uncovering several corruption cases, including the infamous La Línea and Transurbano scandals as well as others that have drawn the ire of government officials.

The first of these scandals came to light in 2015, when more than twenty government officials—including Guatemalan President Otto Pérez Molina, Vice President Roxana Baldett, and the director and former director of the country's customs agency—were accused of participating in a corruption scheme that gave importers a tax break in exchange for monetary kickbacks.[71] Soon after, thousands of Guatemalans joined in mass protests to denounce the corrupt government officials. The Guatemalan congress proceeded to remove President Pérez Molina's immunity, and he was subsequently arrested. The scandal was dubbed La Línea (*The Line*) because when importers wanted to avoid tax payments, they would call a specific landline phone number to begin the process. After the illicit payments were collected, custom officials involved in the fraud scheme would be notified about which containers did not need to pay the import taxes and would ensure that inspectors involved in this scheme were assigned to review those specific shipments. The CICIG estimated that this corrupt network—led by the vice president's former private secretary—generated around $328,000 per week. In 2018, Vice President Roxana Baldetti was found guilty and given a 15-year sentence for her involvement in an unrelated fraudulent state contract to decontaminate a Guatemalan lake.

A second scandal became public in 2018 and centered on contracts related to the Transurbano, a public transport project designed for the country's capital. Public prosecutors and the CICIG accused former President Álvaro Colom, several of his ministers, and the management of the association of bus operating companies of conspiring to defraud the state. They were arrested in February of 2018. Reported irregularities associated with the government-subsidized project included, among others, approval of the contract without bidding or proper prior review procedures, bribes allegedly paid by the company that sold the buses, and fraud and embezzlement related to the implementation of a prepay ticket system.

On several occasions, the CICIG also denounced the illegal financing of political parties by corrupt and criminal groups. In 2017, the attorney general and the CICIG alleged that President Jimmy Morales, who had assumed power a year earlier after campaigning on a pledge to root out corruption, had violated campaign finance laws and asked the Supreme Court to strip him of his presidential immunity. A few months earlier, his brother and son had been arrested after local prosecutors and the CICIG accused them of providing false receipts that defrauded the country's general property registry. President Morales proceeded to declare the chief of the CICIG persona non grata and tried to expel him from the country, but the constitutional court nullified the president's order.[72]

In 2018, President Morales sought to shut down the CICIG altogether and to prevent its chief from returning to the country. In a show of force, armed military vehicles surrounded the headquarters of the CICIG. President Morales's decision led to widespread anti-corruption protests and another ruling by the constitutional court unfavorable to the president. However, the government continued to prevent the CICIG chief from entering the country, triggering a constitutional crisis that highlights the enormous difficulties faced by prosecutors and anti-corruption activists in Guatemala.

Other Major Scandals

Many other major scandals have surfaced over the last few years. One of the most famous is the Lava Jato (*Car Wash*) scandal in Brazil, which began as a money-laundering investigation and then expanded to uncover widespread corruption at the state-run Petrobras oil company and illegal dealings of the construction conglomerate Odebrecht as well as other corrupt activities undertaken by private companies in collusion with powerful politicians. The Lava Jato scandal followed a prior vote-buying scandal dubbed the Mensalao (*the big monthly payment*), which involved illegal payments to legislators from the funds of state-owned companies in exchange for their support for government legislation. Both scandals created the political context that triggered the impeachment of Brazilian President Dilma Rousseff and led to the imprisonment of former President Lula da Silva, his chief of staff, two of his former finance ministers, a former speaker of the Chamber of Deputies, a former governor of Rio de Janeiro, top executives of Petrobras, top executives at Odebrecht, and several other politicians and businesspeople. In March of 2019, former President Michel Temer was also arrested on corruption charges as part of the Lava Jato investigation. Prosecutors accused him of taking bribes in exchange for a contract to build a nuclear power plant.[73]

Another recent corruption scandal centered on influence-peddling inside the Peruvian judiciary. In 2018, leaked audio appeared to show five judicial officials—a Supreme Court justice, three members of the judicial council, and the chief justice of a regional court—making illegal backroom deals involving favorable rulings in criminal cases and appointments and promotions inside the judiciary. In one of the recordings, Supreme Court Justice César Hinostroza asks about a defendant accused of raping a young child: "What do you all want? For the sentence to be reduced or [for the accused to] be declared innocent?"[74] The scandal resulted in the resignations of the minister of justice (who is heard talking to Hinostroza in one of the compromising audio files), the head of Peru's judicial branch, and the president of the judicial council, among others. Judge Hinostroza was dismissed in September of 2018, amid new allegations that he played a prominent role in a criminal organization operating within the judicial branch. Although he was forbidden to leave the country, he escaped the following month and was subsequently detained in Spain.

In Argentina, a major corruption scandal surfaced in 2018. It started when reporters from the newspaper *La Nación* obtained a series of notebooks belonging to the driver of a high-ranking official in the public works ministry that provided detailed accounts of illegal payments made by various businesspeople to members of President Cristina Fernández de Kirchner's government. The driver's notebooks narrated the daily activities of his boss, including frequent rides to pick up bags of cash dispensed by companies that had been awarded government contracts. The revelations led to the detention of several businesspeople and former public officials named in the notebooks. Prosecutors alleged that at the top of this corrupt network, which was dedicated to exchanging government contracts for bribes and illegally financing political candidates, was former President Fernández de Kirchner.

In short, cases of grand corruption have been reported widely by the press over the last decade. They have uncovered a deep web of corruption that involves not only public officials but also prominent businesspeople. Bribes, kickbacks, money laundering, judicial corruption, and illegal campaign financing are the central components of these scandals. Some see these cases as evidence that anti-corruption programs are finally starting to work, while others are concerned about the potential for weakening support for democracy. This ongoing debate is unlikely to be resolved anytime soon.

Conclusions

Corruption is a significant problem in Latin America, negatively affecting the everyday lives of many of its citizens, the workings of governments, and the region's economy. The inability to deal with corruption may ultimately undermine support for democracy and make authoritarian options more desirable to citizens frustrated with the status quo.

This chapter began by defining corruption and illustrating some of the activities typically associated with it. It then moved to address some of the causes and consequences of corruption highlighted in the specialized literature. Regime characteristics, the rule of law, transparency, press freedom, natural resources, poverty, and cultural factors were identified as relevant factors affecting levels of corruption. The chapter also highlighted many adverse consequences, such as fewer private and foreign investments, erosion in the public's confidence in democratic institutions, poor government services, and a favorable context for criminal activities.

Latin American countries have implemented several reforms designed to combat corruption. Some have been aimed at improving the ability to uncover corruption and protecting whistleblowers, while others have focused on decreasing incentives to engage in corruption in the first place. This chapter has also shown that corruption is not equally prevalent in all Latin American countries. In several countries, corruption is widespread; in a few, it is less common. Assessing levels of corruption is, of course, difficult, as the discussion of corruption measures underlined; nonetheless, the available indicators contribute to illustrating the pervasiveness of petty and grand corruption across the region.

The major corruption scandals described in the last section of this chapter exemplify the magnitude of these activities and the difficulties involved in the fight against corruption. They show how individuals in positions of power abuse their authority at the expense of the many and how public officials and private businesses often collude to break the law. Many consider that the region is at a historic crossroads in the fight against corruption. New legal tools are in place, the public appears to demand greater accountability, and the international fight against corruption seems to have gained momentum. Yet, many of the underlying causes of corruption are difficult to eradicate. How governments and civil society tackle this problem will have significant consequences for the political and economic future of the region.

Key Terms

Anti-corruption efforts 277
Clientelism 258
Corruption 256
Corruption scandals 256

Inter-American Convention
    against Corruption 267
Patronage 258
Public procurement 263
Transparency 259

Bibliographic Recommendations

Kevin Casas-Zamora and Miguel Carter. 2017. *Beyond the Scandals: The Changing Context of Corruption in Latin America.* Washington, DC: Inter-American Dialogue.

"Falling Apart? Why Latin America's Corruption Crackdown Is at Risk—and How to Save It." *Americas Quarterly* 13(3), Special Report. [2019]

Ray Fisman and Miriam A. Golden. 2017. *Corruption: What Everyone Needs to Know.* New York: Oxford University Press.

Brian J. Fried, Paul Lagunes, and Atheendar Venkataramani. 2010. "Corruption and Inequality at the Crossroad: A Multimethod Study of Bribery and Discrimination in Latin America." *Latin America Research Review* 45(1): 76–97.

Stephen D. Morris and Joseph L. Klesner. 2010. "Corruption and Trust: Theoretical Considerations and Evidence from Mexico." *Comparative Political Studies* 43(10): 1258–1285.

Klaus Schwab and Xavier Sala-i-Martin. 2017. *The Global Competitiveness Report, 2017–2018.* Geneva, Switzerland: World Economic Forum.

Web Resources

Transparency International: https://www.transparency.org

World Bank, Worldwide Governance Indicators: http://www.govindicators.org

World Justice Project: https://worldjusticeproject.org/

Civil Liberties and Press Freedom

I n June of 1997, the Supreme Court of Chile upheld an earlier court decision that prohibited the screening of the film *The Last Temptation of Christ*. The courts had decided that the film, which was based on a novel by Nikos Kazantzakis and directed by Martin Scorsese, distorted Christ's image and could possibly destroy individuals' deeply felt religious beliefs and, as a result, prohibited its exhibition to all audiences in the country. A few months later, a group of civil rights lawyers filed a petition with the Inter-American Commission on Human Rights (IACHR), alleging that by censoring the film, the Chilean state had violated the American Convention on Human Rights. The Commission proceeded to submit the case to the Inter-American Court after the Chilean state failed to follow its recommendation that the country should eliminate censorship and allow the showing of the film. In February of 2001, the court delivered a verdict: It found that "in censoring the film, Chile had violated its international obligation to respect freedom of thought and expression."[1] The court noted that freedom of expression is a necessary condition for society to be adequately informed and that, except for cases in which such an action was aimed at morally protecting children, censorship of public entertainment was a violation of freedom of thought and expression.[2] This landmark ruling was the first freedom of expression judgment of the Inter-American Court. Chile obeyed the court's decision, amended its constitution accordingly, and the film was finally exhibited in that country for audiences over 18 years of age.

The resolution of this matter strengthened freedom of expression in Chile. It was a significant step forward for a country that, until 1990, had been governed by a military dictatorship that disregarded fundamental civil liberties. In the last decades of the 20th century, as most Latin American countries moved from authoritarianism to democracy, respect for basic freedoms improved. But subsequent progress has not been uniform. Citizens in some parts of Latin America enjoy extensive individual freedoms that are protected by constitutional provisions and enforced by the government. Others, however, face daily life with significant limitations regarding individual rights. These shortcomings not only weaken citizens' protections from the abuse of powerful actors but also harm the quality of democracy.

This chapter focuses on civil liberties in Latin America. It describes those freedoms typically considered fundamental by political thinkers, reviews their justification, and examines how Latin American countries measure up in protecting these rights. Learning about how Latin American countries safeguard the liberties of their citizens and the occurrence of significant violations of such rights illuminates essential aspects of the lives of ordinary Latin Americans and the challenges faced by political activists, public officials, and the press. This chapter also complements the discussion of political rights presented in Chapter 7 as well as the examination of social and gender equality presented in the next chapter.

What Are Civil Liberties?

Political philosophers have debated the precise meaning of *liberty* for centuries. One particularly apt definition was advanced by Thomas Jefferson, who wrote that "rightful liberty is unobstructed action according to our will, within limits drawn around us by the equal rights of others."[3] He expressly rejected the notion of restricting the scope of liberty to "within the limits of the law," because he recognized that the law is "often but the tyrant's will, and always so when it violates the right of an individual."[4] The idea that individuals possess some **natural rights**—privileges to which all are entitled—was a central belief of the Enlightenment philosophers. John Locke, one of the most influential thinkers of that period, identified life, liberty, and ownership of property as natural rights. The Declaration of the Rights of Man and of the Citizen, which followed the French revolution, postulated that all individuals had the unalienable rights to liberty, property, safety, and resistance against oppression. The notion of natural rights also permeated the ideas of the North American revolutionaries and was subsequently incorporated into the Constitution of the United States as a series of amendments—the Bill of Rights—that guaranteed individuals' liberties, such as freedom of speech, religion, and press.

After independence, many Latin American nations integrated the idea of individual rights into their early constitutions, drawing from the examples of France and the United States. But these constitutions complemented the introduction of individual rights with a series of duties required to preserve society, which could be seen as, in practice, constraining the idea of inalienable rights.[5] In the late 19th century, Juan Bautista Alberdi, an Argentine diplomat and political theorist who had seen firsthand how the strongmen ruling most of post-independence South America had systematically violated individuals' liberties, cautioned that personal freedom required the absence of absolute power in the hands of the state.[6]

The potential conflict between individual liberty and authority is an important theme in political philosophy. Theorists in the classical liberal tradition embrace an interpretation of liberty in which an individual is said to be free if no other individual or group of persons interfere with his or her actions. This is typically referred to as a *negative* concept of liberty. The central premise is that the defining feature of liberty is the absence of coercion by others. As a result, **negative rights** limit individuals as well as the government from forcibly intruding on the actions of others.

In contrast, the concept of **positive rights** is based on the idea that freedom requires the ability to act. Liberty, from this perspective, requires autonomy, the capacity for self-realization. As a result, a positive right obliges others (most often the state) to provide some benefit to the bearer of that right. Examples of positive rights include the right to free education, free healthcare, social welfare, and adequate housing. There is a vibrant debate among political philosophers about the compatibility of positive and negative rights and to what extent positive rights imply constraints on freedom.

Civil liberties typically refer to a set of core freedoms that mostly fall within the concept of negative rights. There is no agreed-upon list, but most include the following: the right to life, liberty, freedom of religion, freedom of assembly, equal protection under the law, freedom of speech, freedom of the press, and the right to property. The human rights literature usually classifies these freedoms as first-generation rights, with the positive rights previously mentioned being second-generation rights. All Latin American countries, except for Cuba, have ratified the 1969 American Convention on Human Rights, which includes both the core civil liberties and various positive rights.

The right to life stipulates that no one shall be arbitrarily deprived of life. It is enshrined in Article 3 of the Universal Declaration of Human Rights, Article 6 of the International Covenant on Civil and Political Rights (ICCPR), and Article 4 of the American Convention of Human Rights (ACHR). It is also explicitly included in the constitutions of many Latin American countries. Common understanding of this right allows for exceptions in cases of legitimate self-defense or when law enforcement uses proportionately appropriate force. It is debatable whether legal capital punishment that follows due process of law violates the right to life. Both the ICCPR and the ACHR permit the use of capital punishment under certain circumstances, but human rights organizations such as Amnesty International and Human Rights Watch consider it a violation of an unalienable right. As of 2019, the death penalty remains legal in Cuba, which undertook the last executions in 2003. Guatemala's constitution allows it, but recent rulings by the country's constitutional court have eliminated crimes punishable by death, thereby making it inapplicable in practice. In Brazil, Chile, El Salvador, and

Peru, capital punishment remains a possibility in military courts during times of war.

The right to liberty prohibits slavery and forced labor and requires that no person be subjected to arbitrary arrest or detention by others. Anyone deprived of liberty by arrest or detention according to the law should be entitled to due process. Consequently, an individual cannot be detained for a long period without charges being filed and a trial. According to some interpretations, this right extends to the conditions under which an individual is detained, including the right of detainees to remain silent when questioned. This is one of the reasons why torture is considered a violation of an individual's civil liberties. International treaties, such as the ICCPR and ACHR, have established that no one shall be subjected to cruel, inhuman, or degrading punishment or treatment. In December of 1985, Latin American countries, once again with the exception of Cuba, signed the Inter-American Convention to Prevent and Punish Torture, which mandates that torture is a violation of an individual's fundamental human rights.

Freedom of religion gives individuals the right to practice religion or no religion at all. Accordingly, no individual should be coerced by others or the state to practice a religion or punished for practicing a religion (or none). It differs from freedom of conscience because it goes beyond the right to follow one's own beliefs to include the free exercise of religion. Freedom of religion does not require the lack of a state religion, but it prevents governments from engaging in conduct that limits individuals from worshiping, practicing, teaching, and observing their religious beliefs alone or with others.

The right to **peaceful assembly** ensures that individuals can gather and collectively express themselves, promote ideas, or petition the government. It gives people the freedom to meet and organize demonstrations without government interference. While this right is enshrined in international human rights conventions, such as the ICCPR and the ACHR, it is commonly agreed that it can be restricted with justification in the interest of national security, public safety, or public order. But while the government may impose some restrictions on the time, place, and manner of peaceful assembly, it should not prevent citizens from organizing and making their voices heard in public demonstrations. This right is closely linked to freedom of association, which gives individuals the right to join together for political, social, labor, or other reasons, and the terms are sometimes used interchangeably.

Freedom of speech entails the right to speak freely without being censored or hindered by the state or any other authority. It requires the government not to punish individuals for their speech. The notion that individuals have a fundamental right to free speech predates the French revolution and the United States Bill of Rights. The concept can be traced back to ancient Greece: It was praised by Homer and identified by Pericles as an advantage of Athens over Sparta.[7] Erasmus, one of the leading thinkers of the Renaissance, wrote more than five centuries ago that "in a free state, tongues too should be free."[8] One of the first clear endorsements of the need for free speech for all was articulated in a series of essays entitled *Cato's Letters*, written by John Trenchard and Thomas Gordon in the early 18th century.[9] To them, freedom of speech was a fundamental right of every person, a barrier against tyranny and oppression, and essential to free government.

Freedom of the press entails the liberty to report, publish, and circulate material without restrictions. **Press freedom** can be restricted by libel and obscenity laws, which may be acceptable when narrowly defined; this, however, is not always the case. More troubling are censorship and defamation laws that shield government officials, such as the **desacato laws** that were once common in Latin America. Violence against journalists and threats demanding self-censorship by journalists are examples of infringements of press freedom, as is a government-controlled media.

The right to free speech, freedom of the press, peaceful assembly, and freedom of association are important components of a broader right to free expression. **Freedom of expression** has been defined as the "freedom to seek, receive and impart information and ideas of all kinds, regardless of frontiers, either orally, in writing or in print, in the form of art, or through any other media."[10] While some narrowly defined restrictions, such as those preventing speech that may directly incite physical harm of others (creating a clear and present danger), are considered acceptable by most, a majority of countries impose broader restrictions that free expression advocates consider excessive. How some of these limits have hindered free expression in Latin America will be discussed later in this chapter.

Equal protection under the law is the right of individuals to be treated equally by the law. It is intended to guarantee that individuals would not be discriminated by the government, regardless of race, ethnicity, gender, religion, disability, social status, or other characteristics. It requires that a person not be discriminated against in the enjoyment of any right granted to individuals under national law. The right to equal protection is included in most constitutions as well as in international human rights treaties. However, the scope of this right and its implementation have varied greatly over time and across countries. While the protection it grants to racial and ethnic minorities is well understood, jurisprudence varies greatly with regards to the ever-expanding number of other groups with claims against laws that deliberately discriminate against them.

Lastly, we have the right to property. At a minimum, it entails not only the individual right to own property but also that no one should be arbitrarily deprived of his or her property. It was considered a fundamental human right by Enlightenment philosophers such as John Locke and by American and French revolutionaries as well as by constitution writers in 19th-century Latin America. But this right has always been controversial, and there exists a lively debate about defining appropriate constraints. Disagreements about it led to its exclusion from the ICCPR in 1966, mainly as a result of opposition from the Soviet Union and other Eastern bloc countries. It became part of the ACHR, which stated that no person should be deprived of his or her property "except upon payment of just compensation, for reasons of public utility or social interest," and conformed to the procedures established by law.[11] But even then, debate ensued about how *social interest* should be interpreted. Examples abound of governments abusing the justification of social interest to deprive individuals of their property. Aversion to consider the right to property as a fundamental right stems from the view that it privileges the wealthy elites, perpetuates social inequality, and impedes income redistribution. Yet, for many, property gives people the means to preserve their dignity, make independent decisions, and enjoy their other rights.[12] There is strong evidence that the protection of **property rights** is important to economic development, as will be noted further in this chapter.

The connection between civil liberties and democracy has also been a matter of debate. The introduction of this chapter noted that as Latin American countries moved toward democracy, civil liberties were strengthened. But some, such as the philosopher Isaiah Berlin, have argued that democracy and civil liberties are not necessarily connected. While recognizing that democracy may provide a better guarantee of the preservation of civil liberties than other regimes, he posited that certain autocracies could allow a large measure of personal freedom, just as certain democracies may suppress them.[13] As we saw in Chapter 2, minimalist definitions of democracy usually do not include protection of civil liberties as a defining trait; more-complex procedural definitions—such as the one advanced by Scott Mainwaring and Aníbal Pérez-Liñán—and maximalist definitions, in turn, include civil liberties as essential traits. This latter perspective is consistent with the view of many political thinkers that, together with political rights, civil liberties form the cornerstone of a democratic society.

The next sections of this chapter examine how Latin American countries fare with regard to these civil liberties. Discussions of gender and social inequality are a central component of the next chapter and consequently will not be examined here.

The Right to Life and Liberty

Latin America suffers from high levels of violence and **insecurity**. Despite holding only about 8 percent of the world's population, in 2016, approximately one third of homicides took place in this region.[14] The perpetrators of violence include not only criminal organizations but also security forces and armed political groups. Except for cases of self-defense and in the administration of justice, violence goes against the right to life. It lessens individual freedom.

Cross-national differences are illustrated in Figure 11.1, which shows the average 2010–2017 index for security and safety published by three reputed

FIGURE 11.1 ● Security and Safety, 2010–2017

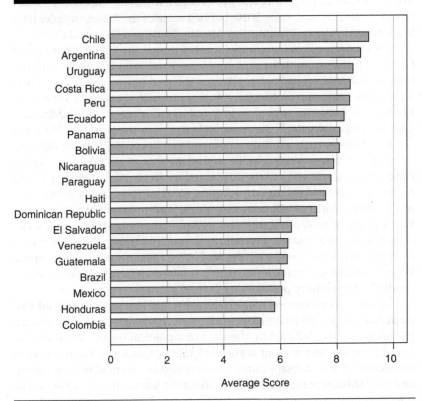

Average Score

Source: Ian Vásquez, and Tanja Porčnik. 2019. *The Human Freedom Index 2019: A Global Measurement of Personal, Civil, and Economic Freedom.* Washington, DC: The Cato Institute, the Fraser Institute, and the Friedrich Naumann Foundation for Freedom.

organizations.[15] Each country's score is based on information on intentional homicides, disappearances, deaths from armed conflicts, the intensity of conflicts, terrorism fatalities and injuries, and women's security and safety.[16] Higher numbers indicate countries with more favorable levels of safety and security.

According to this index, the highest-ranked Latin American country is Chile, which appears positioned only slightly below the United States (not listed in the figure). Other sources show Chile as the country with the fewest homicides in the region.[17] In the index for security and safety, it is followed closely by Argentina and Uruguay. These three countries, which also have a comparatively high level of per capita income, are often considered the safest in Latin America.

At the bottom of the regional ranking is Colombia, which has experienced a high level of violence over the last decades. The country's civil conflict led to an enormous number of victims, including more than 215,000 civilians killed between 1958 and 2018.[18] The level of violence in Colombia has decreased substantially since it peaked in the 1990s but remains comparatively high. Insecurity is also a major problem in Honduras, which has experienced wide-spread criminality and, since 2010, has had some of the highest murder rates in the world.[19] Also badly ranked are Mexico, Brazil, and Guatemala.

The Mexican advocacy group Citizen Council for Public Security and Criminal Justice compiled a ranking of the 50 cities in the world with the highest murder rates in 2018 (excluding those in war zones). It found that 15 of these cities were in Mexico, 14 were in Brazil, six were in Venezuela, two were in Colombia, two were in Honduras, one was in El Salvador, and one was in Guatemala.[20] The most violent city in the world in 2018 was Tijuana, Mexico, with a murder rate equal to 138 per 100,000 inhabitants.

Political violence tends to spike around the time of elections. During the campaign season leading to the 2018 elections in Mexico, for example, 152 politicians were assassinated in addition to 51 of their family members.[21] In Colombia, during 2018, a year in which both presidential and congres-sional elections took place, a total of 172 human rights activists and social leaders were assassinated, according to the country's public defender.[22] In Honduras, a contested election in 2017 triggered mass protests and a violent government crackdown, which resulted in 31 people being killed, mostly by the military police.[23]

Another major violation of the right to life and liberty is the **forced disappearance** of individuals (*desaparición forzada*), which takes place when a person is secretly abducted by the state or a political organization without legal protection and without acknowledgment of such detention. Many of the victims of forced disappearance are tortured or executed with impunity, and their families are kept in the dark about the fate of their loved ones. The forced disappearance of political opponents was a common tactic employed by the security forces in Argentina (1976–1983) and Chile (1973–1990) when these countries were ruled by military dictatorships, and in Guatemala and El Salvador during the civil conflict in the 1980s. More recently, thousands of people in Colombia and Mexico have suffered from this terrible crime.

Colombia's National Center of Historical Memory compiled data that indicates that between 1970 to the end of 2018, around 80,000 people were forcibly disappeared.[24] According to its analysis, the worst years appeared to have been between 1996 and 2005.[25] The main perpetrators, accord-ing to the available information, were paramilitary groups and, to a lesser extent, the guerrillas (who often preferred kidnapping victims for ransom over forced disappearances).

In Mexico, the government announced in 2019 that the estimated number of individuals missing and forcefully disappeared over the prior two decades was around 20,000.[26] Most were the victims of the drug war that has plagued the country since the early 21st century. The disappear-ances have been carried out primarily by organized crime, but the mili-tary and the police have also been accused of disappearing individuals. In September of 2014, one infamous case involved the disappearance of 43 students from a teacher training college in the town of Ayotzinapa in the Mexican state of Guerrero. The students were taken into custody by members of the municipal police, who handed them over to a local drug gang. The Mexican government believes that the missing students were subsequently killed. In early 2019, a new national commission dedicated to finding people who have disappeared began its work. Before this, the search for the disappeared had been carried out mostly by family members, with little government help.

The right to life and liberty is also undermined by the use of torture. As noted earlier, torture is prohibited by international law and regional treaties. Nonetheless, some governments turn a blind eye when their security forces utilize torture or avoid taking necessary steps to prevent it and to prosecute those who carry out such heinous acts.

Figure 11.2 presents an index measuring the use of torture in the period 2000–2018.[27] It was compiled by the Varieties of Democracy (V-Dem) project

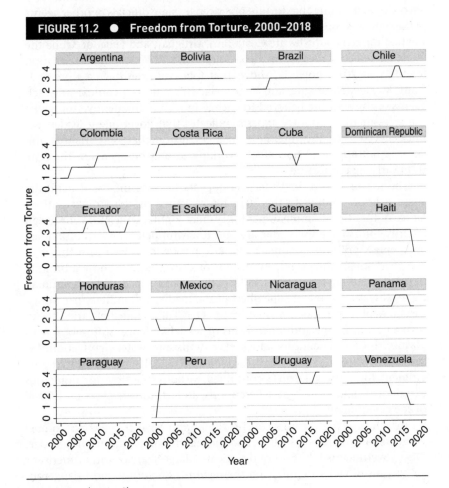

FIGURE 11.2 ● Freedom from Torture, 2000–2018

Source: V-Dem (version 9).

based on the evaluations of country experts. According to this source, *torture* is defined as the purposeful inflicting of extreme pain, whether mental or physical, with the aim of extracting information or intimidating victims who are incarcerated. It focuses on torture practiced by state officials or other agents of the state (e.g., police, security forces, prison guards, and paramilitary groups). Countries are ranked from 0 to 4. Countries where torture is practiced systematically and is incited and approved by government leaders receive a score of 0. Countries where torture is practiced frequently but is often not incited or approved by top government leaders receive a score of 1. Countries where torture is practiced occasionally but is typically not approved by top government leaders receive a score of 2. Countries where torture is practiced in a few isolated cases but is not incited or approved by top government leaders receive a score of 3. Countries where torture is nonexistent receive a score of 4.

By the end of the 2000–2018 period, most Latin American countries had a score of 3, meaning that torture practiced by state officials or other agents of the state was considered an isolated phenomenon. Over the entire period, the best ranked countries are Costa Rica, Uruguay, and Ecuador, while the worst ranked countries are Mexico, Colombia, and Venezuela. Information for the year 2018, however, shows that four countries have a score of 1: Haiti, Mexico, Nicaragua, and Venezuela. This reflects a context in which agents of the state are believed to engage in torture frequently. And while the assessment of country experts indicates that government leaders are not believed to be directing these practices, it nonetheless asserts that officials do not appear to be actively working to prevent agents of the state from carrying out torture.

The use of torture in Venezuela appears to have increased markedly since 2012. According to the 2018 report issued by the United Nations Office of the High Commissioner for Human Rights (OHCHR), Venezuelan security forces have used arbitrary and unlawful detentions to intimidate and repress political opponents or "any person perceived as a threat to the government for expressing dissent or discontent."[28] Those arbitrarily deprived of their freedom include political and social activists, human rights advocates, students, members of the media, and military personnel. Instances of torture documented by the OHCHR included electric shocks, severe beatings, rape and other forms of sexual violence, suffocation with plastic bags and chemicals, mock executions and water deprivation.[29] A subsequent report by the OHCHR (published in 2019) indicated that government forces in Venezuela continued to be responsible for numerous extrajudicial killings, arbitrary detentions, and the torture of people critical of the government.[30]

To sum up, the region's constitutional and legal frameworks compel governments to protect the lives and the security of its citizens. In practice, most governments fall short of this ideal. A large share of Latin Americans are victims of violent crime, and the region is one of the most dangerous in the world. Individuals' inherent right to life requires governments to actively work to prevent extrajudicial killings, torture, and forced disappearances. While some countries in the region show significant progress in these areas and their citizens' right to life is, for the most part, protected, others have failed. As a consequence, their citizens face recurrent physical violence perpetrated by the state's security forces or other powerful non-state actors.

Free Expression, Peaceful Assembly, and Religious Freedom

The ability to express oneself without fear of retribution is a fundamental human right. During most of the 20th century, Latin Americans faced numerous restrictions that prevented them from the full enjoyment of this right. Authoritarian governments often persecuted, repressed, and exiled individuals who expressed dissenting political views. The region as a whole has improved significantly in this area, although substantial differences persist across countries. Respect for the right of peaceful assembly has also generally improved. Yet, as will be noted, it remains absent or severely restricted in a few countries. For the most part, the region scores well in terms of **religious freedom**, even if there is still room for improvement. This section examines how Latin American countries fare on these three critical rights, starting with freedom of belief.

A global study on religious freedom conducted in 2016 by the Pew Research Center found that the Americas (i.e., Latin America, Canada, and the United States) comprise the region of the world with the lowest levels of government restrictions on religion and the lowest levels of social hostilities involving religion.[31] Interestingly, all Latin American countries, except for Cuba and Mexico, rank better than the United States on the former measure, and all Latin American countries, except for Bolivia and Mexico, rank better than the United States on the latter measure. Other indicators, such as the one compiled by the French ministry of the economy (the Institutional Profiles Database) to evaluate the freedom to establish and operate religious organizations and the one on religious freedom compiled by the V-Dem project, also tend to rank Latin American countries rather positively in comparison to countries in other regions of the world. Also relevant is the result of a survey of Latin American Jewish leaders conducted in 2018, which found that anti-Semitism was not a major concern for most Latin American Jews.[32]

Cuba is one Latin American country that has traditionally adopted a hostile position toward religious freedom. There is ample evidence that the Cuban government has threatened and harassed members of religious groups advocating for greater religious and political freedom.[33] In 2015, for example, several churches were demolished, a large number of churches were declared illegal, and hundreds of civil society activists were forcibly prevented from attending religious services.[34] In Cuba, religious groups and associations are regulated by the Office of Religious Affairs, which is part of the Central Committee of the Cuban Communist Party. Religious groups have accused this entity of acting in an antagonistic and arbitrary manner and of interfering in their internal activities.[35] Cuba is the only Latin American country that prohibits private schooling, including schools run by religious groups.[36]

There is greater regional variation regarding freedom of expression and assembly than in the area of religious freedom. Freedom of expression is fundamental to the full realization of human beings: It provides individuals with the right to share their views with others and is essential for the exercise of other fundamental freedoms. Freedom to peacefully assemble, publicly or privately, ensures that people can gather, advocate for change, and raise awareness about issues that matter to them. The rights to freedom of expression and assembly lie at the heart of democratic societies and allow individuals to articulate their ideas, aspirations, and grievances as well as to seek change through peaceful demonstrations.

In comparison to people in other parts of the world, Latin Americans are very supportive of free speech, press freedom, and Internet freedom, as Figure 11.3 shows.[37] For instance, 69 percent of people in Latin America agree with the view that it is very important that people can say what they want without government censorship. This number is only slightly lower than in the United States (71 percent) and higher than in Europe (65 percent) and the global median (56 percent). In addition, 71 percent of people in Latin America believe that it is very important that the media is allowed to report the news without government censorship, more than in the United States (67 percent) and Europe (61 percent), and above the global median (55 percent). The numbers are somewhat lower when the question refers to people's use of the Internet without government censorship (61 percent) but is still higher than the global median (50 percent) and other world regions except for the United States (69 percent).

Freedom House (FH), as part of the civil liberties component of its freedom rating, classifies countries according to whether individuals are free to express their personal views on political or other sensitive subjects without fear of surveillance or retribution. It also classifies countries according to whether there is freedom of assembly. The scores range from 0 to 4, with higher numbers indicating greater respect for these freedoms. Figure 11.4 presents scores for each country for 2019.

The countries ranking highest in both of these dimensions are Argentina, Chile, Costa Rica, Panama, and Uruguay. The first four also fall at the top of the Freedom of Expression Index developed by the V-Dem project. In short, country experts tend to agree that in these countries, people are free to discuss political matters at home and in public and that there is freedom of academic and cultural expression.

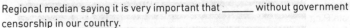

FIGURE 11.3 ● **Support for Free Speech, Freedom of the Press, and Internet Freedom**

Regional median saying it is very important that _____ without government censorship in our country.

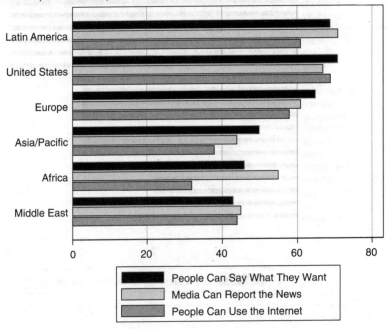

Source: Pew Research Center, Spring 2015 Global Attitudes Survey.

According to FH, the most significant restrictions to freedom of expression and assembly are in Cuba and Venezuela. These two countries are also ranked at the bottom of the aforementioned Freedom of Expression Index elaborated by the V-Dem project. Individuals in these two countries lack freedom of speech and are often persecuted and punished by their respective governments for expressing dissenting views. Cuba outlaws political pluralism, prevents opposition candidates from running in elections, represses independent civil groups, and restricts academic freedom. The Cuban Commission for Human Rights and National Reconciliation, an independent organization that tracks politically motivated arbitrary detentions, usually reports thousands of such cases every year.[38] According to Amnesty International, arbitrary arrests, discriminatory firings from state jobs, and harassment in self-employment are commonly used to silence criticism, while Human Rights Watch reports that the Cuban government regularly uses arbitrary detentions and "repressive tactics, including beatings, public shaming, travel restrictions, and termination of employment

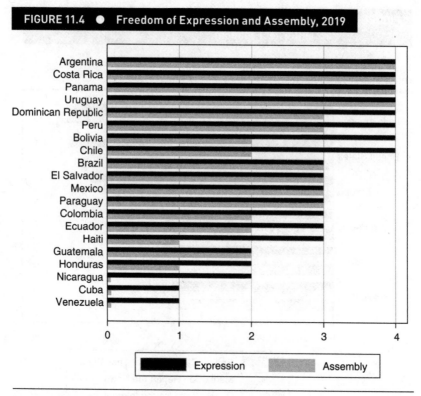

FIGURE 11.4   ●   Freedom of Expression and Assembly, 2019

Source: Freedom House 2020.

against critics."[39] The Venezuelan government has also been singled out for suppressing its critics and limiting freedom of assembly. The government of this country routinely represses dissent, violently crushing protests, detaining opponents, prosecuting civilians in military courts, and disqualifying political opponents from running for office.[40] Venezuela's judicial system is also frequently used by the government to suppress dissent.[41]

Nicaragua and Honduras are two Latin American countries that also rank poorly in terms of freedom of expression and assembly. In Nicaragua, after massive anti-government protests started in 2008, the police and armed pro-government groups began a violent repression that resulted in over 300 deaths and thousands of injured people. Since then, hundreds of demonstrators have been detained by the police, and according to Human Rights Watch, many of them "were subject to torture and other ill-treatment, including electric shocks, severe beatings, fingernail removal, asphyxiation, and rape."[42] In Honduras, environmental and land rights activists are regularly attacked, intimidated, and threatened.[43] For instance, in 2016, Berta Cáceres, the indigenous environmental defender and cofounder of Civic Council of Popular and Indigenous Organizations of Honduras, was assassinated by individuals linked to the security forces. According to court documents, her murder was ordered by executives of the energy company Desa, allegedly as retaliation for delays and monetary losses linked to protests led by Cáceres.[44] The IACHR reported that political demonstrations, land claims, and protests against development projects are often violently suppressed by the government and that those taking part in them are subject to stigmatization, arrest, and criminal proceedings, which it saw as contravening fundamental principles of international human rights law.[45]

To summarize, Latin Americans tend to enjoy a comparatively high level of religious freedom and express strong support for freedom of expression. Most countries ranked fairly well on this latter dimension, with eight out of 20 receiving FH's highest possible score. But in a few countries, citizens' freedom of expression is significantly restricted. Freedom of assembly is even more constrained, which is particularly problematic for individuals' ability to exercise their political rights. A critical aspect of freedom of expression not yet discussed is the right to a free press; the next section examines this matter.

Press Freedom

Press freedom facilitates the free flow of ideas and exposes individuals to a broad array of information and opinions. A free press helps to monitor the behavior of government officials and can investigate and reveal their transgressions. As such, it plays a crucial role in a democratic society. The right of the press to report and comment without restrictions can be thought of as a logical by-product of freedom of expression.

Threats to press freedom can come in a variety of forms. Governments may use censorship or other legal restrictions to prevent the dissemination of information they dislike. They can also use their financial resources and prosecutorial discretion to coerce media companies. Threats to press freedom can also come from criminal organizations, corrupt businesses, and violent political groups that want to prevent the press from disclosing information or opinions they deem inconvenient. Sadly, physical intimidation and violence against journalists are far too common.

In some Latin American countries, being a journalist is a particularly dangerous profession. According to the Committee to Protect Journalists, between 2010 and 2019, a total of 82 journalists or media workers were killed in this region.[46] The largest number of deaths occurred in Mexico (32), followed by Brazil (25), and Colombia (10).[47] Newspaper buildings in Mexico have been set on fire and attacked by gunmen on numerous occasions. In Colombia, a car bomb hit Caracol Radio in August 2010, injuring 43 people. Media outlets have also been targeted in Bolivia, Brazil, Honduras, Nicaragua, and Venezuela.

The legal framework can hamper press freedom in different ways. One type of restriction stems from libel and **slander laws**, which are usually meant to protect individuals from malicious falsehoods but can also be used to curb press freedom. That is the case with desacato (i.e., contempt or insult) laws. These rules allow public officials to sue those whom they believe have defamed their honor or otherwise hurt their reputation. Individuals found guilty of such offenses often must pay substantial fines and are sometimes imprisoned. The ultimate purpose of these laws is to intimidate critics of public officials.

The IACHR has found desacato laws incompatible with the American Convention on Human Rights. It has stated that such rules lend themselves to abuse and are utilized "to silence unpopular ideas and opinions, thereby repressing the debate that is critical to the effective functioning of democratic institutions."[48] It recommended that states amend their criminal libel, slander, and defamation laws in such a way that only civil penalties could be imposed for offenses against public officials. Furthermore, it stated that liability for offenses against public officials should only be incurred if there is proof of actual malice, meaning when "the author of the statement in question acted with the intention to cause harm, was aware that the statement was false, or acted with reckless disregard for the truth or falsity of the statement."[49]

The first Latin American country to abolish its desacato law was Argentina in 1993, followed by Paraguay (1997), Costa Rica (2002), Peru (2003), Chile (2001 and 2005), Panama (2007), Nicaragua (2007), Uruguay (2009), and Ecuador (2014). In Honduras (2005), Guatemala (2006), and Bolivia (2012), desacato laws were abolished after the countries' high courts found them to be unconstitutional.[50] Mexico, which did not have a specific desacato law but instead had a broad provision stating that an offense against a public official was an aggravating factor, eventually decriminalized offenses against honor (2007) and slander and libel (2011).[51]

Desacato laws have been used against journalists and others who make statements considered offensive to public officials. The original case that eventually led to the repeal of the desacato law in Argentina began after a federal judge found journalist Horacio Vertbisky guilty of defaming a member of the Supreme Court in a newspaper article in which he called the judge *asqueroso* (disgusting). In another well-known case, Cuban journalist Bernardo Arévalo Padrón was sentenced to six years in jail for writing articles considered insulting toward Fidel Castro and the president of the Cuban National Assembly. Many political prisoners in Cuban jails have been formally convicted of desacato against public officials. According to Human Rights Watch, in the city of Rio de Janeiro in Brazil, where the armed forces often patrol neighborhoods, many civilians have been subjected to military courts for allegedly disrespecting soldiers under a desacato clause in the military criminal code.[52] As of 2019, desacato laws remained in place in Brazil, Cuba, the Dominican Republic, El Salvador, Haiti, and Venezuela.

Other types of legislation, such as those punishing offenses against honor or preventing speech that incites hatred, foments anxiety, or alters the public order, have also been utilized by public officials to limit the freedom of expression of their critics. For example, in September of 2011, a Venezuelan judge ordered the arrests of the editor and publisher of the Venezuelan weekly publication, *Sexto Poder*, and the temporary ban of the magazine. The judge decided that the cover, showing six Venezuelan government officials as cabaret dancers, amounted to hate speech that insulted the officials and the institutions they represented and threatened the stability of the Venezuelan government.[53]

Defamation and **libel laws** that shield government officials from criticism and threaten journalists with jail time also have detrimental consequences for press freedom. One illustrative example is the severe punishment leveled against three directors and a former columnist of the Ecuadorian newspaper, *El Universo*; in 2011, they were sentenced to three years in jail and fined $40 million for calling then-President Rafael Correra a dictator.[54] Another is the 10-year sentence leveled against Honduran journalist David Romero Ellner for defaming a former prosecutor when reporting on alleged corruption in the country's social security administration (upheld by the Honduran Supreme Court in 2019).[55]

Press freedom may also be threatened by the discretionary use of funds for official advertisements. As a result of declining profits and weak advertising revenues, in many countries, the print media is dangerously dependent on official advertisement purchased by the government. The lack of comprehensive regulations and oversight leaves government officials with a great deal of leeway in using advertising funds to influence media coverage. Controversies surrounding the discretionary use of public advertisement surface frequently in many Latin American countries. In Argentina, for years, governments have been accused of using advertising to prop up media groups that publish favorable editorial lines while withholding support from those adopting critical stances.[56] Similar accusations have been leveled against the governments of Bolivia, Mexico, Nicaragua, Peru, and Venezuela.

The IACHR has criticized the arbitrary and discriminatory placement of official advertising to pressure, punish, or reward media outlets and has advocated in favor of legislation that explicitly prohibits it.[57] Decisions on this subject by the Argentine and Mexican Supreme Courts have had limited success in fostering nonarbitrary and transparent regulations of official advertising expenditures. In 2018, the Peruvian Congress passed a law banning all official advertisement in private media outlets. Such a drastic measure, which took away a significant source of income from media groups and redirected it to state media outlets, was criticized by a number of media organizations, the Special Rapporteur for Freedom of Expression of the IACHR, and the country's president, which advocated instead for clear, nondiscriminatory regulations.[58] In the end, the bill was declared unconstitutional by Peru's Constitutional Tribunal.

The two best-known nongovernmental organizations measuring press freedom across the world are Reporters Without Borders (RWB), based in France, and FH, based in the United States. The World Press Freedom Index elaborated by RWB combines quantitative data on abuses and acts of violence against journalists with responses from experts regarding "pluralism, media independence, media environment and self-censorship, legislative framework, transparency, and the quality of infrastructure that supports the production of news and information."[59] The Freedom of the Press Score elaborated by FH utilizes expert analyses centered on three broad categories: the legal environment, which includes laws and regulations that could influence media content and the extent to which they are used to restrict the media's ability to operate; the political environment, which evaluates the degree of political influence in the content of news media as well as harassment and reprisals against journalists by the state and other actors; and the economic environment for the media, including the structure, concentration, and transparency of media ownership.[60]

Figure 11.5 summarizes the average RWB scores for the period 2013–2019, which can range from 0 to 100, with lower numbers indicating greater freedom of the press. These scores are highly correlated with the scores provided by FH. In both indices, the Latin American countries with the best scores are Costa Rica, Uruguay, and Chile. These countries are also

FIGURE 11.5 ● Press Freedom, 2013–2019

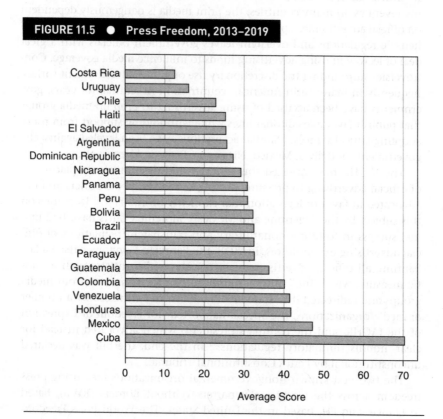

Source: Reporters Without Borders, World Press Freedom Index (2013 to 2019).

very well positioned in comparison to countries in other parts of the world. Cuba, a country where press freedom has been absent for decades, has the worst score in the region. Other Latin American countries badly ranked by both organizations are Mexico, Honduras, and Venezuela. Overall, the average score for Latin American countries is slightly above the world average.

While scores capturing levels of democracy for Latin America have increased since the early 1990s, those referring to media freedom appear to have declined. Particularly relevant are findings that show press freedom declining in countries that have few institutional checks on executive power and countries that are facing financial crises and increasing in countries with higher levels of judicial independence and where executives are constrained by opposition parties in the legislature.[61] There is also evidence that Latin America's populist presidents have been inclined to turn against the mainstream media, weakening their ability to serve as watchdogs of democracy.[62] Prior research has also shown that countries where freedom of the press is greater tend to have lower levels of corruption and better governance.[63]

Property Rights

Enlightenment thinkers such as John Locke, David Hume, and Adam Smith considered the right to property a natural right, on par with the right to life and liberty, freedom of speech, and religious liberty. This was also the view of John Adams and James Madison, founding fathers of the United States, who emphasized the central importance of property rights. Leading intellectual figures of 19th-century Latin American constitutionalism, such as Argentine Juan Bautista Alberdi, Chilean/Venezuelan Andrés Bello, and Colombian José María Samper, also believed in strong protections of property rights.

For classical liberalism, property rights not only include the right to ownership of personal property but also the right to private ownership of productive property. They protect an individual's right to hold and trade property and to engage in such activities as starting a business or forming a corporation. Property rights are part of a larger set of economic liberties advocated by classic liberalism, which also includes the right to freely choose an occupation and freedom of contract formation.

The justification of property rights advocated by classical liberals is based on the ideas of self-ownership and social utility. The concept of self-ownership stems from the belief in individual sovereignty—that is, the notion that individuals have a rightful dominion over themselves. This implies, among other things, the right of individuals to decide what to do with their own bodies and to express their own thoughts. Furthermore, it implies that individuals also own their labor and the benefits each earns from working. This was the view of John Locke, who believed that by combining one's labor with external elements (e.g., goods or resources), individuals develop ownership of those things.[64] As a result of their value-creating labor, individuals buy and dispose of the goods they own through voluntary exchange.

The most common justification of property rights, however, is consequentialist: A system that protects private property provides greater social utility than one without property rights. Classical liberals, among others, argue that protection of property rights brings about benefits to the population as a whole. For instance, they maintain that such protection increases investment and economic productivity, favors the efficient use of resources, encourages individual initiative and experimentation, enhances independence and self-reliance, and promotes a culture that values hard work. Cross-country empirical analyses have shown an association between higher levels of economic development and stronger property rights.[65] Better defined property rights have also been shown to increase economic growth among developing countries.[66]

Putting property rights on par with other civil liberties, as classical liberals do, is controversial. As early as the 18th century, Rousseau noted that property rights and the commercial society they foster contribute to significant class divisions and inequality. Some, such as Karl Marx and his followers, rejected the liberal tradition and its core set of civil liberties, which they saw as disguising an exploitative society. Other thinkers within liberalism also questioned the primacy of economic liberties. This perspective, which began in the 19th century and gained significant prominence in the 20th century, is often referred to as *high liberalism* or *left-liberalism*. Unregulated economies are seen by left-liberals as biased in favor of the rich, augmenting income inequality, underproviding public goods, severely limiting the opportunities of large numbers of poor people, and ultimately leading to an unjust society. For political philosophers writing within this liberal current, such as John Rawls, basic civil and political liberties retain central importance in the formation of a just society, but in terms of property, only the right to personal property and occupational choice make the cut. Excluded from this list are ownership rights in productive property and free economic contracts, which are central to classical liberals and libertarians. High liberals believe that economic liberties should be regulated or constrained in order to secure important social goals, particularly redistribution targeted at achieving social justice.[67]

Latin American constitutions drafted in the 19th century tended to follow tenets of classical liberalism in establishing strong protections for property rights. Both the Chilean Constitution of 1833 and the Argentine Constitution of 1853 are good examples. Alberdi, the father of the Argentine constitution and a classical liberal, stated that "every regulation that, under the pretense of organizing the exercise of economic liberty, restricts it and encroaches upon it, attacks both the Constitution and national wealth."[68] The constitutional article securing property rights in the Argentine constitution drew extensively from Alberdi's writings on the subject.

In the early 20th century, however, a new wave of constitution writing, influenced by the incorporation of the middle and working classes into politics and motivated by concerns over social justice, led to significant changes to property rights. This reformist movement sought to incorporate social protections previously disregarded. It began with the Mexican

Constitution of 1917 and was followed by reforms in Brazil (1937), Bolivia (1938), Cuba (1940), Uruguay (1942), Ecuador (1945), Guatemala (1945), Argentina (1949), and Costa Rica (1949).[69]

In addition to allowing for the **expropriation** of private property in cases of public need and with compensation—as in earlier liberal constitutions—the Mexican Constitution of 1917 included a clause granting the government the power to regulate private property for social benefit. It also incorporated the explicit mandate of achieving a more equitable distribution of public wealth. In the following years, the Mexican government pursued a significant land reform that redistributed landholdings in excess of a statutory limit.

The idea of the social function of property, first articulated by the French jurist Leon Duguit in the early 20th century, was incorporated into many Latin American constitutions. The arguments in favor of it fit well with the views of left-liberalism. For example, when, in the mid-1960s, Chilean President Eduardo Frei Montalva sent to congress his constitutional reform bill seeking to change property rights, he argued that the constitutional protection of property was a mockery if, in practice, it made property inaccessible to the majority of the population.[70] In Chile, as in other Latin American countries, politicians pursued constitutional changes to property rights in order to undertake major redistributive programs. With this reform, Frei Montalva was seeking greater freedom to expropriate land and limit the size of landholdings as part of an agrarian reform program. When Bolivia reformed its constitution in 2009, not only did it stipulate that property must serve a social function, it also noted that an individual's right to property should not go against "the collective interest" and that transferring national resources that are the "social property of the Bolivian people" to companies, people, or foreign states could be considered an act of treason.[71] The following year, the Bolivian government expropriated four electricity-generating companies.

Private owners and investors may receive compensation after their property has been expropriated by the government. For example, United States companies were eventually adequately compensated after Mexico seized foreign-owned oil assets in 1938.[72] But this has not always been the case. The restoration of diplomatic relations between Cuba and the United States in 2015, for instance, spurred negotiations to settle decades-old outstanding property claims from many United States citizens and companies whose assets were confiscated after the 1959 revolution. Recent litigations between foreign companies and the governments of Argentina, Bolivia, Ecuador, and Venezuelan regarding the expropriation of foreign assets have led to several adverse legal rulings against these Latin American nations.

When governments seize the property of their own citizens or local companies, it is the national courts that become involved, and adequate compensation may be more difficult to achieve. This has been the case in Venezuela under presidents Hugo Chávez and Nicolás Maduro, where hundreds of expropriations of local companies, land, and buildings have taken place, many without any compensation. The arbitrary seizure of property in Venezuela was in full display during an infamous episode of Hugo Chávez's weekly television show, broadcasted in 2010. In it, he is seen walking in the main square of the capital, inquiring about the ownership of the buildings surrounding it. After being reassured by the city's mayor that one particular theater is already in the state's hands, Chávez turns his attention to the building next door. After learning that the building belongs to a local jeweler, he orders, "Expropriate it." He then proceeds to issue similar off-the-cuff instructions regarding other privately owned buildings.[73] This episode illustrates an arbitrary approach to determine the public's need and assert the collective interest.

Data on the protection of property rights in Latin America illustrate significant cross-country differences. Figure 11.6 provides information on the risk of expropriation (black bars) and property rights (gray bars). The first measure comes from the insurance agency, Credendo Group, which is a world leader in the market of insuring companies against various types of political risks. The scale ranges from 1 to 7, with lower numbers indicating a higher risk of expropriation.[74] The measure reflects country scores in early 2019. The second measure comes from the World Economic Forum and captures expert assessments of property rights protection included in their 2019 Global Competitiveness Report. The scale also ranges from 1 to 7, with higher numbers indicating better property rights protections.

According to these indicators, Chile and Uruguay exhibit the lowest risks of expropriation and the highest scores in property rights protection. These two countries are also placed at the top of other property rights rankings, such as the one created by the Heritage Foundation. They exhibit the best possible score in terms of expropriation risk and, in terms of property rights, are ranked 32 and 42 (respectively) out of the 141 countries evaluated by the World Economic Forum. Also well placed are Costa Rica and Panama. In short, in these four countries, property rights are well-protected.

At the other end of the spectrum, we have Venezuela and Bolivia, which have the highest risk of expropriation, and, together with Haiti, the lowest scores in property rights protection. Moreover, Venezuela ranks at the very bottom of the property rights ranking of 141 countries built by the World Economic Forum. Cuba, which is not included in the index for property rights, also ranks very poorly in terms of expropriation risk. Since the revolution, Cuba has denounced private property, which was virtually eliminated in the 1960s. However, the country's 2019 constitutional reform formally recognized the right to private property, ending (at least in some limited measure) its long-standing opposition.

To sum up, there are different philosophical views about the place of property rights alongside other civil liberties. For classical liberals and libertarians, property rights are essential for individual liberty, but left-liberals believe rights over productive property and other economic rights should be regulated or constrained to achieve social goals. As this section has shown, Latin American countries vary significantly in the extent to which they protect property rights. Empirical studies have shown that property rights promote economic growth, but politicians have incentives to restrict these protections when they seem incompatible with other political goals.

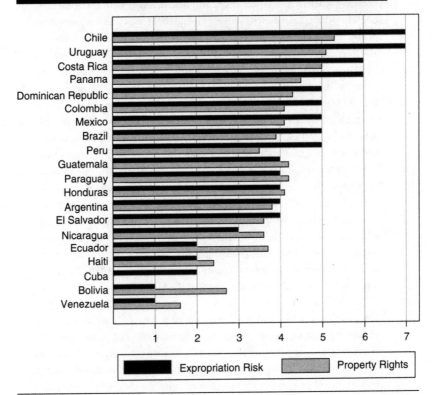

FIGURE 11.6 ● Expropriation Risk and Property Rights Protection

Source: Expropriation Risk, Credendo Group (2019); Property Rights, World Economic Forum (2019).

Conclusions

The idea that individuals possess some basic rights to which they are entitled originated in ancient Greece and became a defining component of classical liberal thought during the Enlightenment period. In Latin America, this notion was embraced by leading constitutional thinkers during the 19th century. Drawing from the examples of France and the United States, many Latin American nations incorporated the idea of civil liberties into their early constitutions. International and regional human rights conventions, as well as contemporary constitutions, explicitly include language protecting individual rights to life and liberty, religion, expression, assembly, a free press, and property. This chapter reviewed these rights and examined the extent to which Latin American countries protect these liberties.

Learning whether governments in Latin America safeguard these liberties, fall short in their attempt, or actively violate them improves our knowledge of the region and their citizens. It informs us not only about individuals' freedoms but also about the quality of democracy, the effectiveness of governments, the limits on state power, and whether public officials abide by international human rights norms. This chapter has shown how the right to life and liberty, protected by constitutional provisions, is too often infringed upon by violent state and non-state actors. In some Latin American countries, extraordinarily high levels of crime, the use of torture, and forced disappearances have had a devastating effect on people's lives. This chapter has also shown significant cross-national differences in terms of free speech protections and the right to peaceful assembly. In countries such as Argentina, Chile, Costa Rica, and Uruguay, citizens enjoy strong protections to exercise these rights, but in others, such as Cuba, Venezuela, and Honduras, there are significant restrictions in place to silence individuals and prevent them from protesting. In terms of religious freedom, cross-national differences are less salient, and there is agreement that the region fares well in comparison to other parts of the world.

The chapter concluded with a discussion of property rights. It noted the philosophical disagreements regarding the protection of private property and its place alongside other civil liberties. As with other rights, differences within the region are significant. Since economists tend to underscore the importance of property rights for economic growth, these distinctions may ultimately have salient long-term effects. Some of the underlying ideas informing different approaches to property rights are also associated with alternative views on equality. The next chapter delves into the topic of social and gender inequality, complementing this chapter's analysis of civil liberties and the earlier discussion on suffrage rights.

Key Terms

Civil liberties 287	Peaceful assembly 288
Freedom of expression 289	Positive rights 287
Insecurity 290	Press freedom 289
Natural rights 286	Property rights 290
Negative rights 287	Religious freedom 295

Bibliographic Recommendations

Taylor C. Boas. 2012. "Mass Media and Politics in Latin America." In J. I. Dominguez and M. Shifter (eds.), *Constructing Democratic Governance in Latin America*. Baltimore: The Johns Hopkins University Press.

Marisa Kellam and Elizabeth A. Stein. "Silencing Critics: Why and How Presidents Restrict Media Freedom in Democracies." *Comparative Political Studies* 49(1): 36–77.

Jessica McCormick. 2016. "The Last Temptation of Christ (Olmedo Bustos et al.) v. Chile." *Loyola of Los Angeles International and Comparative Law Review* 38(4): 1189–1203.

Office of the United Nations High Commissioner for Human Rights. 2018. *Human Rights Violations in the Bolivarian Republic of Venezuela: A Downward Spiral with No End in Sight*. Available at https://www.ohchr .org/Documents/Countries/VE/VenezuelaReport2018_EN.pdf

Piero Stanig. 2015. "Regulation of Speech and Media Coverage of Corruption: An Empirical Analysis of the Mexican Press." *American Journal of Political Science* 59(1): 175–193.

Web Resources

Freedom House: https://freedomhouse.org/

Human Rights Watch: https://www.hrw.org/

Reporters Without Borders: https://rsf.org/en

12

Income Inequality, Poverty, and the Gender Gap

People in Jardim Paulista, an affluent neighborhood in São Paulo, Brazil, can count themselves fortunate. Their life expectancy is about 82 years old.[1] When they need to see a primary care physician, they can quickly do so. Maternal and child mortality rates are comparatively low, and only about 1 percent of babies are born to teenage mothers. The neighborhood has museums, movie theaters, and a very low crime rate. In contrast, those living in Cidade Tiradentes, a poor neighborhood in the far east of São Paulo, face a far grimmer reality. Their life expectancy is only 58 years old. When they want to see a primary care physician, the typical wait time is 46 days. Maternal and child mortality are comparatively high, and over 16 percent of new mothers are teenagers. The neighborhood, which lacks museums and movie theaters, has a high crime rate. It is home to Santa Etelvina, one of the largest public housing complexes in Latin America, made up of dozens of rundown apartment blocks with a history of gang violence. The number of homicides is seven times higher in Cidade Tiradentes than in Jardim Paulista, and the rate of violence against women is more than 40 times higher. Household income in Jardim Paulista is over 13 times that of Cidade Tiradentes.[2] Although the two neighborhoods are less than 23 miles apart, the life prospects of their children appear to be worlds away.

The inequality present in the city of São Paulo is indicative of the country as a whole. Brazil is home to the greatest number of billionaires in Latin America as well as the greatest number of the region's poor. Disparities in wealth between the rich and the poor are enormous in a region long known for its high economic inequality.

From the early 20th century until the early 21st century, Latin America was the most unequal region of the world, a dire distinction that it now shares with sub-Saharan Africa. High levels of inequality hinder develop-ment and make **poverty** reduction considerably more difficult. Most Latin Americans consider extreme disparities in wealth a serious problem; many academics, social activists, religious leaders, and politicians agree. Reducing **income inequality**, ending poverty, and promoting gender equality are three of the 17 sustainable development goals adopted by world leaders in 2015 during a historic meeting of the United Nations. The Organization of American States has also publicly committed itself to combating poverty, lessening economic disparities, and promoting gender equality.

Our understanding of Latin America would be incomplete without an examination of the inequality present among its population. It has been a persistent trait of the region and a source of social tension. This chapter analyzes social disparities in Latin America, focusing primarily on income and gender inequality. The first part traces the origin of Latin American inequality and asks whether income inequality is a moral problem. After a discussion of several issues associated with high disparities in income and the potential benefits of reducing such disparities comes a review of inequality and poverty trends in the region. The first part ends with an examination of the factors that influence poverty levels and income inequality. The second part delves into gender inequalities, outlining the progress women have made in the areas of **education** and health and the harm inflicted by a lack of safety and by pervasive violence. Participa-tion in public office and the labor market are addressed next, including the **gender pay gap** and differences between men and women regarding unpaid work and an independent source of income.

Income Inequality

Income inequality remains remarkably high in Latin America despite some significant improvements since the early 21st century. Latin America and sub-Saharan Africa are the most unequal regions in the world. The standard measure used to quantify inequality in the distribution of income is the **Gini coefficient**. It is an index that ranges from 0 (everyone has the same income) to 1 (one person has all the income and everyone else has no income). Therefore, the lower the Gini coefficient, the more equal the country's income distribution. In 2017, the average Gini coefficient in Latin America and the Caribbean was calculated to be around 0.51, which was much higher than the world average (estimated to be 0.37 in 2013).[3] Brazil and Honduras, the most unequal countries in the region in 2017, were among the most unequal in the world.

When did Latin America become so unequal? Economic historians note that income inequality rose significantly in the second part of the 19th century when Latin America began to expand its export sector.[4] At that time, the well-off benefited greatly from their control of land and mineral resources. The economic returns to land—where ownership was rather concentrated—increased greatly in comparison to the economic returns to labor.[5] By the 1920s, the economic boom of the past decades had led income inequality to historic highs.[6] Unlike the most industrialized countries, which underwent a great leveling of income distribution from the 1920s to the 1970s, the region did not reverse its earlier course.[7] As a result, during the 20th century, Latin America became the most unequal region in the world.

Such large disparities in income raise an important question: Is income inequality a moral problem? As expected, there are many different answers. Some believe it is not. They argue that what really matters is poverty and that the distribution of wealth itself is either of little importance or the by-product of natural differences among individuals. To put it differently, rather than disparities in income, human suffering is the real challenge. In the words of political philosopher Harry G. Frankfurt, "From a moral point of view, economic inequality does not really matter very much, and our moral political concepts may be better focused on ensuring that people have enough."[8] Many believe that it is morally wrong for a country that has the financial resources to tackle poverty not to act to address the suffering of the poor. This latter point is particularly persuasive with regards to poor children, who, through no fault of their own, face severe deprivation.

Other answers to this question focus on opportunity rather than outcomes. One perspective holds that inequality of opportunity is morally wrong because it is fundamentally unfair. While most people may concede that perfect equality of opportunity is both unfeasible and likely problematic in itself, they still regard large disparities in opportunities as unjust. Gross inequalities of opportunity are often the result of unfairness in the institutional framework within which societies operate rather than the outcome of differences in individuals' efforts, ambitions, and choices, which are ubiquitous in human life. Equality of opportunity requires that the regime in place strives to prevent employment discrimination and to provide individuals with such things as a good education, health care, and access to credit.[9] According to this view, whether the children of those at the bottom of the income distribution have sufficient opportunities to ascend the ladder to success is a moral issue.

Another perspective, associated with the views of political philosopher John Rawls, claims that inequality can be morally justified only when it benefits society, particularly those who are most vulnerable. In his well-known book, *A Theory of Justice*, Rawls argued that if the system in place provides both fair equality of opportunity and the greatest benefit to the least-advantaged members of society, then the inequality it produces can be justifiable.[10]

But for others, high levels of income inequality are categorically immoral. This is the position of Oxfam, one of the largest charitable organizations dedicated to alleviating poverty worldwide. It is also a position defended by the clergy in many Latin American countries. For example, when Pope Francis was the archbishop of Buenos Aires, he denounced the "unjust economic structures that give rise to great inequalities" and argued that the disparities they produced were especially immoral in countries that have the "conditions for avoiding or correcting such harm."[11]

Increases in inequality are also likely to shift political power, boosting the influence of the wealthy. Huge disparities in income, the argument goes, give the well-off the means to manipulate the rules of the game in a way that diminishes the political and economic rights of those with low incomes.

Of course, morality is not the only concern raised by income inequality. Before reviewing inequality and poverty trends across Latin America, the next section discusses a few of the negative outcomes that have been associated with income inequality.

Why Is Income Inequality Considered a Problem?

Most Latin Americans consider the levels of income inequality in their societies unjust. Public opinion data have illustrated how widespread this view is: Data from the 2018 Latinobarómetro survey revealed that on average, 80 percent of respondents considered the distribution of income in their country unfair or very unfair.[12] The numbers go from a low of 65 percent in Bolivia to a high of almost 91 percent in Venezuela, showing that most Latin Americans remain unhappy with the degree of inequality that exists in their countries.

Extant research has indicated that there are at least three problematic outcomes linked to income inequality: reducing poverty becomes more difficult, individuals become less likely to trust one another, and there are fewer opportunities for social mobility across generations. Also, there is some evidence that income inequality promotes conflict and reduces growth, but these associations remain disputed.[13]

First, the impact of economic growth on reducing poverty is lower in the context of greater income inequality.[14] We expect economic growth to not only bring about an improvement in average incomes, a lowering of unemployment, and an encouraging context for firms to invest but also to lift people out of poverty. Inequality plays an important role in mediating the effect of economic growth on poverty reduction.[15] In more unequal societies, economic growth is less effective in helping people move out of poverty. Put differently, more unequal countries convert one percentage point of growth in average income into a smaller reduction in poverty than do countries that have a more equal income distribution.[16]

Second, greater inequality appears to lower trust in others. The importance of interpersonal trust to cooperation, economic transactions, and the health of a democracy is discussed in Chapter 9 of this book. When inequalities in the distribution of income are seen as the result of personal connections, inheritance, racism, corruption, or political favoritism rather than merit, individuals are likely to perceive them as unfair. This phenomenon tends to lower people's trust in others and in the government. Moreover, great disparities in income usher in great differences between the values of those at the top and the bottom, which reduce people's general sense of trust.[17] Recent studies lend support to the idea that income inequality reduces interpersonal trust.[18]

Third, high income inequality has detrimental effects on social mobility across generations.[19] This means that in more unequal societies, children from low-income families have less opportunity to move up the ladder and surpass their parent's earnings than in more equal societies.[20] Evidence has also emerged showing that in the presence of greater inequality, young people from poorer backgrounds are more likely to drop out of high school, which negatively impacts their ability to prosper economically down the road.[21] When upward social mobility is absent, many skills and potential talents are not utilized, supplemental income programs may strain public resources, social cohesion is weakened, and life satisfaction among those at the lower end of the income distribution declines. An instructive report on economic mobility in Latin America conducted by the World Bank concluded that the low levels of intergenerational mobility found in the region are associated with income inequality.[22]

Many studies have also linked income inequality with political turmoil, but the evidence remains contested. The claim that inequality in wealth distribution promotes violent conflict has a long history. Aristotle in ancient Greece, James Madison in the *Federalist Papers*, Alexis de Tocqueville and Karl Marx in the 19th century, and numerous modern and contemporary political scientists, economists, and sociologists have argued that economic inequality breeds political conflict. The argument stems from the belief that high levels of economic inequality foster dissatisfaction with the existing socio-economic status quo and demands for radical changes, which increase the likelihood of political instability, violence, and civil conflict.[23] The evidence of this causal relation, however, remains inconclusive.[24] While there is weak support for the claim that income inequality among individuals promotes the onset of conflict,[25] there is stronger evidence that economic inequality between ethnic, religious, or regional groups increases the chances of political violence.[26]

Numerous studies have underlined the complex link between inequality and economic growth. Some of them have found that income inequality negatively affects economic growth, except in poor countries.[27] But others have found income inequality to decrease per capita income and shorten the duration of economic growth cycles, regardless of initial conditions.[28] Christine Lagarde, the former chief of the International Monetary Fund, wrote in an op-ed published in 2016 that "countries that have managed to reduce excessive inequality have enjoyed both faster and more sustainable growth."[29]

One strand of research on inequality distinguishes between opportunity and effort. The former consists of circumstances beyond an individual's control (e.g., race, gender, region of birth, and family background) while the latter comprises freewill choices (e.g., risks taken in entrepreneurship activities) and personal abilities. Inequality of opportunity favors individuals from privileged social origins rather than those with more talent, which means that individuals at the bottom of the income distribution have fewer opportunities to access things such as credit or a quality education because of predetermined factors unrelated to their actions and aptitudes. In contrast, inequalities resulting from differences in effort may encourage people to work harder and invest in education. Economists Gustavo A. Marrero and Juan G. Rodríguez find that "the impact of overall inequality on economic performance is ambiguous because the two main components of inequality have opposite effects on growth": Inequality of opportunity harms it, while inequality of effort benefits it.[30]

In short, aside from the moral question raised by high disparities in income, there are specific detrimental outcomes that make inequality an unwanted societal trait. Reducing inequality, however, is a challenging undertaking. Before discussing how it is influenced by public policies and the economic context, the next two sections provide an overview of income inequality and poverty across Latin America.

Trends in Income Inequality

During the last two decades of the 20th century, income inequality increased in most Latin American countries.[31] This trend, however, was reversed at the beginning of the 21st century. This is illustrated in Figure 12.1, which shows the Gini coefficient for 17 Latin American countries for the period 2000–2017.[32] As the table shows, all countries, except for Costa Rica, reduced income inequality. The change was most impressive in the case of Bolivia, which, in 2000, was the most unequal country in the region. As of 2017, Brazil is the most unequal country in the region, with a Gini coefficient of 0.53. Honduras, Panama, and Colombia, which have a Gini coefficient of around 0.50, also fare poorly, despite having improved their record since the beginning of the 21st century.

The lowest levels of income inequality are found in El Salvador (Gini = 0.38), Uruguay (Gini = 0.39), and Argentina (Gini = 0.41). All three countries have a distribution of income slightly more equal than that of the United States which, in 2016, had a Gini coefficient equal to 0.42.[33] Despite these changes, every country in Latin America had Gini coefficients above those found in all countries of the European Union as well as in other high-income countries such as Canada, Australia, and Japan.

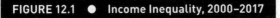

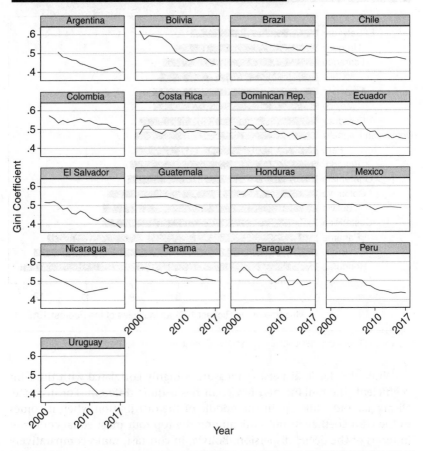

FIGURE 12.1 ● Income Inequality, 2000–2017

Source: LAC Equity Lab, SEDLAC, and World Development Indicators (June 2019).

Another indicator of inequality is the **decile dispersion ratio**. It measures the ratio of the average income for the richest 10 percent (the 90th percentile) to that of the poorest 10 percent (the 10th percentile). This can be interpreted as the income of the rich in the form of multiples of that of the poor. Data on inequality based on the 90 to 10 decile dispersion for 17 Latin American countries are shown in Figure 12.2.[34]

For the region as a whole, the average income decile dispersion is 8.5. In other words, the income of the richest 10 percent is about 8.5 times the income of the poorest 10 percent. The most unequal countries according to this measure are Honduras (decile dispersion = 12.9), Brazil (decile dispersion = 12.3), and Panama (decile dispersion = 11.7). At the other end, the most equal are El Salvador (decile dispersion = 5.5), Uruguay (decile dispersion = 6.2), and Nicaragua (decile dispersion = 6.7).

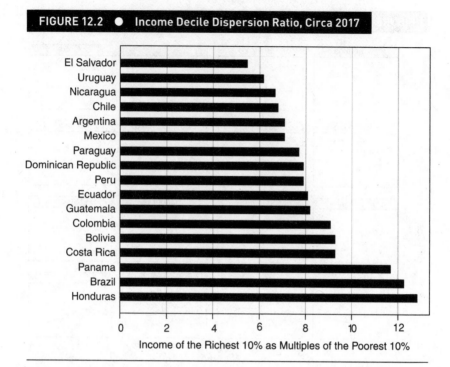

FIGURE 12.2 ● Income Decile Dispersion Ratio, Circa 2017

Income of the Richest 10% as Multiples of the Poorest 10%

Source: LAC Equity Lab, SEDLAC, and World Development Indicators, April 2019.

While the decile dispersion measure is highly correlated with the Gini coefficient, the ranking of a few countries is quite different. For instance, Nicaragua and Chile are in the middle of the distribution when it comes to the Gini coefficient but rank among the top four most equal countries in terms of the decile dispersion. Bolivia, in contrast, ranks comparatively worse in terms of the decile dispersion measure than in terms of the Gini coefficient. Part of the reason for this discrepancy is that the decile dispersion measure focuses solely on incomes at the top and the bottom of the distribution, ignoring those in the middle, while the Gini coefficient considers the entire distribution.

When examining this indicator over time, we find that from the early 2000s to 2017, all 17 Latin American countries experienced decreasing levels of rich–poor income dispersion. The average change in the region was around 6 points. The most significant changes occurred in Bolivia and Panama, followed by El Salvador and Colombia. The country with the smallest change in income dispersion during this period was Costa Rica. Uruguay also experienced relatively little change, but it is worth noting that this country had the lowest level of income dispersion in the early 2000s and remained among the most equal in 2017.

To sum up, the evidence shows that, despite remaining a region with a highly unequal distribution of income, Latin America has made a notable shift toward lower inequality in the first two decades of the 21st century. We have also shown important differences within the region, with some countries remaining much more unequal than others. Together with information on poverty, a topic addressed in the next section, the figures presented here provide an illuminating picture of Latin America's social context.

Poverty Rates

The proportion of Latin Americans living in poverty remains high. According to the Economic Commission for Latin America and the Caribbean (ECLAC), in 2018, 30.1 percent of the region's population was classified as poor.[35] This number, while high, is significantly better than the rate of poverty in 2002, which stood at 45.4 percent of the population. The proportion of the population classified as extremely poor was 10.7 percent in 2018, a slight improvement from 2002, when the rate was 12.2 percent.

Each country measures poverty in a different manner, which makes comparisons difficult. To overcome this problem, ECLAC uses a common methodology to provide a regional perspective that is as comparable as possible. A person is classified as poor when the per capita income of that person's household is below the poverty line, which is the minimum income needed to meet a person's basic needs. Extreme poverty reflects a situation in which the per capita income of the household is not enough to buy a food basket that satisfies its basic nutritional needs. Table 12.1 provides ECLAC information on poverty and extreme poverty in 18 Latin American countries.

The country with the lowest poverty rate is Uruguay, where less than 3 percent of the population is classified as poor. It is followed by Chile, with close to 11 percent of its population below the poverty line. Next are Panama and Costa Rica. Extreme poverty is lowest in Uruguay, with only 0.1 percent of the population falling into this category. It is also low in Chile, Argentina, and Peru, which have rates below 4 percent.

TABLE 12.1 ● Poverty and Extreme Poverty			
Country	Year	Percentage in Poverty	Percentage in Extreme Poverty
Argentina	2018	24.4	3.6
Bolivia	2018	33.2	14.7
Brazil	2018	19.4	5.4
Chile	2017	10.7	1.4
Colombia	2018	29.9	10.8
Costa Rica	2018	16.2	4.0
Dominican Republic	2018	22.0	5.0

(Continued)

TABLE 12.1 ● (Continued)			
Ecuador	2018	24.2	6.5
El Salvador	2018	34.5	7.6
Guatemala	2014	50.5	15.4
Honduras	2018	55.8	19.4
Mexico	2018	41.5	10.6
Nicaragua	2014	46.3	18.3
Panama	2018	14.5	6.2
Paraguay	2018	19.5	6.5
Peru	2018	16.8	3.7
Uruguay	2018	2.9	0.1
Venezuela	2014	28.3	12.0

Source: Economic Commission for Latin America and the Caribbean (ECLAC). 2019. *Social Panorama of Latin America 2019*. Santiago, Chile: United Nations; Economic Commission for Latin America and the Caribbean (ECLAC). 2018. *Medición de la pobreza por ingresos: actualización metodológica y resultados*. Santiago, Chile: United Nations.

At the other end of the ranking are Honduras and Guatemala, with poverty rates above 50 percent of the population. Nicaragua and Mexico also fare quite badly, with poverty rates above 40 percent. The highest rates of extreme poverty are in Honduras, Nicaragua, and Guatemala, where more than 15 percent of the population lives in such conditions. Rates of extreme poverty are also high in Bolivia and Venezuela.

An alternative indicator of poverty used extensively measures the percentage of people living on less than a specific dollar figure a day. According to the World Bank, for upper-middle-income countries, that amount is $5.50 per person a day.[36] Figure 12.3 shows data on the percentage of the population living on less than this amount a day in 17 Latin American countries for the period 2000–2017.

As the figure shows, the proportion of people living on less than $5.50 a day has shrunk significantly since the beginning of the 21st century. All these Latin American countries, except for Guatemala, made visible improvements. When comparing the earliest to the latest available data, we find the largest reductions in poverty in Bolivia (from 62.1 percent to 24.7 percent), Colombia (from 60.5 percent to 27.6 percent), and Ecuador (from 52.5 percent to 23.9 percent).

According to this indicator, the countries with the lowest proportion of poor in the population are Uruguay and Chile, which coincides with

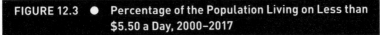

FIGURE 12.3   ●   Percentage of the Population Living on Less than $5.50 a Day, 2000–2017

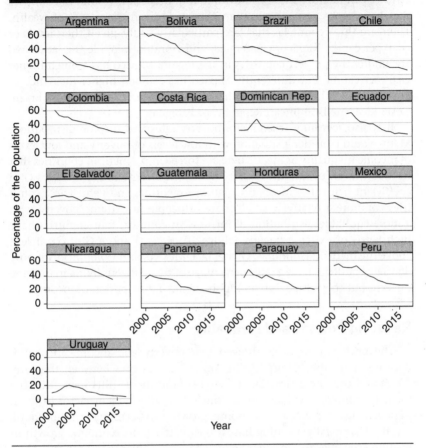

Source: LAC Equity Lab, SEDLAC, and World Development Indicators (June 2019).

the findings stemming from the previously discussed measure of poverty provided by ECLAC. In Uruguay, only 2.9 percent of its population lives on less than $5.50 a day, while in Chile, the figure is 6.4 percent. The following three countries with the lowest proportion of poor are Argentina, Costa Rica, and Panama, in this order.

At the other end, the countries with the largest share of poor in the population are Honduras, Guatemala, and Nicaragua, which also fare badly according to the indicator discussed previously. In Honduras, the percentage of the population living on less than $5.50 a day is about 50 percent, and in Guatemala, it is close to 49 percent.

Both poverty measures presented here strongly correlate with country data on gross domestic product (GDP) per capita, which is a measure of the country's economic output divided by population. GDP per capita is the most common measure utilized to represent a country's level of prosperity. Based on a simple bivariate association between GDP per capita and poverty, we can identify those countries that underperform—that is, countries that have more poor people than expected, given their level of wealth. There are three countries that fare particularly badly, given their levels of GDP per capita: Mexico, Guatemala, and Honduras. While the latter two are among the poorest countries in the region, Mexico has a much higher GDP per capita. Put differently, Mexico has a much higher incidence of poverty than other countries with a lower GDP per capita, such as Brazil, Costa Rica, the Dominican Republic, or Paraguay.

It is also revealing to compare poverty rates and income distribution. Many would consider a situation with low levels of poverty and low levels of income inequality as ideal. There are three Latin American countries that have low levels of extreme poverty (below 5 percent) and also have a Gini coefficient below the median: Uruguay, Argentina, and Peru. These countries combine a relatively small share of people in extreme poverty with a more equitable distribution of income. In contrast, four countries have high levels of extreme poverty (above 10 percent) and a Gini coefficient above the median: Honduras, Guatemala, Mexico, and Colombia. Not only do these countries have a large percentage of their citizens living in extreme poverty, but they also exhibit a highly unequal distribution of income.

Reducing Poverty and Inequality

The prior two sections showed that poverty and income inequality declined markedly in most Latin American countries between the early 2000s and the late 2010s. The reasons behind these shifts have been the focus of numerous studies. Most conclude that the main factor explaining decreases in poverty is economic growth.[37] As economist Dani Rodrik put it, "Historically, nothing has worked better than economic growth in enabling societies to improve the life chances of their members, including those at the very bottom."[38] In 18 of the 20 years between 2000 and 2019, Latin America experienced positive GDP growth.

Another contributing factor to the decline in poverty has been a reduction in income inequality. Although less significant than the rise of average incomes, its contribution is still considered crucial for preventing a backslide during less favorable economic contexts.[39]

Declining inequality during the first part of the 21st century has been attributed to two different processes: a change in relative wages benefiting workers at the bottom of the income distribution and improvements in government transfers.[40]

The wages of affluent and low-income workers may become more equal as a result of "good" or "bad" developments. For example, if wages decline for all workers but less abruptly for those at the bottom of the income distribution, then wages should become more equal. Yet, this is clearly a negative development for all workers. Economists have concluded that the move toward greater wage equality that took place in Latin America from about 2002 until the first part of the 2010s was the result of a "good" process. It came about as a result of increasing wages that benefited workers at the top and the bottom of the income ladder but were particularly advantageous to the lowest-paid workers.[41]

A decline in the skill premium—the added income provided by more years of education and work experience—is the most common explanation for the equalizing effect of wage improvements. While more-educated and more-experienced workers continued to receive higher wages than less-educated and inexperienced workers, the difference became less pronounced.[42] Another explanation is that unskilled workers benefited from increases in domestic demand[43] as a result of improvements in terms of trade[44]—itself a consequence of a price boom in the commodities exported by Latin American countries and the flow of capital into the region.[45]

Government transfers were the second channel contributing to improvements in income distribution. The most salient of these government initiatives targeting the poor were **conditional cash transfer (CCT) programs** and noncontributory social pensions.[46]

CCTs have been widely credited with reducing both poverty and inequality in the region. CCTs distribute cash payments to low-income families when they participate in educational, health, nutrition, or other services that are considered beneficial to overcoming poverty. So, they support consumption among the poor while encouraging the accumulation of human capital. They began in the mid-1990s, first in Brazil, then in Chile, and later in Mexico. Currently, almost all countries in Latin America have some form of CCT program.

Many Latin American countries have also put noncontributory social pensions in place, which consist of monetary transfers by the government to elderly and disabled individuals who have not worked in the formal labor market or have not made contributions toward social security during their working life. Many Latin Americans work in the **informal sector**, where they and their employers do not contribute to the set of health, pension, and other related programs commonly required by labor legislation. For this and other reasons, more than half of the Latin American population is not covered by established contributory pension systems. The noncontributory pension programs were put in place to try to fill the gap in social security generated by this problem. While only a few countries in the region had these programs in the 1990s, they are now a staple across the region.

In addition to CCTs and pensions, other policies are often promoted to help reduce income inequality. Before concluding, we will briefly review the potential benefits and challenges of four such policies: increasing the **minimum wage**, establishing protections for job losses, improving access to education, and tax reform.

Increases in the minimum wage are often advocated to reduce income inequality. They can help raise low-wage workers above the poverty line and reduce the gap between high and low earners. Increases in the minimum wage are more likely to attain their desired effect when the economy is growing. The impact of minimum wage increases on income inequality, however, is affected by the proportion of individuals employed in the informal sector (i.e., where productive activities by employers and employees are not taxed, regulated, or registered by the government). In countries where many people work in the informal sector, as is the case in Latin America, increases in the minimum wage have a limited effect on improving the earnings of low-income individuals. In some instances, raising the minimum wage may exacerbate distributional inequities. This would be the case, for example, if it increases unemployment or moves workers from the formal to the informal sector, where wages are typically lower.

Another approach is to put in place policies that protect individuals from job losses. Most Latin American countries have sought to achieve this goal by requiring **severance payments** (i.e., a lump sum payment given to a worker when they are laid off or fired for an unjust cause). Large severance payments often lead to unintended consequences. For example, they create incentives for firms to shorten job tenures, litigate the cause of separation, and hire permanent workers under temporary contracts, all of which ultimately hinder productivity and discourage the creation of formal employment.[47] Unemployment insurance, funded by regular payments made by employers for their employees, is considered a better instrument to smooth income disparities, improve productivity, lower costs associated with litigation, and promote formal employment of longer duration.[48]

Few countries in Latin America have unemployment insurance in place and, in those that do, less than half of the workforce is covered. Unemployment insurance can be a better instrument than severance payments to protect workers during unemployment. However, its potential benefits can be rather minor in countries where a large share of jobs remains in the informal sector. In those instances, many workers would not enjoy coverage or may have incentives to claim unemployment benefits even while working in the informal sector.

Many also advocate expanding education as a strategy to reduce income inequality. We know that increasing education has a favorable impact on an individual's income. Education does help to lift people out of poverty, but the relationship between education and income inequality is rather complex.[49]

Consider the following: If one additional year of education adds, let us say, 10 percent to a person's wage on average, the impact that it will have on income inequality depends on whether this return differs among people at different levels of education. If the gain in income from the extra year of schooling is greater at higher levels of schooling, then increasing education will lead to increases in inequality. This phenomenon has been labeled "the paradox of progress" because education expansion is accompanied by greater inequality.[50] Economists describe this education–earnings relationship as concave.

In contrast, if the gain in income from the extra year of schooling is lower at higher levels of schooling, then increasing education will reduce inequality. Economists describe this education–earnings relationship as convex. The evidence with regards to Latin America shows that the returns to tertiary education increased significantly in the 1990s, contributing to inequality, but then fell in the subsequent two decades, helping to reduce income disparities.[51]

One promising approach to tackling economic disparities is to focus on decreasing educational inequality. More precisely, policies aimed at closing the educational gap between the rich and the poor, reducing dropout rates, and increasing the educational attainment of less-well-off social groups are likely to reduce income inequality.

Lastly, experts have suggested that changes to the tax system can also help to make the distribution of income more equitable.[52] Taxes raise revenues that finance transfers to low-income people as well as expenditures on health and education. Tax evasion and avoidance is a major problem in Latin American countries; improving enforcement should provide significant additional resources that could be used to boost the opportunities available to the poor.

It would also be beneficial for countries to rely less on **consumption taxes** and more on income and property taxes.[53] Taxes on consumption, which are predominant in most Latin American countries, place a greater burden on middle- and low-income groups than on more well-off individuals.

Increasing income taxes on the wealthy, which is a common demand when attempting to reduce inequality, is not as simple a solution as it may sound. Latin American countries already have progressive income tax systems, which require those with higher incomes to pay a larger share. For instance, it has been estimated that, in most Latin American countries, 90 percent or more of income tax has been collected from individuals with the highest 20 percent of incomes.[54]

The maximum rates in the tax codes are not very low (they range between 25 percent and 40 percent), but the actual rates paid by those with high incomes are much lower because of exemptions and deductions as well as tax evasion.[55] Increasing enforcement, eliminating exemptions, and raising taxes on capital income may bring about more revenue. But many economists are skeptical about the effectiveness of changes in income tax rates as a strategy to improve inequality. Taxes change relative prices and alter the decisions made by individuals and businesses. Excessively high taxes can hurt growth, increase unemployment, foster tax evasion, and push people toward the informal sector.

In conclusion, we have reviewed the most prominent explanations for the decline in poverty and income inequality in Latin America during the early 21st century. Economic growth has been the main engine in reducing poverty in the region. Improvements in income inequality have also helped. While Latin America is still a region with high disparities in wealth, in the first two decades of this century, most countries reduced income inequality. One significant reason behind this change was an improvement in wages, which primarily benefited those with lower incomes. Also relevant were government transfers, such as CCTs and noncontributory pensions.

These instruments should also prove valuable to help the poor in more difficult economic contexts, preventing a backslide to greater inequality. Also, this section briefly reviewed other potential policy instruments to reduce income inequality—increasing the minimum wage, establishing protections for job loss, enhancing access to education, and tax reform. Improving our understanding of the connection between policies and socio-economic outcomes should make us more aware of the difficulties entailed in designing programs to reduce poverty and income inequality.

The Gender Gap

Social inequality is exacerbated by the disadvantages confronted by women. Despite significant improvements over the last decades, women continue to face major obstacles to their development, which have negative consequences for their personal freedom as well as for society at large. Unequal opportunities in education and the labor market, for instance, can make it harder for women to compete on an equal footing with men. It is also fundamentally unfair. Reducing gender-based disparities can improve economic performance, reduce poverty, advance the goal of equal rights, and help prevent violence against women.

Latin America is a region with high levels of violence and widespread perceptions of insecurity, as noted in Chapter 11. About two thirds of adult women in Latin America report not feeling safe walking alone at night in the areas where they live.[56] The levels of violence against women are also unacceptably high. The term **femicide**—the assassination of women because of their gender—has been used in reference to gender-related killings.[57] Most of the intentional homicides of women in Latin America are femicides, and most of these are committed by an intimate or former intimate partner.[58] Intimate partner violence is pervasive in Latin America. The proportion of women (aged 15–49) in the region reporting physical or sexual violence by an intimate partner ranges from about one in seven to more than half.[59]

In 2015, a group of women in Argentina began to organize and march against gender-based violence. This movement, which rallied under the slogan *Ni Una Menos* (*Not One Less*), organized the first-ever mass strike of women in response to the murder of a pregnant 16-year-old girl who had been beaten to death by her boyfriend. Since then, the movement has spread to many other Latin American countries and has developed links with several organizations fighting for women's rights. This activism has contributed to the enactment of legislation that specifically criminalizes femicide.

One of the biggest obstacles in the quest to achieve greater equality between men and women is deep-rooted attitudes. Public opinion surveys show that a large proportion of the world population believes that wife-beating is justified. One survey question, compiled by UNICEF and the World Bank, asks women whether a husband/partner is justified in hitting or beating his wife/partner for any of the following five reasons: arguing with him, refusing to have sex, burning food, going out without telling him, or neglecting the children.[60] The share of Latin American women who believe a husband is justified in beating his wife is much lower than the world average. Yet, in some countries for which data are available, the share is disturbingly high. For example, the proportion of women answering yes to such a question is around 17 percent in Haiti, 16 percent in Bolivia, 14 percent in Nicaragua, and 12 percent in Honduras.

Attitudes regarding gender roles in the family are also informative of the challenges ahead. For example, in 2014, the Pew Research Center conducted a survey in Latin America that asked people whether they agreed with the statement, "A wife must always obey her husband."[61] The percentage of respondents who completely or mostly agreed with this statement appears in Table 12.2. The results show that although women are less likely

TABLE 12.2 ● Percentage Who Agree That a Wife Must Obey Her Husband		
Country	Men	Women
Argentina	34	28
Bolivia	67	51
Brazil	70	58
Chile	30	19
Colombia	56	45
Costa Rica	51	46
Dominican Republic	84	77
Ecuador	61	54
El Salvador	71	65
Guatemala	82	78
Honduras	82	79
Mexico	49	41
Nicaragua	74	63
Panama	75	65
Paraguay	58	43
Peru	58	45
Uruguay	26	21
Venezuela	72	58

Source: Pew Research Center. 2014.

than men to agree with such an assertion, in most countries, a majority of both men and women embrace traditional mores about gender roles in the family. In only four countries—Chile, Uruguay, Argentina, and Mexico—did more people disagree than agree with this statement.

Gender equality demands not only tackling the problem of violence and sexism but also creating opportunities for the empowerment of women. One related area in which Latin America has made significant progress is in women's education. Literacy rates are only slightly higher for men, but this is primarily the result of differences among older adults. For people aged 15 to 24, there is virtually no gender difference, and literacy rates for young women are above 98 percent in most countries.[62] The distribution of years of education within each gender is also fairly equal: The same proportion of women and men are classified as having low levels of education (about 46 percent), and women slightly overperform men in terms of having high levels of education (20 percent of women versus 18 percent of men).[63] Moreover, in secondary and tertiary education, the enrollment rates of women actually surpass those of men.

Despite these improvements in literacy rates and enrollment in educational institutions, women remain underrepresented in science, technology, engineering, and mathematics (STEM) disciplines. Only 35 percent of graduates in these areas are women.[64] These disciplines offer the best prospects for employment; fewer women in these fields means lower opportunities in the kind of skills required by the new technological environment.

Another crucial area with noticeable improvements is health. Between 1990 and 2015, all Latin American countries, except Venezuela, reduced maternal mortality rates. Eleven countries cut rates by more than 50 percent. In Peru, for instance, the maternal mortality rate dropped from 251 per 100,000 live births to 68. The best performers were Uruguay and Chile, which, in 2015, had a maternal mortality rate of 15 and 22 respectively.[65] In addition, the proportion of women receiving at least some prenatal care also increased and is now higher than 95 percent in most countries in the region. There is still substantial room for improvement, but progress in this area is evident.

Also important is paid maternity leave, which gives women greater autonomy, has positive health effects on infants and their mothers, and brings economic security to families facing this major life event. Currently, all Latin American countries have legislation in place making paid maternity leave mandatory, with almost all countries offering at least 12 weeks of such leave.

Most examinations of gender inequality pay particular attention to two categories: women in public office and economic opportunities. The rest of this chapter reviews the gender gap as it applies to these two areas.

Women in Public Office

Most countries around the world have never had a female head of government or state. Latin America is no different. As of 2019, only seven Latin American countries have had a female head of government: Argentina, Brazil, Chile, Costa Rica, Haiti, Nicaragua, and Panama.[66] The first woman president in Latin America was Isabel Martínez de Perón in Argentina. She had been elected vice president and became the head of state after the death of her husband, Juan Perón, in 1974. Martínez de Perón was deposed from power in a military coup in March of 1976. The first elected female president was Violeta Chamorro, who became Nicaragua's head of state in 1990 and stayed in power until the end of her term in January 1997. Since then, five other women have been elected president: Mireya Moscoso in Panama (1999–2004), Michelle Bachelet in Chile (2006–2010 and 2011–2016), Cristina Fernández de Kirchner in Argentina (2007–2011 and 2011–2015), Laura Chinchilla in Costa Rica (2010–2014), and Dilma Rousseff in Brazil (2014–2018). In Haiti, which has a semi-presidential system, two women have been elected prime minister: Claudette Werleigh (1995–1996), and Michèle Pierre-Louis (2008–2009).

In comparison to other parts of the world, Latin America has done much better in terms of the share of women elected to congress. The representation of women has been boosted by legislation requiring political parties to nominate a specific percentage of women to congress. As noted in Chapter 6 of this book, gender quotas were first introduced in Argentina in 1991 and, in subsequent years, almost all Latin American countries adopted some version of them. In Latin America, the average share of women in the lower or single chamber of congress was 29.3 percent in 2019. This number is higher than the share of women in the lower or single chambers of Europe (28.6 percent), the United States (23.5 percent), or other regions of the world. In the upper chambers, the Latin American average is 23.7 percent, which is close to the world average of 24.1 percent. Information on each of the 20 Latin American countries is presented in Table 12.3.

Five Latin American countries have more than 40 percent of women in their single or lower chambers. In Cuba's parliament and Bolivia's lower chamber, there are more women than men. In the upper chambers, Bolivia and Mexico are the only ones that come close to gender parity. The worst performer is Haiti, where women make up less than 3 percent in the lower chamber and less than 4 percent in the Senate. Brazil and Paraguay also exhibit a significant gender gap.

Women are not only underrepresented as heads of government but also as members of the executive cabinet. On average, women make up about one fourth of cabinet appointments. The percentages for each country are shown in Table 12.4. These data show that Nicaragua in the period 2012–2017 is the only case in which the share of women in the cabinet came close to parity. Next comes Chile in the period 2014–2018, when women held 36.2 percent of cabinet appointments. The lowest shares were in Brazil in the period 2011–2014, when only 5 percent of cabinet appointments were held by women.

TABLE 12.3 ● Percentage of Women in Congress, 2019		
Country	Single House or Lower House	Senate
Argentina	38.8	41.7
Bolivia	53.1	47.2
Brazil	15.0	14.8
Chile	22.6	23.3
Colombia	18.1	20.4
Costa Rica	45.6	~
Cuba	53.2	~
Dominican Republic	26.8	9.4
Ecuador	38.0	~
El Salvador	31.0	~
Guatemala	19.0	~
Haiti	2.5	3.6
Honduras	21.1	~
Mexico	48.2	49.2
Nicaragua	44.6	~
Panama	18.3	~
Paraguay	15.0	20.0
Peru	30.0	~
Uruguay	22.2	25.8
Venezuela	22.2	~

Source: Inter-Parliamentary Union, January 2019.

The composition of the highest courts also exhibits a wide gender gap. On average, only 30 percent of seats in these courts go to female judges. Information from each country as of 2017 appears in Table 12.4. Gender parity, or close to it, was only achieved in the highest courts of Cuba, Guatemala, Venezuela, and Ecuador. In Uruguay, the share of women judges also was comparatively high (40 percent).

The different measures of women's participation in public office are not highly correlated, but some countries rank high in more than one

TABLE 12.4 ● Women in Cabinets and High Courts			
	Women in the Cabinet		Percentage of Women in the Highest Tribunal (2017)
Country	Period	Percentage	
Argentina	2011–2015	11.1	20.0
Bolivia	2010–2015	27.8	33.3
Brazil	2011–2014	4.9	18.2
Chile	2014–2018	36.2	23.8
Colombia	2014–2018	27.6	13.0
Costa Rica	2014–2018	32.4	31.6
Cuba	2011–2016	25.0	55.0
Dominican Republic	2012–2016	18.2	17.6
Ecuador	2013–2017	33.3	47.6
El Salvador	2014–2019	20.0	33.3
Guatemala	2012–2016	21.7	53.8
Haiti	2004–2006	29.0	–
Honduras	2014–2018	21.7	33.3
Mexico	2012–2018	18.8	18.2
Nicaragua	2012–2017	47.1	31.3
Panama	2014–2019	19.0	11.1
Paraguay	2013–2018	29.4	22.2
Peru	2011–2016	31.8	21.1
Uruguay	2010–2015	35.7	40.0
Venezuela	2013–2019	22.3	50.0

Source: ECLAC, CEPALSTAT (2018).

indicator, such as Cuba, Nicaragua, Costa Rica, and Ecuador. Others rank poorly in more than one indicator, such as Brazil, Panama, and Haiti; however, all three of these countries have had women as heads of government. Nonetheless, it is clear that despite improvements over time and significant achievements in comparison to other parts of the world, women in Latin America remain underrepresented in public office. Increasing the presence of women in political office not only promotes the empowerment of women but has also been associated with greater advocacy for women's and children's interests[67] and higher investment in health and social welfare.[68]

Economic Participation and the Income Gap

For a very long time, cultural and legal conventions restricted the entry of women into the labor force. To be considered as part of the labor force, a person must be either employed or actively seeking a job. Women's participation in the labor market is not only an important contributor to economic development and family income but also empowers women at home and in society at large.

The participation of women in the labor force expanded significantly over the last fifty years. In 1960, only two out of ten women in Latin America were part of it. By 1990, the share of women in the workforce had increased to a regional average of 45 percent, and in 2018, it reached 57 percent, which is higher than the world average of 53 percent.[69]

This growth follows a global trend that has been connected with changes in governmental regulations and people's attitudes, including the erosion of the social stigma attached to married women working. In Latin America, adult women are now more educated, have fewer children, and are more likely to be single than a few decades ago, all of which have been associated with greater participation in the labor market.[70]

Another useful indicator to illustrate the economic participation of women is the female share of the total labor force. As expected, this indicator also captures the improvements seen in the incorporation of women over the last few decades. In 1990, women in Latin America made up around 35 percent of the total labor force, but by 2018, their share had grown to almost 41 percent, which is slightly higher than the world average of 39 percent.[71]

To more fully understand the economic participation of women, it is important to recognize the importance of unpaid work. Unpaid work includes time spent caring for one's home and family members (e.g., children, the elderly, and persons with disabilities) or supporting another household. Although indispensable, this activity is frequently devalued by society. Available data show that in Latin America, women spend over five hours a day (on average) on unpaid work, while men spend a bit less than two hours a day.[72]

Differences in remuneration are also commonplace. The gender pay gap is a much-discussed measure of the inequality of wages between men and women. The cumulative impact of lower wages can be substantial, hindering women's ability to save and buy a home and leading to lower pensions and a higher incidence of poverty in old age.

One way to calculate this difference is by measuring the proportion of male wages women earn. If this indicator equals 100, it means that, on average, women earn as much as men. If it equals 75 percent, it means that the gender gap is 25 percent. Figure 12.4 presents data for 18 Latin American countries, showing the salary of women as a percentage of the salary of men at the beginning of the 2000s and the end of the 2010s.[73]

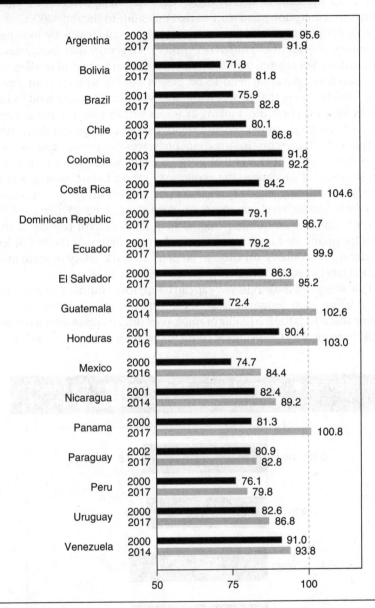

FIGURE 12.4 ● Salary of Women as a Percentage of the Salary of Men

Country	Year	Value
Argentina	2003	95.6
	2017	91.9
Bolivia	2002	71.8
	2017	81.8
Brazil	2001	75.9
	2017	82.8
Chile	2003	80.1
	2017	86.8
Colombia	2003	91.8
	2017	92.2
Costa Rica	2000	84.2
	2017	104.6
Dominican Republic	2000	79.1
	2017	96.7
Ecuador	2001	79.2
	2017	99.9
El Salvador	2000	86.3
	2017	95.2
Guatemala	2000	72.4
	2014	102.6
Honduras	2001	90.4
	2016	103.0
Mexico	2000	74.7
	2016	84.4
Nicaragua	2001	82.4
	2014	89.2
Panama	2000	81.3
	2017	100.8
Paraguay	2002	80.9
	2017	82.8
Peru	2000	76.1
	2017	79.8
Uruguay	2000	82.6
	2017	86.8
Venezuela	2000	91.0
	2014	93.8

Source: ECLAC, CEPALSTAT (2018).

In almost all Latin American countries, the gender pay gap has diminished over time. At the beginning of the 21st century, the average salary of women was about 82 percent that of men, but by the late 2010s, that number was 92 percent. This means that the pay gap was reduced from 18 percent to 8 percent, which is a substantial improvement. Moreover, in five countries—Costa Rica, Guatemala, Honduras, Panama, and Ecuador—the average wages of women were about the same or slightly higher than the average wages of men. No Latin American country had reached that milestone in the early 2000s.

Calculating differences between male and female wages by looking at all workers irrespective of differences other than gender may mask relevant information. For example, in Latin America, the percentage of workers with high levels of education tend to be greater among women than among men. We also know that people with more years of schooling tend to have higher salaries. Therefore, looking at wages within groups having similar levels of education can be very informative in terms of gender differences.

Figure 12.5 presents information on wages by gender and years of schooling in 2017. It shows that once we examine wages for people with similar levels of education, the gender pay gap in Latin America is larger than previously suggested. The gender pay gap within groups of workers who have similar levels of education goes from about 21 percent to 17 percent, which is substantially higher than the 8 percent pay gap derived from the unadjusted measure shown in the prior figure. At the lowest level of education, women earn close to 80 percent of the salary of men; at the highest level of education, that figure comes close to 83 percent.

Calculations of the gender pay gap can be improved further if we have additional information besides education. For instance, age is another important feature that affects the job profile of employees, since it approximates the labor market experience of individuals. Furthermore, prior research has shown that

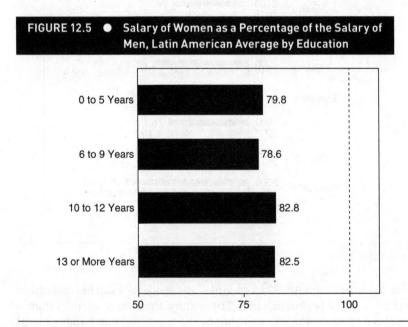

FIGURE 12.5 ● Salary of Women as a Percentage of the Salary of Men, Latin American Average by Education

0 to 5 Years   79.8

6 to 9 Years   78.6

10 to 12 Years   82.8

13 or More Years   82.5

50   75   100

Source: ECLAC, CEPALSTAT (2018).

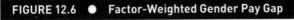

FIGURE 12.6 ● Factor-Weighted Gender Pay Gap

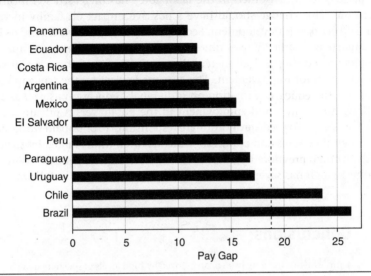

Source: International Labour Organization. 2018. *Global Wage Report 2018/19*, Geneva: ILO.

women are more likely than men to work part-time and in the public sector, which is important to take into consideration. The International Labour Organization, which is part of the United Nations, has developed a factor-weighted pay gap measure that incorporates information on workers' education, age, full-time versus part-time status, and public versus private sector employment. Figure 12.6 shows the gap between women's and men's wages in 11 Latin American countries based on this measure.

The differences in women's to men's wages estimated by this method are larger than those provided by the unadjusted method previously shown. In total, nine of the eleven Latin American countries included in this study have a gender pay gap below the world average, which equals 18.8 percent (shown as a dashed vertical line in Figure 12.6). The smallest gap based on the factor-weighted measure is in Panama, where women earn (on average) 11 percent less than men. Three other countries have a gender pay gap of between 10 percent and 15 percent: Ecuador, Costa Rica, and Argentina. All four of these countries rank better than the United States, where the factor-weighted gender pay gap is 15.3 percent. The widest gaps are in Brazil (26.4 percent) and Chile (23.7 percent).

The picture presented so far would be incomplete without pointing out that many women do not have an income of their own. In Latin America, 29 percent of women ages 15 and older do not have their own source of income.[74] The proportion of men in that situation is about 11 percent. Economic dependence restricts women's individual freedom and opportunities, undermines their ability to secure health benefits and education, and makes them more vulnerable to domestic violence.

To conclude, this section has identified four important findings. First, the participation of women in the labor force has increased significantly over time. This change should have a positive impact on family income and help economic development. Second, the pay gap between genders has also improved markedly over time. This is most evident when comparing the unadjusted wages of all men and women. However, there is still substantial room for improvement. This was made clear by the pay gap measures adjusted using information on individuals' education as well as age, working-time status, and employment in the public versus private sector. Third, women carry a disproportionate responsibility for unpaid work, such as household chores and childcare, which is often undervalued by society. Lastly, women are more likely than men to lack an independent source of income, which has several harmful consequences for their well-being.

Conclusions

Latin America has long been characterized by high levels of social inequality, and many of its countries have a sizeable portion of their population living in poverty. Reducing income and gender inequalities and ending poverty are some of the greatest challenges facing governments in the region. The evidence presented in this chapter shows substantial improvements: a marked reduction in poverty and extreme poverty since at least the 1990s and a more equitable distribution of income since the beginning of the 21st century. And yet, there is still much to be done. High levels of income inequality undermine social mobility across generations, exacerbate distrust among individuals, and make poverty reduction more difficult. Inequality of opportunity has also been found to hurt economic growth. Leveling the playing field is not only a matter of fairness but also a concern of most Latin Americans.

This chapter presented an overview of poverty and inequality trends over time and across Latin American countries. They illustrate how the region has changed and how major cross-national differences persist. Our discussion also addressed the causes of these changes and some common policy prescriptions. It underlined the benefits of economic growth and the importance of targeted government transfers.

Progress also demands efforts to tackle the persistent inequalities faced by women. Visible improvements in health, education, and participation in the labor market are encouraging, but substantial gaps remain in other areas. Latin American women are often the victims of violence and, in most instances, this violence is perpetrated by partners or former partners. Latin American countries have passed legislation penalizing femicides, but legal weapons are not enough; biased practices and attitudes regarding gender roles pose a major obstacle to achieving greater equality. Improving the representation of women in public office should help, while the shrinking of the gender pay gap should contribute to women's economic empowerment. Increased activism by Latin American women and favorable attitudes regarding gender equality by the youngest generations are welcome developments in the pursuit of a fairer society.

Key Terms

Conditional cash transfers
   (CCTs) 323
Decile dispersion ratio 317
Education 312
Femicide 326

Gender pay gap 312
Gini coefficient 312
Income inequality 312
Informal sector 323
Poverty 312

Bibliographic Recommendations

ECLAC. 2019. *Social Panorama of Latin America 2019*. Santiago, Chile: United Nations.

Francisco H. G. Ferreira, Julián Messina, Jamele Rigolini, Luis-Felipe López-Calva, Maria Ana Lugo, and Renos Vakis. 2013. *Overview: Economic Mobility and the Rise of the Latin American Middle Class*. Washington, DC: World Bank.

Nora Lustig, Luis F. Lopez-Calva, and Edmundo Ortiz-Juarez. 2013. "Deconstructing the Decline in Inequality in Latin America." Policy Research Working Paper 6552. World Bank, Washington DC.

Julián Messina and Joana Silva. 2018. "Wage Inequality in Latin America: Understanding the Past to Prepare to the Future." *Latin American Development Forum*. Washington, DC: World Bank.

Jeffrey G. Williamson. 2015. "Latin American Inequality: Colonial Origins, Commodity Booms, or a Missed Twentieth-Century Leveling?" *Journal of Human Development and Capabilities* 16(3): 324–341.

World Economic Forum. 2018. *The Global Gender Gap Report 2018*. Geneva: Author.

Web Resources

Economic Commission for Latin America and the Caribbean (ECLAC), CEPALSTAT: https://estadisticas.cepal.org/cepalstat/Portada.html

LAC Equity Lab at The World Bank: https://www.worldbank.org/en/topic/poverty/lac-equity-lab1/overview

Socio-Economic Database for Latin America and the Caribbean (CEDLAS and The World Bank): http://www.cedlas.econo.unlp.edu.ar/wp/en/estadisticas/

World Development Indicators: http://datatopics.worldbank.org/world-development-indicators/

• Glossary •

19th of April Movement (M-19): an urban guerilla group in Colombia formed in the early 1970s and demobilized in 1990 that advocated for a populist nationalism of the left.

26th of July Movement (M-26-7): a Cuban political organization created in 1955 and led by Fidel Castro, which would eventually overthrow the authoritarian regime of President Fulgencio Batista in 1959. Its name originated from a failed attack on the Moncada army barracks on July 26, 1953.

Audiencia: the highest appellate court in Spanish America, which also had some legislative and executive functions.

Administrative decree: a type of executive decree that codifies ministerial decisions.

Amendatory veto: a type of veto power that gives the president the power to not only delete parts of a bill but also to add text or amendments to it.

Anti-drug certification process: after the passage of an anti-drug bill in 1986, the United States began conducting a controversial process by which it certifies whether a government in a major drug-producing or drug-transit country is cooperating in anti-narcotic efforts. If a country is decertified, it risks losing foreign assistance from the United States and having the United States oppose loan requests in multilateral development banks.

Authoritarianism: a non-democratic form of government. It is typically characterized by the absence of both competitive elections to choose the country's rulers and alternation in power. More encompassing definitions also refer to limited political participation and recurrent government violations of fundamental rights.

Bay of Pigs invasion: a failed military invasion of Cuba by an exile force trained and funded by the CIA that took place in April of 1961. The principal landing occurred at a beach named Playa Girón in the Bay of Pigs.

Bicameralism: the practice of having a congress with two separate legislative chambers.

Block veto: a type of veto power that gives the president the power to reject a bill in its entirety.

Cabildos: town councils in Spanish America, composed of magistrates and councilors and empowered with some judicial duties and the ability to manage town lands, impose local taxes, issue building permits, and coordinate the formation of self-defense forces.

Castas: the caste system put in place in the Spanish colonies after the abolishment of indigenous slavery, which entailed a set of rights and responsibilities based on ethnicity.

Civil liberties: a set of core freedoms that mostly fall within the concept of negative rights.

Clientelism: refers to the distribution of selective benefits in exchange for electoral support.

Closed-list proportional representation: a type of proportional election rule where voters cast a single vote for a party list composed of ranked candidates. Votes are aggregated by party, and seats are distributed to parties according to their share of the vote. If a party wins seats, these are allocated to the candidates of the party according to their ranking on the list. Voters cannot alter the ranking of candidates on the party list.

Cold War: denotes the state of hostility that existed between the United States and the Soviet Union from the end of World War II until the unification of Germany (1990) or the dissolution of the Soviet Union (1991), depending on the source.

Compulsory voting: a legal requirement making voting mandatory.

Conditional cash transfer (CCT) programs: government programs that distribute cash payments to low-income families when they participate in educational, health, nutrition, or other services that are considered beneficial to overcoming poverty.

Conference committees: temporary committees formed in bicameral congresses to resolve differences in the text of a particular bill that has passed both chambers.

Conquistadores: soldiers and explorers used by Spain and Portugal to lead the conquest of the Americas during the early phase of colonization.

Conservatives: in post-independence Latin America, individuals who supported a strong central government, advocated for trade protectionism, and sought to preserve a central role for the Catholic Church and a stratified social system.

Constitutional courts: high courts that resolve disputes over the interpretation and application of the constitution.

Constitutions: provide a set of rules, rights, and fundamental principles that determine the structure of the state as well as the powers, limits, and responsibilities of the institutions of government.

Consumption taxes: taxes levied on the purchase of goods and services.

Contras: an anti-Sandinista fighting force backed by the United States and some Latin American countries, which emerged in 1979 and officially disbanded in 1990.

Control of Corruption Index (CCI): one of the best-known indicators of corruption, compiled by the World Bank.

Corruption Perception Index (CPI): one of the best-known indicators of corruption, compiled by the anti-corruption organization, Transparency International.

Corruption: the abuse of public office for private benefit.

Council of the Indies: a supreme governing body created in 1524 by King Charles V to oversee Spain's colonies in the Americas.

Court-packing: an attempt by the political branches to pack the high court with additional appointees, usually by increasing the required number of judges in it.

Decile dispersion ratio: a measure of income inequality based on the ratio of the average income for the richest 10 percent (the 90th percentile) to that of the poorest 10 percent (the 10th percentile), which can be interpreted as the income of the rich in the form of multiples of that of the poor. It can also be calculated for other percentiles.

Decree-law: a type of executive decree that gives the president broad authority to legislate, usually in cases of urgency or exceptional contexts.

Delegated decree: a type of executive decree in which congress chooses to temporarily cede authority to the president to legislate on certain specified matters.

Democracy: a system of government that, at a minimum, requires competitive elections to choose the country's rulers and alternation in power. Definitions of democracy range from minimal to maximal, depending on whether the operationalization of the concept is based solely on procedural aspects or whether standard practices, political outcomes, and societal beliefs are also considered.

Democratic norms: a series of attitudes believed to favor democracy.

Desacato laws: allow public officials to sue those whom they believe have defamed their honor or otherwise hurt their reputation.

Descriptive representation: the extent to which representatives resemble their constituents, usually in reference to identifying features such as gender, ethnicity, and race.

District magnitude: the number of seats assigned to a district at election time. It tells us the number of candidates that will be elected to represent a district.

Dominant-party regime: an authoritarian regime in which control over policy, leadership selection, and the security apparatus is in the hands of a ruling party.

Encomienda: a system employed by Spain in the early phase of colonization, which entailed the provision of land or a grant of labor or tribute from indigenous people to the conquistadores.

Erga omnes: Latin phrase meaning "toward all"; in legal terminology, it means that court decisions, usually about legal rights or obligations, apply to all.

Export-led growth: the expansion of income and jobs as a result of export growth.

Expropriation: the taking of property from its owner by the state or other public authority.

Farabundo Martí National Liberation Front (FMLN): the principal guerrilla force in El Salvador, formed in 1980. It later became a political party.

Femicide: assassination of a woman because of her gender.

Forced disappearance: occurs when a person is secretly abducted by the state or a political organization without legal protection and without acknowledgment of such detention.

Gender quotas: the (usually legal) requirement that parties nominate a specific number or share of female candidates in an election.

Gini coefficient: an index used to quantify inequality in the distribution of income that ranges from 0 (everyone has the same income) to 1 (one person has all the income and everyone else has no income).

Good Neighbor Policy: articulated by President Franklin Delano Roosevelt in 1933. It sought to depart from previous interventionist approaches and instead emphasize the principle of nonintervention and deepening economic ties between Latin American countries and the United States.

Grand corruption: acts of corruption that occur at a high level of government and affect policy formulation, distort existing policies, impact state resources, or influence the functioning of the state.

Guatemalan National Revolutionary Unity (URNG): an umbrella organization formed in 1982 that included the major guerrilla groups of Guatemala: the Guerrilla Army of the Poor (EGP), the Revolutionary Organization of Armed People (ORPA), the Rebel Armed Forces (FAR), and the Guatemalan Party of Labor (PGT). It later became a political party.

Guerrilla: a member of an irregular military force fighting against conventional armed forces. In Latin America, the term guerrillas usually refers to left-wing armed revolutionary movements.

Ideology: refers to a set of beliefs according to which individuals evaluate the political context and guide their political stances. Ideologies are typically composed of some established principles about such things as the role of government in the economy, the consequences of free markets, the primacy of individual liberties, or the implementation of income redistribution policies.

Incomplete list system: a type of majoritarian electoral rule where voters cast a single vote for a party list; the winning list gets its candidates elected, and the list coming in second gets a share of its candidates elected.

Indirect military regime: a regime in which formal political leaders are chosen through competitive elections but the military either prevents parties that would attract large numbers of voters from participating or controls key policy choices. Some consider such regimes authoritarian, while others classify them as hybrids, semi-democratic, or semi-authoritarian.

Informal sector: economically productive activities, usually undertaken by own-account workers and microenterprises, that do not comply with formal regulations pertaining to fiscal, employment, or other matters and are not monitored by the government.

Institutions: formal rules and informal norms that constrain political, economic, and social interactions, thereby establishing the "rules of the game." Political institutions also refer to organizations such as legislatures or courts, which structure governance.

Inter partes: Latin phrase meaning "between the parties"; in legal terminology, this means that court decisions are only binding upon the parties involved in the case at hand.

Inter-American Convention Against Corruption: the first international convention that sought to address the problems of corruption. It was adopted by members of the Organization of American States in 1996 and became effective in 1997.

Interpelaciones: a Spanish term indicating the oversight prerogative available to the legislature to call ministers or other high-ranking officials to answer questions on matters under their purview.

Interpersonal trust: refers to trust in others. It has been associated with a host of positive political and economic outcomes, including stable democracy.

Iran–Contra Affair: a political scandal in the United States during the second Reagan administration that involved government officials selling arms to Iran, which was prohibited by an arms embargo, to free American hostages held in Lebanon and redirecting part of the proceeds to fund the Contras, which was forbidden by Congress.

Judicial authority: the power given to courts and judges to hear cases and render verdicts and to interpret, enforce, and invalidate laws and other statues.

Judicial crises: refer to crises triggered when one of the political branches threatens to alter or succeeds in altering the composition of the high court via impeachment, forced resignation, court-packing, or other mechanisms.

Judicial independence: a court is considered independent when its judges make decisions sincerely according to their own ideas of what the law requires, without undue political or private pressures conditioning such decisions.

Judiciary's legitimacy: the willingness of individuals to accept the decisions and coercive authority of courts, irrespective of whether they agree or not with its decisions.

Juntas: councils or committees formed for administrative or government purposes.

Left-to-right dimension: a useful shortcut to contrast some core political principles. It distinguishes between those who favor (left) and those who oppose (right) state intervention in the economy. It also differentiates between those who favor policies to counteract inequality (left) and those who see inequality as natural and outside the scope of desirable government intervention (right).

Legislative autonomy: refers to the ability of congress to exercise its main functions independently of the executive.

Legislative effectiveness: refers to the ability to coordinate on matters on which legislators agree and make decisions concerning matters in which they have differing and conflictive preferences.

Legislative organization: refers to the offices and procedures that regulate the legislative process.

Legislatures: an organized, deliberative body with lawmaking authority.

Libel laws: regulations meant to compensate individuals for damages to their reputations as a result of published statements that can be proven to be untrue, which may result in jail time for the offender in some countries.

Liberals: in post-independence Latin America, individuals who supported a decentralized federal structure, advocated for free trade, and sought to curtail the influence and privileges of the Catholic Church.

Majoritarian electoral systems: a family of electoral formulas that tends to amplify the share of seats for the leading party and penalizes minor parties. Examples of majoritarian formulas used in Latin America are plurality rule, majority runoff, and the incomplete list system.

Majority runoff: an electoral rule that requires the winning candidate to receive more than 50 percent of the vote. If no candidate passes this threshold, a second election, known as a runoff, is held between the top two vote-getters and whoever has the most votes in the second round wins.

Mérida Initiative: a security cooperation agreement between the United States and Mexico, signed into law in 2008 and designed to combat transnational organized crime, improve law enforcement cooperation, and prevent arms and drug trafficking across the border.

Mestizos: people of mixed indigenous and European descent.

Military coup: the abrupt overthrow of a government by the armed forces or a military faction.

Military junta: a military council or committee controlling the government, usually after a military coup.

Military regimes: authoritarian regimes in which control over policy, leadership selection, and the security apparatus are in the hands of a military institution.

Minimum wage: the minimum amount of remuneration that an employer is required by law to pay a worker for work performed during a given period.

Mixed-member electoral system: an electoral rule that combines both majoritarian and proportional rules to elect members of the same legislative chamber.

Monroe Doctrine: a major tenet of foreign policy in the United States, articulated by President James Monroe in 1823. It promised that the United States would not interfere in European affairs, warned European powers than any intervention in the Western Hemisphere would be viewed as an act of aggression against the United States, and declared that no other nation could establish a colony in this region.

Mulattos: individuals of mixed white and black ancestry.

National Liberation Army (ELN): a Colombian guerrilla organization formed in 1964 by communist activists and students who had trained in Cuba and were inspired by that country's revolution.

Natural rights: inalienable rights that all individuals are entitled to, regardless of whether they are codified in the legal system or not.

Negative rights: rights that limit individuals as well as the government from forcibly intruding on the actions of others.

North American Free Trade Agreement (NAFTA): a free trade agreement between the United States, Canada, and Mexico, which went into effect on January 1, 1994. It had a significant impact, boosting trade and investment and furthering economic integration among the three member countries. In 2018, the three countries agreed on a deal to replace NAFTA with a new agreement called the United States–Mexico–Canada Agreement (USMCA).

Oligarchic regime: a regime in which leaders are chosen through competitive elections but most of the adult population is disenfranchised. It is typically considered a type of authoritarian regime.

Open-list proportional representation: a type of proportional representation rule in which voters can show a preference for a specific candidate or candidates within a party list. Votes are aggregated by party, and seats are distributed to parties according to their share of the vote. Preferential votes help to determine which candidates within a party list win the seats.

Organization of American States (OAS): a continental organization formed in 1948 to address interhemispheric affairs diplomatically, defend the territorial integrity and sovereignty of its members, and encourage cooperation.

Panama Canal Treaty (of 1977): also known as the Carter-Torrijos Treaty; it comprised two separate agreements: a renegotiation of the Panama Canal Treaty and a new neutrality treaty. The first required the United States to relinquish control of the canal on December 31, 1999, at which time the operation of the canal would shift to Panama, while the second established the canal as a neutral water passage and gave the United States permanent authority to defend it if this status were to be threatened.

Paramilitary forces: armed groups with a military-type structure, which are sometimes illegal. In Colombia, it usually alludes to the right-wing forces organized in opposition to the leftist guerrillas, such as the United Self-Defense Forces (AUC).

Parliamentarism: a form of government where the head of government (prime minister) is separate from the head of state (usually a figurehead president or a monarch), the government is run by a cabinet (comprised of a prime minister and the other ministers) and is chosen indirectly by parliament, and the government depends on the confidence of parliament to remain in power.

Partial veto: a type of veto power wherein the president can reject specific parts of a bill.

Patronage: the exchange of public employment for electoral support.

Peninsulares: Spanish-born individuals residing in colonial Latin America.

Personal vote: refers to contexts where politicians pursue votes based on their personal characteristics rather than on the reputation of their party.

Personalist regimes: authoritarian regimes in which control over policy, leadership selection, and the security apparatus are in the hands of a narrower group centered around an individual dictator.

Petty corruption: also called bureaucratic or administrative corruption. It refers to small-scale corruption involving low- and mid-level public officials; it usually occurs when public officials interact with ordinary citizens and tends to involve less money than grand corruption.

Plan Colombia: a plan negotiated between the United States and Colombia and approved by the U.S. Congress in 2000 that provided military and economic assistance to help the Colombian government combat drugs and organized crime.

Plurality rule: an electoral rule where voters cast a single vote for one candidate, and the candidate with the most votes wins. It can be used for presidential or congressional elections. When used for congressional elections, competition usually takes place in single-member districts (i.e., each with district magnitude = 1).

Political culture: refers to the beliefs, values, and attitudes shared by people in a society, which give meaning to various political processes and shape political behavior.

Political tolerance: refers to the acceptance of the rights of others—typically members of the opposition, dissidents, and individuals from marginalized groups. It is an aspect of political attitudes that has been linked to democratic norms.

Positive rights: rights that oblige others (most often the state) to provide some benefit to the bearer of that right.

Presidentialism: a form of government characterized by a popularly elected president as chief executive, fixed terms in office for the president and the legislative assembly, and a president with some lawmaking authority who names and leads the cabinet.

Proportional representation: an electoral rule that assigns seats to parties according to their share of the vote in multimember districts.

Public procurement: government acquisitions of goods and services; an area where opportunities for corruption are usually plentiful.

Recall referendum: a constitutional provision that allows for a popular referendum that may cut short the term of office of an elected official.

Reduced-threshold runoff: a variation of the majority runoff electoral formula, which establishes a threshold of less than 50 percent of the vote for a candidate to win the election in a first round. If the candidate with the most votes does not pass this required threshold, there is a runoff election among the top two vote-getters. The threshold requirement number varies by country.

Regulatory decree: a type of executive decree that specifies how a law is supposed to be implemented (i.e., the instrumentation or modus operandi of a piece of legislation).

Religious freedom: gives individuals the right to practice religion or no religion at all without coercion by others or the state.

Repartimiento: a system of draft labor used in Spanish America, which gave some colonists the right to recruit a share of the indigenous population to work for a prescribed period of time. In Peru, it was called mita.

Revolutionary Armed Forces of Colombia (FARC): the most prominent guerilla group in Colombia, which was formed in 1964 by Manuel Marulanda and other communist militants. It reached a peace agreement with the Colombian government in 2016 and subsequently transformed into a political party.

Roll-call votes: usually refers to the recorded votes taken by legislators on the floor of the chamber.

Roosevelt Corollary to the Monroe Doctrine: articulated by President Theodore Roosevelt in 1904; it asserted that the United States could exercise "international police power" in Latin American countries that engage in "chronic wrongdoing," which included failing to pay international creditors as well as significant internal disorder.

Royal patronage (patronato real): an arrangement between the Catholic Church and the monarchies of Spain and Portugal that gave the monarchs of both nations control over major church appointments and the establishment of dioceses in the colonies in exchange for organizing and financing evangelization in the new colonial territories.

Sandinista National Liberation Front (FSLN): a Nicaraguan guerrilla movement formed in 1961, which eventually led the revolutionary movement that deposed the authoritarian government of Anastacio Somoza Debayle in 1979. It later became a political party.

Semi-democracy: an intermediate category between democracy and authoritarianism. It is usually characterized by having contested elections but partially lacking some political rights or civil liberties.

Semi-presidentialism: a form of government characterized by a president who has some lawmaking powers, direct elections to choose the president, and a prime minister who serves as head of government and who needs the confidence of a parliamentary majority to remain in power.

Severance payments: a lump sum payment given to a worker when they are laid off or fired for an unjust cause.

Slander laws: regulations meant to compensate individuals for damages to their reputations as a result of oral statements that can be proven to be untrue, which may result in jail time for the offender in some countries.

Substantive representation: activities that legislators undertake to advance the interests and demands of their constituents.

Term limits: regulations that limit the number of terms an elected official (e.g., a legislator) can serve.

Transparency policies: policies aimed at improving the capacity of the public to monitor public officials, thereby reducing opportunities for public officials to engage in corruption; it requires access to information about the financial transactions and decisions made by governments.

Treaty of Tordesillas: a treaty signed between Spain and Portugal in 1494, which resolved controversies over land in the Americas by establishing a line of demarcation along a meridian 370 leagues west of the Cape Verde islands; the territories to the west of the line would be ruled by Spain and those to the east by Portugal.

U.S. Agency for International Development (USAID): an agency of the U.S. federal government in charge of administering civilian foreign aid and development assistance, established in 1961 by President John F. Kennedy.

Viceroy: the most senior official in colonial Latin America, who ruled as the king's representative.

Votes of no confidence: in a parliamentary country, a vote of no confidence usually leads to the removal of the government from office (the prime minister and the rest of the cabinet but not the head of state). In Peru, considered a presidential country, the constitution allows the cabinet chief and individual ministers to introduce a confidence motion linked to a bill. If the Peruvian Congress rejects the motion of confidence (with its associated bill), the entire cabinet or the individual minister making the motion must resign.

• Notes •

Preface

1. Philip B. Taylor. 1956. "The Guatemalan Affair." *American Political Science Review* 50(3): 87–806.

Chapter 1: Colonial Legacy and the Post-Independence Period

1. Adam Przeworski. 2009. "The Mechanics of Regime Instability in Latin America." *Journal of Politics in Latin America* 1(1): 5–36.

2. John Lynch. 1955. "Intendants and Cabildos in the Viceroyalty of La Plata, 1782–1810." *The Hispanic American Historical Review* 35(3): 337–362; John H. Elliott. 1984. "Spain and America in the Sixteenth and Seventeenth Centuries." In Leslie Bethell (ed.), *The Cambridge History of Latin America*, Volume I. London: Cambridge University Press, pp. 287–340.

3. Joseph Smith. 2013. *A History of Brazil, 1500–2000.* New York: Routledge, p. 8.

4. Josep M. Barnadas. 1984. "The Catholic Church in Colonial Spanish America." In Leslie Bethell (ed.), *The Cambridge History of Latin America*, Volume I. London: Cambridge University Press, pp. 511–540.

5. Eduardo Hoornaert. 1984. "The Catholic Church in Colonial Brazil." In Leslie Bethell (ed.), *The Cambridge History of Latin America*, Volume I. London: Cambridge University Press, pp. 541–556.

6. The terms *natives* and *indigenous people* are used interchangeably in this text.

7. Victor Bulmer-Thomas. 2014. *The Economic History of Latin America since Independence.* New York: Cambridge University Press, p. 24.

8. Ibid.

9. Peter Bakewell. 1984. "Mining in Colonial Spanish America." In Leslie Bethell (ed.), *The Cambridge History of Latin America*, Volume I. London: Cambridge University Press, pp. 105–151.

10. D. A. Brading and Harry E. Cross. 1972. "Colonial Silver Mining: Mexico and Peru." *The Hispanic American Historical Review* 52(4): 545–579.

11. Andrés Reséndez. 2016. *The Other Slavery: The Uncovered Story of Indian Enslavement in America.* Boston: Houghton Mifflin Harcourt, p. 62.

12. Nils Jacobsen. 1993. *Mirages of Transition: The Peruvian Altiplano, 1780–1930.* Berkeley: University of California Press, p. 92.

13. Kendall Brown. *A History of Mining in Latin America: From the Colonial Era to the Present.* Albuquerque: University of New Mexico Press, p. 43.

14. John H. Coatsworth. 2005. "Structures, Endowments, and Institutions in the Economic History of Latin America." *Latin American Research Review* 40(3): 126–144.

15. John H. Coatsworth. 2006. "Political Economy and Economic Organization." In Victor Bulmer-Thomas, John H. Coatsworth, and Roberto Cortés Conde (eds.), *The Cambridge Economic History of Latin America,* Volume I. New York: Cambridge University Press, pp. 237–273.

16. Alex Borucki, David Eltis, and David Wheat. 2015. "Atlantic History and the Slave Trade to Spanish America." *American Historical Review* 120(2): 433–461.

17. John Lynch. 1985. "The Origins of Spanish American Independence." In Leslie Bethell (ed.), *The Cambridge History of Latin America,* Volume III. London: Cambridge University Press, pp. 3–50.

18. John H. Coatsworth. 2008. "Inequality, Institutions, and Economic Growth in Latin America." *Journal of Latin American Studies* 40(3): 545–569.

19. Ibid.

20. The figure includes population in the highlands and lowlands. Sherburne F. Cook and Woodrow Borah. 1971. *Essays in Population History: Mexico and the Caribbean,* Volume 1. Berkeley: University of California Press.

21. Linda A. Newson. 1993. "The Demographic Collapse of Native Peoples of the Americas, 1492–1650." *Proceedings of the British Academy* 81: 247–288.

22. Alex Borucki, David Eltis, and David Wheat. 2015. "Atlantic History and the Slave Trade to Spanish America." *American Historical Review* 120(2): 433–461.

23. Ibid.

24. Stanley L. Engerman and Kenneth L. Sokoloff. 1997. "Factor Endowments, Institutions, and Differential Paths of Growth among New World Economies: A View from Economic Historians of the United States." In Stephen Haber (ed.), *How Latin America Fell Behind.* Stanford CA, Stanford University Press, pp. 260–304.

25. John H. Elliott. 2006. *Empires of the Atlantic World: Britain and Spain in America 1492–1830.* New Haven: Yale University Press, pp. 171–172.

26. Ibid.

27. Anthony John R. Russell-Wood. 1982. *The Black Man in Slavery and Freedom in Colonial Brazil.* London: Palgrave Macmillan.

28. Leslie B. Rout, Jr. 1976. "Race and Slavery in Brazil." *The Wilson Quarterly* 1(1): 73–89.

29. Alexander Von Humboldt. 1811. *Political Essay on the Kingdom of New Spain.* London: Longman, Hurst, Rees, Orme, and Brown, p. 205.

30. John H. Coatsworth. 2008. "Inequality, Institutions, and Economic

Growth in Latin America." *Journal of Latin American Studies* 40(3): 545–569.

31. John Lynch. 1985. "The Origins of Spanish American Independence." In Leslie Bethell (ed.), *The Cambridge History of Latin America*, Volume III. London: Cambridge University Press, pp. 3–50.

32. Michael P. Costeloe. 1986. *Response to Revolution: Imperial Spain and the Spanish American Revolutions, 1810–1840.* New York: Cambridge University Press, p. 120.

33. John Lynch. 1985. "The Origins of Spanish American Independence." In Leslie Bethell (ed.), *The Cambridge History of Latin America*, Volume III. London: Cambridge University Press, pp. 3–50.

34. John H. Elliott. 2006. *Empires of the Atlantic World: Britain and Spain in America 1492–1830.* New Haven: Yale University Press, pp. 172–173.

35. Robert H. Bates, John H. Coatsworth, and Jeffrey G. Williamson. 2007. "Lost Decades: Post Independence Performance in Latin America and Africa." *Journal of Economic History* 67(4): 917–943.

36. Leonardo Prados de la Escosura. 2006. "The Economic Consequences of Independence in Latin America." In Victor Bulmer-Thomas, John H. Coatsworth, and Roberto Cortés Conde (eds.), *The Cambridge Economic History of Latin America*, Volume I. New York: Cambridge University Press, pp. 463–504.

37. Ibid.

38. Data in 2011 U.S. dollars comes from the Maddison Project Database, version 2018. Jutta Bolt, Robert Inklaar, Herman de Jong, and Jan Luiten van Zanden. 2018. "Rebasing 'Maddison': New Income Comparisons and the Shape of Long-Run Economic Development." Maddison Project Working Paper 10. Available online at https://www.rug.nl/ggdc/historicald evelopment/maddison/releases/ maddison-project-database-2018

39. Douglass North, William Summerhill, and Barry Weingast. 2000. "Order, Disorder, and Economic Change: Latin America versus North America." In Bruce Bueno de Mesquita and Hilton Root (eds.), *Governing for Prosperity.* New Haven: Yale University Press, pp. 17–58.

40. Frank Safford. 1985. "Politics, Ideology, and Society in Post-Independence Spanish America." In Leslie Bethell (ed.), *The Cambridge History of Latin America*, Volume III. London: Cambridge University Press, pp. 347–422.

41. Jose Murilo de Carvalho. 1982. "Political Elites and State Building: The Case of Nineteenth-Century Brazil." *Comparative Studies in Society and History* 24(3): 378–399.

42. Adam Przeworski and Carolina Curvale. 2008. "Does Politics Explain the Economic Gap between the United States and Latin America?" In Francis Fukuyama (ed.), *Falling Behind: Explaining the Development Gap between Latin America and the United States.* New York: Oxford University Press, pp. 99–133.

43. Victor Bulmer-Thomas. 2014. *The Economic History of Latin America since Independence.* New York: Cambridge University Press, p. 79.

44. James Mahoney. 2001. "Path-Dependent Explanations of Regime Change: Central America in Comparative Perspective." *Studies in Comparative International Development* 36(1): 111–141.

45. Aldo A. Lauria-Santiago. 1999. *An Agrarian Republic: Commercial Agriculture and the Politics of Peasant Communities in El Salvador, 1823–1914.* Pittsburgh: University of Pittsburgh Press, p. 193.

46. Leonardo Prados de la Escosura. 2006. "The Economic Consequences of Independence in Latin America." In Victor Bulmer-Thomas, John H. Coatsworth, and Roberto Cortés Conde (eds.), *The Cambridge Economic History of Latin America*, Volume I. New York: Cambridge University Press, pp. 463–504.

47. Angus Madisson. 2003. *The World Economy: Historical Statistics.* Paris: OECD.

48. Maddison Project Database, version 2018. Jutta Bolt, Robert Inklaar, Herman de Jong and Jan Luiten van Zanden. 2018. "Rebasing 'Maddison': New Income Comparisons and the Shape of Long-Run Economic Development." Maddison Project Working Paper 10.

49. James Mahoney. 2001. *The Legacies of Liberalism: Path Dependence and Political Regimes in Central America.* Baltimore: The Johns Hopkins University Press, p. 13.

50. James Mahoney. 2001. "Path-Dependent Explanations of Regime Change: Central America in Comparative Perspective." *Studies in Comparative International Development* 36(1): 111–141.

Chapter 2: Political Regimes and Democratic Stability

1. Karl R. Popper. 1945 [1971]. *The Open Society and Its Enemies*, Volume I. Princeton: Princeton University Press, p. 124.

2. Larry Diamond. 1999. *Developing Democracy: Towards Consolidation.* Baltimore: The John Hopkins University Press, p. 3.

3. Robert A. Dahl. 1989. *Democracy and Its Critics.* New Haven: Yale University Press, pp. 83–96.

4. Joseph Schumpeter. 1942 [2006]. *Capitalism, Socialism, and Democracy.* London: Routledge, p. 269.

5. Adam Przeworski. 1999. "A Minimalist Conception of Democracy: A Defense." In I. Shapiro and C. Hacker-Cordón (eds.), *Democracy's Value.* Cambridge: Cambridge University Press, pp. 23–55.

6. José Antonio Cheibub, Jennifer Gandhi, and James Raymond Vreeland. 2010. "Democracy and Dictatorship Revisited." *Public Choice* 143(1–2): 67–101.

7. Carles Boix, Michael Miller, and Sebastian Rosato. 2013. "A Complete Data Set of Political Regimes, 1800–2007." *Comparative Political Studies* 46(12): 1523–1554.

8. Larry Diamond. 1999. *Developing Democracies: Towards Consolidation.* Baltimore: John Hopkins University Press, pp. 13–15.

9. Scott Mainwaring and Aníbal Pérez-Liñán. 2013. *Democracies and Dictatorships in Latin America: Emergence, Survival, and Fall*. New York: Cambridge University Press, pp. 65–66.

10. Details on the methodology used and further information on country rankings is available at https://freedomhouse.org

11. Freedom House. 2019. *Freedom in the World*, [web report] p. 9. Available at https://freedomhouse.org

12. Ibid., p. 13.

13. The Economist Intelligence Unit. 2019. *Democracy Index 2018: Me too? Political Participation, Protest and Democracy*. Available at http://www.eiu.com

14. Barbara Geddes, Joseph Wright, and Erica Frantz. 2014. "Autocratic Breakdown and Regime Transitions: A New Dataset." *Perspectives on Politics* 12(1): 313–331.

15. His hand-picked successor, Joaquín Balaguer, who was president at that time, was deposed from power a year later.

16. Barbara Geddes, Joseph Wright, and Erica Frantz. 2014. "Autocratic Breakdown and Regime Transitions: A New Dataset." *Perspectives on Politics* 12(1): 313–331.

17. The Economist Intelligence Unit's Democracy Index classified them as non-democratic hybrid regimes. For an argument that Chávez presided over a competitive authoritarian regime, see Scott Mainwaring. 2012. "From Representative Democracy to Participatory Competitive Authoritarianism: Hugo Chávez and Venezuelan Politics." *Perspectives on Politics* 10(4): 955–967.

18. Seymour M. Lipset. 1959. "Some Social Requisites for Democracy: Economic Development and Political Legitimacy." *American Political Science Review* 53(1): 69–105.

19. David L. Epstein, Robert H. Bates, Jack Goldstone, Ida Kristensen, and Sharyn O'Halloran. 2006. "Democratic Transitions." *American Journal of Political Science* 50(3): 551–569; Carles Boix. 2011. "Democracy, Development, and the International System." *American Political Science Review* 105(4): 809–828; Daniel Treisman. 2015. "Income, Democracy, and Leader Turnover." *American Journal of Political Science* 59(4): 927–942; Fabrice Murtin and Romain Wacziarg. 2014. "The Democratic Transition." *Journal of Economic Growth* 19(2): 141–181.

20. Adam Przeworski. 2019. *Crises of Democracy*. New York: Cambridge University Press, p. 33.

21. Peter Smith. 2005. *Democracy in Latin America*. New York: Oxford University Press, pp. 50–53.

22. Scott Mainwaring and Aníbal Pérez-Liñán. 2013. *Democracies and Dictatorships in Latin America: Emergence, Survival, and Fall*. New York: Cambridge University Press, pp. 278–279.

23. Daron Acemoglu, Simon Johnson, James E. Robinson, and Pierre Yared. 2008. "Income and Democracy." *American Economic Review* 98(3): 808–842.

24. Guillermo O'Donnell. 1973. *Modernization and Bureaucratic-Authoritarianism: Studies in South American*

Politics. Berkeley: University of California Press.

25. Ko Maeda. 2010. "Two Modes of Democratic Breakdown: A Competing Risks Analysis of Democratic Durability." *The Journal of Politics* 72(4): 1129–1143.

26. Stephan Haggard and Robert R. Kaufman. 1995. *The Political Economy of Democratic Transitions*. Princeton: Princeton University Press, pp. 45–74.

27. Daron Acemoglu, Simon Johnson, and James Robinson. 2001. "The Colonial Origins of Comparative Development: An Empirical Investigation." *The American Economic Review* 91(5): 1369–1401; Daron Acemoglu, Simon Johnson, James Robinson, and Pierre Yared. 2008. "Income and Democracy." *The American Economic Review* 98(3): 808–842.

28. Polity IV Project. *Political Regime Characteristics and Transitions, 1800–2015*. Retrieved December 28, 2015 from https://www.systemicpeace.org/polity/polity4.htm

29. Matthew S. Shugart and John M. Carey. 1992. *Presidents and Assemblies: Constitutional Design and Electoral Dynamics*. New York: Cambridge University Press, p. 148.

30. Aníbal Pérez-Liñán, Nicolás Schmidt, and Daniela Vairo. 2019. "Presidential Hegemony and Democratic Backsliding in Latin America, 1925–2016." *Democratization* 26(4): 606–625.

31. Gabriel Almond and Sidney Verba. 1963. *The Civic Culture: Political Attitudes and Democracy in Five Nations*. Princeton: Princeton University Press; John Higley and Michael Burton. 1989. "The Elite Variable in Democratic Transitions and Breakdowns." *American Sociological Review* 54(1): 17–32; Ronald Inglehart. 1990. *Cultural Shift in Advanced Industrial Societies*. Princeton: Princeton University Press.

32. Kingsley Davis. 1942 [1951]. "Political Ambivalence in Latin America." In Ashner N. Christensen (ed.), *The Evolution of Latin American Government*. New York: Henry Hold, pp. 224–247. Quote is from p. 240.

33. Howard Wiarda. 2001. *The Soul of Latin America*. New Haven: Yale University Press.

34. Howard J. Wiarda and Margaret MacLeish Mott. 2003. "Introduction: Interpreting Latin America's Politics on Its Own Terms." In Howard J. Wiarda and Margaret MacLeish Mott (eds.), *Politics and Social Change in Latin America: Still a Distinct Tradition?* 4th edition. Westport: Praeger Publishers, pp. 1–14. Quote from p. 6. See also Howard J. Wiarda. 2001. *The Soul of Latin America: The Cultural and Political Tradition*. New Haven: Yale University Press.

35. Samuel P. Huntington. 1991. *The Third Wave of Democratization in the Late Twentieth Century*. Norman: University of Oklahoma Press, p. 76.

36. Edward Bell. 2008. "Catholicism and Democracy: A Reconsideration." *Journal of Religion & Society* 10: 1–22.

37. Seymour Martin Lipset. 1994. "The Social Requisites of Democracy Revisited: 1993 Presidential

Address." *American Sociological Review* 59(1):1–22.

38. Eduardo Alemán and Yeaji Kim. 2015. "The Democratizing Effect of Education." *Research & Politics*, https://doi.org/10.1177/205316 8015613360

39. Ryan E. Carlin, Gregory J. Love, Matthew M. Singer, Daniel Zizumbo-Colunga, and Amy Erica Smith. 2012. "Political Legitimacy and Democratic Values." In M.A. Seligson, A. E. Smith, and E. Zechmeister (eds.), *The Political Culture of Democracy in the Americas, 2012: Towards Equality of Opportunity, Americas Barometer Survey by the Latin American Public Opinion Project.* Nashville: Vanderbilt University, pp. 189–216.

40. Data on authoritarianism is from the political regime data set of Mainwaring and Pérez-Liñán. Data on illiteracy in 1900 comes from the Montevideo–Oxford Latin American Economic History Database (http://moxlad-staging.herokuapp.com/home/en).

41. Barbara Geddes. 1999. "What Do We Know About Democratization after Twenty Years?" *Annual Review of Political Science* 2: 115–144.

42. Nancy Bermeo. 2003. *Ordinary People in Extraordinary Times: The Citizenry and the Breakdown of Democracy.* Princeton: Princeton University Press.

43. Scott Mainwaring and Aníbal Pérez-Liñán. 2013. *Democracies and Dictatorships in Latin America: Emergence, Survival, and Fall.* New York: Cambridge University Press, pp. 35–43.

44. Carles Boix. 2011. "Democracy, Development, and the International System." *American Political Science Review* 105(4): 809–828.

45. Samuel P. Huntington. 1991. *The Third Wave of Democratization in the Late Twentieth Century.* Norman: University of Oklahoma Press, pp. 3–30.

Chapter 3: Guerrillas and Revolutions

1. Jorge Castañeda. 2006. "Latin America's Left Turn." *Foreign Affairs* 85 (May–June): 28–43.

2. Mauricio Florez-Morris. 2007. "Joining Guerrilla Groups in Colombia: Individual Motivations and Processes for Entering a Violent Organization." *Studies in Conflict and Terrorism* 30(7): 615–634.

3. Gordon Tullock. 1971. "The Paradox of Revolution." *Public Choice* 11(1): 89–100.

4. Samule L. Popkin. 1979. *The Rational Peasant: The Political Economy of Rural Society in Vietnam.* Berkeley: University of California Press, pp. 259–266.

5. Stathis N. Kalyvas and Matthew Adam Kocher. 2007. "How 'Free' Is Free Riding in Civil Wars? Violence, Insurgency, and the Collective Action Problem." *World Politics* 59(2): 117–216.

6. Human Rights Watch. 2003. *You'll Learn Not to Cry: Child Combatants in Colombia.* New York: Human Rights Watch, pp. 29–31; José Miguel Vivanco. "A Challenge to FARC's Narrative on Child Recruitment." *Human*

Rights Watch, March 11, 2019. Available at https://www.hrw.org/news/2019/03/11/challenge-farcs-narrative-child-recruitment#; see also the Report (Boletín) 2343 issued by the office of Colombia's Attorney General (Fiscal General) on July 16, 2018, available at https://www.fiscalia.gov.co/colombia/fiscal-general-de-la-nacion/fiscalia-realiza-segunda-entregade-informes-a-la-jurisdiccion-especial-de-paz/

7. Jack Goldstone. 1994. "Is Revolution Individually Rational?" *Rationality and Society* 6(1): 39–166.

8. Michael Taylor. 1988. "Rationality and Revolutionary Collective Action." In Michael Taylor (ed.), *Rationality and Revolution*. New York: Cambridge University Press, pp. 63–97.

9. Morris Silver. 1974. "Political Revolution and Repression: An Economic Approach." *Public Choice* 17: 63–97.

10. Elisabeth Jean Wood. 2001. "The Emotional Benefits of Insurgency in EL Salvador." In Jeff Goodwin, James M. Jasper, and Francesca Polletta (eds.), *Passionate Politics: Emotions and Social Movements*. Chicago: The University of Chicago Press, pp. 267–281.

11. Ibid., p. 268.

12. Timothy P. Wickham-Crowley. 1992. *Guerrillas and Revolution in Latin America: A Comparative Study of Insurgents and Regimes since 1956*. New Jersey: Princeton University Press, p. 51.

13. Jeff Goodwin. 2001. *No Other Way Out: States and Revolutionary Movements, 1945–1991*. New York: Cambridge University Press.

14. See also Jeff Goodwin and Theda Skocpol. 1989. "Explaining Revolutions in the Contemporary Third World." *Politics and Society* 17(4): 489–509.

15. Barbara Geddes. 1999. "What Do We Know About Democratization after 20 Years?" *Annual Review of Political Science* 2(1): 115–144.

16. Jeff Goodwin. 2001. *No Other Way Out: States and Revolutionary Movements, 1945–1991*. New York: Cambridge University Press, p. 144.

17. Timothy P. Wickham-Crowley. 1992. *Guerrillas and Revolution in Latin America: A Comparative Study of Insurgents and Regimes since 1956*. New Jersey: Princeton University Press, p. 119.

18. Ibid., p. 140.

19. Herbert L. Matthews. 1975. *Revolution in Cuba: An Essay in Understanding*. New York: Charles Scribner's Sons, p. 100.

20. Timothy P. Wickham-Crowley. 1992. *Guerrillas and Revolution in Latin America: A Comparative Study of Insurgents and Regimes since 1956*. New Jersey: Princeton University Press, p. 191.

21. Herbert L. Matthews, "Cuban Rebel Is Visited in Hideout." *New York Times*, February 24, 1957, pp. 1, 34.

22. Julie Marie Bunck. 1994. *Fidel Castro and the Quest for Revolutionary Culture in Cuba*. University Park: The Pennsylvania State University Press, p. 34.

23. Mervin Block. 1962. "The Night Castro Unmasked." *Columbia Journalism Review* 1(2): 5–10.

24. Matilde Zimmermann. 2000. *Sandinista: Carlos Fonseca and the Nicaraguan Revolution.* Durham: Duke University Press, p. 6.

25. Timothy P. Wickham-Crowley. 1992. *Guerrillas and Revolution in Latin America: A Comparative Study of Insurgents and Regimes since 1956.* New Jersey: Princeton University Press, 96–99.

26. Jeffrey Paige. 1985. "Cotton and Revolution in Nicaragua." In Peter Evans, Dietrich Reuschemeyer, and Evelyn Huber (eds.), *States versus Markets in the World System.* Thousand Oaks: SAGE, pp. 91–114.

27. "Nicaraguans Accused of Profiteering on Help the U. S. Sent after Quake." *New York Times,* March 23, 1977, p. 10.

28. "National Mutiny in Nicaragua." *New York Times,* July 30, 1978, Section SM, p. 4.

29. Alan Riding, "Somoza's Foes Honor Editor Murdered a Year Ago." *New York Times,* January 11, 1979, p. 9.

30. Thomas W. Walker and Christine J. Wade. 2017. *Nicaragua: Emerging from the Shadow of the Eagle,* 6th edition. Boulder: Westview Press, p. 69.

31. Jeff Goodwin. 2001. *No Other Way Out: States and Revolutionary Movements, 1945–1991.* New York: Cambridge University Press, p. 194.

32. James C. Dunkerley. 1988. *Power in the Isthmus. A Political History of Modern Central America.* London: Verso, p. 232.

33. Timothy P. Wickham-Crowley. 1992. *Guerrillas and Revolution in Latin America: A Comparative Study of Insurgents and Regimes since 1956.* New Jersey: Princeton University Press, p. 268.

34. Casualties data taken from Bethany Lacina and Nils Petter Gleditsch. 2005. "Monitoring Trends in Global Combat: A New Dataset of Battle Deaths." *European Journal of Population* 21(2–3): 145–166.

35. Silvia L. Saravia-Matus and Jimmy Saravia-Matus. 2009. "Agrarian Reform: Theory and Practice. The Nicaraguan Experience." *Encuentro* 84: 21–43.

36. Max Spoor. 1990. "Rural Employment and Agrarian Markets in Transition: Nicaragua (1979–89)." *The Journal of Peasant Studies* 17(4): 520–545.

37. "Catholic Radio Shut for Indefinite Period by Sandinista Order." *New York Times,* January 3, 1986; available at https://www.nytimes.com/1986/01/03/world/catholic-radio-shut-for-indefinite-period-by-sandinista-order.html

38. Jeff Goodwin. 2001. *No Other Way Out: States and Revolutionary Movements, 1945–1991.* New York: Cambridge University Press, p. 195; Timothy P. Wickham-Crowley. 1992. *Guerrillas and Revolution in Latin America: A Comparative Study of Insurgents and Regimes since 1956.* New Jersey: Princeton University Press, p. 286; Mark Everingham. 1996.

Revolution and the Multiclass Coalition in Nicaragua. Pittsburgh: University of Pittsburgh Press, pp. 97–103.

39. Elisabeth J. Wood. 2000. *Forging Democracy from Below: Insurgent Transitions in South Africa and El Salvador.* New York: Cambridge University Press, p. 47.

40. John A. Booth, Christine J. Wade, and Thomas W. Walker. 2015. *Understanding Central America,* 6th edition. Boulder: Westview Press, p. 144.

41. Michael J. Hennelly. 1993. "US Policy in El Salvador: Creating Beauty or the Beast." *Parameters* 23(1): 59–69.

42. Congressional Quarterly Almanac. 1984. [Online Edition.] Available at https://library.cqpress.com/cqalmanac/document.php?id=cqal84-1151564

43. Cynthia J. Arnson. 2013. "In El Salvador, a Military and Police Campaign Attacking Civilians." In Alexander Cruden (ed.), *El Salvador and Guatemala.* New York: Greenhaven Press, pp. 30–38.

44. Tim Golden. "Accord Reached to Halt Civil War in El Salvador." *New York Times,* January 1, 1992, pp. 1, 7.

45. Information available in The National Security Archive, The George Washington University. Available at https://nsarchive2.gwu.edu/NSAEBB/NSAEBB11/docs/

46. By that time, FAR had reorganized itself, changed its name to Revolutionary Armed Forces, and broken its alliance with the PGT.

47. John A. Booth, Christine J. Wade, and Thomas W. Walker. 2015.

Understanding Central America, 6th edition. Boulder: Westview Press, p. 176.

48. Jeff Goodwin. 2001. *No Other Way Out: States and Revolutionary Movements, 1945–1991.* New York: Cambridge University Press, p. 207.

49. James Gerstenzang and Juanita Darling, "Clinton Gives Apology for U.S. Role in Guatemala." *Los Angeles Times,* March 11, 1999.

50. "Revolutionary Armed Forces of Colombia." *Mapping Militant Organizations.* Stanford University. Available at https://cisac.fsi.stanford.edu/mappingmilitants/profiles/revolutionary-armed-forces-colombia-farc

51. Jennifer S. Holmes, Sheila Amin Gutiérrez de Piñeres, and Kevin M. Curtin. 2008. *Guns, Drugs, and Development in Colombia,* Austin: University of Texas Press, pp. 95–96; Fabio Sánchez and Mario Chacón. 2005. "Conflict, State and Decentralisation: From Social Progress to an Armed Dispute for Local Control, 1974–2002." Crisis States Research Centre working Papers series 1 (70). Crisis States Research Centre, London School of Economics and Political Science, London, UK.

52. "National Liberation Army." Mapping Militant Organizations. Stanford University. Available at https://cisac.fsi.stanford.edu/mappingmilitants/profiles/national-liberation-army-eln

53. "April 19 Movement." *Mapping Militant Organizations.* Stanford University. Available at https://cisac.fsi.stanford.edu/mappingmilitants/profiles/april-19-movement

54. Centro Nacional de Memoria Histórica. 2016. *BASTA YA! Colombia:*

Memories of War and Dignity. Bogota: CNMH, p. 42.

55. Diana Jean Schemo. "Colombia's Death-Strewn Democracy." *New York Times,* July 24, 1997, p. A8.

56. "Colombia Cierra 2017 con la Tasa de Homicidio Más Baja Desde 1975: Mindefensa." *El Heraldo,* December 17, 2017.

57. "Preocupa el Número de Guerrilleros del ELN." *El Tiempo,* April 20, 2019. Available online at https://www.semana.com/confidenciales/articulo/numero-de-guerrilleros-del-eln-en-2019/609989

Chapter 4: U.S.–Latin America Relations

1. Brian Loveman. 2016 "U.S. Foreign Policy toward Latin America in the 19th Century." *Oxford Research Encyclopedia of Latin American History.* Oxford University Press. doi: 10.1093/acrefore/9780199366439.013.41

2. J. Fred Rippy. 1937. "The Initiation of the Customs Receivership in the Dominican Republic." *The Hispanic American Historical Review* 17(4): 419–457.

3. Richard Haas. 2017. *A World in Disarray: American Foreign Policy and the Crisis of the Old Order.* New York: Penguin Press, p. 39.

4. Abraham F. Lowenthal. 1970. "The United States and the Dominican Republic to 1965: Background to Intervention." *Caribbean Studies* 10(2): 30–55.

5. Ibid.

6. Piero Gleijeses. 2014. "Hope Denied: The US Defeat of the 1965 Revolt in the Dominican Republic." Working Paper #72, Cold War International History Project, Washington DC: Woodrow Wilson international Center for Scholars.

7. In addition, it is likely that domestic politics played some role in the decision to intervene, given President's Johnson's intent on appearing tough against communists and the potential electoral costs of failing to act if communist factions were to emerge triumphant out of the conflict. On this subject, see Howard J. Wiarda. 1980. "Review: The United States and the Dominican Republic: Intervention, Dependency, and Tyrannicide." *Journal of Interamerican Studies and World Affairs* 22(2): 247–260.

8. Director of Central Intelligence. *Soviet Policies and Activities in Latin America and the Caribbean,* June 23, 1982, p. 4. [Approved for release through the Historical Review Program of the CIA on 1994.] Available at https://www.cia.gov/library/readingroom/

9. Peter Shearman. 1985. "The Soviet Union and Grenada under the New Jewel Movement." *International Affairs* 61(4): 661–673; John Quigley. 1987. "The United States Invasion of Grenada: Stranger than Fiction." *University of Miami Inter-American Law Review* 18(2): 271–352.

10. Hal Brands. 2010. *Latin America's Cold War.* Cambridge: Harvard University Press, p. 16.

11. David M. Barret. 2001. "Congress, the CIA, and Guatemala, 1954." *Studies in Intelligence* 10: 23–31.

12. Max Paul Friedman. 2010. "Fracas in Caracas: Latin American Diplomatic Resistance to United States Intervention in Guatemala in 1954." *Diplomacy & Statecraft* 21(4): 669–689.

13. Central Intelligence Agency. 2000. *CIA Activities in Chile.* General report available online at https://www.cia.gov/library/reports/general-reports-1/chile/

14. Congressional ratification was needed because Allende won a plurality but not a majority of the vote.

15. Central Intelligence Agency. 2000. *CIA Activities in Chile.* General report available online at https://www.cia.gov/library/reports/general-reports-1/chile/

16. For example, the U.S. spearheaded the OAS suspension of Cuba's membership in 1962. The OAS also agreed to send troops to the Dominican Republic after the landing of U.S. forces in 1965.

17. Robert A. Pastor. 1992. *The Carter Administration and Latin America: A Test of Principle.* Atlanta: The Carter Center, Emory University.

18. Ibid.

19. Ibid.

20. Larry Rother. "Most Latin Nations, Ending Reticence, Backed Deposed Panamanian." *New York Times,* February 27, 1988; Sol M. Linowitz. "A Strategy to Oust Panama's Leader." *New York Times,* April 26, 1988.

21. George de Lama. "Déjà vu in Latin America." *Chicago Tribune.* December 24, 1989, p. 4.

22. Richard L. Millett. 1990. "The Aftermath of Intervention: Panama 1990." *Journal of Interamerican and World Affairs* 32(1): 1–15.

23. John M. Border. "Clinton Offers His Apologies to Guatemala." *The New York Times,* March 11, 1999.

24. David Scott Palmer. 2006. *U.S. Relations with Latin America during the Clinton Years.* Gainesville: University of Florida Press, pp. 33–34.

25. The original provisions for the anti-drug certification process were established by the Foreign Assistance Act of 1961.

26. United Nations Office on Drugs and Crime. 2015. *Colombia: Coca Cultivation Survey, 2014.* Bogota, Colombia: UNODC.

27. Abraham F. Lowenthal. 1992. "Changing U.S. Interests and Policies in a New World." In Jonathan Hartlyn, Lars Schoultz, and Augusto Varas (eds.), *The United States and Latin America in the 1990s: Beyond the Cold War.* Chapel Hill: University of North Carolina Press, pp. 64–85.

28. Cooperation was not "immediate" and "unconditional" as demanded in a United Nations Security Council Resolution.

29. Hector Tobar and Marla Dickerson. "Mexico and Chile Walk a Tightrope." *Los Angeles Times,* March 13, 2003.

30. Terry F. Buss. 2008. *Haiti in the Balance.* Washington, DC: Brookings Institution's Press, p. 39.

31. Maureen Taft-Morales and Clare Ribando Seelke. 2008. "Haiti:

Developments and U.S. Policy since 1991 and Current Congressional Concerns." *Congressional Research Service Report for Congress* (Order Code RL32294).

32. John Lichfield an Andrew Buncombe. "Aristide Plans to Sue France and the US." *The Independent*, March 11, 2004.

33. Jorge I. Dominguez. 2005. "Bush Administration Policy: A View toward Latin America." *ReVista* (Spring/Summer): 3–5.

34. Jeffrey D. Sachs. "From His First Day in Office, Bush Was Ousting Aristide." *Los Angeles Times*, March 4, 2004.

35. Helen Cooper and Marc Lacey. "In a Coup in Honduras, Ghosts of Past U.S. Policies." *New York Times*, June 29, 2009.

36. "The Honduras Conundrum." [Editorial], *New York Times*, December 5, 2009, p. A18.

37. "Documents Show C.I.A. Knew of a Coup Plot in Venezuela." *New York Times,* December 3, 2004, Section A, p. 4.

38. Javier Corrales and Carlos A. Romero. 2013. *U.S.–Venezuela Relations since the 1990s.* New York: Routledge, pp. 49–51.

39. For example, the slide to authoritarianism encouraged Mercosur—the trade bloc composed of Argentina, Brazil, Paraguay, and Uruguay—to suspend Venezuela's membership and gave way to a new round of sanctions from the U.S. and Canadian governments as well as the European Union.

40. In 2017, the Venezuelan government held an election for a constituent assembly, which was boycotted by the opposition and considered fraudulent by many election experts. The pro-government constituent assembly proceeded to take over the powers of the opposition-led national assembly.

41. Vivian Salama. "U.S. Expands Sanctions Against Venezuela into an Embargo." *Wall Street Journal*, August 11, 2019.

42. Juliet Eliperin and Karen De Young. "Obama Addresses the Cuban Nation: 'It Is Time Now for Us to Leave the Past Behind.'" *The Washington Post*, March 22, 2016.

43. Steve Holland and Sofia Menchu. "Guatemala Agrees to New Migration Measures to Avoid Trump Sanctions Threat." *Reuters*, July 26, 2019.

44. Andrew Kohut. "Reviving America's Global Image." *Pew Research Center*, March 5, 2010. Available at http://www.pewglobal.org/2010/03/05/reviving-americas-global-image/

45. Richard Wike, Bruce Stokes, Jacob Poushter, and Janell Fetterolf. 2017. "U.S. Image Suffers as Publics around World Question Trump's Leadership." *Pew Research Center*, June 26, 2017. Available at https://www.pewresearch.org/global/2017/06/26/u-s-image-suffers-as-publics-around-world-question-trumps-leadership/

Chapter 5: Latin American Presidentialism

1. A full text of *Federalist 51* can be accessed at https://billofrightsinstitute.org/founding-documents/primary-source-documents/the-federalist-papers/federalist-papers-no-51/

2. Matthew S. Shugart and John M. Carey. 1992. *Presidents and Assemblies: Constitutional Designs and Electoral Dynamics*. New York: Cambridge University Press, p. 19.

3. Matthew S. Shugart. 2006. "Comparative Executive-Legislative Relations." In R. A. W. Rhodes, Sarah A. Binder, and Bert A. Rockman (eds.), *The Oxford Handbook of Political Institutions*. New York: Oxford University Press, pp. 344–365.

4. It usually requires the consent of the head of state.

5. Juan J. Linz. 1990. "The Perils of Presidentialism." *Journal of Democracy* 1(1): 51–69; Juan J. Linz. 1992. "Presidential or Parliamentary Democracy: Does It Make a Difference?" In Juan J. Linz and Arturo Valenzuela (eds.), *The Failure of Presidential Democracy*. Baltimore: The Johns Hopkins University Press, pp. 3–87.

6. Scott Mainwaring. 1993. "Presidentialism, Multipartyism and Democracy: The Difficult Combination." *Comparative Political Studies* 26(2): 198–228.

7. Juan J. Linz. 1990. "The Perils of Presidentialism." *Journal of Democracy* 1(1): 51–69. Quote from p. 62.

8. José A. Cheibub. 2002. "Minority Governments, Deadlock Situations, and the Survival of Presidential Democracies." *Comparative Political Studies* 35(3): 284–312.

9. José A. Cheibub, Adam Przeworski, Sebastián M. Saiegh. 2004. "Government Coalitions and Legislative Success under Presidentialism and Parliamentarism." *British Journal of Political Science* 34(4): 565–587.

10. Alícia Adserà and Carles Boix. 2008. "Constitutions and Democratic Breakdowns." In José M. Maravall and Ignacio S. Cuenca (eds.), *Controlling Governments*. New York: Cambridge University Press, pp. 247–301.

11. Matthew S. Shugart and John M. Carey. 1992. *Presidents and Assemblies: Constitutional Designs and Electoral Dynamics*. New York: Cambridge University Press, pp. 44–49.

12. This is the case when the executive has a parliamentary majority. In the case of a parliamentary system with a fragmented party system and considerable parliamentary initiative, the coercive capacity shifts from the executive to the assembly.

13. Matthew S. Shugart. 1999. "Presidentialism, Parliamentarism, and the Provision of Collective Goods in Less-Developed Countries." *Constitutional Political Economy* 10(1): 53–88.

14. The president cannot dismiss the prime minister or dissolve the national assembly.

15. A president cannot dismiss the lower chamber during the last year of the term in office.

16. The president cannot dissolve congress during the last year of the term.

17. In Venezuela, the president can also delegate to the executive vice president other responsibilities. For example, in early 2017, President Nicolás Maduro via decree delegated major responsibilities to Vice President Tareck El Aissami, including the ability to undertake expropriations and modify budgetary allocations.

18. While censure votes never took place when the government enjoyed a comfortable majority in congress, they occurred on three occasions after the 2015 election gave the opposition control of congress. However, the increasingly authoritarian government led by President Nicolás Maduro, with the support of the subservient Supreme Court, disregarded these votes of censure.

19. In the prior constitution, censured ministers had to offer their resignations to the president, who could reject them. Since 2009, a minister censured by congress is fired and the president does not intervene.

20. The Radical Party (UCR), in the opposition at that time, sought to install a semi-parliamentary system of government whereby a popularly elected president with relevant legislative powers would coexist with a chief of cabinet elected by parliament and subject to its confidence. The governing party at the time, the Peronist Party (PJ), rejected the move to a semi-presidential system, preferring to maintain the status quo. In the end, both parties compromised and agreed to create the position of cabinet chief.

21. In Ecuador, the recall cannot take place the first or last year of a presidential term; in Bolivia, it can only take place after half of the president's term in office has passed and before the last year; in Venezuela, it can only occur after half of the president's term in office has passed.

22. The type of veto that rejects the entire bill is also referred to as a *block* or *absolute* veto.

23. The U.S. also allows a "pocket veto," which occurs when the president does not sign a bill while congress is adjourned for the stipulated ten-day period. In such a case, congress must reintroduce and pass the bill again to overcome the president's objection.

24. In the case of Brazil, it must happen in a joint session rather than in each chamber separately.

25. However, the vast majority of U.S. states give their governors some type of line-item veto.

26. George Tsebelis and Eduardo Alemán. "Presidential Conditional Agenda Setting Power in Latin America." *World Politics* 57(3): 396–420.

27. In the case of Ecuador, urgencies are restricted to bills on economic matters.

28. Kenneth R. Meyer. 1999. "Executive Orders and Presidential Power." *Journal of Politics* 61(2): 445–466.

29. The other two constitutional grounds are common crimes and crimes in the exercise of his duties.

30. This list does not include the ouster of Ecuadorean President Jamil Mahuad in 2002 because the military played an active role in the process, and as a result, this event is considered a coup. The ouster of Honduran President Manuel Zelaya in 2009 is excluded from the list for the same reason.

31. "Constitutional Coup by Congress Ousts Gutiérrez on Wave of Popular Protests." *Latin American Weekly Reports*, April 26, 2005.

32. Haitian President Jean-Bertrand Aristide also resigned in 2004 (see Chapter 4), but he is not included in this list because, at the time, his government was considered authoritarian.

33. Anatoly Kurmanaev. "Election Fraud Aided Evo Morales, International Panel Concludes." *New York Times*, December 5, 2019. Available https://www.nytimes.com/2019/12/05/world/americas/evo-morales-election.html; "Evo Morales: Overwhelming Evidence of Election Fraud in Bolivia, Monitors Say." *BBC News*, December 6, 2019. Available at https://www.bbc.com/news/world-latin-america-50685335

34. Gabriel Hetland. "Many Wanted Morales Out. But What Happened in Bolivia Was a Military Coup." *The Guardian*, November 13, 2019.

35. David Pion-Berlin. "Why Bolivian President Evo Morales' Resignation Was Not a Coup." *The Globe Post*, November 13, 2019. Available at https://theglobepost.com/2019/11/13/bolivia-no-coup/

36. Aníbal Pérez-Liñán and John Polga-Hecimovich. 2017. "Explaining Military Coups and Impeachments in Latin America." *Democratization* 24(5): 839–858.

37. Christopher A. Martínez. 2017. "Presidential Survival in South America: Rethinking the Role of Democracy." *International Political Science Review* 38(1): 40–55.

38. Young Hun Kim and Donna Bahry. 2008. "Interrupted Presidencies in Third Wave Democracies." *The Journal of Politics* 70(3): 807–822; Michael E. Álvarez and Leiv Marsteintredet. 2010. "Presidential and Democratic Breakdowns in Latin America: Similar Causes, Different Outcomes." In M. Llanos and L. Marsteintredet (eds.), *Presidential Breakdowns in Latin America. Causes and Outcomes of Executive Instability in Developing Democracies*. New York: Palgrave Macmillan, pp. 33–52; Margaret E. Edwards. 2015. "Understanding Presidential Failure in South America." *Latin American Politics and Society* 57(2): 111–131; Aníbal Pérez-Liñán and John Polga-Hecimovich. 2017. "Explaining Military Coups and Impeachments in Latin America." *Democratization* 24(5): 839–858.

39. Kathryn Hochstetler and Margaret E. Edwards. 2009. "Failed Presidencies: Identifying and Explaining a South American Anomaly." *Journal of Politics in Latin America* 1(2): 31–57.

40. Aníbal Pérez-Liñán and John Polga-Hecimovich. 2017. "Explaining Military Coups and Impeachments in Latin America." *Democratization* 24(5): 839–858; Young Hun Kim and Donna Bahry. 2008. "Interrupted Presidencies in Third Wave Democracies." *The Journal of Politics* 70(3): 807–822; Michael E. Álvarez, and Leiv Marsteintredet. 2010. "Presidential and Democratic Breakdowns in Latin America: Similar Causes, Different Outcomes." In M. Llanos and L. Marsteintredet (eds.), *Presidential Breakdowns in Latin America. Causes and Outcomes of Executive Instability in Developing Democracies.* New York: Palgrave Macmillan, pp. 33–52.

41. Margaret E. Edwards. 2015. "Understanding Presidential Failure in South America." *Latin American Politics and Society* 57(2): 111–131.

42. Gretchen Helmke. 2017. *Institutions on the Edge: The Origins of Inter-Branch Crises in Latin America.* New York: Cambridge University Press, pp. 89–91.

43. Aníbal Pérez-Liñán and John Polga-Hecimovich. 2017. "Explaining Military Coups and Impeachments in Latin America." *Democratization* 24(5): 839–858; Young Hun Kim and Donna Bahry. 2008. "Interrupted Presidencies in Third Wave Democracies." *The Journal of Politics* 70(3): 807–822.

44. Kathryn Hochstetler and Margaret E. Edwards. 2009. "Failed Presidencies: Identifying and Explaining a South American Anomaly." *Journal of Politics in Latin America* 1(2): 31–57.

45. Leiv Marsteintredet. 2014. "Explaining Variation of Executive Instability in Presidential Regimes: Presidential Interruptions in Latin America." *International Political Science Review* 35(2): 173–194.

46. Aníbal Pérez-Liñán. 2007. *Presidential Impeachment and the New Political Instability in Latin America.* New York: Cambridge University Press, p. 211.

47. Arturo Valenzuela. 2004. "Latin American Presidencies Interrupted." *Journal of Democracy* 15(4): 5–19.

Chapter 6: Legislatures in Latin America

1. Alexander T. Edelman. 1969. *Latin American Government and Politics: The Dynamics of a Revolutionary Society.* Homewood, Ill.: Dorsey Press, 1969, pp. 443–444.

2. Brian Crisp and Rachael E. Ingall. 2002. "Institutional Engineering and the Nature of Representation: Mapping the Effects of Electoral Reform in Colombia." *American Journal of Political Science* 46 (4): 733–748.

3. Carlos Pereira and Bernardo Muller. 2004. "The Cost of Governing: Strategic Behavior of the President and Legislators in Brazil's Budgetary Process." *Comparative Political Studies* 37(7): 781–815.

4. Michelle M. Taylor. 1992. "Formal versus Informal Incentive Structures and Legislator Behavior: Evidence from Costa Rica." *The Journal of Politics* 54(4): 1055–1073.

5. Eduardo Alemán, Margarita M. Remírez, and Jonathan B. Slapin. 2017. "Party Strategies, Constituency Links, and Legislative Speech." *Legislative Studies Quarterly* 42(4): 637–659.

6. For example, proportional representation with large district magnitude (to be discussed in the next chapter) has been linked to greater opportunities for the election of women legislators.

7. Jennifer M. Piscopo. 2015. "States as Gender Equality Activists: The Evolution of Quota Laws in Latin America." *Latin American Politics and Society* 57(3): 27–49.

8. Leslie A. Schwindt-Bayer. 2010. *Political Power and Women's Representation in Latin America.* New York: Oxford University Press, pp. 131–154.

9. Susan Franceschet and Jennifer M. Piscopo. 2008. "Gender Quotas and Women's Substantive Representation: Lessons from Argentina." *Politics & Gender* 4(3): 393–425; Mala Htun, Marina Lacalle, and Juan Pablo Micozzi. "Does Women's Presence Change Legislative Behavior? Evidence from Argentina." *Journal of Politics in Latin America* 5(1): 95–125; Jennifer M. Piscopo. 2018. "Beyond Hearth and Home: Female Legislators, Feminist Policy Change, and Substantive Representation in Mexico." *Revista Uruguaya de Ciencia Política* 23(2): 87–110.

10. Tiffany D. Barnes. 2012. "Gender and Legislative Preferences: Evidence from the Argentine Provinces." *Politics & Gender* 8(4): 483–507.

11. Karl Kurtz, Bruce Cain, and Richard G. Niemi (eds.). 2007. *Institutional Change in American Politics: The Case of Term Limits.* Ann Arbor: University of Michigan Press.

12. Mark P. Jones, Sebastián Saiegh, Pablo T. Spiller, and Mariano Tomassi. 2002. "Amateur Legislators-Professional Politicians: The Consequences of Party-Centered Electoral Rules in a Federal System." *American Journal of Political Science* 46(3): 656–669.

13. Eduardo Alemán and George Tsebelis (eds.). 2016. *Legislative Institutions and Lawmaking in Latin America.* New York: Oxford University Press, p. 230.

14. Ibid., p. 231.

15. Ibid., p. 232; Andréa Marcondes de Freitas. 2016. "Unboxing the Active Role of the Legislative Power in Brazil." *Brazilian Political Science Review* 10(2), e0004. [Epub.] Accessed August 8, 2016, from https://dx.doi.org/10.1590/1981-38212016000200004

16. Sebastian M. Saiegh. 2010. "Active Players or Rubber Stamps? An Evaluation of the Policymaking Role of Latin American Legislatures." In Carlos Scartascini, Ernesto Stein, and Mariano Tomassi (eds.), *How Democracy Works. Political Institutions, Actors, and Arenas in Latin American Policymaking.* Washington DC: IDB—Harvard University Press, pp. 47–76.

17. Gary W. Cox and Scott Morgenstern. 2001. "Latin America's Reactive Assemblies and Proactive

Presidents." *Comparative Politics* 33(2): 171–189.

18. They can be found in Argentina (only for the cabinet chief), Bolivia, Brazil, Chile, Colombia, Costa Rica, Ecuador, El Salvador, Guatemala, Honduras, Mexico, Nicaragua, Panama, Paraguay, Peru, the Dominican Republic, Uruguay, and Venezuela.

19. In others, such as the Guatemalan congress and the Uruguayan House of Representatives, a favorable vote by a majority of their membership is sufficient for the creation of an investigative committee.

20. Carlos Santiso. 2004. "Legislatures and Budget Oversight in Latin America: Strengthening Public Finance Accountability on Emerging Democracies." *OECD Journal on Budgeting* 4(2):47–76.

21. Oliver Cover and Sazan Meran. 2013. *Watchdogs? The Quality of Legislative Oversight of Defence in 82 Countries.* Defence and Security Programme, Transparency International UK, September 2013.

22. Eduardo Alemán. 2015. "Legislative Organization and Outcomes." In Jennifer Gandhi and Rubén Ruiz-Rufino (eds.), *The Routledge Handbook of Comparative Political Institutions.* London: Routledge, pp. 145–161.

23. Mariana Llanos and Detlef Nolte. 2003. "Bicameralism in the Americas: Around the Extremes of Symmetry and Incongruence." *The Journal of Legislative Studies* 9(3): 54–86.

24. Ibid.

25. In Colombia, the composition of the conference committee is in the hands of the authorities of the chamber.

26. In Argentina, if the chamber of origin disagrees with the version of the bill passed by the revising chamber, it can successfully insist on passing its version of the bill by a majority vote. However, if the revising chamber had passed its version by a two-thirds majority, then the chamber of origin can only prevail if its version of the bill is also supported by a two-thirds majority; otherwise, the version passed by the revising chamber wins. In Brazil, after the revising chamber modifies a bill, the chamber of origin can insist on its version and win by a majority vote. In Paraguay, if there is no agreement on which version of the bill should be passed, the revising chamber can prevail by a vote of a majority of its members. In Mexico and the Dominican Republic, if disagreement between chambers over the final version of the bill cannot be resolved, the bill is rejected. However, in Mexico, both chambers can agree to pass a version of the bill that excludes the matters about which disagreement persisted.

27. In Bolivia, after 30 days of inaction by the revising chamber, the bill passed by the chamber of origin is forwarded to the joint meeting of both chambers, where members of congress can vote to pass the bill.

28. Keith Krehbiel. 1994. "Legislative Organization." *Journal of Economic Perspectives* 18(1): 113–128.

29. Herbert Döring. 1995. "Time as a Scarce Resource: Government Control of the Agenda." In Herbert Döring (ed.), *Parliaments and Majority Rule in Western Europe*. New York: St. Martin's Press, pp. 223–246. Quote is from p. 242.

30. Eduardo Alemán and George Tsebelis. 2016. "Introduction: Legislative Institutions and Agenda Setting." In E. Alemán and G. Tsebelis (eds.), *Legislative Institutions and Lawmaking in Latin America*. Oxford University Press, pp. 1–31.

31. Malcom Shaw. 1998. "Parliamentary Committees: A Global Perspective." *The Journal of Legislative Studies* 4(1): 225–251.

32. Brian F. Crisp, Maria C. Escobar-Lemmon, Bradford S. Jones, Mark P. Jones, and Michelle M. Taylor-Robinson. 2009. "The Electoral Connection and Legislative Committees." *The Journal of Legislative Studies* 15(1): 35–52.

33. Mark P. Jones, Sebastián Saiegh, Pablo T. Spiller, and Mariano Tomassi. 2002. "Amateur Legislators, Professional Politicians: The Consequences of Party-Centered Electoral Rules in a Federal System." *American Journal of Political Science* 46(3): 656–669.

34. Carlos Pereira and Bernardo Mueller. 2004. "A Theory of Executive Dominance of Congressional Politics: The Committee System in the Brazilian Chamber of Deputies." *The Journal of Legislative Studies* 10(1): 9–49. Quote is from p. 30.

35. Inter-American Development Bank. 2006. *The Politics of Policies: Economic and Social Progress in Latin America, 2006*. IADB: Washington DC, p. 55.

36. For example, votes are recorded often in Brazil, Chile, and Peru, but less regularly in countries such as Bolivia and Venezuela.

37. John M. Carey. 2007. "Competing Principals, Political Institutions, and Party Unity in Legislative Voting." *American Journal of Political Science* 51(1): 92–107.

38. Ibid.

39. Carlos Pereira and Bernardo Muller. 2004. "The Cost of Governing: Strategic Behavior of the President and Legislators in Brazil's Budgetary Process." *Comparative Political Studies* 37(7): 781–815.

40. Because in most instances internal rules of procedure offer ways for individual legislators to try to force a vote on a bill not scheduled by the chamber's authorities, the leaders of the majority party also need to prevent their co-partisans from dissenting and joining others to overrule their scheduling decisions. Thus, party discipline can prevent the passage of motions to force votes on bills the leadership does not want to schedule.

41. Gary W. Cox, and Mathew D. McCubbins. 2005. *Setting the Agenda: Responsible Party Government in the US House of Representatives*. New York: Cambridge University Press, p. 12.

42. Mark P. Jones and Wonjae Hwang. 2005. "Party Government in Presidential Democracies: Extending Cartel Theory Beyond the U.S. Congress." *American Journal of Political Science* 49(2): 267–282.

43. Eduardo Alemán. 2006. "Policy Gatekeepers in Latin American Legislatures." *Latin American Politics and Society* 48(3): 125–155.

44. Octavio Amorim Neto, Gary W. Cox, and Mathew D. McCubbins. 2003. "Agenda Power in Brazil's Camara dos Deputados, 1998–98." *World Politics* 55(4): 550–578.

45. Mona M. Lyne 2008 *The Voter's Dilemma and Democratic Accountability: Latin America and Beyond.* University Park: The Pennsylvania University Press. pp. 200–201.

46. John M. Carey. 2009. *Legislative Voting Unity and Accountability.* New York: Cambridge University Press, pp. 140–150.

47. Eduardo Alemán, Aldo F. Ponce, and Iñaki Sagarzazu. 2011. "Legislative Parties in Volatile, Nonprogrammatic Party Systems: The Peruvian Case in Comparative Perspective." *Latin American Politics and Society* 53(3): 57–81.

48. This figure was created using roll-call data for the period 1994–1998.

Chapter 7: Elections and Electoral Rules

1. William Blackstone. 1979. *Commentaries on the Laws of England: A Facsimile of the First Edition of 1765–1769,* Volume 1. Chicago: The University of Chicago Press, p. 165.

2. Ibid.

3. In the U.S., tax-based requirements for voting were common in several states until the middle of the 19th century.

4. Quoted in Valentín Paniagua Corazao. 2003. "El Derecho de Sufragio en el Perú." *Elecciones* 2: 61–89, p. 72.

5. Provincia de Buenos Aires. 1891. *Debates de la Convención Constituyente, Tomo 1, Octubre de 1882 hasta Marzo de 1888.* Buenos Aires: El Censor, pp. 175–177.

6. Manuel Vicente Villarán. 1962. "El Indio y la Geografía Electoral." Páginas Escogidas. Lima: Talleres Gráficos P.L. Villanueva, p. 234.

7. Manuel Murillo Toro. 1979. "El Sufragio Universal." In Jorge Mario Eastman (ed.), *Manuel Murillo Toro: Obras Selectas.* Bogota: Imprenta Nacional, pp. 89–96.

8. Quoted in Luciana de Privitellio. 2012. "¿Qué Reformo la Reforma? La Quimera contra la Maquina y el Voto Secreto y Obligatorio." *Estudios Sociales* 43: 29–58, p. 36.

9. Ana Lau Jaiven and Roxana Rodríguez Bravo. 2017. "Women's Suffrage and the Mexican Constitution of 1917. A Historical Review." *Política y Cultura* 48: 57–81.

10. Gretchen Helmke and Bonnie M. Meguid. 2012. "Endogenous Institutions: The Origins of Compulsory Voting Laws." Working Paper.

11. Mauricio Bugarin and Adriana Portugal. 2015. "Should Voting be Mandatory? The Effects of Compulsory Voting Rules on Candidates' Political Platforms." *Journal of Applied Economics* 18(1): 1–19.

12. Miguel Carreras. 2016. "Compulsory Voting and Political Engagement (Beyond the Ballot Box): A Multilevel Analysis." *Electoral Studies* 43: 158–168.

13. William A. Galston. 2011. "Telling Americans to Vote, or Else." *New York Times*, November 6, p. SR9.

14. Richard Katz. 1997. *Democracy and Elections*. Oxford: Oxford University Press, p. 247.

15. Jason Brennan. 2014. "Should We Force the Drunk to Drive?" In Jason Brennan and Lisa Hill (eds.), *Compulsory Voting: For and Against*. New York: Cambridge University Press, pp. 83–110.

16. Mauricio Morales Quiroga and Gonzalo Contreras. 2017. "¿Por Qué se Aprobó el Voto Voluntario en Chile? Razones y Argumentos que Impulsaron la Reforma." *Revista Chilena de Derecho y Ciencia Política* 6(2): 1–37. doi: 10.7770/RCHDYCP-V8N2=ART1216.

17. A candidate who can be defeated by every other candidate in a one-to-one competition is called a *Condorcet loser* in the social choice literature. Plurality rule violates the Condorcet loser criterion, which requires that such a candidate may not be able to win an election.

18. Matt Golder. 2006. "Presidential Coattails and Legislative Fragmentation." *American Journal of Political Science* 50(1): 34–48.

19. Miguel Carreras. 2018. "Presidential Institutions and Electoral Participation in Concurrent Elections in Latin America." *Political Studies* 66(3): 541–549.

20. Cynthia McClintock. 2018. *Electoral Rules and Democracy in Latin America*. Oxford: Oxford University Press, pp. 8–9.

21. Josep M. Colomer. 2004. "The Americas: General Overview." In Josep M. Colomer (ed.), *The Handbook of Electoral System Choice*. New York: Palgrave Macmillan, pp. 81–109.

22. Javier Corrales and Michael Penfold. 2014. "Manipulating Term Limits in Latin America." *Journal of Democracy* 25(4): 157–168.

23. Some authors call this type of preferential system a *closed and flexible list* or a *closed and unblocked list* rather than *open list* because voters can only choose candidates from one party list.

24. In this case, the vote for the party is only considered in the process of assigning seats to parties but has no effect on the distribution of seats among candidates within a party.

25. Ecuador also has two overlapping tiers of districts (as is the case in Guatemala and Nicaragua, previously discussed), one of which is a national district covering the entire country.

26. The ranking of candidates is done by the parties before the election.

27. This type of plurality rule is sometimes called *majority block voting* or *multiple non-transferable vote*.

28. In the case of Bolivia, the ballot to elect deputies in the multimember district is linked to the vote to elect the country's president and senators. This means that voters cannot split the ticket: They choose one party for president, Senate, and (the multimember district) part of the Chamber of Deputies.

29. This refers to the district magnitude for elections to the lower chamber.

30. A classic example is Arend Lijphart. 1990. "The Political Consequences of Electoral Laws, 1945–85." *American Political Science Review* 84(2): 481–496.

31. As Douglas W. Rae noted long ago, the relationship is curvilinear: Increases in district magnitude lead to proportionality increasing at a decreasing rate. Douglas W. Rae. 1967. *The Political Consequences of Electoral Laws.* New Haven: Yale University Press, p. 153.

32. Michael Gallagher. 1991. "Proportionality, Disproportionality, and Electoral Systems." *Electoral Studies* 10(1): 33–51.

33. The Senate also has an additional special district for indigenous peoples that allocate two seats. Including that district does not change the results and has almost no impact on the disproportionality index for this chamber.

34. The data are from the following elections: Colombia, 2014; Paraguay, 2013; Costa Rica, 2014; Panama, 2014; and the Dominican Republic, 2016.

35. John M. Carey. 2007. "Competing Principals, Political Institutions, and Party Unity in Legislative Voting." *American Journal of Political Science* 51(1): 92–107.

36. David M. Primo and James M. Snyder Jr. 2010. "Party Strength, the Personal Vote, and Government Spending." *American Journal of Political Science* 54(2): 354–370.

37. Joseph W. Robins. 2010. "The Personal Vote and Turnout." *Electoral Studies* 29(4): 661–672.

38. Pippa Norris. 2004. *Electoral Engineering: Voting Rules and Political Behavior.* Cambridge: Cambridge University Press, pp. 240–242.

39. Matthew S. Shugart, Melody E. Valdini, and Kati Suominen. 2005. "Looking for Locals: Voter Information Demands and Personal Vote-Earning Attributes of Legislators under Proportional Representation." *American Journal of Political Science* 49(2): 437–449.

40. John M. Carey and Matthew S. Shugart. 1995. "Incentives to Cultivate a Personal Vote: A Rank Ordering of Electoral Formulas." *Electoral Studies* 14(4): 417–439.

41. John M. Carey and Matthew S. Shugart. 1995. "Incentives to Cultivate a Personal Vote: A Rank Ordering of Electoral Formulas." *Electoral Studies* 14(4): 417–439; Audrey André and Sam Depauw. 2014. "District Magnitude and the Personal Vote." *Electoral Studies* 35: 102–114.

42. José Antonio Cheibub and Gisela Sin. 2020. "Preference Vote and Intra-Party Competition in Open List PR Systems." *Journal of Theoretical Politics* 32(1): 70–95.

Chapter 8: The Judiciary

1. This definition of judicial crises comes from Gretchen Helmke. 2017. *Institutions on the Edge: The Origins and Consequences of Inter-Branch Crises in Latin America.* New York: Cambridge University Press, p. 142.

2. Ibid., p. 30.

3. John Ferejohn, Frances Rosenbluth, and Charles Shipan. 2007. "Comparative Judicial Politics." In Carles Boix and Susan C. Stokes (eds), *The Oxford Handbook of Comparative Politics*. New York: Oxford University Press, pp. 727–751.

4. Cristina Costantini. "Honduran President Fears Coup, Four Supreme Court Judges Fired." *ABC News*, December 12, 2012. Available at https://abcnews.go.com/ABC_Univision/News/honduran-congress-fires-supreme-court-judges/story?id=17944425

5. "Venezuela: Chávez's Authoritarian Legacy." *Human Rights Watch*, March 5, 2013. Available at https://www.hrw.org/news/2013/03/05/venezuela-chavezs-authoritarian-legacy

6. Leonardo Vivas, Noam Chomsky, and Charlie Clements. "One of Chávez's Most Arbitrary Acts Has Finally Been Reversed." *New York Times*, July 22, 2019. Available at https://www.nytimes.com/2019/07/22/opinion/maria-lourdes-afiuni-chomsky-venezuela.html

7. Baron de Montesquieu, Charles Louis de Secondat. 1784 [2001]. *The Spirit of Laws*. Translated by Thomas Nugent. Ontario: Batoche Books, p. 173

8. Adams's views were included in his drafts of the Massachusetts constitution and incorporated into the text passed in 1780.

9. Julio Ríos Figueroa. 2011. "Institutions for Constitutional Justice in Latin America." In Gretchen Helmke and Julio Ríos Figueroa (eds.), *Courts in Latin America*. New York: Cambridge University Press, pp. 27–54.

10. Erika Moreno, Brian F. Crisp, and Matthew S. Shugart. 2003. "The Accountability Deficit in Latin America." In Scott Mainwaring and Christopher Welna (eds.), *Democratic Accountability in Latin America*. New York: Oxford University Press, pp. 79–131.

11. See, for instance, the information provided in the following website from the Brazilian government: http://www.brazil.gov.br/government/how-the-government-works/federal-judiciary-branch

12. The number of candidates on the ballot was 36 for each court.

13. The judicial council may select two additional members from lists proposed by labor and business organizations. Members of the judicial council may be dismissed before their term is over with the vote of two thirds of members of congress.

14. Gretchen Helmke and Jeffrey Staton. 2011. "The Puzzling Judicial Politics of Latin America: A Theory of Litigation, Judicial Decisions, and Inter-Branch Conflict." In Gretchen Helmke and Julio Ríos Figueroa (eds.), *Courts in Latin America*. New York: Cambridge University Press, pp. 306–331.

15. Daniel M. Brinks and Abby Blass. 2018. *The DNA of Constitutional Justice in Latin America: Politics, Governance, and Judicial Design*. New York: Cambridge University Press, p. 46.

16. Julio Ríos Figueroa. 2011 "Institutions for Constitutional Justice in Latin America." In Gretchen Helmke and Julio Ríos Figueroa (eds.), *Courts in Latin America*. New York: Cambridge University Press, pp. 27–54.

17. The required majority is not in the constitution but in the rules of the Peruvian congress (Article 89.i).

18. Julio Ríos Figueroa. 2011. "Institutions for Constitutional Justice in Latin America." In Gretchen Helmke and Julio Ríos Figueroa (eds.), *Courts in Latin America*. New York: Cambridge University Press, pp. 27–54.

19. For example, constitutional provisions in Argentina and Mexico prohibit the political branches from reducing the salaries of Supreme Court judges while they are in office.

20. Jenna Bednar, William N. Eskridge Jr., and John Ferejohn. 2001. "A Political Theory of Federalism." In John Ferejohn, Jack N. Rakove, and Jonathan Riley (eds.), *Constitutional Culture and Democratic Rule*. New York: Cambridge University Press, pp. 223–270.

21. McNollgast. 2006. "Conditions for Judicial Independence." *Journal of Contemporary Legal Issues*, 15(1): 105–127. For an argument challenging the assertion that fragmentation favors judicial independence, see Lisa Hilbink. 2012. "The Origins of Positive Judicial Independence." *World Politics* 64(4): 587–621.

22. Rebecca Bill Chávez, John A. Ferejohn, and Barry R. Weingast. 2011. "A Theory of the Political Independent Judiciary: A Comparative Study of the United States and Argentina." In Gretchen Helmke and Julio Ríos Figueroa (eds.), *Courts in Latin America*. New York: Cambridge University Press, pp. 219–247.

23. Druscilla Scribner. 2011. "Courts, Power, and Rights in Argentina and Chile." In Gretchen Helmke and Julio Ríos Figueroa (eds.), *Courts in Latin America*. New York: Cambridge University Press, pp. 248–277.

24. She examines the constitutionality of presidential use of exceptional authority.

25. Julio Ríos-Figueroa. 2007. "Fragmentation of Power and the Emergence of an Effective Judiciary in Mexico, 1994–2002." *Latin American Politics and Society*, 49(1): 31–57.

26. Georg Vanberg. 2001. "Legislative-Judicial Relations: A Game-Theoretic Approach to Constitutional Review." *American Journal of Political Science* 45(2): 346–61.

27. Jeffrey K. Stanton. 2006. "Constitutional Review and the Selective Promotion of Case Results." *American Journal of Political Science* 50(1): 98–112.

28. Catalina Smulovitz and Enrique Peruzzotti. 2000. "Societal Accountability in Latin America." *Journal of Democracy* 11(4): 147–158.

29. Joseph Daniel Ura and Alison Higgins Merrill. 2017. "The Supreme Court and Public Opinion." In Lee Epstein and Stefanie A. Lindquist

(eds.), *The Oxford Handbook of U.S. Judicial Behavior.* Oxford: Oxford University Press, pp. 432–459.

30. Julio Ríos Figueroa. 2011. "Institutions for Constitutional Justice in Latin America." In Gretchen Helmke and Julio Ríos Figueroa (eds.), *Courts in Latin America.* New York: Cambridge University Press, pp. 27–54.

31. Ibid.

32. Except for the case of Chile, this review is based on data presented in Julio Ríos Figueroa (Ibid.).

33. Teresa M. Miguel-Stearns. 2015. "Judicial Power in Latin America: A Short Survey." *Legal Information Management* 15(2): 100–107.

34. It is debatable how restricted this last path actually is. A *writ of unconstitutionality*, as it is called in Chilean jurisprudence, allows a plaintiff to petition the constitutional court to exercise abstract constitutional review (a posteriori), which would make this path open rather than restricted. However, this can take place only after the court has ruled on the same matter using concrete constitutional review. In fact, the Constitutional Tribunal seldom decides on writs of unconstitutionality filed by individuals.

35. The Chilean Constitutional Tribunal may have a slight edge over the Bolivian one because it has one procedure for abstract review that is semi-closed.

36. Daniel M. Brinks and Abby Blass. 2018. *The DNA of Constitutional Justice in Latin America: Politics, Governance,* *and Judicial Design.* New York: Cambridge University Press, p. 302.

37. Lydia Tiede and Susan Achury. 2019. "Challenging Authorities' (In)action via Amparos." In Susan Sterett and Lee Walker (eds.), *Research Handbook on Law and Courts.* Cheltenham, UK: Edward Elgar Publishing, pp. 130–144; Allan R. Brewer-Carías. 2009. *Constitutional Protection of Human Rights in Latin America: A Comparative Study of Amparo Proceedings.* New York: Cambridge University Press.

38. For information on rulings from the Constitutional Tribunal of Colombia, see https://www.corteconstitucional.gov.co/english/

39. Lydia Tiede and Susan Achury. 2019. "Challenging Authorities' (In)action via Amparos." In Susan Sterett and Lee Walker (eds.), *Research Handbook on Law and Courts.* Cheltenham, UK: Edward Elgar Publishing, pp. 130–144.

40. Elizabeth J. Zechmeister and Noam Lupu (eds.). 2019. *Pulse of Democracy.* Nashville, TN: LAPOP, p. 35.

41. Cuba is not included in this survey.

42. Ryan Carlin. 2017. "Democratic Orientations in the Americas." In Mollie J. Cohen, Noam Lupu, and Elizabeth J. Zechmeister (eds.). *The Political Culture of Democracy in the Americas, 2016/2017: A Comparative Study of Governance and Democracy, Latin American Public Opinion Project.* Nashville: Vanderbilt University, pp. 129–144.

43. Ryan Salzman and Adam Ramsey. 2013. "Judging the Judiciary:

Understanding Public Confidence in Latin American Courts." *Latin American Politics and Society* 55(1): 73–95.

44. Gretchen Helmke. 2017. *Institutions on the Edge: The Origins and Consequences of Inter-Branch Crises in Latin America.* New York: Cambridge University Press, p. 30.

45. Shawnette Rochelle and Jay Loschky. "Confidence in Judicial Systems Varies Worldwide." *Gallup News*, October 22, 2019. Available at https://news.gallup.com/poll/178757/confidence-judicial-systems-varies-worldwide.aspx

46. Pilar Domingo. 2004. "Judicialization of Politics or Politicization of the Judiciary? Recent Trends in Latin America." *Democratization* 11(1): 104–126.

47. Amanda Driscoll and Michael J. Nelson. 2018. "There Is No Legitimacy Crisis: Public Support for Judicial Institutions in Modern Latin America." Working Paper, Florida State University.

48. World Justice Project. 2019. WJP Rule of Law Index 2019, p. 11. Available at https://worldjusticeproject.org/our-work/publications/rule-law-index-reports/wjp-rule-law-index-2019

49. Cuba, which ranks at the bottom of the prior ranking, is excluded from the analysis provide by the World Justice Project.

50. Sandra Day O'Connor. 2006. "Remarks on Judicial Independence." *Florida Law Review* 58(1): 1–6.

Chapter 9: Political Culture

1. Gabriel Almond and Sidney Verba. 1963. *The Civic Culture.* Thousand Oaks: SAGE.

2. Ronald Inglehart. 2003. "How Solid Is Mass Support for Democracy—And How Can We Measure It?" *PS: Political Science & Politics* 36(1): 51–57.

3. Larry Diamond. 1999. *Developing Democracy: Towards Consolidation.* Baltimore: The Johns Hopkins University Press, p. 175.

4. John A. Booth and Mitchell A. Seligson. 2009. *The Legitimacy Puzzle in Latin America: Political Support and Democracy in Eight Nations.* New York: Cambridge University Press, p. 244.

5. Nicola Fuchs-Schündeln and Matthias Schündeln. 2015. "On the Endogeneity of Political Preferences: Evidence from Individual Experience with Democracy." *Science* 347(6226): 1145–1148.

6. John A. Booth and Patricia Bayer Richard. 2015. *Latin American Political Culture: Public Opinion and Democracy.* Los Angeles: CQ Press, p. 186.

7. Ibid., pp. 36–38.

8. Scott Mainwaring and Aníbal Pérez-Liñán. 2013. *Democracies and Dictatorships in Latin America: Emergence, Survival, and Fall.* New York: Cambridge University Press.

9. John A. Booth and Patricia Bayer Richard. 2015. *Latin American Political Culture: Public Opinion and Democracy.* Los Angeles: CQ Press, p. 186.

10. Seymour Martin Lipset. 1959. "Some Social Requisites of Democracy: Economic Development and Political Legitimacy." *American Political Science Review* 53(1): 69–105. Quote is from p. 79.

11. Richard Wike, Katie Simmons, Bruce Stokes, and Janell Fetterolf. "Globally, Broad Support for Representative and Direct Democracy." *Pew Research Center,* October 16, 2017. Available at http://www.pewresearch.org/

12. Ryan E. Carlin. 2006. "The Socioeconomic Roots of Support for Democracy and the Quality of Democracy." *Revista de Ciencia Política* 26(1): 48–66.

13. Ryan E. Carlin and Matthew M. Singer. 2011. "Support for Polyarchy in the Americas." *Comparative Political Studies* 44(11): 1500–1526. Quote is from p. 1502.

14. Michael Coppedge. 2012. *Democratization and Research Methods.* New York: Cambridge University Press, p. 247.

15. The percentages are based on the total number of respondents who answered the questions (i.e., it excludes those who did not answer or did not know).

16. Ryan E. Carlin and Matthew M. Singer. 2011. "Support for Polyarchy in the Americas." *Comparative Political Studies* 44(11): 1500–1526; John A. Booth and Patricia Bayer Richard. 2015. *Latin American Political Culture: Public Opinion and Democracy.* Los Angeles: CQ Press, pp. 29–31.

17. Ronald Inglehart. 2003. "How Solid Is Mass Support for Democracy—And How Can We Measure It?" *PS: Political Science & Politics* 36(1): 51–57.

18. John A. Booth and Patricia Bayer Richard. 2015. *Latin American Political Culture: Public Opinion and Democracy.* Los Angeles: CQ Press, p. 153.

19. Inter-American Commission on Human Rights. 2015. *Violence against Lesbian, Gay, Bisexual, Trans and Intersex Persons in the America.* Organization of American States, Doc. 36.

20. Natalia Letki. 2018. "Trust in Newly Democratic Regimes." In Eric M. Uslaner (ed.), *The Oxford Handbook of Social and Political Trust.* New York: Oxford University Press, pp. 335–356; William Mishler and Richard Rose. 2001. "What Are the Origins of Political Trust? Testing Institutional and Cultural Theories in Post-Communist Societies." *Comparative Political Studies* 34(1): 30–62.

21. Ronald Inglehart. 1977. *The Silent Revolution: Changing Values and Political Styles among Western Publics.* Princeton: Princeton University Press; Robert Putnam. 1993. *Making Democracy Work.* Princeton: Princeton University Press.

22. William Mishler and Richard Rose. 2001. "What Are the Origins of Political Trust? Testing Institutional and Cultural Theories in Post-Communist Societies." *Comparative Political Studies* 34(1): 30–62.

23. Michel J. Crozier, Samuel P. Huntington, and Joji Watanuki. 1975. *The Crisis of Democracy: Report on the Governability of Democracies to the Trilateral Commission.* New York: New York University Press, p. 162.

24. OECD. 2017. *Government at a Glance 2017.* Paris: OECD Publishing, p. 214.

25. William Mishler and Richard Rose. 2001. "What Are the Origins of Political Trust? Testing Institutional and Cultural Theories in Post-Communist Societies." *Comparative Political Studies* 34(1): 30–62.

26. Gabriela Catterberg and Alejandro Moreno. 2006. "The Individual Bases of Political Trust: Trends in New and Established Democracies." *International Journal of Public Opinion Research* 18(1): 31–48.

27. "Beyond Distrust: How Americans View Their Government." *Pew Research Center,* November 23, 2015. Available at https://www.peo ple-press.org/2015/11/23/beyond -distrust-how-americans-view-their -government/

28. Ronald Inglehart. 1977. *The Silent Revolution: Changing Values and Political Styles among Western Publics.* Princeton: Princeton University Press.

29. Russell J. Dalton and Doh Chull Shin. 2014. "Reassessing the Civic Culture Model." In Russell J. Dalton and Christian Welzel (eds.), *The Civic Culture Transformed: Form Allegiant to Assertive Citizens.* New York: Cambridge University Press, pp. 91–115. Quote is from p. 101.

30. Russell J. Dalton. 2005. "The Social Transformation of Trust in Government." *International Review of Sociology* 15(1): 133–154.

31. Pippa Norris. 1999. "Introduction: The Growth of Critical Citizens?" In Pippa Norris (ed.), *Critical Citizens: Global Support for Democratic Government.* New York: Oxford University Press, pp. 1–30.

32. OECD/CAF/ECLAC. 2018. *Latin American Economic Outlook 2018: Rethinking Institutions for Development.* Paris: OECD Publishing, p. 15.

33. Alberto Alesina and Eliana La Ferrara. 2002. "Who Trusts Others?" *Journal of Public Economics* 85(2): 207–234.

34. Robert Putnam. 1993. *Making Democracy Work.* Princeton: Princeton University Press; Pippa Norris (ed.). 1999. *Critical Citizens: Support for Democratic Government.* New York: Oxford University Press.

35. Ronald Inglehart. 1999. "Trust, Well-Being and Democracy." In Mark Warren (ed.), *Democracy and Trust.* Cambridge: Cambridge University Press, pp. 88–120.

36. Marta Lagos. 2001. "Between Stability and Crisis in Latin America." *Journal of Democracy* 12(1): 137–145.

37. Edward N. Muller and Mitchell A. Seligson. 1994. "Civic Culture and Democracy: The Question of Causal Relationships." *American Political Science Review* 88(3): 635–652.

38. Abby Córdova. 2011. "The Role of Social Capital in Citizen Support for Governmental Action to Reduce Economic Inequality." *International Journal of Sociology* 41(2): 28–49.

39. Charles L. Davis, Roderic Ai Camp, and Kenneth M. Coleman. 2004. "The Influence of Party Systems on Citizens' Perceptions of

Corruption and Electoral Response in Latin America." *Comparative Political Studies* 37(6): 677–703.

40. Mathew L. Layton. 2010. "Trust in Elections." *AmericasBarometer Insights Series,* Volume II. Nashville: Vanderbilt University, pp. 39–44.

41. John A. Booth and Patricia Bayer Richard. 2015. *Latin American Political Culture: Public Opinion and Democracy.* Los Angeles: CQ Press, p. 64.

42. Miguel Carreras. 2013. "The Impact of Criminal Violence on Regime Legitimacy in Latin America." *Latin American Research Review* 48(3): 85–107.

43. Joseph L. Klesner. 2007. "Social Capital and Political Participation in Latin America: Evidence from Argentina, Chile, Mexico, and Peru." *Latin America Research Review* 42(2): 1–32.

44. OECD. 2016. *Society at a Glance 2016: OECD Social Indicators.* Paris: OECD Publishing, p. 128.

45. Juan Pablo Luna and Cristóbal Rovira Kaltwasser. 2014. "The Right in Contemporary Latin America: A Framework for Analysis." In Juan Pablo Luna and Cristóbal Rovira Kaltwasser (eds.), *The Resilience of the Latin American Right.* Baltimore: Johns Hopkins University Press, pp. 1–24, p. 3.

46. Ronald Inglehart. 1997. *Modernization and Postmodernization: Cultural, Economic, and Political Change in 43 Societies.* Princeton: Princeton University Press, p. 238.

47. Elizabeth Zechmeister. 2006. "What's Left and Who's Right? A Q-Method Study of Individual and Contextual Influences on the Meaning of Ideological Labels." *Political Behavior* 28(2): 151–173.

48. Elizabeth Zechmeister and Margarita Corral. 2010. "El Variado Significado de 'Izquierda' y 'Derecha' en América Latina." *Perspectivas desde el Barómetro de las Américas* 38. LAPOP.

49. Nina Wiesehomeier and David Doyle. 2012. "Attitudes, Ideological Associations and the Left–Right Divide in Latin America." *Journal of Politics in Latin America* 4(1): 3–33.

50. The same is the case in Haiti, with the exception that a larger percentage of respondents do not place themselves on the left–right spectrum.

51. The numbers are based on the averages for each of the 19 Latin American countries included in the surveys.

Chapter 10: Corruption

1. "El Expresidente Salvadoreño Saca, Condenado a 10 Años de Cárcel por Desviar Más de 300 Millones." *El País,* September 13, 2018.

2. Sam Roberts. "Francisco Flores, Tainted Ex-President of El Salvador, Dies at 56." *New York Times,* February 2, 2016.

3. Dan Collyns. "Peru President Pedro Pablo Kuczynski Resigns amid Corruption Scandal." *The Guardian,* March 21, 2018.

4. "Peru Top Court Says Ex-President Humala Must Be Freed from Jail." *Reuters*, April 26, 2018.

5. Kevin Casas-Zamora and Miguel Carter. 2017. *Beyond the Scandals: The Changing Context of Corruption in Latin America*. Washington, DC: Inter-American Dialogue.

6. Oskar Kurer. 2015. "Definitions of Corruption." In Paul M. Heywood (ed.), *Routledge Handbook of Political Corruption*. New York: Routledge, pp. 30–41.

7. Ibid., p. 38.

8. Bo Rothstein and Aiysha Varraich. 2017. *Making Sense of Corruption*. Cambridge, UK: Cambridge University Press, pp. 55–56.

9. The survey was conducted by the nongovernmental organization *Acción Ciudadana Frente a la Pobreza* (https://democraciasinpobreza.mx/inicio/) and reported widely in the press.

10. Carlos Melendez. 2014. *Honduras, Elecciones 2013: Compra de Votos y Democracia*. Tegucigalpa, Honduras: Lithopress Industrial.

11. Dominik H. Enste and Christina Heldman. 2017. *Causes and Consequences of Corruption: An Empirical Overview*. Köln, Germany: Cologne Institute for Economic Research, IW Report.

12. Martin Paldam. 2002. "The Big Pattern of Corruption. Economics, Culture and the Seesaw Dynamics." *European Journal of Political Economy* 18(2): 215–240.

13. Laurence Whitehead. 2000. "High-Level Political Corruption in Latin America: A 'Transitional' Phenomenon?" In Joseph S. Tulchin and Ralph H. Espach (eds.), *Combating Corruption in Latin America*. Washington, DC: Woodrow Wilson Center, pp. 107–129.

14. Lorenzo Pellegrini and Reyer Gerlagh. 2008. "Causes of Corruption: A Survey of Cross-Country Analyses and Extended Results." *Economics of Governance* 9(3): 245–263; Danila Serra. 2006. "Empirical Determinants of Corruption: A Sensitivity Analysis." *Public Choice* 126: 225–256; Daniel Treisman. 2000. "The Causes of Corruption: A Cross-National Study." *Journal of Public Economics* 76(3): 399–457.

15. Hamid Mohtadi and Terry L. Roe. 2003. "Democracy, Rent Seeking, Public Spending and Growth." *Journal of Public Economics* 87(3): 445–466.

16. Michael T. Rock. 2009. "Corruption and Democracy." *Journal of Development Studies* 45(1): 55–75.

17. Axel Dreher, Christos Kotsogiannis, and Steve Mccorriston. 2009. "How Do Institutions Affect Corruption and the Shadow Economy?" *International Tax and Public Finance* 16(6): 773–796.

18. Randall G. Holcombe and Christopher J. Bordeaux. 2015. "Regulation and Corruption." *Public Choice* 164(1): 75–85; Nicholas A. Lash and Bala Batavia. 2013. "Government Economic Intervention and

Corruption." *The Journal of Developing Areas* 47(2): 1–15.

19. Barbara Kowalczyk-Hoye. 2011. *Promoting Revenue Transparency: 2011 Report on Oil and Gas Companies.* Berlin, Germany: Transparency International. Available at https://www.transparency.org/whatwedo/publication/promoting_revenue_transparency_2011_report_on_oil_and_gas_companies

20. Kenneth Rapoza. "Brazil's Petrobras Not a Victim of Corruption, But a Participant." *Forbes*, August 29, 2017. Available at https://www.forbes.com/sites/kenrapoza/2017/08/29/brazils-petrobras-not-a-victim-of-corruption-but-a-participant/#77a700b264c2

21. "Oil Company Corruption Scandal Threatens Ecuador's Political Elite." *Insight Crime,* November 7, 2016. Available at https://www.insightcrime.org/news/brief/oil-company-corruption-scandal-threatens-ecuador-political-elite/

22. "Carlos Pareja Yannuzzelli y Tres Personas Más Sentenciadas a 6 Años y 8 Meses de Cárcel por Tráfico de Influencias." *El Universo,* September 13, 2019. Available at https://www.eluniverso.com/noticias/2019/09/13/nota/7516657/carlos-pareja-yannuzzelli-tres-personas-mas-sentenciadas-6-anos-8

23. Nabamita Dutta and Sanjukta Roy. 2016. "The Impact of Press Freedom and Media Outreach on Corruption." *Economic Modelling* 58: 337–236; Shyamal K. Chowdhury. 2004. "The Effect of Democracy and Press Freedom on Corruption: An Empirical Test." *Economic Letters* 85(1): 93–101.

24. Cheryl W. Gray and Daniel Kaufmann. 1998. "Corruption and Development." *Finance & Development* 35(1): 7–10.

25. Robert Putnam. 2000. *Bowling Alone: The Collapse and Revival of American Community.* New York: Simon & Schuster, pp. 2–23.

26. Johann Graf Lambsdorff. 2002. "Making Corrupt Deals: Contracting in the Shadow of the Law." *Journal of Economic Behavior and Organization* 48(3): 221–241.

27. Eric M. Uslaner. 2002. *The Moral Foundations of Trust.* Cambridge: Cambridge University Press, pp. 220–221.

28. Eric M. Uslaner. 2004. "Trust and Corruption." In Johann Graf Lambsdorff, Markus Taube, and Matthias Schramm (eds.), *The New Institutional Economics of Corruption: Norms, Trust, and* Reciprocity. London: Routledge, pp. 76–92.

29. Paolo Mauro. 1995. "Corruption and Growth." *The Quarterly Journal of Economics* 110(3): 681–712; Andrzej Cieślik and Łukasz Goczek. 2018. "Control of Corruption, International Investment, and Economic Growth—Evidence from Panel Data." *World Development* 103: 323–335.

30. For evidence that corruption increases dropout rates in primary schools, see Sanjeev Gupta, Hamid R. Davoodi, and Erwin R. Tiongson.

2001. "Corruption and the Provision of Health Care and Education Services." In Arvind K. Jain (ed.), *The Political Economy of Corruption*. London: Routledge, pp. 111–141.

31. Paulo Mauro. 1998. "Corruption and the Composition of Government Expenditure." *Journal of Public Economics* 69: 263–279.

32. Vito Tanzi. "Corruption: Arm's Length Relationships and Markets." In Gianluca Fiorentini and Sam Peltzman (eds.), *The Economics of Organized Crime*. Cambridge: Cambridge University Press, pp. 161–180.

33. Sanjeev Gupta, Hamid Davoodi, and Rosa Alonso-Terme. 2002. "Does Corruption Affect Income Inequality and Poverty?" *Economics of Governance* 3(1): 23–45.

34. World Bank. 2001. *World Development Report 2000/2001: Attacking Poverty*. New York: Oxford University Press, p. 102.

35. Ibid.

36. Ray Fisman and Miriam A. Golden 2017. *Corruption: What Everyone Needs to Know*. New York: Oxford University Press, pp. 95–96.

37. Sanjeev Gupta, Hamid Davoodi, and Rosa Alonso-Terme. 2002. "Does Corruption Affect Income Inequality and Poverty?" *Economics of Governance* 3(1): 23–45.

38. Luis Enrique Pedauga, Lucien David Pedauga, and Blanca L. Delgado-Márquez. 2017. "Relationships between Corruption, Political Orientation, and Income Inequality: Evidence from Latin America." *Applied Economics* 49(17): 1689–1705; Brian J. Fried, Paul Lagunes, and Atheendar Venkataramani. 2010. "Corruption and Inequality at the Crossroad: A Multimethod Study of Bribery and Discrimination in Latin America." *Latin America Research Review* 45(1): 76–97.

39. Stephen Dobson and Carlyn Ramlogan-Dobson. 2012. "Why Is Corruption Less Harmful to Income Inequality in Latin America?" *World Development* 40(8): 1534–1545.

40. Bianca Clausen, Aart Kraay, and Zsolt Nyiri. 2011. "Corruption and Confidence in Public Institutions: Evidence from a Global Survey." *The World Bank Economic Review* 25(2): 212–249.

41. Stephen D. Morris and Joseph L. Klesner. "Corruption and Trust: Theoretical Considerations and Evidence from Mexico." *Comparative Political Studies* 43(10): 1258–1285.

42. United Nations Office on Drugs and Crime. 2017. *World Drug Report 2017*. United Nations publication, p. 3.

43. Edgardo Buscaglia and Jan van Dijk. 2003. "Controlling Organized Crime and Corruption in the Public Sector." *Forum on Crime and Society* 3(1&2): 3–34.

44. International Monetary Fund. *Corruption: Costs and Mitigating Strategies*. Staff Discussion Note, May 16, 2016.

45. Adriana García. 2016. *Transparency in Mexico: An Overview of Access to*

Information Regulations and their Effectiveness at the Federal and State Level. Washington, DC: Wilson Center, Mexico Institute Report.

46. Susan Rose-Ackerman, an expert in the study of corruption, suggests that giving bonuses to officials who achieve procurement goals can help substitute for illegal payoffs; see Susan Rose-Ackerman. 2004. "Governance and Corruption." In Bjørn Lomborg (ed.), *Global Crises, Global Solutions.* Cambridge: Cambridge University Press, 301–362.

47. Auralice Graft, Stefaan Verhulst, and Andrew Young. 2016. "Brazil's Open Budget Transparency Portal: Making Public How Public Money Is Spent." *GOVLAB Report.* Available at http://odimpact.org/case-brazils-open-budget-transparency-portal.html

48. USAID. 2017. "Combatting Corruption among Civil Servants: Interdisciplinary Perspectives on What Works." Research and Innovation Grants Working Papers Series.

49. Carl Dahlström, Victor Lapuente, and Jan Teorell. 2012. "The Merit of Meritocratization: Politics, Bureaucracy, and the Institutional Deterrents of Corruption." *Political Research Quarterly* 65(3): 656–668; Nicholas Charron, Carl Dahlström, Mihaly Fazekas, and Victor Lapuente. 2017. "Careers, Connections, and Corruption Risks: Investigating the Impact of Bureaucratic Meritocracy on Public Procurement Processes." *The Journal of Politics* 79(1): 89–104.

50. Christian Schuster. 2014. *Strategies to Professionalize the Civil Service Lessons from the Dominican Republic.* Washington, DC: Inter-American Development Bank, Technical Note 688.

51. Americas Society/Council of the Americas Report. 2018. "Latin America's Battle Against Corruption: A Path Forward." Available at https://www.as-coa.org/articles/latin-americas-battle-against-corruption-path-forward

52. Interpol. 2002. *Global Standards to Combat Corruption in Police Forces/Services.* Available at https://policehumanrightsresources.org/content/uploads/2001/01/Global-Standards-to-Combat-Corruption-in-Police-Forces-Services.pdf?x68217

53. "Casi 2 Mil Policías Reprebaron Pruebas del Polígrafo." *La Prensa,* November 4, 2015. Available at https://www.laprensa.hn/honduras/897459-410/casi-2-mil-polic%C3%ADas-reprobaron-pruebas-del-pol%C3%ADgrafo

54. Christopher Sherman, Martha Mendoza, and Garance Burke. "Honduras's National Police Chief Helped Cartel Move 1,700 lbs. of Cocaine, Report Says." *Chicago Tribune,* January 26, 2018.

55. Kevin Casas-Zamora. 2016. "The State of Political Finance Regulations in Latin America." International IDEA Discussion Paper. Stockholm, Sweden: International Institute for Democracy and Electoral Assistance, p. 13.

56. Kevin Casas-Zamora and Daniel Zovatto. 2015. *The Cost of Democracy: Campaign Finance Regulation in Latin America.* Washington, DC:

Brookings Institution, Policy Brief Series.

57. "Consenso Entre Varios Líderes Políticos Para Eliminar Fueros de los Parlamentarios." *El Observador,* April 2, 2018. Available at https://www.elobservador.com.uy/nota/consenso-entre-varios-lideres-politicos-para-eliminar-fueros-de-los-parlamentarios-20184221330

58. Randall C. Archibald. "Politics Enables Mexican Fugitive to Defang a Law." *New York Times,* December 15, 2010, p. A1.

59. Kevin Casas-Zamora and Miguel Carter. 2017. *Beyond the Scandals: The Changing Context of Corruption in Latin America*. Washington, DC: Inter-American Dialogue.

60. See the OAS website, Anticorruption Portal of the Americas, for related information: http://www.oas.org/en/sla/dlc/mesicic/documentos.html

61. Transparency International indices are available at https://www.transparency.org

62. Information on this indicator and data are available at http://info.worldbank.org/governance/wgi/#home

63. World Bank Enterprise Surveys are available at http://www.enterprisesurveys.org/data

64. "Corruption in Latin America: Democracy to the rescue." *The Economist,* March 12, 2015. Available at https://www.economist.com/the-americas/2015/03/12/democracy-to-the-rescue

65. Lindsay Mayka and Amy Erica Smith. "Could Corruption Investigations Undermine Democracy in Latin America?" *Vox,* May 17, 2018.

66. Jorge G. Castañeda. "Has Latin America's Crusade against Corruption Gone Too Far?" *New York Times,* April 15, 2018.

67. "Lo Que Debe Saber del Escándalo de Corrupción de Odebrecht." *Revista Semana,* January 24, 2017.

68. "Former Brazilian Leader Lula to Face Fifth Corruption Trial." *Reuters,* December 19, 2016.

69. "Alan García: Peru's Former President Kills Himself Ahead of arrest." *BBC News,* April 17, 2019.

70. "Panama Says Odebrecht Paid Ex-President's Sons $49 Million." *Reuters,* November 9, 2017.

71. Michael Lohmuller. "Guatemala's Government Corruption Scandals Explained." *InSight Crime,* June 21, 2016.

72. "Guatemala Court Says President Must Allow Return of Anti-Corruption Chief." *The Guardian,* September 17, 2018.

73. Ernesto Londoño and Letícia Casado. "Former President Michel Temer of Brazil Is Arrested in Bribery Probe." *New York Times,* March 21, 2019.

74. "Juez Ofreció Reducción de Pena Para Violador de Menor." *La República,* July 8, 2018. Available at https://larepublica.pe/politica/1274842-juez-cesar-hinostroza-ofrecio-reduccion-pena-violador-menor-video/

Chapter 11: Civil Liberties

1. Caralina Botero Marino and Michael J. Camilleri. 2011. "Freedom of Expression in Latin America: The Inter-American Human Rights System." *ReVista* 10(2): 21–22. Quote comes from p. 21.

2. Jessica McCormick. 2016. "The Last Temptation of Christ (Olmedo Bustos et al.) v. Chile." *Loyola of Los Angeles International and Comparative Law Review*, 38(4): 1189–1203.

3. "From Thomas Jefferson to Isaac H. Tiffany, 4 April 1819." *Founders Online*, National Archives. Accessed September 29, 2019, https://founders.archives.gov/documents/Jefferson/98-01-02-0303

4. Ibid.

5. Paolo G. Carozza. 2003. "From Conquest to Constitutions: Retrieving a Latin American Tradition of the Idea of Human Rights." *Human Rights Quarterly* 25: 281–313.

6. This idea is expressed in Alberdi's speech, "The Unlimited Power of the State Is the Denial of Individual Freedom," delivered at the graduation ceremony of the Faculty of Law and Social Sciences, University of Buenos Aires on May 24, 1880.

7. Robert Ligon McWhorter. 1951. "The Athenian Democracy." *The Georgia Review* 5(3): 290–299.

8. Erasmus. 1516 [2003]. *The Education of a Christian Prince*. Lisa Jardine (ed.). New York: Cambridge University Press, p. 88.

9. John Trenchard and Thomas Gordon. 1733. *Cato's Letters: Or, Essays on Liberty, Civil and Religious, and Other Important Subjects*. Volumes I–IV. London: W. Wilkins, T. Woodward, J. Walthoe, and J. Peele.

10. Article 19 of the International Covenant on Civil and Political Rights, ratified by the General Assembly of the United Nations on December 16, 1966. Available at https://www.ohchr.org/en/professionalinterest/pages/ccpr.aspx

11. Article 21 of the American Convention on Human Rights. Available at https://www.cidh.oas.org/basicos/english/basic3.american%20convention.htm

12. Rhoda E. Howard-Hassmann. 2013. "Reconsidering the Right to Own Property." *Journal of Human Rights* 12(2): 180–197.

13. Isaiah Berlin. 2006. "Two Concepts of Liberty." In Robert E. Goodin and Philip Pettit (eds.), *Contemporary Political Philosophy*. Oxford: Blackwell Publishing, pp. 369–386.

14. David Luhnow. "400 Murders a Day: The Crisis in Latin America." *The Wall Street Journal*, September 21, 2018, p. 1.

15. It is published by the Fraser Institute, the Friedrich Naumann Foundation for Freedom, and the Cato Institute.

16. Ian Vásquez, and Tanja Porčnik. 2019. *The Human Freedom Index 2019: A Global Measurement of Personal, Civil, and Economic Freedom*. Washington, DC: The Cato Institute, the

Fraser Institute, and the Friedrich Naumann Foundation for Freedom.

17. See, for instance, murder rate data compiled by *InSight Crime*; available at https://www.insightcrime.org

18. Additionally, more than 45,000 combatants were also killed, according to publicly available data compiled by the Observatory of Memory and Conflict, which is part of Colombia's National Center of Historic Memory.

19. OSAC. 2018. *Honduras 2018 Crime & Safety Report*. U.S. Department of State, Bureau of Diplomatic Security. Available at https://www.osac.gov/Content/Report/84d448fd-c42b-462c-91ce-15f4ae5df483

20. Carols Martell. "Study: The 50 Most Violent Cities in the World 2018." *Seguridad, Justicia y Paz*, March 12, 2019. Available at http://seguridadjusticiaypaz.org.mx/seguridad/1567-estudio-las-50-ciudades-mas-violentas-del-mundo-2018

21. AN/IR Drafting, Etellekt. 2018. "152 Politicians Killed; #Elections2018, the Most Violent in the History of the Country: Etellekt." *AristeguiNoticias*. Available at https://m.aristeguinoticias.com/1007/mexico/152-politicos-asesinados-elecciones2018-las-mas-violentas-en-la-historia-del-pais-etellekt/

22. "El Riesgo de los Defensores de Derechos Humanos Merece Mayor Atención del Estado: Defensor." *Defensoria del Pueblo Colombia*, January 10, 2019. Available at http://www.defensoria.gov.co/es/nube/noticias/7716/%E2%80%9CEl-riesgo-de-los-derechos-de-derechos-humanos-merece-mayor-atenci%C3%B3n-del-Estado%E2%80%9D-Defensor-Defensor-del-Pueblo-Carlos-Negret-Defensor%C3%ADa-derechos-humanos.htm

23. Sarah Kinosian. "Families Fear No Justice for Victims as 31 Die in Honduras Post-Election Violence." *The Guardian,* January 2, 2018.

24. "Lo que sabemos de los desaparecidos en Colombia." *Centro Nacional de Memoria Histórica*. Available at http://www.centrodememoriahistorica.gov.co/micrositios/balances-jep/desaparicion.html

25. Ibid.

26. Elias Camhaji. "Tecomán: Una Tragedia Soterrada." *El País*, February 17, 2019. Available at https://elpais.com/internacional/2019/02/16/mexico/1550286797_746567.html

27. Michael Coppedge, John Gerring, Carl Henrik Knutsen, Staffan I. Lindberg, Jan Teorell, David Altman, Michael Bernhard, M. Steven Fish, Adam Glynn, Allen Hicken, Anna Lührmann, Kyle L. Marquardt, Kelly McMann, Pamela Paxton, Daniel Pemstein, Brigitte Seim, Rachel Sigman, Svend-Erik Skaaning, Jeffrey Staton, Steven Wilson, Agnes Cornell, Lisa Gastaldi, Haakon Gjerløw, Nina Ilchenko, Joshua Krusell, Laura Maxwell, Valeriya Mechkova, Juraj Medzihorsky, Josefine Pernes, Johannes von Römer, Natalia Stepanova, Aksel Sundström, Eitan Tzelgov, YitingWang, Tore Wig, and Daniel Ziblatt. 2019. "V-Dem [Country-Year/Country-Date] Dataset v9," Vari

eties of Democracy (V-Dem) Project. https://doi.org/10.23696/vdemcy19.

28. Office of the United Nations High Commissioner for Human Rights. 2018. "Human Rights Violations in the Bolivarian Republic of Venezuela: A Downward Spiral with No End in Sight." Available at https://www .ohchr.org/Documents/Countries/ VE/VenezuelaReport2018_EN.pdf

29. Ibid.

30. "UN Human Rights Report on Venezuela Urges Immediate Measures to Halt and Remedy Grave Rights Violations." *United Nations Human Rights Office of the High Commissioner*, July 4, 2019. Available at https://www.ohchr.org/EN/ NewsEvents/Pages/DisplayNews .aspx?NewsID=24788&LangID=E

31. "Global Uptick in Government Restrictions on Religion in 2016." *Pew Research Center*, June 21, 2018. Available at https://www.pewforum .org/2018/06/21/global-uptick-in -government-restrictions-on-reli gion-in-2016/

32. JTA. "Anti-Semitism Not a Major Concern for Latin American Jews, Survey Finds." *The Times of Israel*, October 9, 2018. Available at https:// www.timesofisrael.com/anti-semi tism-not-a-major-concern-for-latin -american-jews-survey-finds/

33. United States Department of State, Bureau of Democracy, Human Rights, and Labor. "Cuba 2017 International Religious Freedom Report." *International Religious Freedom Report for 2017.* Available at https://www.state.gov/wp- content/uploads/2019/01/Cuba-2.pdf

34. "Cuba: Freedom of Religion or Belief." *Christian Solidarity Worldwide,* December 13, 2018. Available at https://www.csw.org.uk/2018/12/13/ report/4173/article.htm

35. Ibid.

36. An exception is made for schools dedicated to teaching the children of foreign diplomats.

37. Richard Wike. "Americans More Tolerant of Offensive Speech Than Others in the World." *Pew Research Center*, October 12, 2016. Available at http://www.pewresearch.org/ fact-tank/2016/10/12/americans -more-tolerant-of-offensive-speech -than-others-in-the-world/

38. These are typically reported monthly on their website, available at http://ccdhrn.org/

39. Amnesty International. 2018. *Amnesty International Report 2017/18.* London: Amnesty International Ltd., pp. 140–141; Human Rights Watch. 2019. *World Report 2019.* Washington, DC: Human Rights Watch, pp. 164–169.

40. Human Rights Watch. 2019. *World Report 2019.* Washington, DC: Human Rights Watch, pp. 164–169.

41. Amnesty International. 2018. *Amnesty International Report 2017/18.* London: Amnesty International Ltd., pp 140–141.

42. Human Rights Watch. 2020. *World Report 2020.* Washington, DC: Human Rights Watch, p. 423.

43. Amnesty International. 2018. *Amnesty International Report 2017/18.*

London: Amnesty International Ltd., pp 140–141.

44. Nina Lakhani. "Berta Cáceres: Seven Men Convicted of Murdering Honduran Environmentalist." *The Guardian*, November 30, 2018. Available at https://www.theguardian.com/world/2018/nov/29/berta-caceres-seven-men-convicted-conspiracy-murder-honduras

45. Maria Isabel Rivero. "Press Release: IACHR Has Concluded Its Visit to Honduras and Presents Its Preliminary Observations." OAS, August 3, 2018. Available at http://www.oas.org/en/iachr/media_center/PReleases/2018/171.asp

46. This numbers include only those cases where the motive has been confirmed.

47. Data available at Committee to Protect Journalists website: https://cpj.org/data/killed/

48. Inter-American Commission on Human Rights. *Report on the Compatibility of "Desacato" Laws with the American Convention on Human Rights*. OEA/Ser. L/V/II.88, doc. 9 rev. February 17, 1995, pp. 197–212.

49. Ibid.

50. Luis Alejandro Gutiérrez Eklund, Ian Miranda Sánchez, Carlos Andrés Peredo Molina, and Camila Calvi Baldivieso. 2016. "Las Leyes de Desacato y la Difamación Criminal en America Latina." *Revista Internacional de Derechos Humanos* 6(6): 121–144.

51. In Colombia, this type of ordinance was not included in the constitution or its penal code to begin with.

52. Human Rights Watch. 2018. *World Report 2018*. Washington, DC: Human Rights Watch, pp. 91–92.

53. "Press Release R96/11: Office of the Special Rapporteur Expresses Concern over Detention of Journalists and Serious Measures Taken against Magazine in Venezuela for Publishing Article That Offended the Authorities." *Inter-American Commission on Human Rights*, August 31, 2011. Available at http://www.oas.org/en/iachr/expression/showarticle.asp?artID=864&lID=1

54. "Ecuador Court Sentences Journalists to Prison in Presidential Libel Case." *Amnesty International*, July 22, 2011. Available at https://www.amnesty.org/en/latest/news/2011/07/ecuador-court-sentences-journalists-prison-presidential-libel-case/; President Correa ended up pardoning the convicted men.

55. "Honduras Court Upholds Journalist's 10-Year Prison Sentence for Defamation." *Committee to Protect Journalists*, January 15, 2019. Available at https://cpj.org/2019/01/honduras-court-upholds-journalists-10-year-prison-.php

56. Kyle Younker. "Follow the Money: Government Influence on Private Media in Argentina." *The Christian Science Monitor*, March 29, 2012. Available at https://www.csmonitor.com/World/Americas/2012/0329/Follow-the-money-Government-influence-on-private-media-in-Argentina

57. Inter-American Commission on Human Rights. 2011. *Declaration*

of Principles on Freedom of Expression. Available at http://www.oas.org/en/iachr/expression/showarticle.asp?artID=26

58. Fabiana Sanchez. "Edison Lanza: Proyecto (Que Regula la Publicidad en Medios Privados) Genera Discriminación." *Perú 21*, February 1, 2018. Available at https://peru21.pe/politica/edison-lanza-proyecto-regula-publicidad-medios-privados-genera-discriminacion-395927

59. Details about how the Reporters Without Borders' *World Press Freedom Index* is calculated can be found at https://rsf.org/en/world-press-freedom-index

60. Details about how Freedom House calculates its Freedom of the Press scores can be found at https://freedomhouse.org/freedom-press-research-methodology

61. Marisa Kellam and Elizabeth A. Stein. "Silencing Critics: Why and How Presidents Restrict Media Freedom in Democracies." *Comparative Political Studies* 49(1): 36–77.

62. Taylor C. Boas. 2012. "Mass Media and Politics in Latin America." In Jorge I. Dominguez and Michael Shifter (eds.), *Constructing Democratic Governance in Latin America.* Baltimore: The Johns Hopkins University Press, pp. 48–77.

63. Elizabeth A. Stein and Marisa Kellam. 2014. "Programming Presidential Agendas: Partisan and Media Environments That Lead Presidents to Fight Crime and Corruption." *Political Communication* 31(1): 25–52; Piero Stanig. 2015. "Regulation of Speech and Media Coverage of Corruption: An Empirical Analysis of the Mexican Press." *American Journal of Political Science* 59(1): 175–193.

64. John Tomasi. 2012. *Free Market Fairness.* New Jersey: Princeton University Press, p. 5.

65. Daron Acemouglu, Simon Johnson, and James A. Robinson. 2005. "Institutions as a Fundamental Cause of Long-Run Growth." In Philippe Aghion and Steven Durlauf (eds.), *Handbook of Economic Growth*, Volume 1A. Amsterdam: North Holland, pp. 385–472; Richard Roll and John R. Talbott. 203. "Political Freedom, Economic Liberty, and Prosperity." *Journal of* Democracy 14(3): 75–89; Timothy Besley and Maitreesh Ghatak. 2009. "Property Rights and Economic Development." In Dani Rodrik and Mark Rosenzweig (eds.), *Handbook of Development Economics*, Vol. 5. Amsterdam: North Holland, pp. 4525–4595.

66. Daron Acemouglu, Simon Johnson, and James A. Robinson. 2001. "The Colonial Origins of Comparative Development: An Empirical Investigation." *The American Economic Review* 91(5): 1369–1401; Carrie B. Kerekes and Claudia R. Williamson. 2008. "Unveiling de Soto's Mystery: Property Rights, Capital Formation, and Development." *Journal of Institutional Economics* 4(3): 299–325.

67. John Tomasi. 2012. *Free Market Fairness.* New Jersey: Princeton University Press, pp. 44–45.

68. Quoted in José Sebastián Elias. 2014. *The Constitutional Protection of*

Property Rights in Argentina: A Reappraisal of the Doctrine of Economic Emergency. Yale Law School Dissertations, p. 5.

69. Roberto Gargarella. 2014. "Latin American Constitutionalism: Social Rights and the 'Engine Room' of the Constitution." *Notre Dame Journal of International and Comparative Law* 4(1): 9–18.

70. Enrique Evans 1967. *Estatuto del Derecho de Propiedad en Chile.* Santiago: Jurídica de Chile, p. 34.

71. U.S. Department of State. *Bolivia Investment Climate Statement 2015.* Bureau of Economic and Business Affairs. Available at https://2009-2017.state.gov/documents/organization/241699.pdf

72. Noel Maurer. 2011. "The Empire Strikes Back: Sanctions and Compensation in the Mexican Oil Expropriation of 1938." *The Journal of Economic History* 71(3): 590–615.

73. "Hugo Chavez Orders Expropriation of Historic Buildings." *BBC News*, February 8, 2010. Available at http://news.bbc.co.uk/2/hi/americas/8503892.stm

74. The original scale was reversed it to make it compatible with the property rights scale.

Chapter 12: Income Inequality, Poverty, and the Gender Gap

1. Information about the city of São Paulo in Brazil comes from Rede Nosa São Paulo, a Brazilian civil society organization. Data available at https://www.nossasaopaulo.org.br/

2. Philipp Rode, Ricky Burdett, Richard Brown, Frederico Ramos, Kay Kitazawa Antoine Paccoud, and Natznet Tesfay. 2009. *Cities and Social Equity: Inequality, Territory and Urban Form.* London, UK: Urban Age Programme, London School of Economics and Political Science.

3. Data for Latin America and the Caribbean came from the LAC Equity Lab at the World Bank (updated in April 2019), and the world average for 2013 comes from the World Bank. 2016. *Poverty and Shared Prosperity 2016: Taking on Inequality.* Washington, DC: World Bank. doi:10.1596/978-1-4648-0958-3.

4. Leticia Arroyo Abad. 2013. "Persistent Inequality? Trade, Factor Endowments, and Inequality in Republican Latin America." *Journal of Economic History* 73 (1): 38–78; Luis Bértola and Jeffrey G. Williamson. 2006. "Globalization in Latin America Before 1940." In Victor Blumer-Thomas, John H. Coatsworth, and Roberto Cortés Conde (eds.), *The Cambridge Economic History of Latin America*, Volume II. New York: Cambridge University Press, pp. 11–56.

5. Leonardo Prados de la Escosura. 2006. "The Economic Consequences of Independence in Latin America." In Victor Bulmer-Thomas, John H. Coatsworth, and Roberto Cortés Conde (eds.), *The Cambridge Economic History of Latin America*, Volume I. New York: Cambridge University Press, pp. 463–504.

6. Jeffrey G. Williamson. 2015. "Latin American Inequality: Colonial

Origins, Commodity Booms, or a Missed Twentieth-Century Leveling?" *Journal of Human Development and Capabilities* 16(3): 324–341.

7. Ibid.

8. Harry G. Frankfurt. 2015. *On Inequality.* New Jersey: Princeton University Press, p. xi.

9. John Tomasi. 2013. *Free Market Fairness.* New Jersey: Princeton University Press, p. 241.

10. John Rawls. 1971. *A Theory of Justice.* Cambridge: Belknap Press of Harvard University Press.

11. The Editors. "Glaring Inequalities." *America, The Jesuit Review*, May 13, 2013.

12. Results estimated using Latinobarómetro's online analysis tool, available at http://www.latinobarometro.org/lat.jsp

13. The potential link between corruption and income inequality was discussed in Chapter 10.

14. Melanie Allwine, Jamele Rigolini, and Luis F. López-Calva. 2013. "The Unfairness of Poverty Targets." Policy Research Working Paper 6361, Washington, DC: World Bank.

15. Julián Messina and Joana Silva. 2018. *Wage Inequality in Latin America: Understanding the Past to Prepare to the Future.* Latin American Development Forum. Washington, DC: World Bank. doi:10.1596/978-1-4648-1039-8.

16. David De Ferranti, Guillermo E. Perry, Francisco H. G. Ferreira, and Michael Walton. 2004. *Inequality in Latin America: Breaking with History?* Washington, DC: World Bank. Quote is from p. 26.

17. Eric D. Gould and Alexander Hijzen. 2016. "Growing Apart, Losing Trust? The Impact of Inequality on Social Capital." IMF Working Paper 16/176, International Monetary Fund.

18. Ibid. See also Beatrice d'Hombres, Leandro Elia, and Anke Weber. 2013. "Multivariate Analysis of the Effect of Income Inequality on Health, Social Capital, and Happiness." Report EUR 26488, Joint Research Centre of the European Commission; Johan Graafland and Bjorn Lous. 2018. "Income Inequality, Life Satisfaction Inequality and Trust: A Cross Country Panel Analysis." *Journal of Happiness Studies* 20: 1717–1737. Available at https://link.springer.com/article/10.1007%2Fs10902-018-0021-0

19. Renowned economist Alan Krueger has called this relationship "The Great Gatsby Curve." Miles Corak. 2013. "Income Inequality, Equality of Opportunity, and Intergenerational Mobility." *Journal of Economic Perspectives* 27(3): 79–10. doi: 10.2307/41955546

20. OECD. 2018. *A Broken Social Elevator? How to Promote Social Mobility.* Paris: OECD Publishing. doi: https://doi.org/10.1787/9789264301085-en

21. Melissa S. Kearney and Phillip B. Levine. 2014. "Income Inequality, Social Mobility, and the Decision to Drop Out of High School." Working Paper 20195, National Bureau of Economic Research.

22. Francisco H. G. Ferreira, Julián Messina, Jamele Rigolini, Luis-Felipe López-Calva, Maria Ana Lugo, and Renos Vakis. 2013. *Overview: Economic Mobility and the Rise of the Latin American Middle Class.* Washington, DC: World Bank.

23. Alberto Alesina, Silvia Ardagna, Roberto Perotti, and Fabio Schiantarelli. 2002. "Fiscal Policy, Profits, and Investment." *American Economic Review* 92 (3): 571–589.

24. Gunhild Gram Giskemo. 2012. "Exploring the Relationship between Socioeconomic Inequality, Political Instability and Economic Growth: Why Do We Know So Little?" Working Paper 2012:2, Bergen: Chr. Michelsen Institute. For an argument linking high income inequality to crime and violence, see J. Humberto Lopez and Guillermo Perry. 2008. "Inequality in Latin America: Determinants and Consequences." Policy Research Working Paper 4504, World Bank, Washington DC.

25. Paul Collier and Anke Hoeffler. 2004. "Greed and Grievance in Civil War." *Oxford Economic Papers* 56 (4): 563–95.

26. Christopher Cramer. 2003. "Does Inequality Cause Conflict?" *Journal of International Development* 15(4): 397–412; Gudrun Østby. 2008. "Polarization, Horizontal Inequalities, and Violent Social Conflict." *Journal of Peace Research* 45(2): 143–162.

27. Markus Brueckner and Daniel Lederman. 2015. "Effects of Income Inequality on Aggregate Output." Policy Research Working Paper 7317, World Bank, Washington DC.

28. Bebonchu Atems and Jason Jones. 2015. "Income Inequality and Economic Growth: A Panel Var Approach." *Empirical Economics* 48: 1541–1561; Andrew G. Berg and Jonathan D. Ostry. "Inequality and Unsustainable Growth: Two Sides of the Same Coin?" IMF Staff Discussion Note, August 11, 2011. Washington: International Monetary Fund.

29. Christine Lagarde. "Equality Is Key to Global Economic Growth." *Boston Globe*, January 27, 2016.

30. Gustavo A. Marrero and Juan G. Rodríguez. 2016. "Inequality . . . of Opportunity and Economic Performance." In Federal Reserve Bank of St. Louis and Board of Governors of the Federal Reserve System (eds.), *Economic Mobility: Research and Ideas on Strengthening Families, Communities and the Economy.* Washington, DC: Authors, pp. 385–420. Quote is from p. 412.

31. Leonardo Gasparini and Nora Lustig. 2011. "The Rise and Fall of Income Inequality in Latin America." Working Paper 213, The Society for the Study of Economic Inequality (ECINEQ), Mallorca, Spain.

32. The data utilized here have been compiled by the LAC Equity Lab at the World Bank (updated in April 2019), which uses data from SEDLAC and the World Development Indicators. SEDLAC (CEDLAS and the World Bank) undertakes a regional harmonization effort to increase

cross-country comparability, which may result in numbers that differ from official statistics reported by governments and national statistics offices (see http://www.worldbank.org/en/topic/poverty/lac-equity-lab1).

33. Based on World Bank data; see previous footnote.

34. Data for 2017, except for the Dominican Republic (2016), Guatemala (2014), Honduras (2016), and Nicaragua (2014).

35. Economic Commission for Latin America and the Caribbean (ECLAC). 2019. *Social Panorama of Latin America 2018*. Santiago, Chile: United Nations, p. 93.

36. This is expressed in 2011 dollars at purchasing power parity.

37. Nora Lustig, Luis F. Lopez-Calva, and Edmundo Ortiz-Juarez. 2013. "Deconstructing the Decline in Inequality in Latin America." Policy Research Working Paper 6552, World Bank, Washington DC.

38. Dani Rodrik. 2007. *Open Economics, Many Recipes: Globalization, Institutions, and Economic Growth*. Princeton: Princeton University Press, p. 2.

39. Economic Commission for Latin America and the Caribbean (ECLAC). 2019. *Social Panorama of Latin America 2018*. Santiago, Chile: United Nations.

40. Ibid.

41. Julián Messina and Joana Silva. 2018. *Wage Inequality in Latin America: Understanding the Past*

to Prepare to the Future*. Latin American Development Forum. Washington, DC: World Bank. doi:10.1596/978-1-4648-1039-8.

42. Potential reasons include the increase in the relative supply of skilled workers resulting from improvements in education as well as the lesser current value provided by skills acquired during earlier years in the labor market.

43. *Domestic demand* refers to expenditures by households, governments, and firms.

44. *Terms of trade* refers to the relationship between the prices at which a country sells its exports and the prices it pays for its imports.

45. Julián Messina and Joana Silva. 2018. *Wage Inequality in Latin America: Understanding the Past to Prepare to the Future*. Latin American Development Forum. Washington, DC: World Bank. doi:10.1596/978-1-4648-1039-8.

46. Nora Lustig, Luis F. Lopez-Calva, and Edmundo Ortiz-Juarez. 2013. "Deconstructing the Decline in Inequality in Latin America." Policy Research Working Paper 6552, World Bank, Washington DC.

47. Suzanne Duryea, Andrew Morrison, Carmen Pagés, Ferdinando Regalia, Norbert Schady, Emiliana Vegas, and Héctor Salazar. 2017 "Challenges for Social Policy in a Less Favorable Macroeconomic Context." In Luis Bértola and Jeffrey Williamson (eds.), *Has Latin America Changed Direction? Looking Over the Long Run*. New York: Springer, pp. 407–419.

48. Ibid.

49. David Coady and Allan Dizioli. 2017. "Income Inequality and Education Revisited: Persistence, Endogeneity, and Heterogeneity." Working Paper 17/126, International Monetary Fund.

50. François Bourguignon and Francisco H. G. Ferreira. 2005. "Decomposing Changes in the Distribution of Household Incomes: Methodological Aspects." In François Bourguignon, Francisco H. G. Ferreira, and Nora Lustig (eds.), *The Microeconomics of Income Distribution Dynamics in East Asia and Latin America*. Washington, DC: Oxford University Press and the World Bank, pp. 17–46.

51. Sebastián Galiani, Guillermo Cruces, Pablo Acosta, and Leonardo Gasparini. 2017. "Educational Upgrading and Returns to Skills in Latin America: Evidence from a Supply-Demand Framework." Working Paper 127, CEDLAS, Universidad Nacional de La Plata.

52. James E. Mahon Jr. and Marcelo Bergman, with Cynthia J. Arnson. 2015. "The Political Economy of Progressive Tax Reform in Latin America: Comparative Context and Policy Debates." In James E. Mahon, Marcelo Bergman, and Cynthia J. Arnson (eds.), *Progressive Tax Reform and Equality in Latin America*. Washington DC: Woodrow Wilson International Center for Scholars.

53. Economic Commission for Latin America and the Caribbean (ECLAC) and Oxford Committee for Famine Relief (OXFAM). 2016. *Time to Tax for Inclusive Growth*. Santiago, Chile: ECLAC.

54. Michael Hanni, Ricardo Martner, and Andrea Podestá. 2015. "The Redistributive Potential of Taxation in Latin America." *CEPAL Review* 116: 7–26.

55. Ibid.

56. Johanna Godoy. "Latin America: Signs of Progress." *Gallup*, March 8, 2019. Available at https://news.gallup.com/poll/247199/latin-america-signs-progress-change-takes-time.aspx

57. Recording practices regarding femicide vary significantly across countries, which makes cross-national comparisons difficult.

58. Economic Commission for Latin America and the Caribbean. "Notes for Equality N27: Femicide, the Most Extreme Expression of Violence Against Women." *Gender Equality Observatory*, November 15, 2018. Available at https://oig.cepal.org/en/notes/note-equality-ndeg-27-femicide-most-extreme-expression-violence-against-women

59. Sarah Bott, Alessandra Guedes, Ana P. Ruiz-Celis, and Jennifer Adams Mendoza. 2019. "Intimate Partner Violence in the Americas: A Systematic Review and Reanalysis of National Prevalence Estimates." *Pan American Journal of Public Health* 43(26). doi: 10.26633/RPSP.2019.26

60. Data available at https://data.worldbank.org/indicator/SG.VAW.REAS.ZS and https://data.unicef.org/resources/resource-type/datasets/

61. Pew Research Center. 2014. *Religion in Latin America: Widespread Change in a Historically Catholic Region.* Available at http://www.pewforum.org/2014/11/13/religion-in-latin-america/

62. Data from Socio-Economic Database for Latin America and the Caribbean (SEDLAC; CEDLAS and The World Bank). Available at http://www.cedlas.econo.unlp.edu.ar/wp/en/estadisticas/sedlac/estadisticas/#1496165425791-920f2d43-f84a

63. Ibid.; *low* equals 0 to 8 years of education, while *high* equals more than 13 years of education.

64. Economic Commission for Latin America and the Caribbean (ECLAC). 2019. *Social Panorama of Latin America 2018.* Santiago, Chile: United Nations.

65. Data comes from UNICEF. Available at https://data.unicef.org/topic/maternal-health/maternal-mortality/

66. Two others had interim female presidents: Bolivia in 1979–1980 and Ecuador for two days in 1997.

67. UNICEF. 2006. *Women and Children: The Double Dividend of Gender Equality.* New York: UNICEF.

68. Li-Ju Chen. 2010. "Do Gender Quotas Influence Women's Representation and Policies?" *The European Journal of Comparative Economics* 7(1): 13–60.

69. These numbers come from the World Bank, World Development Indicators (updated as of June 28, 2019), and are based on women aged 15 to 64.

70. Leonardo Gasparini, Mariana Marchionni, Nicolás Badaracco, and Joaquín Serrano. 2015. "Female Labor Force Participation in Latin America: Evidence of Deceleration." Working Paper 181, Universidad Nacional de La Plata, Centro de Estudios Distributivos, Laborales y Sociales (CEDLAS), La Plata, Argentina.

71. Data come from the World Bank, World Development Indicators, updates as of June 28, 2019. Labor force comprises people ages 15 and older who supply labor for the production of goods and services during a specified period (World Bank).

72. Data come from ECLAC CEPALSTAT (database), latest year available as of March 13, 2019; available at https://estadisticas.cepal.org/cepalstat/Portada.html

73. Data come from ECLAC, CEPALSTAT and are based on the salaries of people between the ages of 20 and 49 who work 35 or more hours a week and live in urban areas.

74. These figures exclude individuals who are students. Data comes from ECLAC, CEPALSTAT, latest year available as of July 8, 2019; https://oig.cepal.org/es/indicadores/poblacion-sin-ingresos-propios-sexo

• Index •

Acemoglu, Daron, 55
Administrative decree, 140
Afiuni, María Lourdes, 204–205
Aissami, Tareck El, 116
Alarcón, Fabián, 144
Alberdi, Juan Bautista, 286, 303–304
Alfonsín, Raúl R., 142, 147
Allende, Salvador, 66, 102, 131
Al-Qaeda, 111
Amaru, Tupac, 18
Amazonia, indigenous population, 13
Amendatory veto, 138–139
Andes, indigenous population, 13
Anglo-Spanish War, 17
Anti-corruption efforts, 277
Anti-drug certification process, 110
Appointment rules, courts, 205
Árbenz, Jacobo, 60–61, 66, 101
Arce, Manuel José de, 21
Arévalo, Juan José, 101
Argentina
    authoritarian regimes and
        takeovers, 46, 236
    business leaders survey, 272
    confidence in institution, 242
    corruption, 260, 262, 265–266,
        274–275
    democracy, 38–40, 42
    election and electoral rules,
        177–180, 183–187
    GDP per capita (1800-1900), 26
    gender role attitudes, 326–331
    indigenous population (1942), 13
    interpersonal trust, 244
    interruptions to presidents, 142

    judiciary, 209–214, 209, 212
    left-right self-placement, 248
    legislatures, 154–158, 156, 169–170
    Members of Congress, electing
        rules, 189
    Montoneros, 67
    People's Guerilla Army, 67
    People's Revolutionary Army, 67
    perception on America, 120
    post-independence conflicts, 24–27
    poverty, extreme, 319, 321–322
    presidentialism, 133–135, 134,
        137–138, 141–142, 144, 184
    suffrage, restrictions and extensions,
        177, 180
    women in congress, cabinet and
        courts, 330–331
Aristide, Jean-Bertrand, 107–108,
    112–113, 266
Armas, Carlos Castillo, 61
Artigas, José Gervasio, 19–20
Audiencias, 5–7, 18
Authoritarianism, 31, 36–40, 45,
    53–56, 59, 61, 63, 99, 129, 131,
    223, 232, 285
    executive constraints, 55
    illiteracy, 59
    regime types, 49
    See also Specific countries
Aztecs, 4

Bachelet, Michelle, 329
Balaguer, Joaquin A., 100, 142
Baldett, Roxana, 279
Barnes, Tiffany D., 155

Barrios, Justo Rufino, 31

Batista, Fulgencio, 70–74

Battle of Ayacucho, 20

Bay of Pigs invasion, 75

Bello, Andrés, 303

Bicameralism, 152, 163, 165, 171

Blackstone, Sir William, 177–178

Blanco, Guzmán, 32

Blass, Abby, 219

Blix, Hans, 111

Block veto, 138–139

Boix, Carles, 37–39, 50, 52, 62

Bolivia

    authoritarian regime and
        takeovers, 46, 236

    business leaders survey, 272

    confidence in institution, 242

    corruption, 270–272, 274–275

    democracy, 38–39, 42, 44, 45, 54

    gender role attitudes, 327, 329–331

    income inequality, 316–318

    interpersonal trust, 244

    interruptions to presidents, 142

    judiciary, 203–214, 209, 212,
        218–220

    leftist governments, 117–118

    left-right self-placement, 248

    legislatures, 154–156, 158, 164

    Members of Congress, electing
        rules, 189

    National Liberation Army (ELN), 67

    perception on America, 120

    poverty, extreme, 319, 321

    presidentialism and election rules,
        133–135, 144–145, 183–185

    property rights, 305–306

    suffrage, restrictions and extensions,
        177, 180

    War of the Pacific, 25

    War of the Triple Alliance, 24–25

    women in congress, cabinet and
        courts, 330–331

Bolivian Revolution, 48

Bonaparte, Joseph, 16

Bonaparte, Napoleon, 16

Booth, John A., 232–234, 238

Bosch, Juan, 99–100

Bourbon Reforms, 11–12, 17, 21, 33

Brazil

    authoritarian regimes and takeovers,
        46, 236

    business leaders survey, 272

    capital punishment, 287–288

    confidence in institution, 242

    constitutional reforms, 305

    corruption, 256, 260, 262, 265–266,
        274–276, 278

    democracy, 42, 44

    election and electoral rules, 187,
        189, 192, 195

    GDP per capita (1800-1900), 26

    gender role attitudes, 327, 335

    income inequality, 311–312, 316–317

    independence movements, 21–23,
        25–26

    indigenous people, 11–16

    indigenous population (1942), 13

    interpersonal trust, 244

    interruptions to presidents, 142

    judiciary, 205, 207, 209– 212, 215,
        218–219, 221, 224–225

    left-right self-placement, 248

    legislatures, 156, 162, 164–166,
        169–170

    literacy restriction, 179–180

    major scandals, 280

    Members of Congress, electing
        rules, 189

    military regime, 45–46

    National Liberation Action (ALN),
        67

    National Liberation Command
        (COLINA), 67

    perception on America, 120

    political culture, 235–238, 242,
        244–245, 249

population composition
(1570–1825), 14
poverty, extreme, 319, 322–323
president's power, 137–139
Revolutionary Movement 8th
October (MR-8), 67
suffrage, restrictions and extensions,
177, 180–181, 183–184
violence and insecurity, 292,
299–300
women in congress, cabinet and
courts, 329, 330–331
Brinks, Daniel M., 219
Bucaram, Abdalá J., 142, 144, 147
Bush, George H. W., 85, 106–108,
110–113, 115–116

Cabildos, 6, 27
Cádiz Cortes, 16–18, 21
Canada
population composition
(1570–1825), 14
religious freedom, 295
United States–Mexico–Canada
Agreement (USMCA), 118
See also North American Free Trade
Agreement (NAFTA)
Cardenal, Ernesto, 78
Carey, John, 56, 132, 169, 198
Caribbean, indigenous population
(1942), 13
Carlin, Rayan E., 235
Carrera, Rafael, 23
Carter, Jimmy, 103–105, 108
Casas-Zamora, Kevin, 266
Castañeda, Jorge, 66, 277
Castaño, Carlos, 91
Castas, 14
Castro, Fidel, 68, 71–76, 82, 100–101,
104, 300
Castro, Laureano Gómez, 48
Castro, Raúl, 52, 71, 73
Catterberg, Gabriela, 240

Central America, indigenous
population (1942), 13
Central Intelligence Agency (CIA), 61,
74, 100
Cepeda, Manuel Jose, 91
Chamorro, Pedro Joaquín, 77, 81
Chamorro, Violeta, 81, 321
Charles III King of Spain, 15
Charles IV, King, 16
Chávez, Hugo, 52, 62, 114–117,
141, 187, 204–205, 214,
305–306
Chávez, Rebecca Bill, 214
Cheibub, José Antonio, 38–39,
50–51, 131
Chile
authoritarian takeovers, 236
business leaders survey, 272
civil liberties, 285, 287, 291, 296,
305–306
confidence in institution, 242
corruption, 264, 266, 269–271,
273–276, 278
democracy, 36, 38–42, 44–45, 49,
54, 101–102
desacato law, 300
exports, 29
freedom status and democracy
(2018), 42
GDP per capita (1800-1900), 26
gender role attitudes, 327–329,
331, 335
income inequality, 318
indigenous population (1942), 13
interpersonal trust, 244
judiciary, 205, 207, 209–214,
218–219, 221, 224–225
leftist parties, 66
left-right self-placement, 248
legislatures, 151, 154, 156, 159–162,
164–167, 169–170
Members of Congress, electing
rules, 189

Movement of the Revolutionary
Left (MIR), 67
oligarchic republic, 31
perception on America, 120
political culture, 238, 245, 249
post-independent conflicts, 24–25
poverty, extreme, 319,
320–321, 323
presidentialism and election
rules, 128, 131, 137–139,
141, 145, 184
press freedom, 302
suffrage, restrictions and extensions,
177, 179–180, 183–184, 189,
191, 199, 817
U.S. relations, 105, 109, 111–112,
115, 120
War of the Pacific, 25
women in congress, cabinet and
courts, 330–331
Chinchilla, Laura, 329
Civil conflicts (1810-1879), 22
Civil liberties, 40–45, 50, 58, 285–290,
287, 304, 306, 308
classification, 287–290
freedom from torture, 293
freedom of expression and
assembly, 298
freedom of speech, press and
Internet use, 297
free expression, 295–299
peaceful assembly, 295–299
press freedom, 299–303, 302
property rights, 303–307
religious freedom, 295–299
right to life as, 290–295
scope of, 286–287
security and safety 2010-2017, 291
Clientelism, 258
Clinton, Bill, 88, 107–111, 114, 140
Clinton, Hillary, 114
Closed-list proportional
representation, 190, 198–199

Cold War, 35, 61–62, 65, 98–99,
101–103, 105–106, 108, 110,
121–123
Colom, Álvaro, 279
Colombia
authoritarian regime and takeovers,
46, 236
business leaders survey, 272
confidence in institution, 242
corruption, 274–275, 278
democracy, 38–39, 41, 42, 44, 52
GDP per capita (1800-1900), 26
gender role attitudes, 327
interpersonal trust, 244
left-right self-placement, 248
legislatures, 153–156, 158–160, 162,
164, 167
Members of Congress, electing
rules, 189
National Liberation Army (ELN), 67,
88–89, 93
19th April Movement (M-19), 67,
89–91
peace agreements between
government and armed groups,
90–93
perception on America, 120
poverty, extreme, 319, 322
presidentialism and election rules,
133–135, 137–139, 141, 184
Revolutionary Armed Forces of
Colombia (FARC), 67,
88–93
suffrage, restrictions and extensions,
177, 180
United Self-Defense Forces (AUC),
90–92
women in congress, cabinet and
courts, 330–331
Colomer, Josep M., 186
Colonial economic policies
agriculture, types of, 10–11
indigenous slavery, 9, 11

mineral resources, 9–10
trade regulations, 8–9
wage labor, 9
Colonial institutions, 4–8
administrative hierarchy, 6–7
bureaucratic structure, 7
Catholic Church's role, 7–8
Colonial legacy, 3–4
New World in 17th century, 3–4
wars of independence, 4
Colonial societies
black population, demography, 14
caste system, 14–16
class certificates, 15
deaths in war and civil conflicts, 22
growth of exports, 29
indigenous populations, collapse of,
12–13
lack of self-governing institutions, 27
migration pattern, 14
settlers' influence, 15–16, 18
social structure, 14–15
white population, privileges, 15
Compulsory voting, 176, 181–183, 200
Conditional cash transfers (CCTs),
323, 325
Confidence in institutions, 231, 239,
240–241, 243, 245–246, 253, 256,
262, 277
Congressional oversight, 160–162
Conquistadores, 4
Conservatives, 20–23, 27, 33
Constitutional courts, 203–204,
216–219, 223–226
Constitutional review, 216–217, 226
Constitutions, 23, 127–128,
134, 138, 140, 148, 151–152,
160–162, 165, 169, 213, 286–289,
304–307
Consumption taxes, 325
Contested elections, 37, 90
Contra War, 81
Córdova, Abby, 243

Corrales, Javier, 186
Corral, Margarita, 247
Correa, Rafael, 117–118, 187, 301
Corruption
anti-corruption efforts, 263–268,
279–281
causes and consequences, 258–262
forms of, 257
measurement, 268–276
partiality, 258
political elites and, 255–256
public opinion, 257
scandals, 277–281
small-scale, 257
vote buying, 258
World Bank's definition, 256
See also Specific countries
Corruption indices, 262, 268, 270, 273
Open Government Index, 270
Rule of Law, 271
Corruption scandals, 147, 256, 260,
264–266, 277–278, 282
La Línea and Transurbano, 279
Lava Jato (Car Wash), 280
Mensalao (the big monthly
payment), 280
Odebrecht, 277–278, 280
Cortés, Hernán, 4, 16–18, 21
Costa Rica
armed forces, 59
authoritarian takeovers, 236
business leaders survey, 272
confidence in institution, 242
corruption, 266, 269–271, 273,
274–276
democracy (2018), 36, 38–42, 44–45,
49, 233, 296
desacato law, 300
gender role attitudes, 327, 334–335
income inequality, 316, 318
internal conflicts, 23
interpersonal trust, 244–245
judiciary, 221, 224–225

left-right self-placement, 248

legislatures, 151, 153–154, 156, 159–161, 167

Members of Congress, electing rules, 189

oligarchic republic, 31

perception on America, 120

poverty, extreme, 319, 321–322

presidential election rules, 184

presidentialism, 137–139

press freedom, 302

social reforms, 305–306

suffrage, restrictions and extensions, 177, 179–180, 183–185, 187, 196–197

support for the Sandinistas, 78

U.S. relationship, 114–115

violence, 294

women in congress, cabinet and courts, 329, 330–331

Council of the Indies, 4

Court-packing, 203, 213

Cox, Gary W., 160

Creole-led rebellion, 19

Crisp, Brian, 153

Cristiani, Alfredo, 84

Cuba

civil liberties, 287–288

communist party of Cuba (the PSP), 73

conflict with U.S., 74–75, 102, 104, 106, 108, 115, 117–118

democracy, 38–39, 41–42, 44, 45, 49

desacato laws, 300

freedom of expression, 297

freedom status and democracy (2018), 42

GDP per capita (1800-1900), 26

guerrillas, 76–77, 79, 82–83, 89–90

judiciary, 219, 224

missile crisis of 1962, 61, 75, 103

press freedom, 303

religious groups, 295–296

social reforms, 305–306

suffrage extension, 26, 180–181

support for the Sandinistas, 78

under Spain, 3–4, 11, 15, 26

women in congress, cabinet and courts, 329–331

Cuban Missile Crisis, 61, 75, 103

Cuban Revolution, 66, 70, 75–76, 82, 88, 93

Batista, Fulgencio's role, 70–73

U.S. government's role, 71–76

Dahl, Robert A, 35

Debayle, Luis Somoza, 48, 70, 76

Decile dispersion ratio, 317–318

Decree-law, 140

Delegated decree, 141

Democracy

alternative definition, 49

complexity, 40–41

contemporary definition, 36

economic growth, 53–54

EIU's Democracy Index, 2019, 44

from 1901-1950, 38

from 1951-2000, 39

from 2016-2017, 233

maximalist approach, 43–45

minimalist approach, 37–39

non-domestic factors, 61–62

policy making, 55–56

political culture, 56–59

preferences of political elites, 59–61

semi, 41–42

Democracy. See specific countries

Democratic norms, 55, 233–234, 237, 243

Desacato laws, 289–290

D'Escoto, Miguel, 78

Descriptive representation, 154, 171

Devine, Michael, 107

Diamond, Larry, 40, 232

Díaz, Porfirio, 30–31

District magnitude, 194–199

Dominant-party regime, 48–49

Dominican Republic

ambitious law, 264

authoritarian regime and takeovers, 46, 236

business leaders survey, 272

civil liberties, 300

confidence in institution, 242

corruption, 274–275, 278

democracy, 38–39, 42, 44

Dominican Liberation Movement (MLD), 67

gender role attitudes, 327

guerrillas, 89

interpersonal trust, 244

interruptions to presidents, 142

judiciary, 224, 249

left-right self-placement, 248

legislatures, 156, 164–165, 167

Members of Congress, electing rules, 189

perception on America, 120

personalist dictatorship, 47, 62

political culture, 249

poverty, extreme, 319, 322

presidentialism and election rules, 138, 144, 184, 195–197, 199

Revolutionary Movement 14th of June (MR1J4), 67

suffrage, restrictions and extensions, 177, 179–180, 183–184, 187, 191–192

U.S. relationship, 98–100, 108, 112, 119–120

women in congress, cabinet and courts, 330–331

Dorticós, Osvaldo, 73

Doyle, David, 247

Driscoll, Amanda, 221

Drug Eradication Act, 118

Duarte, Jose Napoleón, 83–84

Duhalde, Eduardo A., 142

Dunkerley, James, 78

Echeverría, José Antonio, 72

Economic Commission for Latin America and the Caribbean (ECLAC), 319

Ecuador

authoritarian takeovers, 236

business leaders survey, 272

confidence in institution, 242

corruption, 274–275, 278

democracy, 38–39, 42, 44

desacato law, 300

GDP per capita (1800-1900), 26

gender role attitudes, 327, 334–335

interpersonal trust, 244

interruptions to presidents, 142

judiciary, 205, 221, 224

left-right self-placement, 248

legislatures, 154, 156, 157, 158, 191–192

Members of Congress, electing rules, 189

military coups, 59

perception on America, 120

political culture, 245

poverty, extreme, 320

presidentialism and election rules, 130, 135–136, 139, 144, 147, 184–185, 187

social reforms, 304–305

Spanish rule, 4, 6, 15

suffrage, restrictions and extensions, 177, 179–181, 183

U.S. relationship, 109, 112, 117–118

violence, 294

women in congress, cabinet and courts, 330–331

Education, 12, 15, 57–58, 63, 141, 176, 178, 182, 234, 247, 253, 261, 312, 316, 323–328, 335–336

Edwards, Margaret E., 146

Eisenhower, Dwight D., 61, 74, 101, 140

Elections/electoral system
  compulsory voting, 181–183
  consequences of rules, 194–195
  disproportionality index, 196
  electoral rules for choosing
      presidents, 183–186
  majoritarian rules, 192
  mixed-member systems, 192–194
  19th century, 175
  personal vote *versus* the partisan
      vote, 197–199
  presidential reelection rules,
      186–188
  proportional representation,
      188–192
  rules for electing members of
      congress, 188
  share of votes and seats, 195–197
  suffrage extension, 176–181
  20th century, 175–176
Elías, Jorge A. Serrano, 142, 145, 147
Elliott, J. H., 18
Ellner, David Romero, 301
El Salvador
  authoritarian regime and takeovers,
      46, 236
  business leaders survey, 272
  capital punishment, 287
  civil wars, 47
  confidence in institution, 242
  corruption, 255, 274–275
  democracy, 38–39, 42
  desacato law, 300
  Farabundo Martí National
      Liberation Front (FMLN), 67,
      83–85
  gender role attitudes, 327
  guerilla movement, 65, 68–70, 80,
      82–85, 86, 88, 90
  income inequality, 316–318
  internal conflicts, 23
  interpersonal trust, 244
  judiciary, 224

left-right self-placement, 248
legislatures, 156, 157, 161, 191
Members of Congress, electing
    rules, 189
Nationalist Republican Alliance
    (ARENA) party, 84
People's Revolutionary Army (ERP),
    67, 83
perception on America, 120
political culture, 249
Popular Forces of Liberation (FPL),
    67, 83
poverty, extreme, 320
presidentialism and election rules,
    40, 139, 179, 181, 183–184, 187
suffrage, restrictions and extensions,
    177, 180, 199
U.S. military assistance, 84–85
U.S. relation, 103–105, 107, 115
violence, 292
women in congress, cabinet and
    courts, 330–331
Encomienda, 9
Endara, Guillermo, 106–107
Enlightenment, The, 18
Erga omnes, 217–219, 226
Executive decree power, 136
Executive-legislative deadlock,
    129–131, 137
Export-led growth, 3
Expropriation, 16, 73, 305–307

Farabundo Martí National Liberation
    Front (FMLN), 47, 67, 83
Female economic participation,
    332–336
Femicide, 326, 336
Ferdinand VII, 16–17, 21
Ferejohn, John A., 214
Figueres, José M., 72
Figueroa, Julio Ríos, 214, 218
Flores, Francisco, 255
Flores, Luis Medrano, 77

Forced disappearance, 292
Fox, Vicente, 111
Frankfurt, Harry G., 313
Freedom of expression, 285, 289,
    296–301
Frutos, Nicanor Duarte, 52
Fuchs-Schündeln, Nicola, 233
Fujimori, Alberto, 107, 129, 142, 145,
    147, 255

Galindo, Hermila, 181
Gallagher, Michael, 195
Gandhi, Jennifer, 38
García, Alan, 255, 278
García, Anastasio Somoza, 47, 76, 79
García, Romeo Lucas, 86
Geddes, Barbara, 45, 47–51
Gender gap, 326–328
Gender pay gap, 312, 332–335, 337
Gender quotas, 154, 156, 329
Gini coefficient, 312, 316–318, 322
Godoy, Julio César, 266
González, Manuel, 31
Good Neighbor Policy, 98, 101
Goodwin, Jeff, 70, 78
Gorbachev, Mikhail S., 105, 107
Grand corruption, 272, 277, 281–282
Grau, Raúl A. Cubas, 142, 144
Gray, Cheryl W., 260
Guaidó, Juan, 117
Guardia, Tomás, 31
Guatemala
    authoritarian regime and takeovers,
        46, 236
    business leaders survey, 272
    confidence in institution, 242
    corruption, 260, 274–275, 279–280
    democracy, 38–39, 40, 42, 44, 45–47,
        50–51, 60, 62, 66, 234
    desacato law, 300
    gender role attitudes, 327, 334
    Guatemalan National Revolutionary
        Unity (URNG), 67, 86–88

Guatemalan Party of Labor (PGT), 85
guerilla groups, 68–69, 82–83,
    85–88, 90
Guerrilla Army of the Poor
    (EGP), 67, 86
internal conflicts, 23
interpersonal trust, 244
interruptions to presidents, 142
judiciary, 224
left-right self-placement, 248
legislatures, 157
Members of Congress, electing
    rules, 189
military rule, 27, 237
perception on America, 120
political culture, 239
polítival violence, 292
poverty, extreme, 320, 321–322
presidentialism and election rules,
    31, 40, 133–135, 138, 143–144,
    147, 183–184, 192
Rebel Armed Forces (FAR), 67, 85–86
Revolutionary Organization of
    Armed People (ORPA), 67, 86
social reforms, 305
suffrage, restrictions and extensions,
    177, 180
United Nations Mission, 87
U.S. military aid, 86, 88
U.S. relations, 61, 70, 101, 103, 105,
    107, 109, 115, 119
women in congress, cabinet and
    courts, 330–331
Guatemalan Civil War, 109
Guatemalan National Revolutionary
    Unity (URNG), 47, 67, 86–88
Guerrero, Vicente, 20–21
Guerrilla Movements, 47, 51–52,
    60–61, 65–95, 104, 110, 290, 292
    common motivations, 68–69
    counterinsurgency operations, 70
    major groups, role in, 66–70
    See also Specific countries

Guevara, Ernesto Che, 68, 71, 73, 75–76
Gutiérrez, Lucio E., 142, 144, 147, 205

Haggard, Stephan, 54
Haiti
  authoritarian takeovers, 236
  business leaders survey, 272
  confidence in institution, 242
  corruption, 269–270
  democracy, 38–39, 41–42, 44, 45, 49
  desacato law, 300
  freedom status and democracy (2018), 42
  gender role, 327
  guerrillas, 68
  interpersonal trust, 244–245
  judiciary, 219, 224
  left-right self-placement, 248–249
  presidentialism, 132–133
  U.S. relations, 107–108, 112
  use of torture, 294
  women in congress, cabinet and courts, 329–331
Hamilton, Alexander, 128, 208
Hass, Richard, 99
Helmke, Gretchen, 146, 203, 210, 221
Heredia, Dr. Aditardo, 178
Hidalgo, Manuel, 20
Hidalgo, Matilde, 181
Hinostroza, César, 280–281
Hochstetler, Kathryn, 146
Honduras
  authoritarian takeovers, 236
  business leaders survey, 272
  confidence in institution, 242
  corruption, 258, 265, 274–275
  criminality, 292
  democracy, 38–39, 41, 42, 44, 45, 303
  desacato law, 300
  freedom of expression, 298–299
  gender role attitudes, 327, 334
  guerrillas, 76

  income inequality, 312, 316–317
  internal conflicts, 23
  interpersonal trust, 244
  judiciary, 204, 224–225
  left-right self-placement, 248–249
  legislatures, 157
  liberalism, 31
  Members of Congress, electing rules, 189
  military coups, 59
  perception on America, 120
  poverty, extreme, 320–322
  presidentialism and election rules, 41–42, 138, 184
  suffrage, restrictions and extensions, 177, 179–180, 183–184, 187, 191, 199
  U.S. relations, 80, 114–115
  women in congress, cabinet and courts, 330–331
Humala, Ollanta, 255, 278
Huntington, Samuel P., 62
Hussein, Saddam, 111

Ideology, 66, 89, 232, 246–247
Impeachment, 128, 141–145, 147, 164, 203, 214, 219, 235, 255, 267, 278, 280
Incas, 4
Income gap
  economic participation, 332–336
  See also Income inequality
Income inequality, 30, 66, 115, 249–250, 261–262, 304, 311–319, 312–314, 322–326, 336
  decile dispersion ratio, 317
  in 2000-2017, 317
  population lives on less than $5.50 a day, 321
  problematic outcomes, 314–316
  reduction approaches, 322–326
  trends, 316–319
Incomplete list system, 192, 199

Independence movements
    death in war and civil conflicts,
        22–23
    impact on colonies, 16–17
    intensity of conflicts, 17–22
    international conflicts, 24–25
    local governments role, 17
    political instability, 27–28
    political struggle, 16–17
    Spanish constitution, nullification, 17
    turmoil after, 22–27
Indirect military regime, 47
Informal sector, 323–325
Ingall, Rachael E., 153
Inglehart, Ronald, 232, 238, 240
Insecurity, 10, 290, 292, 326
Inter-American Convention against
        Corruption, 267
International sanctions, 107
Inter partes, 217–219, 226
Interpelaciones, 160
Interpersonal trust, 231, 239–240,
        242–246, 253, 260–261, 314–315
Iran-Contra Affair, 81, 105
Isabella II, 17
Iturbide, Agustín de, 21–22

Jay, John, 128
João, King, 21
Johnson, Simon, 55
Judicial authority, 204, 215–216, 218
Judicial crises, 203
Judicial independence, 44, 204–215,
        223–226, 303
Judicial legitimacy, 220
Judiciary
    appointment process, 205–208
    authority, 215–220
    constitutional courts, evaluations
        on, 222–225
    government power checking by, 225
    higher courts' size, 212–213
    independence, 223

    instruments, combination, 217
    judicial independence, 204–205
    length of tenure, 208–210
    perceptions, 220–222
    political context, 213–215
    public trust, 222
    removal proceedings, 210–212
    See also Specific countries
Junta, 17–20, 79, 84, 107–108

Kaltwasser, Cristóbal Rovira, 246
Kaufmann, Daniel, 260
Kaufman, Robert R., 54
Kennedy, John F., 74–75, 100, 103
Khrushchev, Nikita, 75
Kirchner, Cristina Fernández de,
        262, 281, 329
Kuczynski, Pedro P., 142, 145, 186,
        255, 278
Kurer, Oskar, 257

Lanz, Pedro Díaz, 74
Leal, Jaime Pardo, 91
Left-right dimension, 247, 249, 252
Legislative agenda setting, 139
Legislative autonomy, 151–152
Legislative effectiveness, 152
Legislative organization, 163, 171–172
Legislatures, 56, 136, 151–169,
        171–172, 186
    bicameralism, 163–165
    committees and procedural rules,
        165–168
    definition, 152
    endogenous and exogenous rules,
        163–165
    lawmaking, 158–160
    19th century, 151
    organization, 163–168
    oversight of the executive, 160–162
    representing constituents, 152–158
    20th century, 151
    voting behavior, 168–171

Legitimacy, 27, 54, 57–58, 79, 112, 130–131, 143, 182, 185–186, 215, 220–221, 240, 262

Libel laws, 301

Liberal Revolution, 21

Liberals, 20–21, 23–24, 33, 246, 303–304, 306

Linz, Juan J., 129–131

Lipset, Seymour M., 53, 234

Lobos, Porfirio, 115

Lopez, Francisco Solano, 25

Lozada, Gonzalo Sánchez de, 142

Lugo, Fernando, 142–143

Luna, Juan Pablo, 246

Lynch, John, 18

Madison, James, 127–128, 208

Maduro, Nicolás, 116–117, 305

Mainwaring, Scott, 40–41, 50–52, 54, 56, 61, 234, 290

Majoritarian electoral systems, 175

Majority runoff, 183–185

Marrero, Gustavo A., 316

Marsteintredet, Leiv, 147

Martinez, Maximiliano Hernández, 83

Marulanda, Manuel, 88

Matos, Hubert, 74

Matthews, Herbert L., 73

Maximilian, Archduke, 22

Maximilian I., 23

Mein, John, 86

Mello, Fernando A. Collor de, 142, 144, 147

Menem, Carlos S., 147, 205, 213

Mercado, José Raquel, 89

Mercantilism, 8, 32

Mérida Initiative, 113

Mesa, Carlos D., 142

Mestizos, 10, 12, 14–16, 20

Mexican-American War, 24

Mexican Revolution, 48

Mexico
  authoritarian regime and takeovers, 46, 236
  authoritarian regime (dominate party), 46

Aztecs, 4

business leaders survey, 272

confidence in institution, 242

corruption, 258, 260, 262, 266, 274–276, 278

criminality, 292

democracy, 38–39, 42, 44, 234, 303

desacato laws, 300

dominant-party regime, 48–49

GDP per capita (1800-1900), 26

gender role attitudes, 327, 329

General Transparency and Access to Information Law, 263

guerillas, 85

independence movement, 20–26

indigenous population (1942), 12–13

interpersonal trust, 244

judiciary, 205, 207, 209–214, 212, 218–220, 224

left-right self-placement, 248

legislatures, 155, 156–160, 162, 164–166, 169

Members of Congress, electing rules, 189

military coup, 237

perception on America, 120

poverty, extreme, 320, 322–323

presidentialism and election rules, 138–139, 145, 154, 184, 186–187, 189, 193

press freedom, 299, 301

religious freedom, 295

silver mining, 9

Spanish rule, 15

suffrage, restrictions and extensions, 177, 179–180, 183

U.S. relations, 97–98, 108–113, 115, 118–121, 305

women in congress, cabinet and courts, 330–331

Military coup, 23, 47–48, 59–60, 66, 70–71, 76, 78, 87, 102, 110, 114–115, 131, 141, 145–146, 148–149, 236–237, 329

Military junta, 46, 108

Military regime, 45, 47, 49, 78, 102

Miller, Michael, 37

Minimum wage, 323–326

Miró, José, 73

Mishler, William, 240

mita, 9

Mixed-member electoral systems, 192, 194

modernizing governments, 30–31

Molina, Otto Pérez, 142–143, 147, 279

Monroe Doctrine, 97–98

Montalva, Eduardo Frei, 305

Montenegro, Julio Méndez, 50–51

Montezuma II, 4

Montt, Efraín Rios, 51, 87

Morales, Evo, 117, 145–146, 205, 214

Morales, Jimmy, 279–280

Morelos, José Maria, 20

Moreno, Alejandro, 240

Morgenstern, Scott, 160

Moscoso, Mireya, 329

Mott, Margaret MacLeish, 57

Mulattos, 15–16

Napoleon III, 22

Nationalist Republican Alliance (*Alianza Republicana Nacionalista*, ARENA), 255

Natural rights, 286

Negative rights, 287

Nelson, Michael J., 221

Nicaragua
authoritarian regime and takeovers, 46, 236
business leaders survey, 272
confidence in institution, 242
corruption, 269, 274–276
democracy, 38–39, 41, 42, 44, 45
desacato law, 300
freedom of expression, 298–299, 301
gender role attitudes, 327
guerillas, 65, 68–70, 76–77, 79, 82–83, 85–86, 88, 90
income inequality, 317–318
internal conflicts, 23
interpersonal trust, 244
judiciary, 224–225
left-right self-placement, 248–249, 248
legislatures, 157
Members of Congress, electing rules, 190
perception on America, 120
personalist dictatorship, 47, 62
political stability, 31
poverty, extreme, 320, 321
presidentialism and election rules, 139, 184, 192
Sandinista National Liberation Front (FSLN), 67
suffrage, restrictions and extension, 177, 179–180, 183–184, 187
U.S.relations, 101, 103–106
use of torture, 294
women in congress, cabinet and courts, 329, 330–331

Nicaraguan Revolution, 70, 76, 78–79, 82
Sandinista National Liberation Front (FSLN) movement, 76–82
Somoza families, role in, 76

19th century Latin America
economic growth, 28–31
exports, 28–29
income per capita, 26–27
political order, 28–31

Non-democratic regimes, categories, 45–49

Noriega, Manuel, 106–107

Norris, Pippa, 241
North America
   indigenous population (1942), 13
   See also United States (U.S.)
North American Free Trade Agreement
   (NAFTA), 108, 112, 118
North, Douglass C., 27

Obama, Barack, 113–114, 116,
   118–121, 140
O'Donnell, Guillermo, 54
Oligarchic regime, 48–49
Open-list proportional representation,
   191, 194, 199
Organization of American States
   (OAS), 62, 78, 81, 100, 312
Ortega, Daniel, 81
Osama bin Laden, 111
Osorio, Carlos Arana, 51

Padrón, Bernardo Arévalo, 300
País, Frank, 72
Palmer, Larry, 116
Panama
   authoritarian takeovers, 236
   business leaders survey, 272
   confidence in institution, 242
   corruption, 260, 274–275, 278
   democracy, 38–39, 42, 44
   gender role attitudes, 327
   internal conflicts, 23
   interpersonal trust, 244
   left-right self-placement, 248
   legislatures, 157
   Members of Congress, electing
      rules, 190
   perception on America, 120
   poverty, extreme, 320, 321
   presidential election rules, 184
   suffrage, restrictions and extensions,
      177, 180
   women in congress, cabinet and
      courts, 330–331

Panama Canal Treaty, 104, 106
Paraguay
   authoritarian takeovers, 236
   business leaders survey, 272
   confidence in institution, 242
   corruption, 260, 274–276, 278
   democracy (2018), 39, 42
   desacato law, 300
   freedom of expression, 296
   gender role attitudes, 327, 334–335
   guerrillas, 69, 78
   income inequality, 316–318
   indigenous population (1942), 13
   interpersonal trust, 244
   interruptions to presidents, 142
   judiciary, 224
   left-right self-placement, 248
   legislatures, 154, 157–158, 161
   Members of Congress, electing
      rules, 190
   perception on America, 120
   poverty, extreme, 319–321
   presidentialism and election rules,
      145, 183–184, 187, 194, 196
   property rights, 306
   suffrage, restrictions and extensions,
      177, 180
   U.S. relations, 97, 104, 106–107,
      112–113, 115
   women in congress, cabinet and
      courts, 329–331
Paramilitary forces, 65, 90
Parliamentarism, 129, 132–133,
   147–149
Parrales, Edgar, 78
Partial veto, 138
Patronage, 7, 132, 258–259, 264
Peace agreements, 65, 82, 90, 93
Peaceful assembly, 288–289, 295, 308
Pedro, Dom, 21–22
Pellegrini, Carlos, 179
Penfold, Michael, 186
Peninsulares, 15, 17, 33

Peninsular War, 16
Pérez, Carlos Andrés, 107, 142–143
Pérez-Liñán, Aníbal, 40–41, 50–52, 54,
    56, 61, 146–147, 234, 290
Pernambuco, 11
Perón, Isabel Martínez de, 46, 329
Perón, Juan, 46, 50, 329
Persian Gulf War of 1990-1991, 111
Personalist regime, 47, 49, 70, 78, 82
Personal vote, 197–199
Peru
    authoritarian takeovers, 236
    business leaders survey, 272
    capital punishment, 288
    confidence in institution, 242
    corruption, 255, 260, 264,
        274–276, 278
    democracy, 38–39, 42, 44, 54
    desacato law, 300
    GDP per capita (1800-1900), 26
    gender role attitudes, 327
    guerrillas, 69
    interpersonal trust, 244
    interruptions to presidents, 142
    judiciary, 205, 207, 209–213, 219,
        221, 224
    left-right self-placement, 248
    legislatures, 155, 157–161, 170,
        177–180
    Members of Congress, electing
        rules, 190
    military coups, 60
    National Liberation Army
        (ELN), 67
    perception on America, 120
    political culture, 237, 245
    poverty, extreme, 319, 320, 322
    presidentialism and election rules,
        133–134, 137–139, 141–142, 145,
        183–184, 186–187, 190–191
    press freedom, 301
    Shining Path, 67
    Spanish rule, 4–5, 9, 13, 15, 18–21
    suffrage, restrictions and extensions,
        177, 180
    Túpac Amaru Revolutionary
        Movement (MRTA), 67
    U.S. relations, 109, 112, 115
    War of the Pacific, 25
    women in congress, cabinet and
        courts, 330–331
Petty corruption, 262, 272
Piérola, José Nicolás de, 31
Pinochet, Augusto, 102–103, 105
Pizarro, Carlos, 91
Pizarro, Francisco, 4
Plan Colombia, 110
Plurality rule, 175, 183, 185–186,
    192–199
Polga-Hecimovich, John, 146
political culture
    confidence in institutions, 239–246
    ideological positions, 246–251
    interpersonal trust, 239–246
    political regime 1900-2011, 41
    support of democracy, 232–239
Political elites, 59–63, 215, 241, 247,
    253, 256
Political institutions, 27, 53, 55–57, 63,
    148–149, 172–173, 176, 201, 222,
    226, 240–241, 243, 262
Political tolerance, 58, 234, 239
    citizen's dislikes and, 238
    gay persons running for office
        2016–2017, 239
Popper, Karl, 35
Positive rights, 287
poverty, 322–326
    prevalence, 319–322
    rate and measurement, 319–322
    reduction approaches, 322–326
    See also Specific Countries
Presidential interruptions, 128,
    141–142, 146–148
Presidentialism, 127–141, 147–148,
    203, 226

presidentialism, Latin America
American Presidentialism vs, 136–146
criticism, 128–132
essential characteristics, 133–136
presidential interruptions, 146–148
Presidential term limits, 50, 187
Press freedom, 52, 82, 258, 260, 282,
285, 289, 296, 299–303
Property rights, 12, 16, 55, 74, 92, 102,
216, 261, 271, 290, 303–308
Proportional representation, 175,
188–199
Przeworski, Adam, 37
Public office
women in, 328–332
Public procurement, 263–265, 269

Químper, José María, 178

Ramsey, Adam, 221
Reagan, Ronald, 80–81, 84, 100,
105, 111
Recall referendum, 135
Reduced-threshold runoff, 184
Regime transitions, 46, 49, 53–54, 61
Regulatory decree, 140
Religious freedom, 32, 58, 295–296, 299
Repartimiento, 9–10
Reporters Without Borders (RWB),
301–302
Revolutionary Armed Forces of
Colombia (FARC), 65, 67–68, 88–93
Rice, Condoleezza, 116
Richard, Patricia Bayer, 233–234, 238
Rio Pact, 103
Rivero, Manuel Ray, 72
Rodríguez, Andrés, 51
Rodríguez, Juan G., 316
Rodrik, Dani, 322
Roll-call votes, 168–170
in Chile, 170
Romero, Oscar, 84
Roosevelt Corollary to the Monroe
Doctrine, 98

Rosato, Sebastian, 37
Rothstein, Bo, 258
Rousseff, Dilma, 141–143, 215, 235,
280, 329
Royal patronage (patronato real), 7
Rúa, Fernando de la, 142

Saá, Adolfo Rodriguez, 142
Saca, Elías Antonio, 255
Safford, Frank, 28
Salvadorean Civil War, 82–85
Salzman, Ryan, 221
Samper, Ernesto, 110
Samper, José María, 303
Sandinista National Liberation Front
(FSLN), 67, 76–81, 101
Sandinista Revolution, 48
Sandino, Augusto, 76
San Martín, José de, 20
Santos, Juan Manuel, 89, 92, 186
Schneider, Rene, 102
Schumpeter, Joseph, 37
Schündeln, Matthias, 233
Schwindt-Bayer, Leslie A., 154
Scribner, Druscilla, 214
Seligson, Mitchell A., 232
Semi-democracy, 41, 50–51, 62
Semi-presidentialism, 132
Serrano, Rosalía Arteaga, 142, 144
Severance payments, 324
Shugart, Matthew, 56, 132, 198
Silva, Luiz Inácio Lula da, 215, 256,
262, 267, 278, 280
Singer, Matthew M., 235
Slander laws, 299
Somoza, Anastasio, 47–48, 70, 76–80,
82, 103
Soto, Marco Aurelio, 31
Spain (Spanish America)
population composition
(1570–1825), 14
Spanish revolution of 1820, 21
Staton, Jeffrey, 210
Substantive representation, 154–155

Sucre, Antonio José de, 20
Survey data, 240

Temer, Michel, 280
Tenure of judges, 208–210
Term limits, judges, 31, 50, 155–158, 171, 187, 200, 214
Thousand Days War, 23
Tlaxcalans, 4
Toledo, Francisco, 255, 278
Tolerance, 44, 57–58, 231, 234, 237–239, 253
Toro, Manuel Murillo, 178
Torres, Camilo, 89
Transparency policies, 41, 162, 259, 263–272, 281, 302
Treaty of Tordesillas, 3
Triple Alliance, War of, 24–25
Truman, Harry, 61, 101, 140
Trump, Donald J., 116–121, 140

United Nations Convention against Corruption, 265, 268
United States (U.S.)
  Alliance for Progress., 103
  authoritarian takeovers, 236
  Chile and Mexico, refusal to use of force, 112
  Chilean military *versus,* 102
  CIA involvement, 101–103
  Cold War and aftermath, 99–111
  confidence in institution, 242
  Cuban Interest Sections, 104
  drug crimes, 115–116
  foreign policy, 98, 103 (*See also Specific countries*)
  immigration issues, 119
  intergovernmental relations, 119
  "international police power," 98
  interpersonal trust, 244
  invasion of Grenada, 100, 105
  invasion of Iraq, 119
  Latin American exports to, 98
  left-right self-placement, 248
  military intervention, 98–100
  OAS, creation of, 103
  Panama Canal Treaty, 104
  population composition (1570–1825), 14
  process of democratization, 105
  suffrage restrictions, 177
  Venezuela and, 115–116
  "War on Terror," 111
  weapons of mass destruction (WMDs), 111
United States-Mexico-Canada Agreement (USMCA), 118
Urrutia, Manuel, 73
Uruguay
  authoritarian takeovers, 236
  business leaders survey, 272
  civil war, 25, 27, 29
  confidence in institution, 242
  corruption, 264, 266–267, 269–271, 273, 274–275, 276
  democracy, 36, 38–42, 44, 49, 54, 234–235
  desacato law, 300
  freedom of expression, 296
  GDP per capita (1800-1900), 26
  gender role attitudes, 328
  income inequality, 316–318
  indigenous population (1942), 13
  interpersonal trust, 244–245
  judiciary, 221, 224–225
  left-right self-placement, 248
  legislatures, 157–159, 164–165
  Members of Congress, electing rules, 190
  military coups/dictatorship, 59, 103
  perception on America, 120
  political tolerance, 237–238
  poverty, extreme, 319–322
  presidentialism and election rules, 133–134, 137, 139, 183–184, 187, 190–191
  press freedom, 302

social reforms, 305–306
suffrage, restrictions and extensions,
177, 180–181
Tupamaros, 67
U.S. relations, 108, 120
use of torture, 294
women in congress, cabinet and
courts, 330–331
U.S. Agency for International
Development (USAID), 117–118

Varraich, Aiysha, 258
Velasco, Juan, 60
Venezuela, 27
authoritarian regime, 45
business leaders survey, 272
civil war, 24
confidence in institution, 242
corruption, 260, 269–271, 273,
274–276, 278
creole-led rebellion, 19
democracy, 38–39, 41–42, 44–45,
52, 60
desacato laws, 300
dictatorial regimes, 27, 60, 62
freedom of expression, 297, 299,
301, 303
Fuerzas Armadas de Liberación
Nacional (FALN), 67
GDP per capita (1800-1900), 26
gender role attitudes, 327
guerrillas, 68, 78, 85
income inequality, 314
interpersonal trust, 244
interruptions to presidents, 142
judiciary, 205, 220, 224–225
left-right self-placement, 248
legislatures, 155, 157, 162
Members of Congress, electing
rules, 190
perception on America, 120
political culture, 235–236, 245, 249
political violence, 292

poverty, extreme, 320
presidentialism and election rules,
131, 133–136, 141–143, 155, 157,
183–184, 186–187
property rights, 305–306
regime classification, 52
suffrage, restrictions and extensions,
177, 180
U.S. relations, 98, 108, 112,
114–118, 120
use of torture, 294
women in congress, cabinet and
courts, 330–331
Venustiano, Carranza, 181
Vertbisky, Horacio, 300
Veto powers, 40, 79, 129, 135–139, 138
Viceroy, 5–7, 9, 11, 17–19
Villarán, Manuel Vicente, 178
Votes of no confidence, 148
Vreeland, James Raymond, 38

War deaths (1810-1879), 22
War of the Pacific, 25, 31
War of the Triple Alliance, 24
Weingast, Barry R., 214
Werleigh, Claudette, 329
Wiarda, Howard, 57
Wickham-Crowley, Timothy P., 69–70,
77, 79
Wiesehomeier, Nina, 247
women
economic participation, 332–336
gender cap, 326–328
income gap, 332–336
in public office, 328–332
men's salary comparison, 333–335
Wood, Elisabeth J., 69, 83
World War II, 56, 58, 62, 65, 98–99, 140
Zaldívar, Rafael, 31
Zechmeister, Elizabeth, 247
Zelaya, José Santos, 31
Zelaya, Manuel, 62, 114
Zuazo, Hernán Siles, 142, 147